COURSE 21: THE USUAL

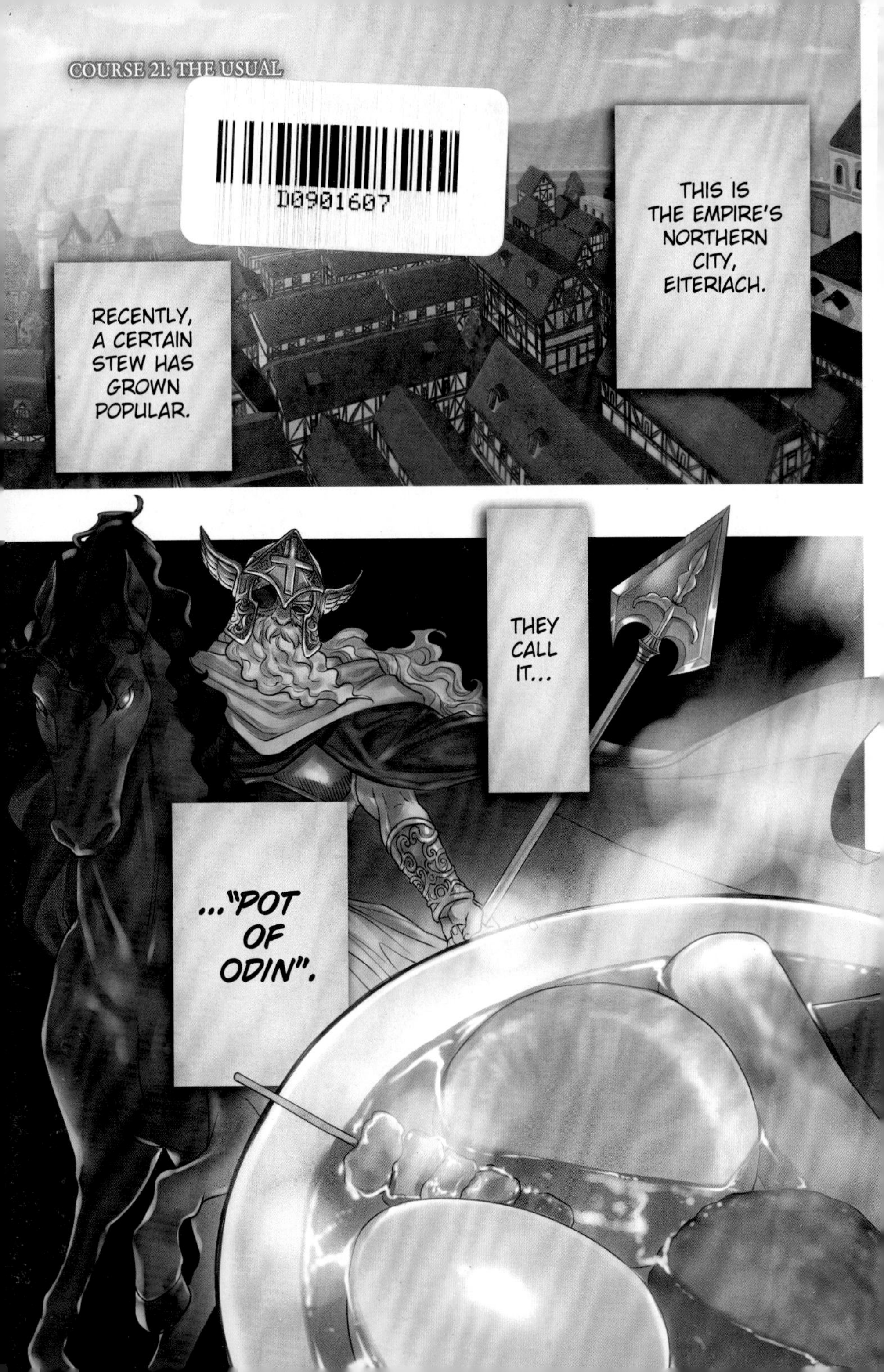
THIS IS THE EMPIRE'S NORTHERN CITY, EITERIACH.
RECENTLY, A CERTAIN STEW HAS GROWN POPULAR.
THEY CALL IT...
..."POT OF ODIN".

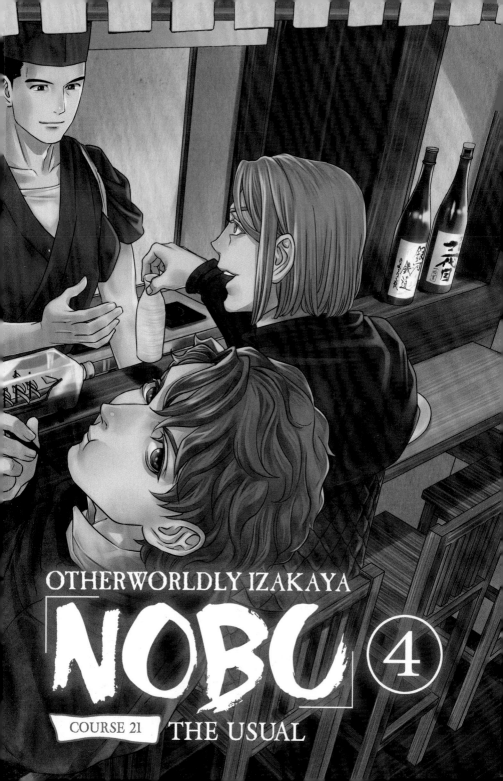

OTHERWORLDLY IZAKAYA

NOBU ④

COURSE 21   THE USUAL

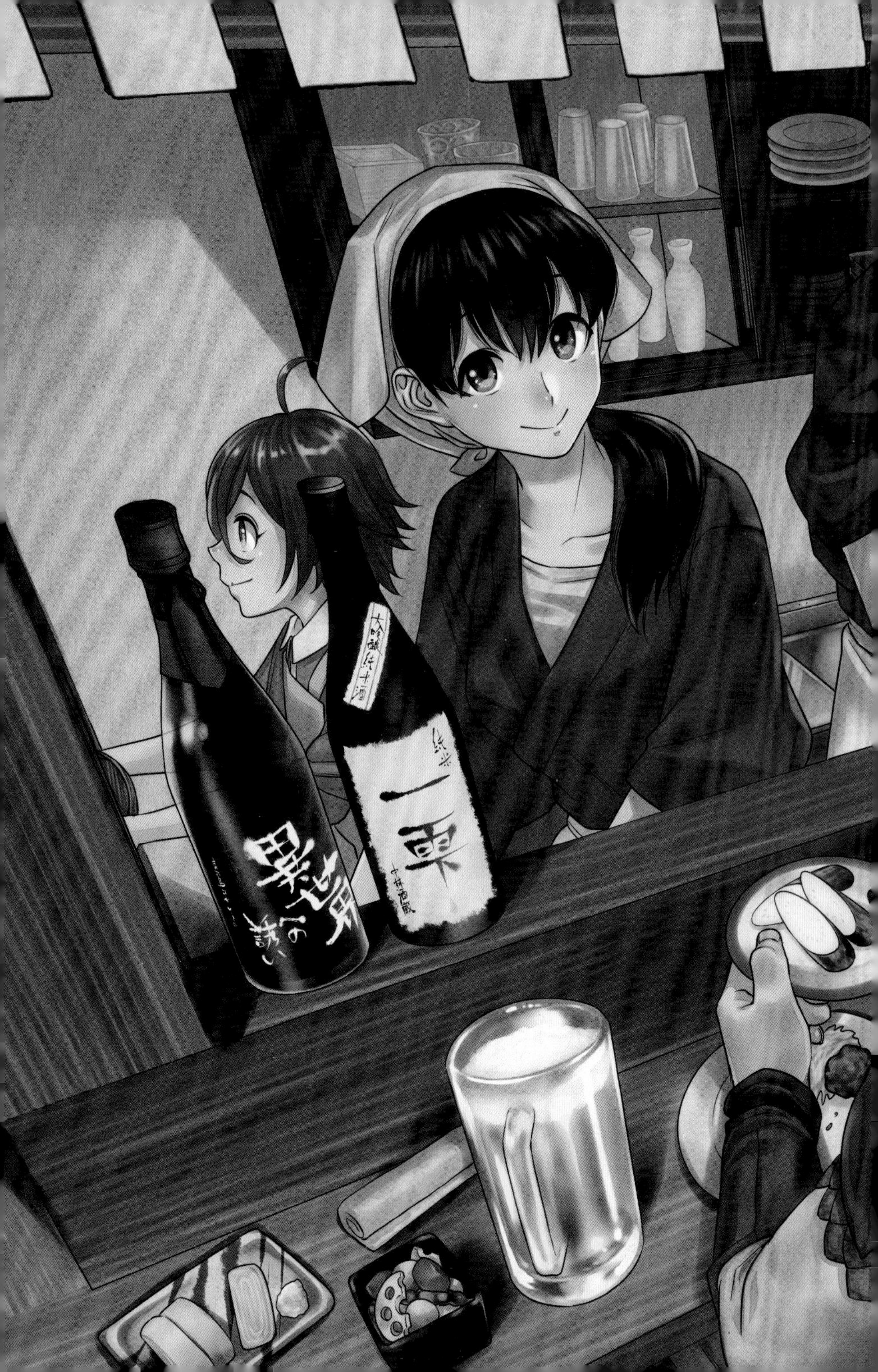
大吟醸純米酒
純米
一栗
中林酒蔵

MENU

OTHERWORLDLY IZAKAYA

NOBU ④

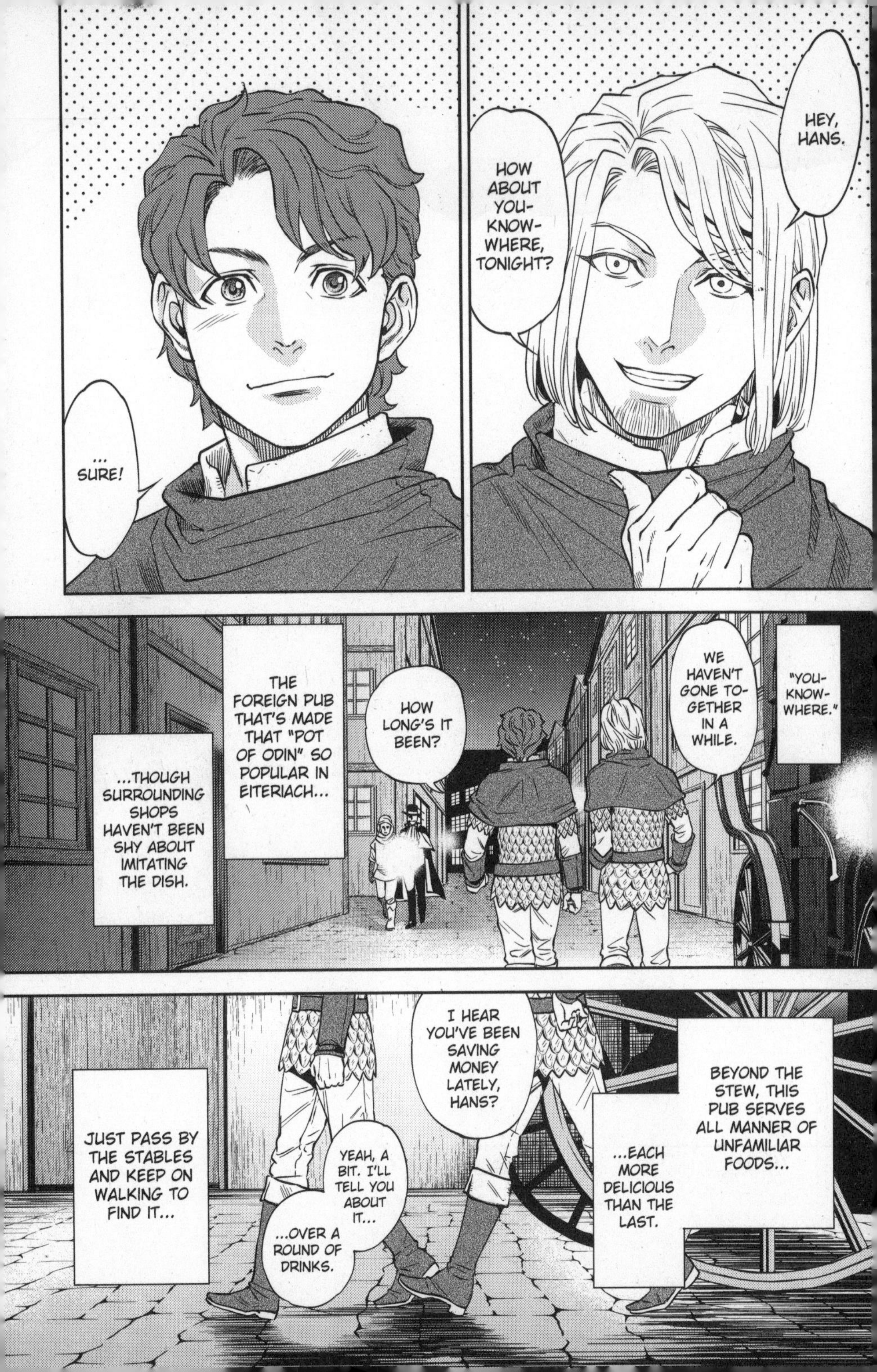
HEY, HANS.
HOW ABOUT YOU-KNOW-WHERE, TONIGHT?
... SURE!
"YOU-KNOW-WHERE."
WE HAVEN'T GONE TO-GETHER IN A WHILE.
HOW LONG'S IT BEEN?
THE FOREIGN PUB THAT'S MADE THAT "POT OF ODIN" SO POPULAR IN EITERIACH...
...THOUGH SURROUNDING SHOPS HAVEN'T BEEN SHY ABOUT IMITATING THE DISH.
BEYOND THE STEW, THIS PUB SERVES ALL MANNER OF UNFAMILIAR FOODS...
...EACH MORE DELICIOUS THAN THE LAST.
I HEAR YOU'VE BEEN SAVING MONEY LATELY, HANS?
YEAH, A BIT. I'LL TELL YOU ABOUT IT...
...OVER A ROUND OF DRINKS.
JUST PASS BY THE STABLES AND KEEP ON WALKING TO FIND IT...

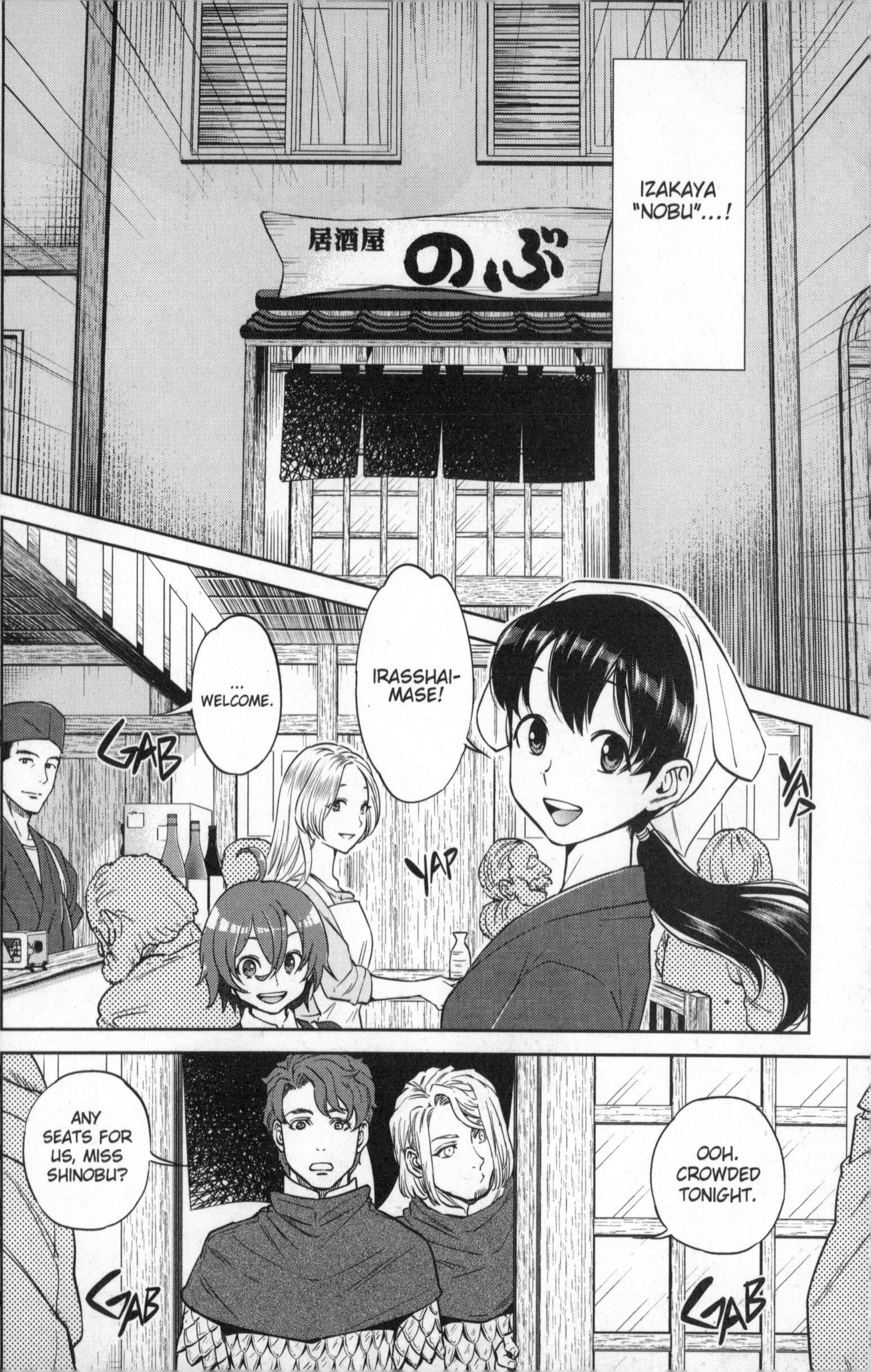
IZAKAYA "NOBU"...!
居酒屋
のぶ
YAP
IRASSHAI-MASE!
YAP
...WELCOME.
GAB
OOH. CROWDED TONIGHT.
GAB
ANY SEATS FOR US, MISS SHINOBU?
GAB

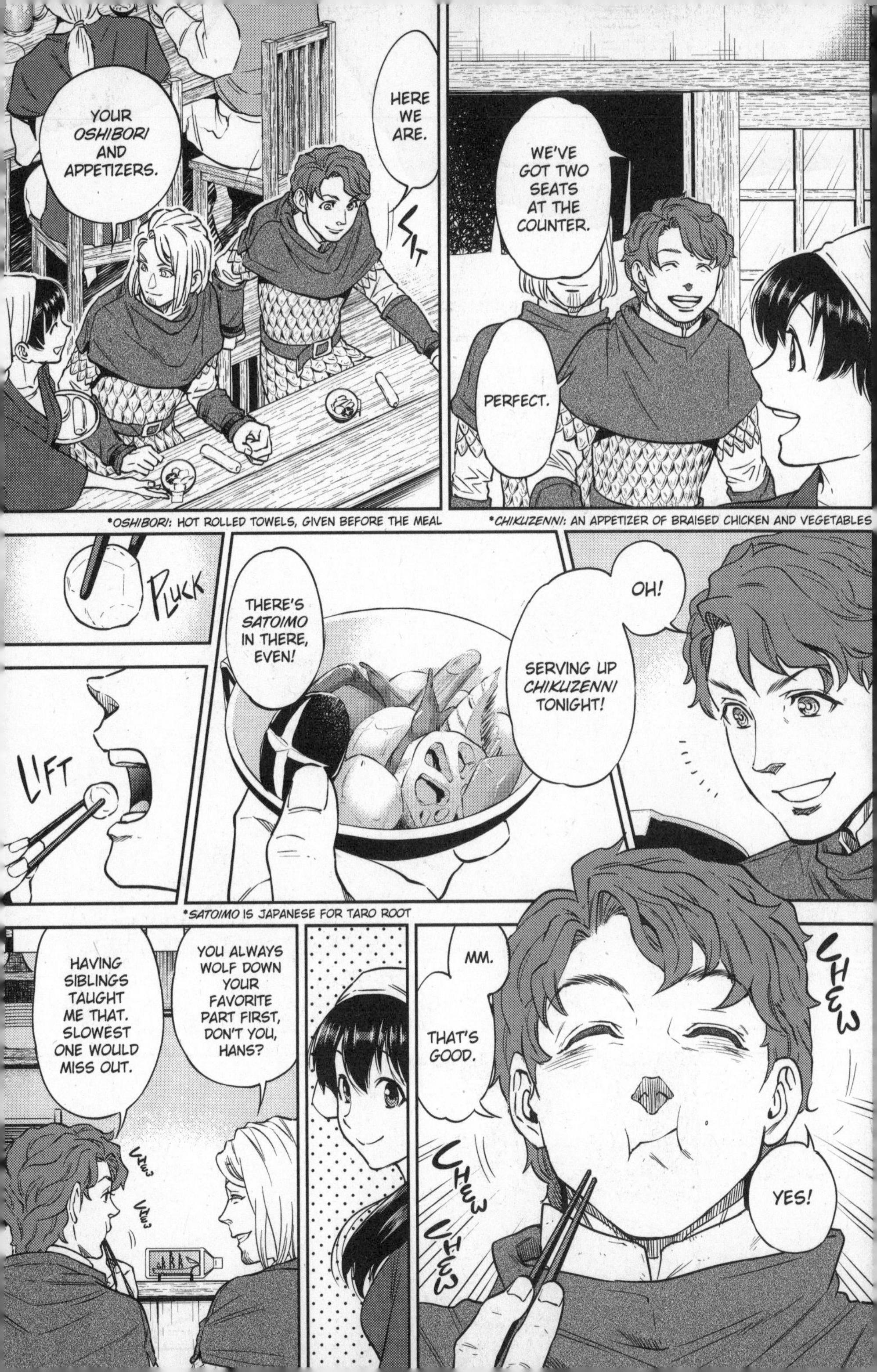
WE'VE GOT TWO SEATS AT THE COUNTER.
PERFECT.
HERE WE ARE.
SLIT
YOUR OSHIBORI AND APPETIZERS.
*CHIKUZENNI: AN APPETIZER OF BRAISED CHICKEN AND VEGETABLES
*OSHIBORI: HOT ROLLED TOWELS, GIVEN BEFORE THE MEAL
OH!
SERVING UP CHIKUZENNI TONIGHT!
THERE'S SATOIMO IN THERE, EVEN!
PLUCK
LIFT
*SATOIMO IS JAPANESE FOR TARO ROOT
CHEW
MM.
THAT'S GOOD.
CHEW CHEW
YES!
YOU ALWAYS WOLF DOWN YOUR FAVORITE PART FIRST, DON'T YOU, HANS?
HAVING SIBLINGS TAUGHT ME THAT. SLOWEST ONE WOULD MISS OUT.

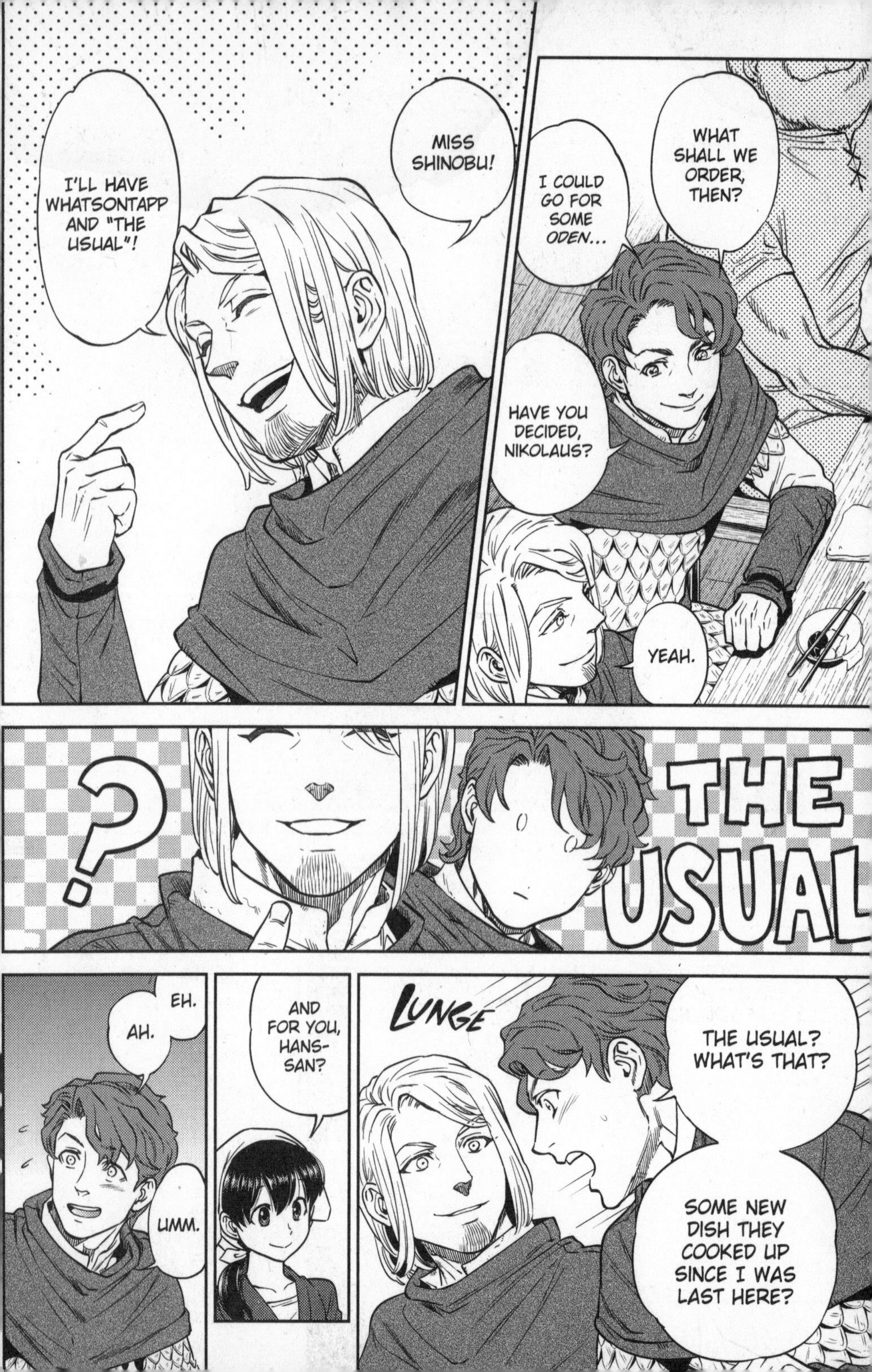
WHAT SHALL WE ORDER, THEN?
I COULD GO FOR SOME ODEN...
HAVE YOU DECIDED, NIKOLAUS?
YEAH.
MISS SHINOBU!
I'LL HAVE WHATSONTAPP AND "THE USUAL"!
THE USUAL
?
THE USUAL? WHAT'S THAT?
LUNGE
SOME NEW DISH THEY COOKED UP SINCE I WAS LAST HERE?
AND FOR YOU, HANS-SAN?
EH.
AH.
UMM.

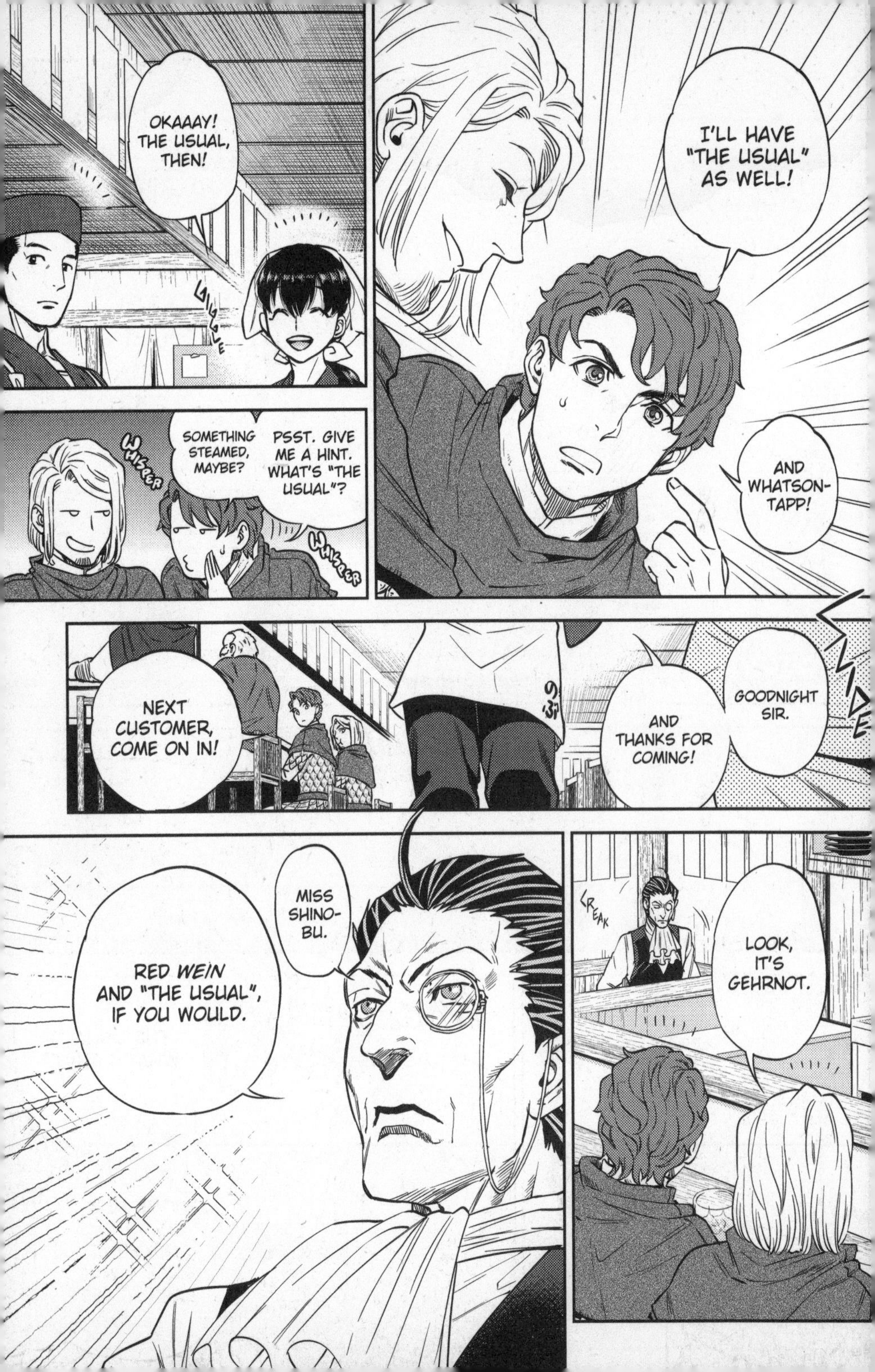
I'LL HAVE "THE USUAL" AS WELL!
AND WHATSON-TAPP!
OKAAAY! THE USUAL, THEN!
PSST. GIVE ME A HINT. WHAT'S "THE USUAL"?
SOMETHING STEAMED, MAYBE?
WHISPER
WHISPER
SLIDE
GOODNIGHT SIR.
AND THANKS FOR COMING!
NEXT CUSTOMER, COME ON IN!
CREAK
LOOK, IT'S GEHRNOT.
MISS SHINO-BU.
RED WEIN AND "THE USUAL", IF YOU WOULD.

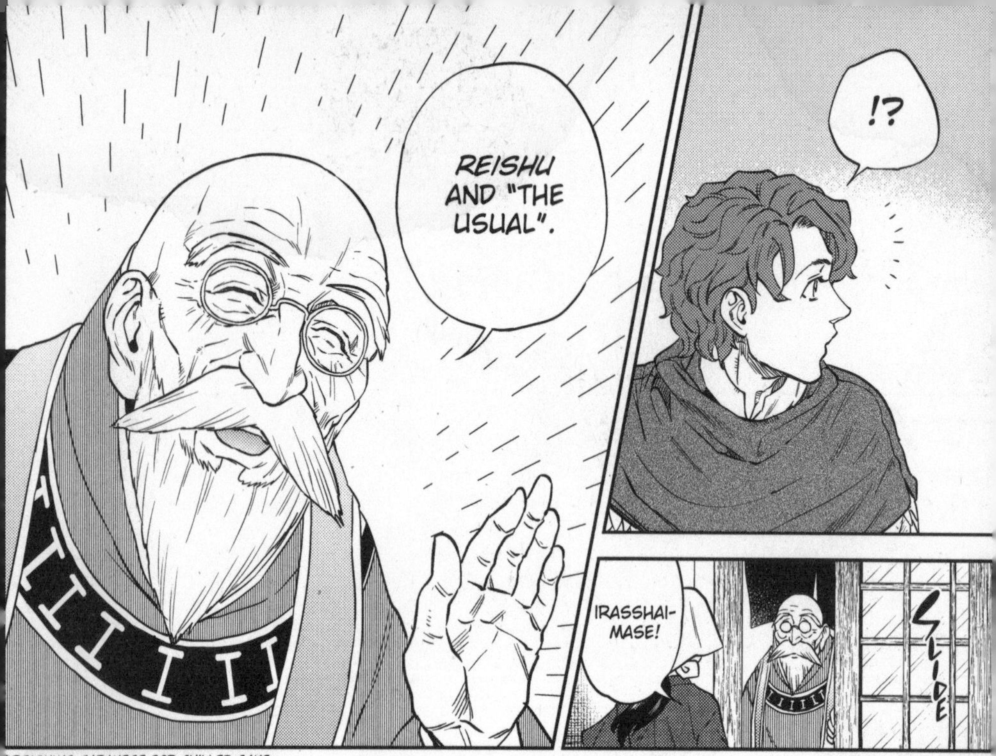
!?
IRASSHAI-MASE!
SLIDE
REISHU AND "THE USUAL".

*REISHU IS JAPANESE FOR CHILLED SAKE.

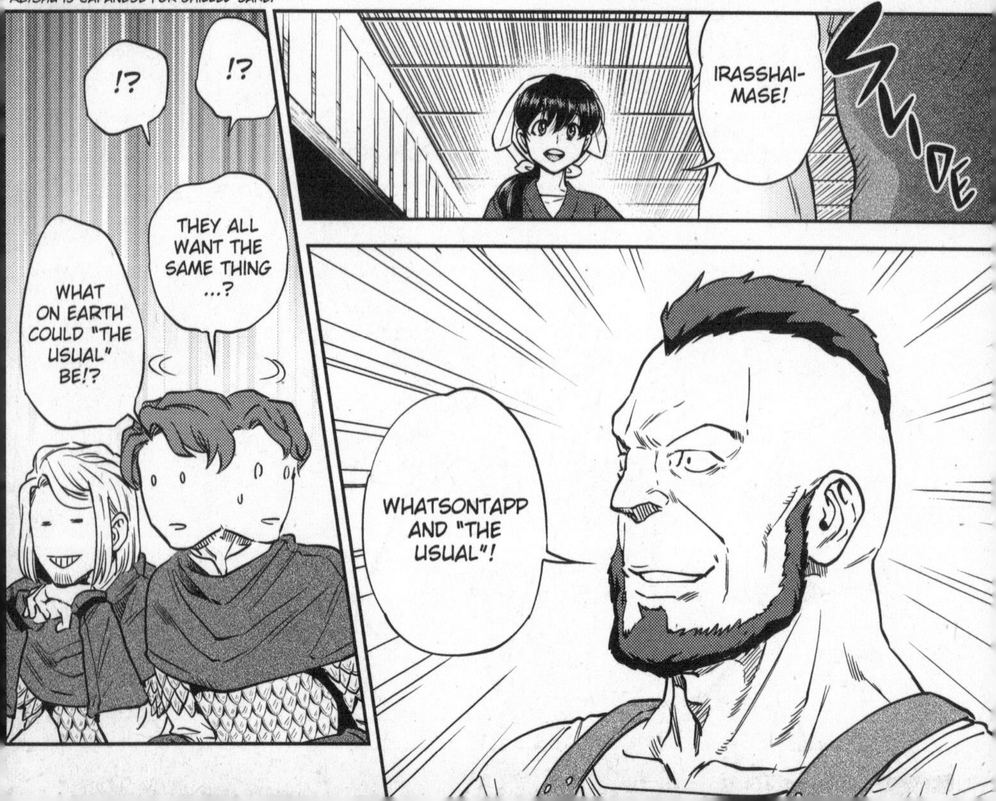
SLIDE
IRASSHAI-MASE!
!?
!?
WHATSONTAPP AND "THE USUAL"!
THEY ALL WANT THE SAME THING ...?
WHAT ON EARTH COULD "THE USUAL" BE!?

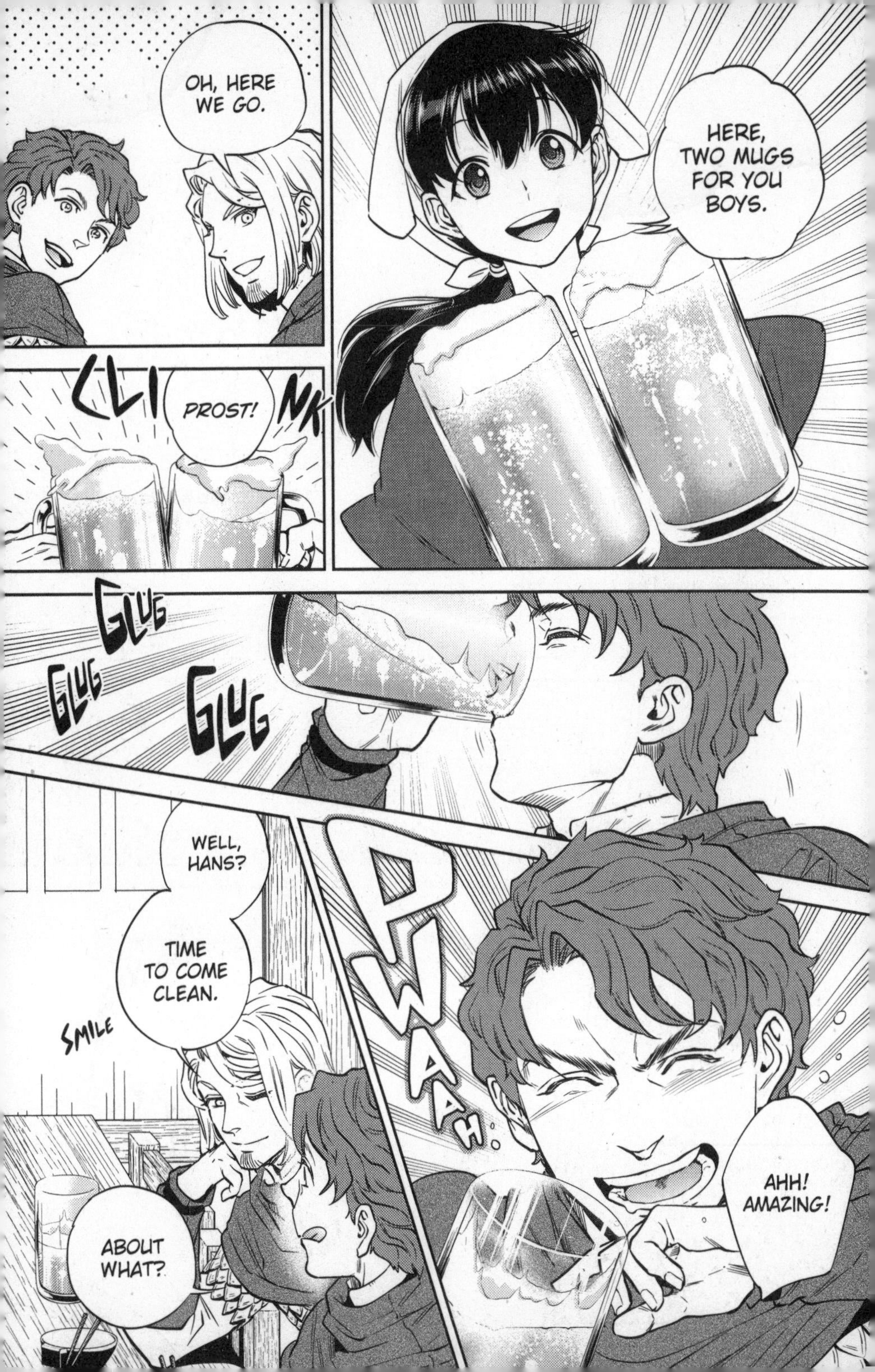
HERE, TWO MUGS FOR YOU BOYS.
OH, HERE WE GO.
CLINK
PROST!
GLUG
GLUG
GLUG
PWAAH
AHH! AMAZING!
WELL, HANS?
TIME TO COME CLEAN.
SMILE
ABOUT WHAT?

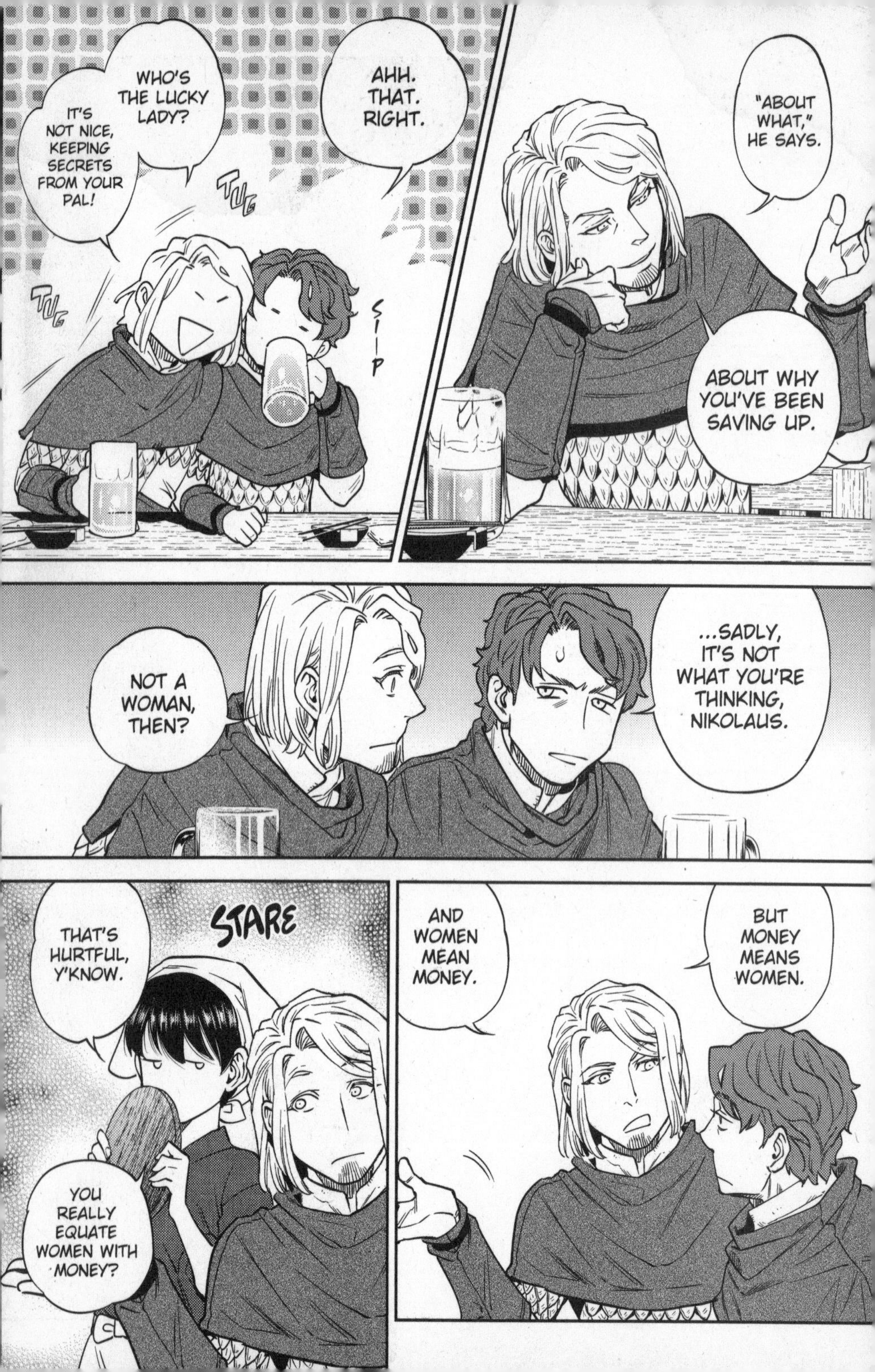
"ABOUT WHAT," HE SAYS.
ABOUT WHY YOU'VE BEEN SAVING UP.
AHH. THAT. RIGHT.
WHO'S THE LUCKY LADY?
IT'S NOT NICE, KEEPING SECRETS FROM YOUR PAL!
TUG
TUG
SIP
...SADLY, IT'S NOT WHAT YOU'RE THINKING, NIKOLAUS.
NOT A WOMAN, THEN?
BUT MONEY MEANS WOMEN.
AND WOMEN MEAN MONEY.
STARE
THAT'S HURTFUL, Y'KNOW.
YOU REALLY EQUATE WOMEN WITH MONEY?

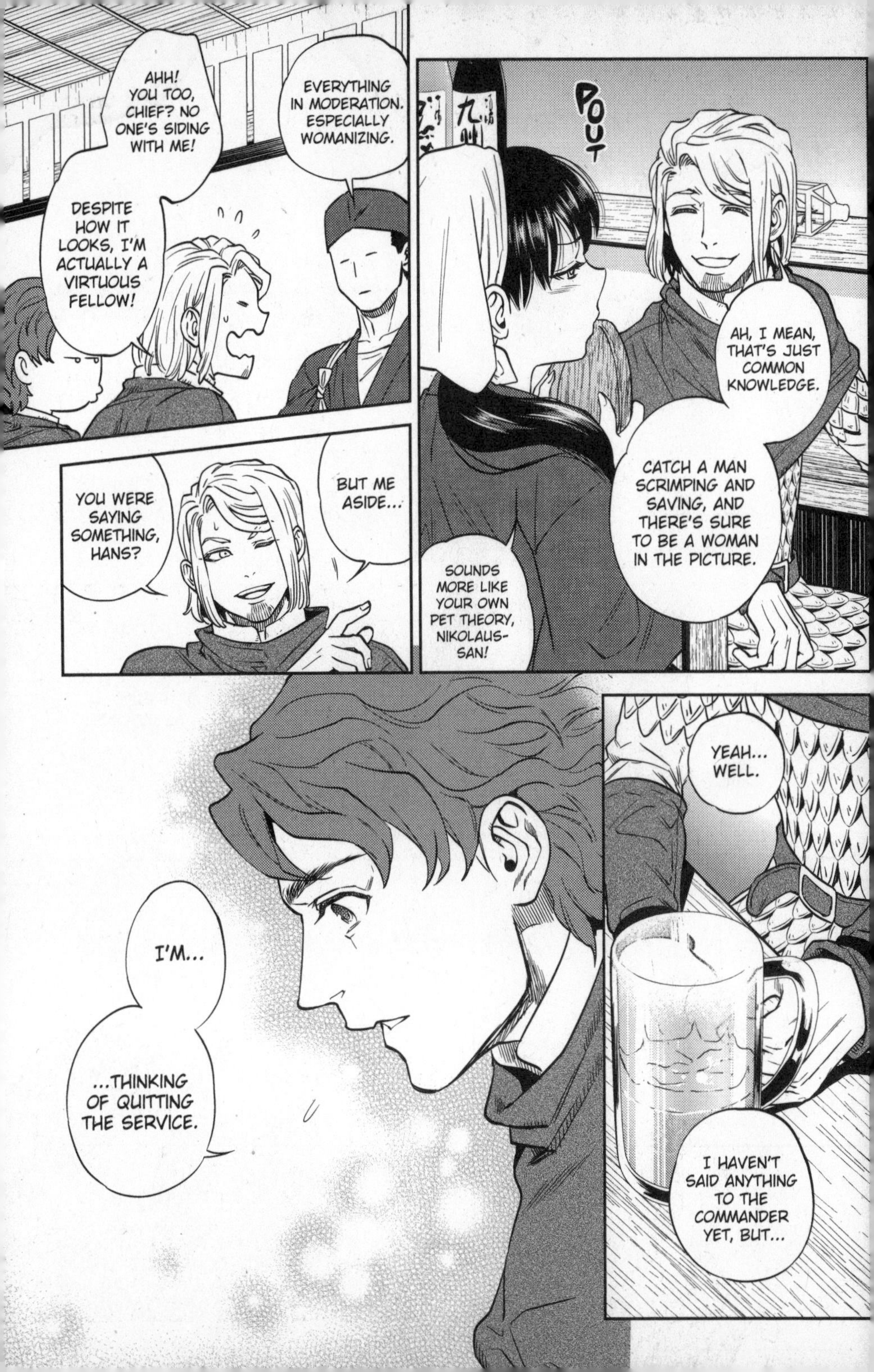
POUT
AH, I MEAN, THAT'S JUST COMMON KNOWLEDGE.
CATCH A MAN SCRIMPING AND SAVING, AND THERE'S SURE TO BE A WOMAN IN THE PICTURE.
SOUNDS MORE LIKE YOUR OWN PET THEORY, NIKOLAUS-SAN!
EVERYTHING IN MODERATION. ESPECIALLY WOMANIZING.
AHH! YOU TOO, CHIEF? NO ONE'S SIDING WITH ME!
DESPITE HOW IT LOOKS, I'M ACTUALLY A VIRTUOUS FELLOW!
BUT ME ASIDE...
YOU WERE SAYING SOMETHING, HANS?
YEAH... WELL.
I HAVEN'T SAID ANYTHING TO THE COMMANDER YET, BUT...
I'M...
...THINKING OF QUITTING THE SERVICE.

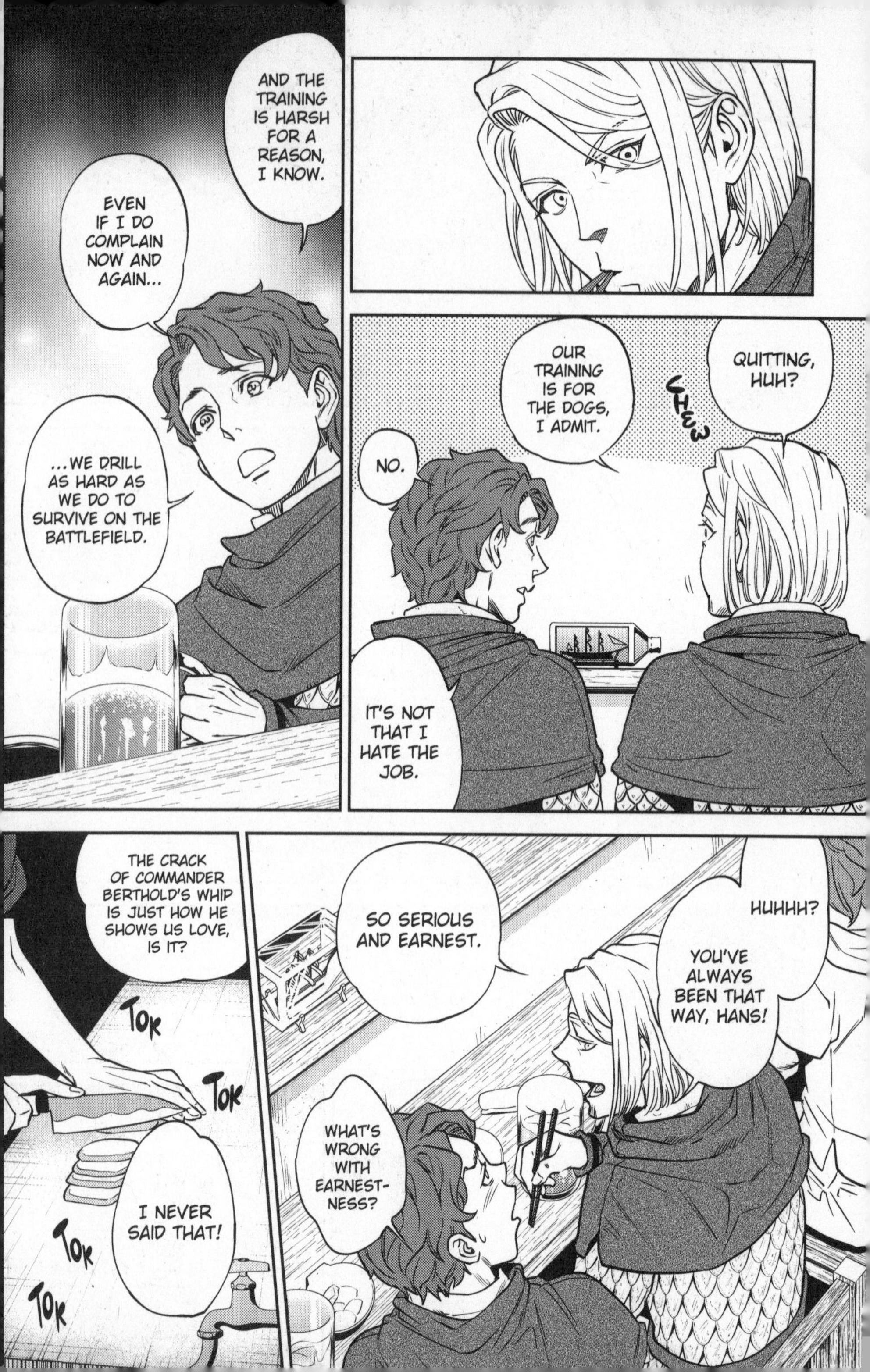
QUITTING, HUH?
CHEW
OUR TRAINING IS FOR THE DOGS, I ADMIT.
NO.
IT'S NOT THAT I HATE THE JOB.
AND THE TRAINING IS HARSH FOR A REASON, I KNOW.
EVEN IF I DO COMPLAIN NOW AND AGAIN...
...WE DRILL AS HARD AS WE DO TO SURVIVE ON THE BATTLEFIELD.
HUHHH?
YOU'VE ALWAYS BEEN THAT WAY, HANS!
SO SERIOUS AND EARNEST.
WHAT'S WRONG WITH EARNEST-NESS?
THE CRACK OF COMMANDER BERTHOLD'S WHIP IS JUST HOW HE SHOWS US LOVE, IS IT?
TOK
TOK
I NEVER SAID THAT!
TOK
TOK

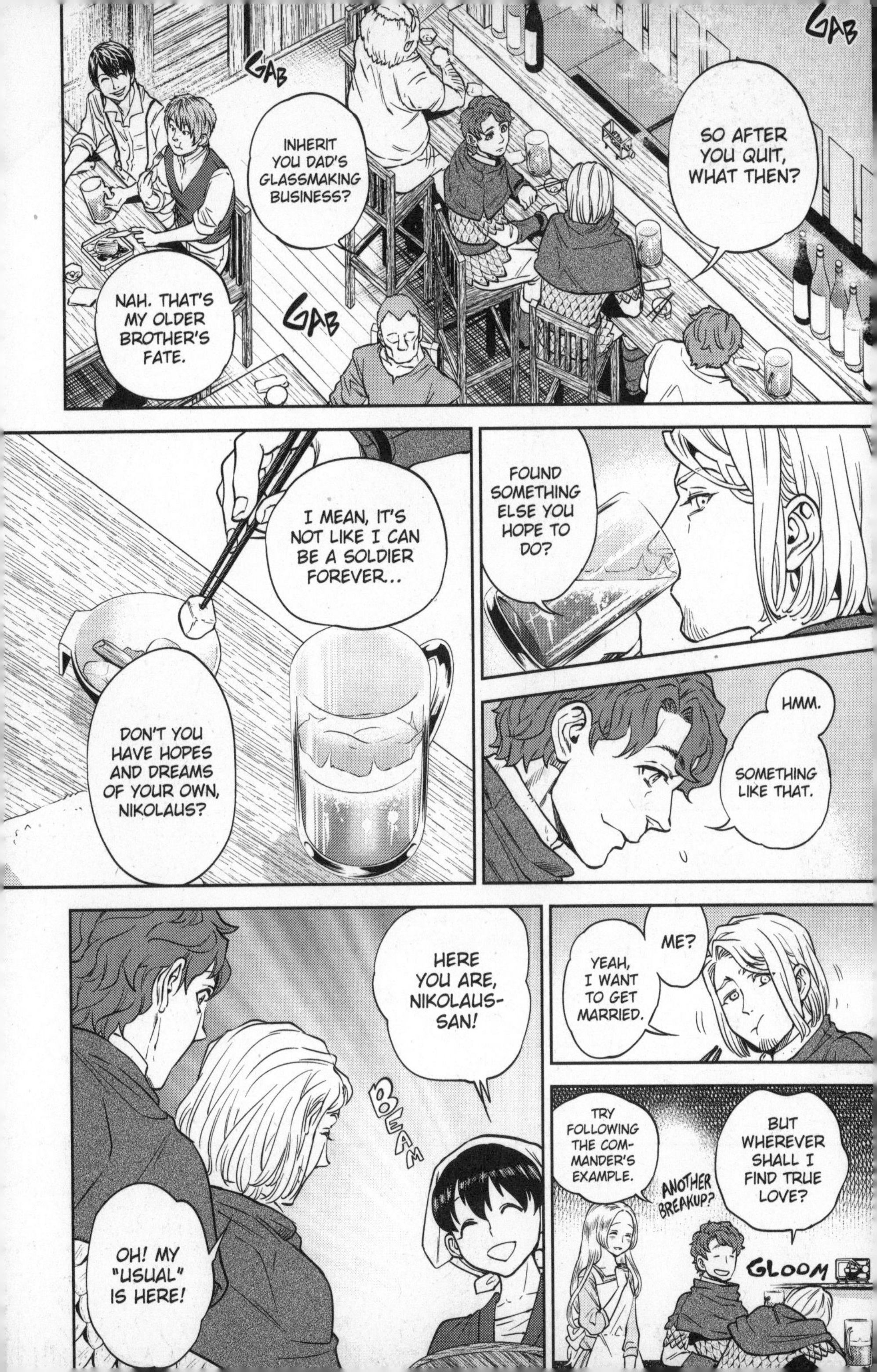
GAB
SO AFTER YOU QUIT, WHAT THEN?
INHERIT YOU DAD'S GLASSMAKING BUSINESS?
GAB
NAH. THAT'S MY OLDER BROTHER'S FATE.
GAB
FOUND SOMETHING ELSE YOU HOPE TO DO?
HMM.
SOMETHING LIKE THAT.
I MEAN, IT'S NOT LIKE I CAN BE A SOLDIER FOREVER...
DON'T YOU HAVE HOPES AND DREAMS OF YOUR OWN, NIKOLAUS?
ME?
YEAH, I WANT TO GET MARRIED.
BUT WHEREVER SHALL I FIND TRUE LOVE?
TRY FOLLOWING THE COM-MANDER'S EXAMPLE.
ANOTHER BREAKUP?
GLOOM
HERE YOU ARE, NIKOLAUS-SAN!
BEAM
OH! MY "USUAL" IS HERE!

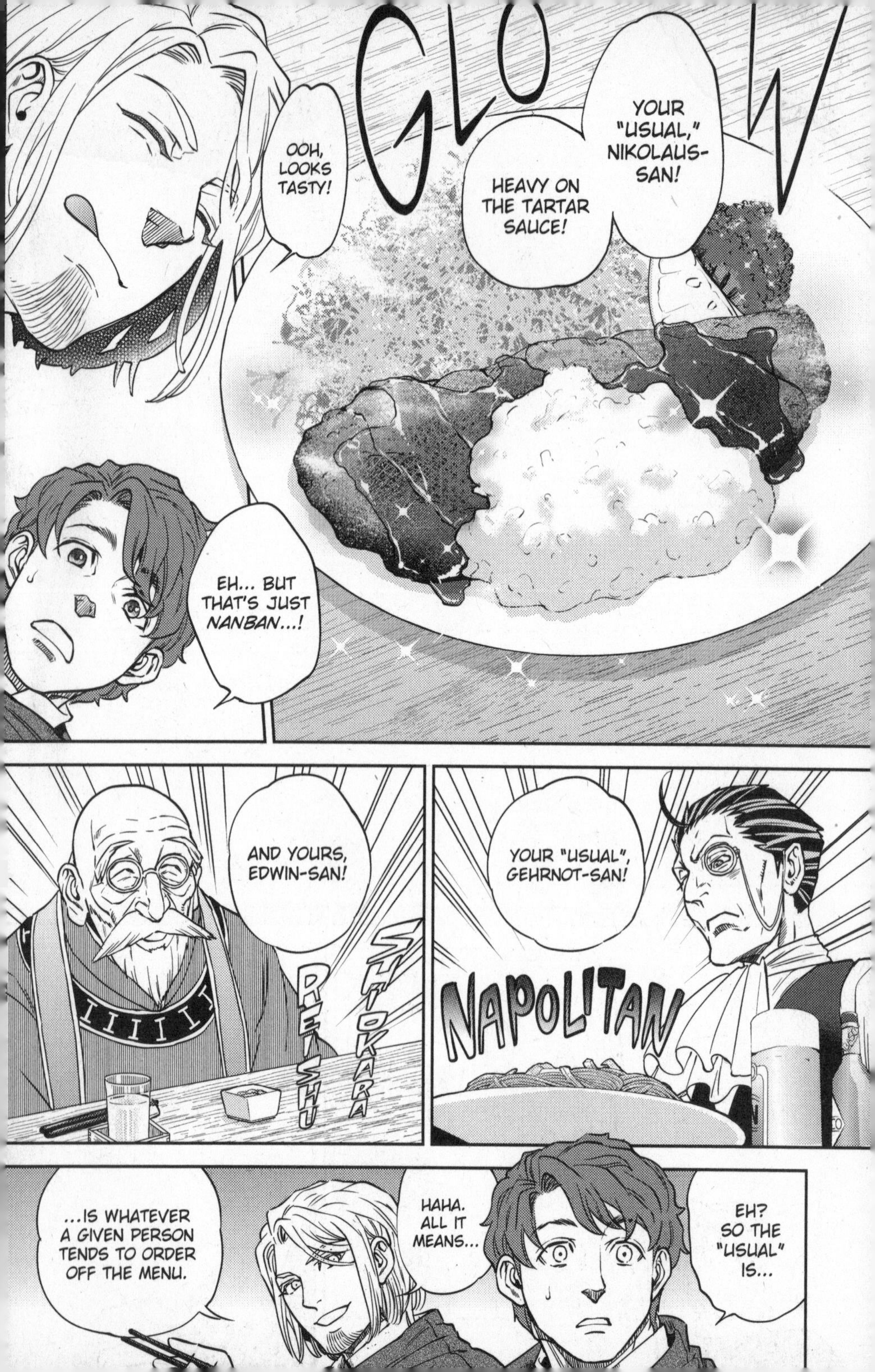
GLOW
YOUR "USUAL," NIKOLAUS-SAN!
HEAVY ON THE TARTAR SAUCE!
OOH, LOOKS TASTY!
EH... BUT THAT'S JUST *NANBAN*...!
YOUR "USUAL", GEHRNOT-SAN!
NAPOLITAN
AND YOURS, EDWIN-SAN!
SHIOKARA
REISHU
EH? SO THE "USUAL" IS...
HAHA. ALL IT MEANS...
...IS WHATEVER A GIVEN PERSON TENDS TO ORDER OFF THE MENU.

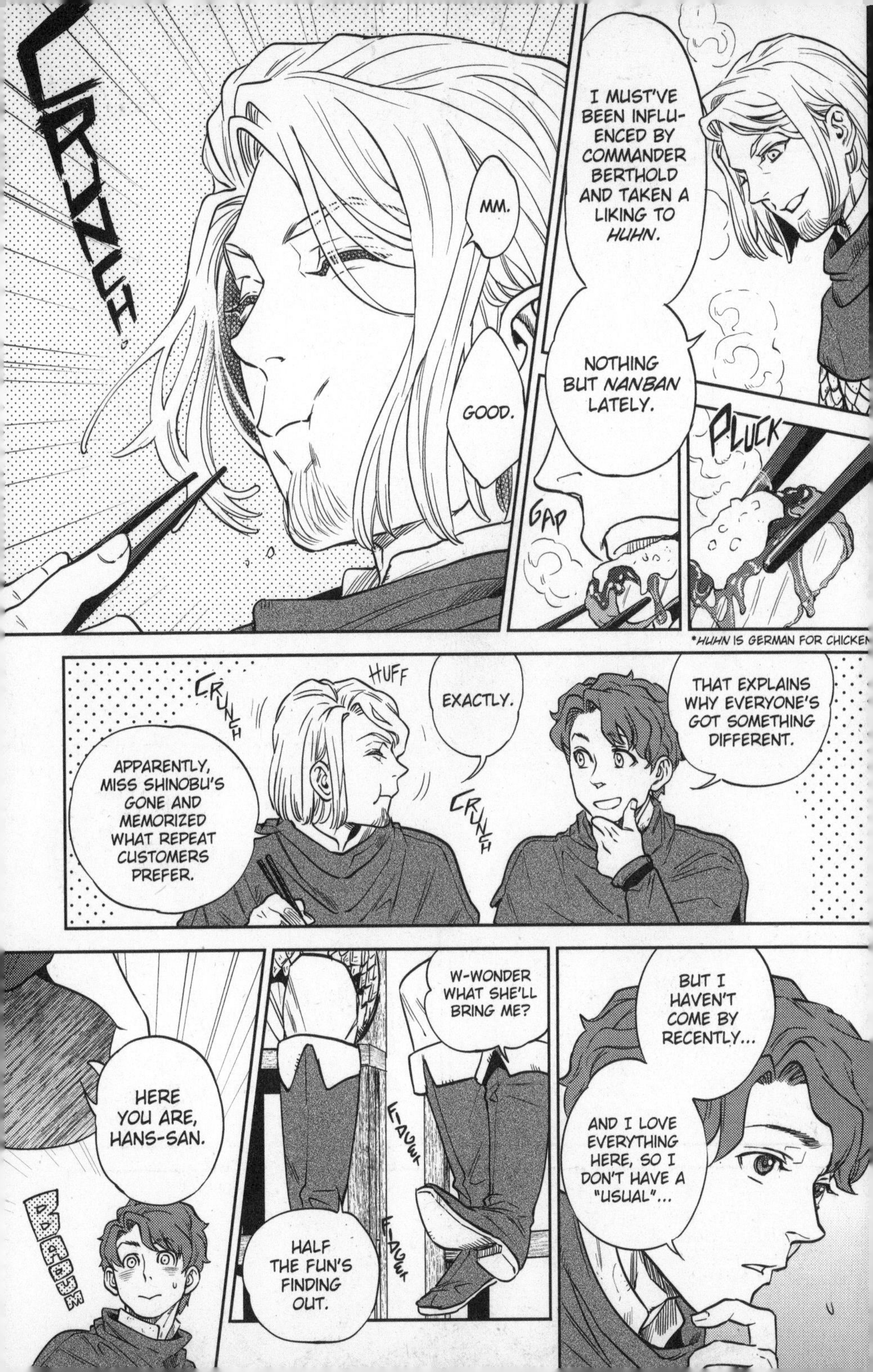
I MUST'VE BEEN INFLUENCED BY COMMANDER BERTHOLD AND TAKEN A LIKING TO *HUHN*.
NOTHING BUT *NANBAN* LATELY.
PLUCK
GAP
MM.
GOOD.
CRUNCH.
*HUHN IS GERMAN FOR CHICKEN
THAT EXPLAINS WHY EVERYONE'S GOT SOMETHING DIFFERENT.
EXACTLY.
HUFF
CRUNCH
APPARENTLY, MISS SHINOBU'S GONE AND MEMORIZED WHAT REPEAT CUSTOMERS PREFER.
CRUNCH
BUT I HAVEN'T COME BY RECENTLY...
AND I LOVE EVERYTHING HERE, SO I DON'T HAVE A "USUAL"...
W-WONDER WHAT SHE'LL BRING ME?
FIDGET
FIDGET
HALF THE FUN'S FINDING OUT.
HERE YOU ARE, HANS-SAN.
BADUM

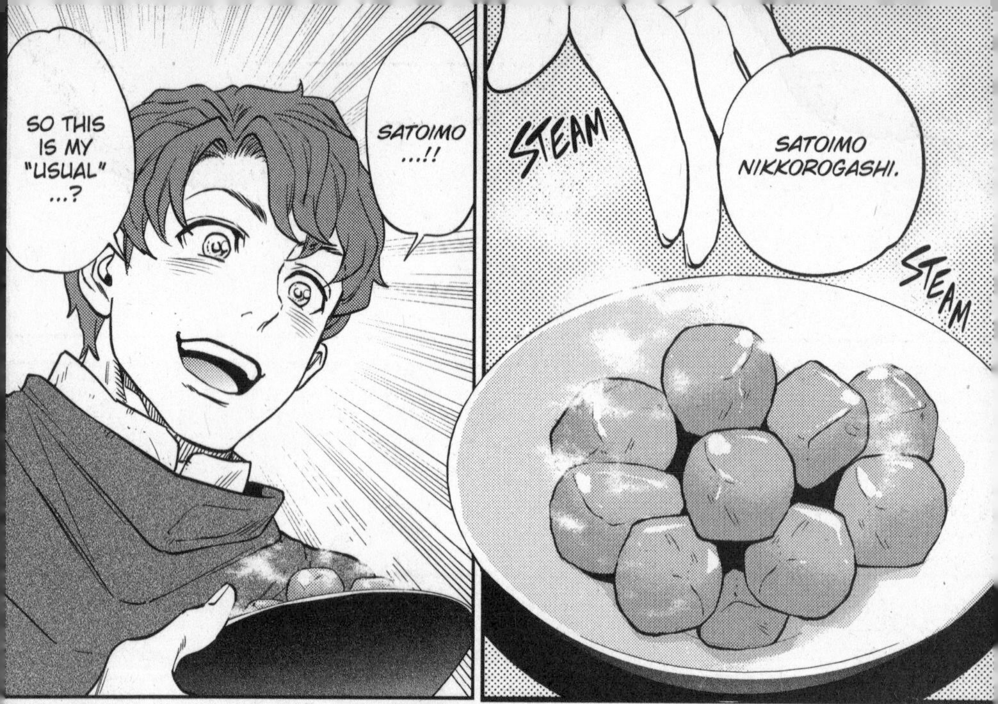
SATOIMO NIKKOROGASHI.
STEAM
STEAM
SATOIMO ...!!
SO THIS IS MY "USUAL" ...?

SATOIMO NIKKOROGASHI: SMALL TARO COOKED AND ROLLED ABOUT IN A THICK, SWEET SAUCE

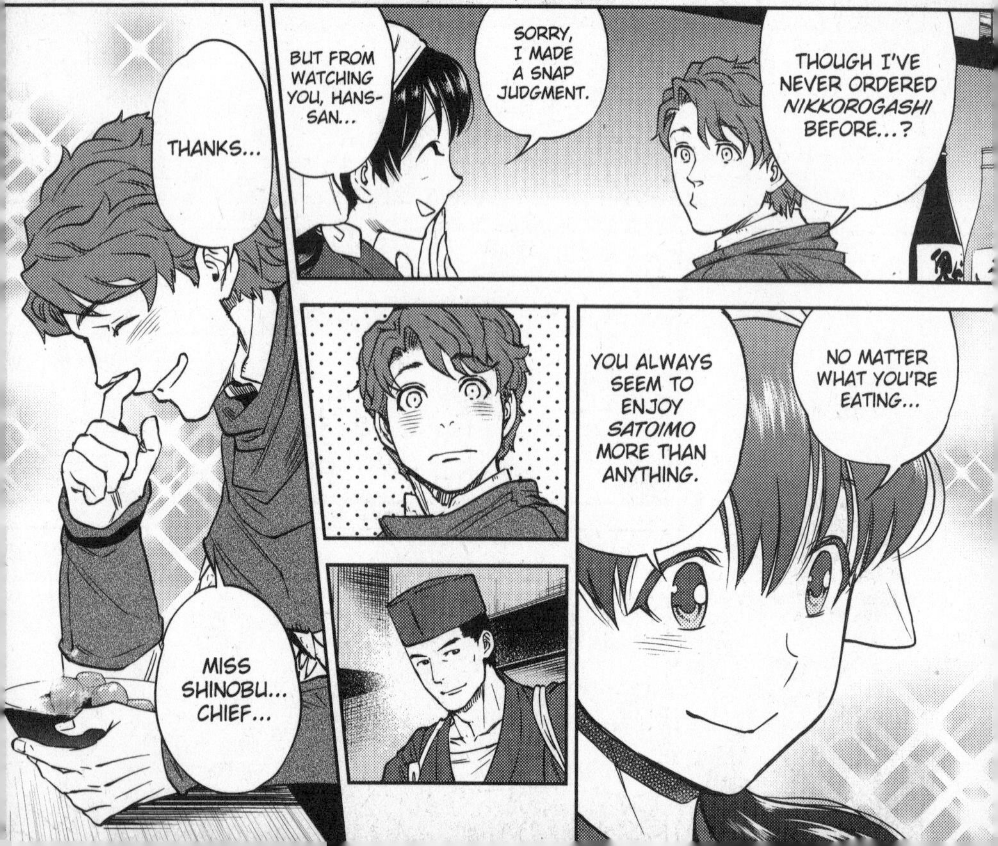
THOUGH I'VE NEVER ORDERED *NIKKOROGASHI* BEFORE...?
SORRY, I MADE A SNAP JUDGMENT.
BUT FROM WATCHING YOU, HANS-SAN...
NO MATTER WHAT YOU'RE EATING...
YOU ALWAYS SEEM TO ENJOY *SATOIMO* MORE THAN ANYTHING.
THANKS...
MISS SHINOBU... CHIEF...

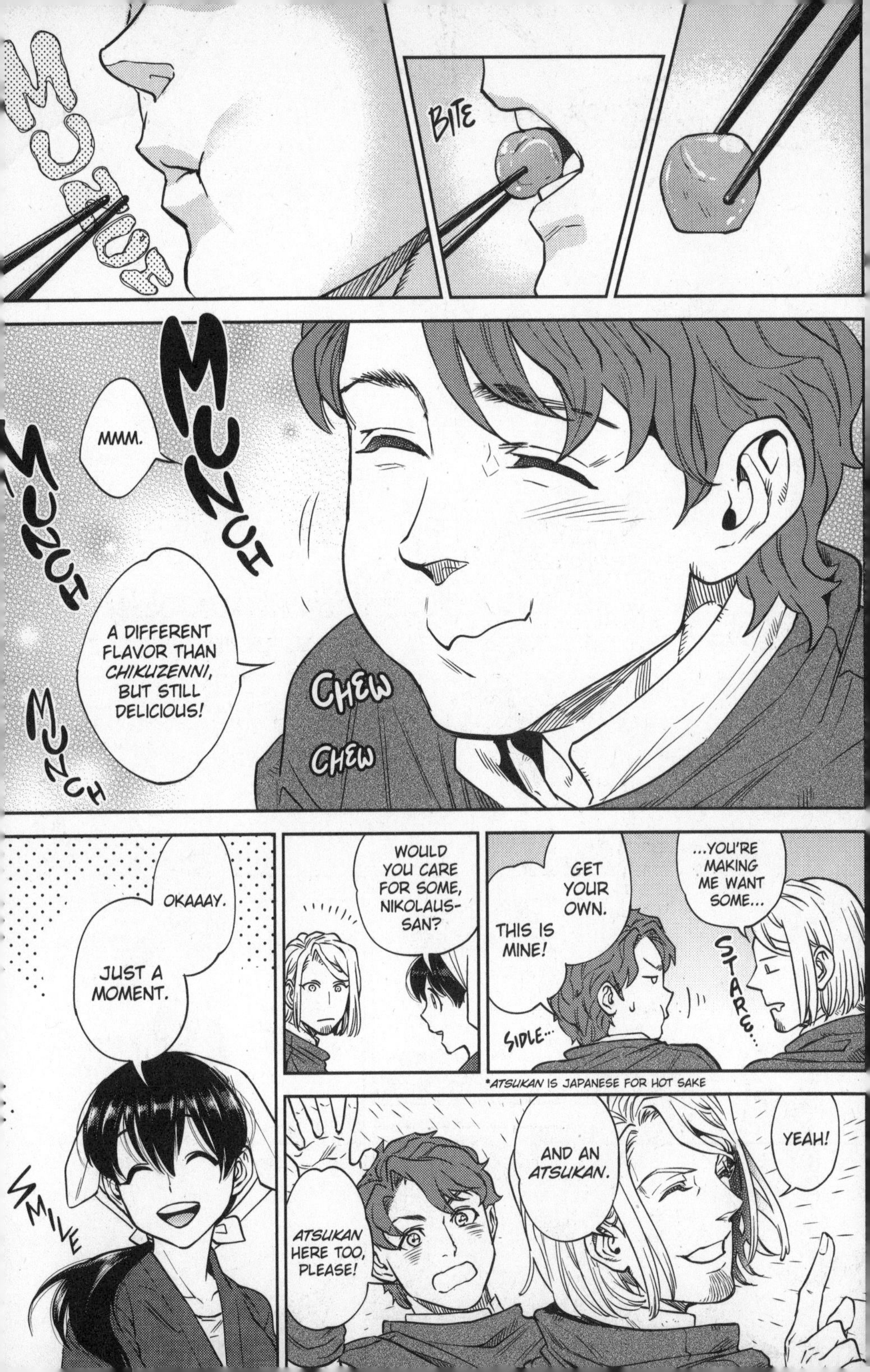
BITE
MUNCH
MUNCH
MMM.
MUNCH
A DIFFERENT FLAVOR THAN *CHIKUZENNI*, BUT STILL DELICIOUS!
CHEW
CHEW
MUNCH
...YOU'RE MAKING ME WANT SOME...
STARE...
GET YOUR OWN.
THIS IS MINE!
SIDLE...
WOULD YOU CARE FOR SOME, NIKOLAUS-SAN?
YEAH!
AND AN *ATSUKAN*.
ATSUKAN HERE TOO, PLEASE!
OKAAAY.
JUST A MOMENT.
SMILE
**ATSUKAN* IS JAPANESE FOR HOT SAKE

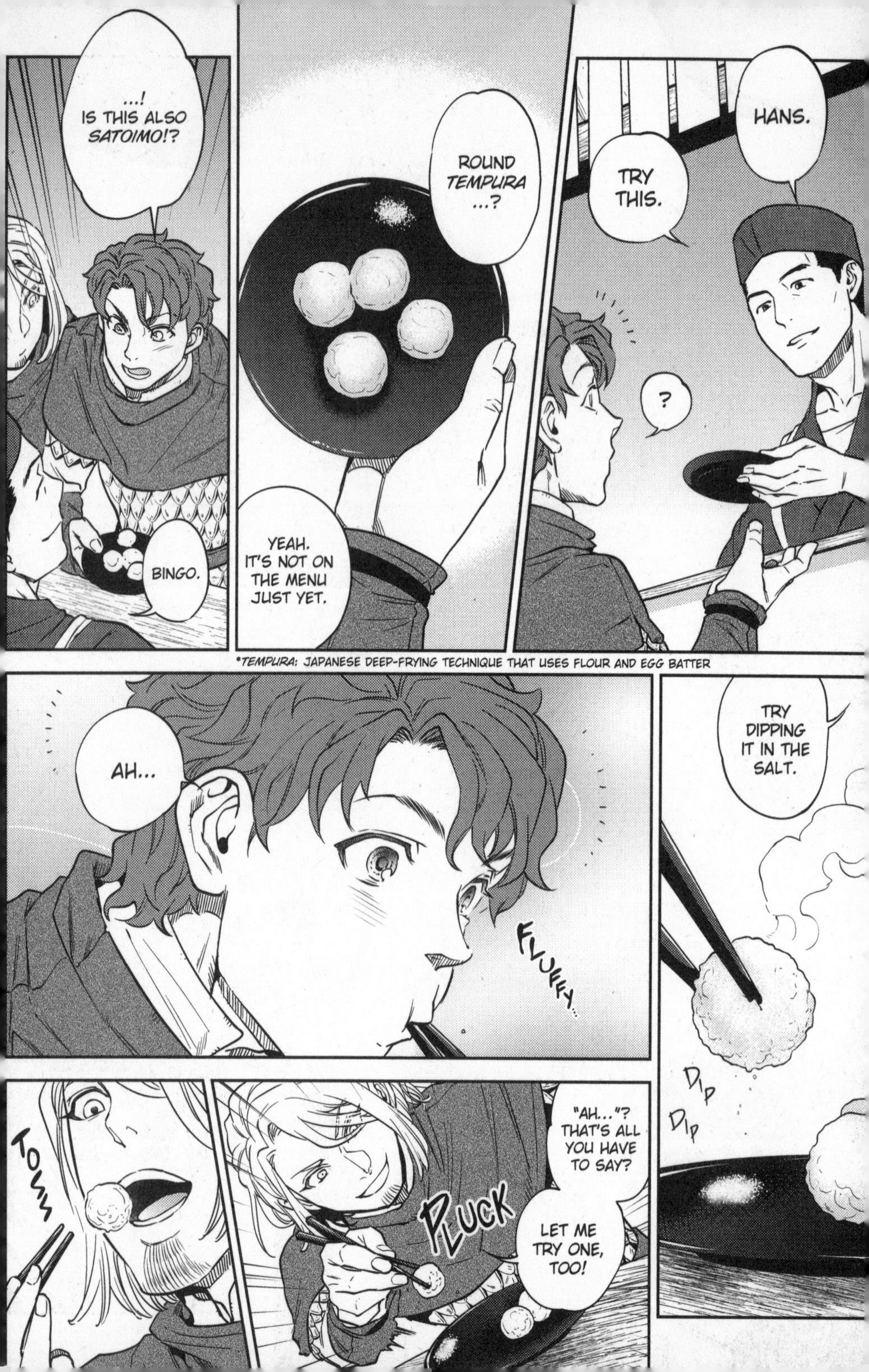
HANS.
TRY THIS.
?
ROUND *TEMPURA* ...?
YEAH. IT'S NOT ON THE MENU JUST YET.
...! IS THIS ALSO *SATOIMO*!?
BINGO.
TRY DIPPING IT IN THE SALT.
DIP
DIP
AH...
FLUFFY...
"AH..."? THAT'S ALL YOU HAVE TO SAY?
PLUCK
LET ME TRY ONE, TOO!
TOSS

**Tempura*: Japanese deep-frying technique that uses flour and egg batter

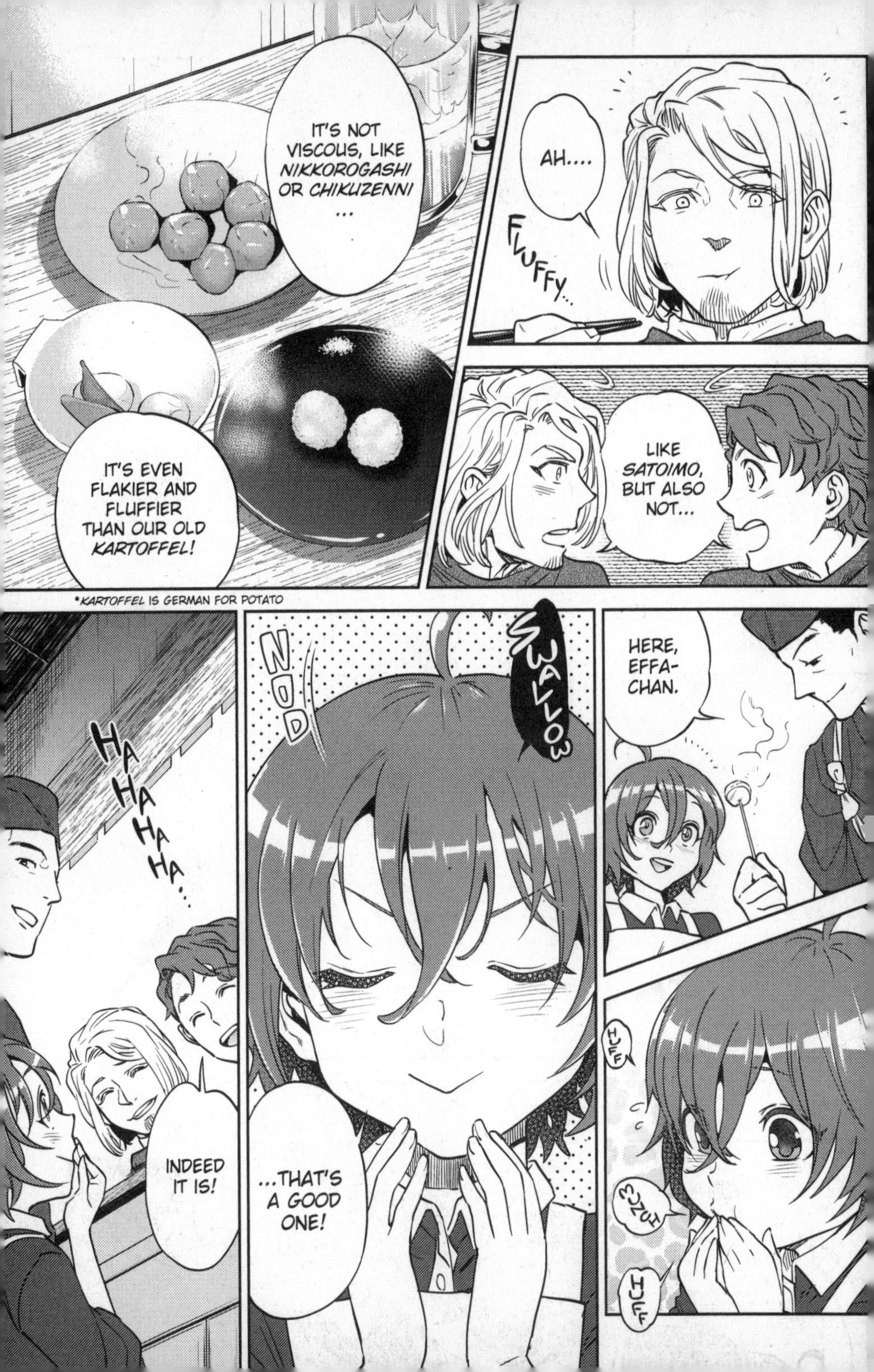
AH....
FLUFFY...
LIKE SATOIMO, BUT ALSO NOT...
IT'S NOT VISCOUS, LIKE NIKKOROGASHI OR CHIKUZENNI ...
IT'S EVEN FLAKIER AND FLUFFIER THAN OUR OLD KARTOFFEL!
*KARTOFFEL IS GERMAN FOR POTATO
HERE, EFFA-CHAN.
HUFF
MUNCH
HUFF
NOD
SWALLOW
...THAT'S A GOOD ONE!
HAHAHAHA...
INDEED IT IS!

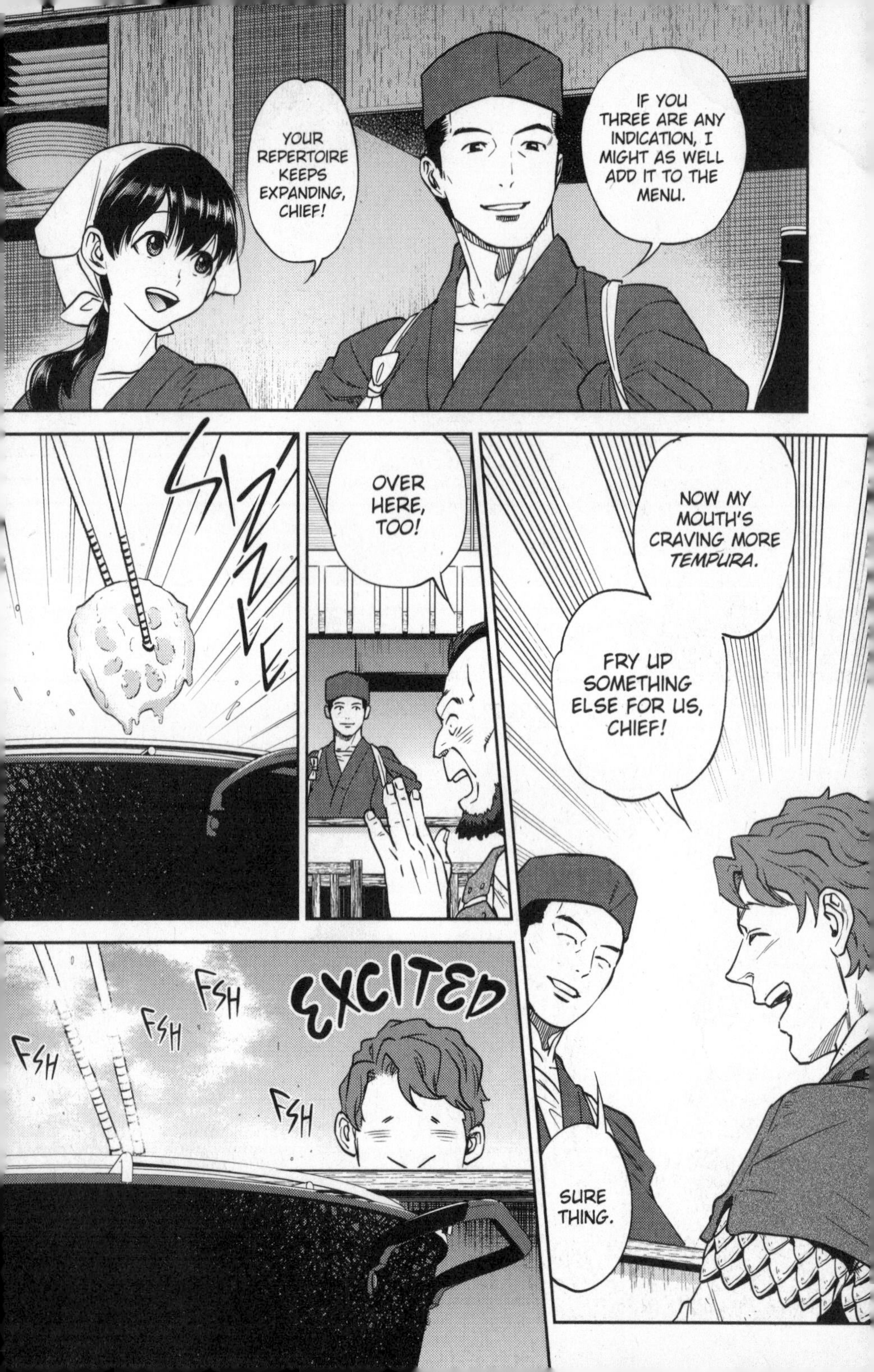
IF YOU THREE ARE ANY INDICATION, I MIGHT AS WELL ADD IT TO THE MENU.
YOUR REPERTOIRE KEEPS EXPANDING, CHIEF!
NOW MY MOUTH'S CRAVING MORE *TEMPURA*.
FRY UP SOMETHING ELSE FOR US, CHIEF!
SURE THING.
OVER HERE, TOO!
SIZZLE
EXCITED
FSH
FSH
FSH
FSH

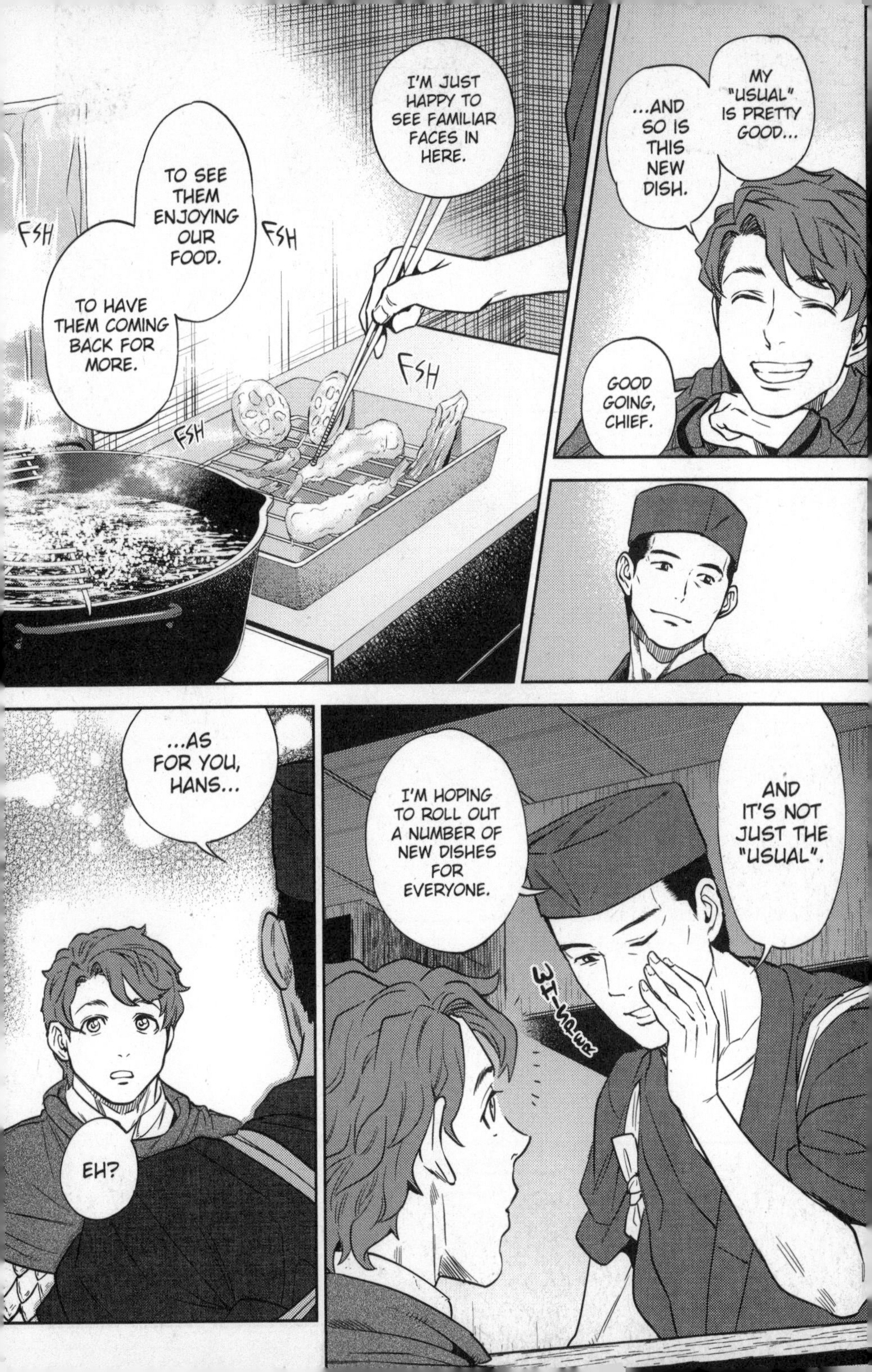

MY "USUAL" IS PRETTY GOOD...
...AND SO IS THIS NEW DISH.
GOOD GOING, CHIEF.
I'M JUST HAPPY TO SEE FAMILIAR FACES IN HERE.
TO SEE THEM ENJOYING OUR FOOD.
FSH
FSH
TO HAVE THEM COMING BACK FOR MORE.
FSH
FSH
AND IT'S NOT JUST THE "USUAL".
I'M HOPING TO ROLL OUT A NUMBER OF NEW DISHES FOR EVERYONE.
...AS FOR YOU, HANS...
EH?

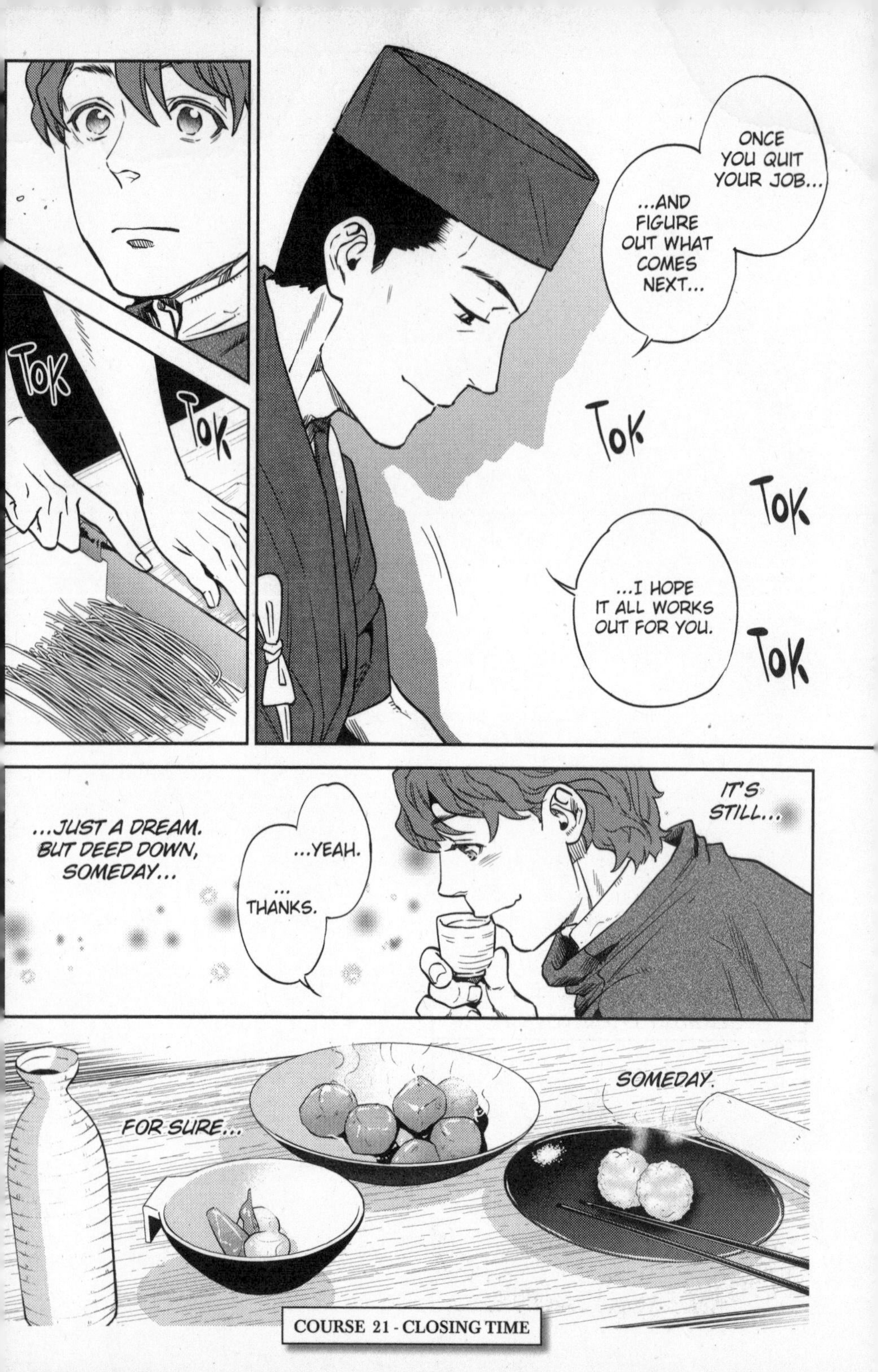
ONCE YOU QUIT YOUR JOB...
...AND FIGURE OUT WHAT COMES NEXT...
TOK
TOK
...I HOPE IT ALL WORKS OUT FOR YOU.
TOK
TOK
TOK
IT'S STILL...
...YEAH.
... THANKS.
...JUST A DREAM. BUT DEEP DOWN, SOMEDAY...
SOMEDAY.
FOR SURE...

COURSE 21 - CLOSING TIME

Satoimo Nikkorogashi

OTHERWORLDLY IZAKAYA

NOBU

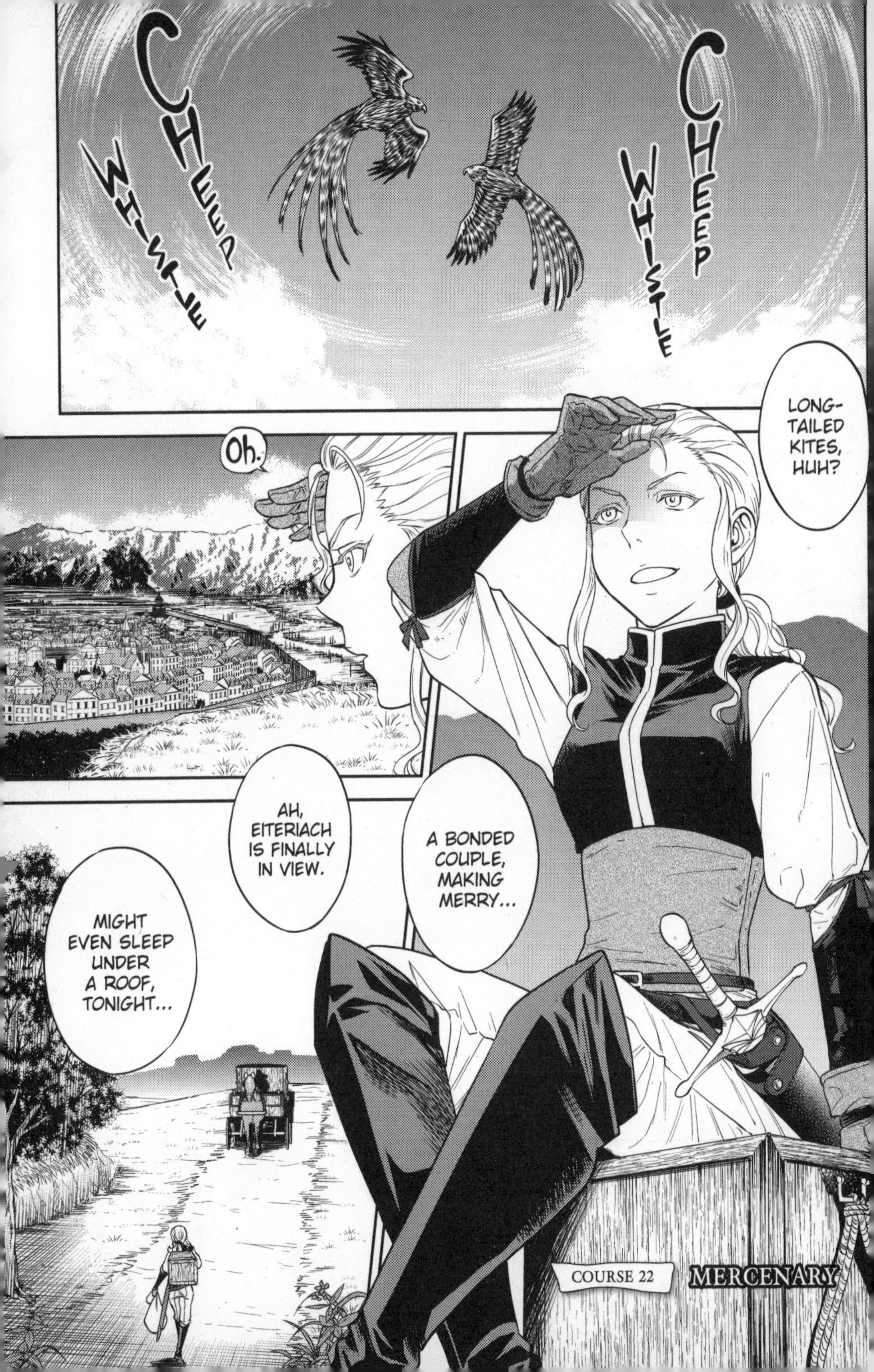
CHEEP
WHISTLE
CHEEP
WHISTLE
LONG-TAILED KITES, HUH?
A BONDED COUPLE, MAKING MERRY...
COURSE 22
MERCENARY
Oh.
AH, EITERIACH IS FINALLY IN VIEW.
MIGHT EVEN SLEEP UNDER A ROOF, TONIGHT...

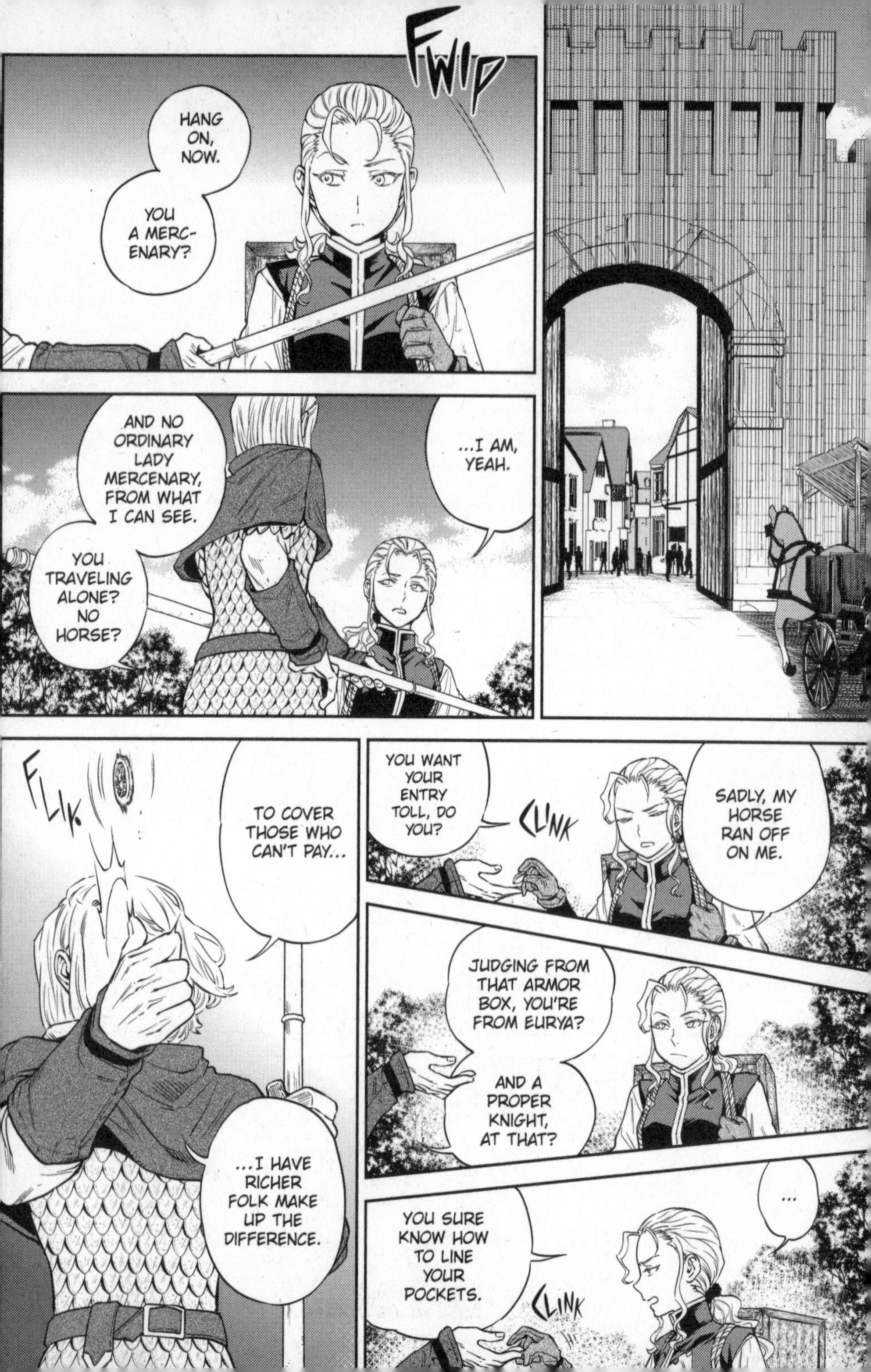
FWIP
HANG ON, NOW.
YOU A MERCENARY?
...I AM, YEAH.
AND NO ORDINARY LADY MERCENARY, FROM WHAT I CAN SEE.
YOU TRAVELING ALONE? NO HORSE?
SADLY, MY HORSE RAN OFF ON ME.
YOU WANT YOUR ENTRY TOLL, DO YOU?
CLINK
JUDGING FROM THAT ARMOR BOX, YOU'RE FROM EURYA?
AND A PROPER KNIGHT, AT THAT?
...
YOU SURE KNOW HOW TO LINE YOUR POCKETS.
CLINK
TO COVER THOSE WHO CAN'T PAY...
...I HAVE RICHER FOLK MAKE UP THE DIFFERENCE.
FLIK

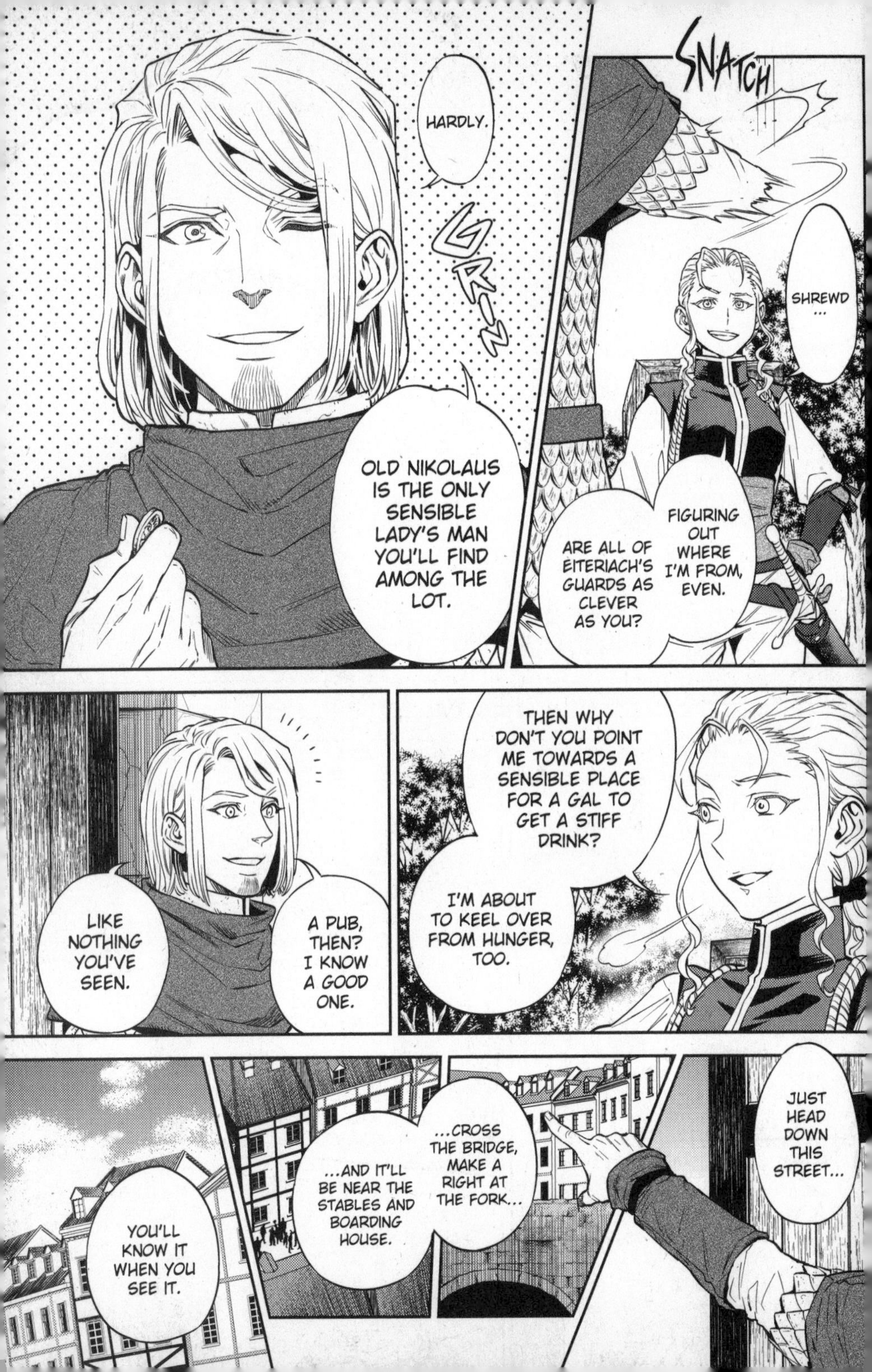
SNATCH
SHREWD...
FIGURING OUT WHERE I'M FROM, EVEN.
ARE ALL OF EITERIACH'S GUARDS AS CLEVER AS YOU?
HARDLY.
GRIN
OLD NIKOLAUS IS THE ONLY SENSIBLE LADY'S MAN YOU'LL FIND AMONG THE LOT.
THEN WHY DON'T YOU POINT ME TOWARDS A SENSIBLE PLACE FOR A GAL TO GET A STIFF DRINK?
I'M ABOUT TO KEEL OVER FROM HUNGER, TOO.
A PUB, THEN? I KNOW A GOOD ONE.
LIKE NOTHING YOU'VE SEEN.
JUST HEAD DOWN THIS STREET...
...CROSS THE BRIDGE, MAKE A RIGHT AT THE FORK...
...AND IT'LL BE NEAR THE STABLES AND BOARDING HOUSE.
YOU'LL KNOW IT WHEN YOU SEE IT.

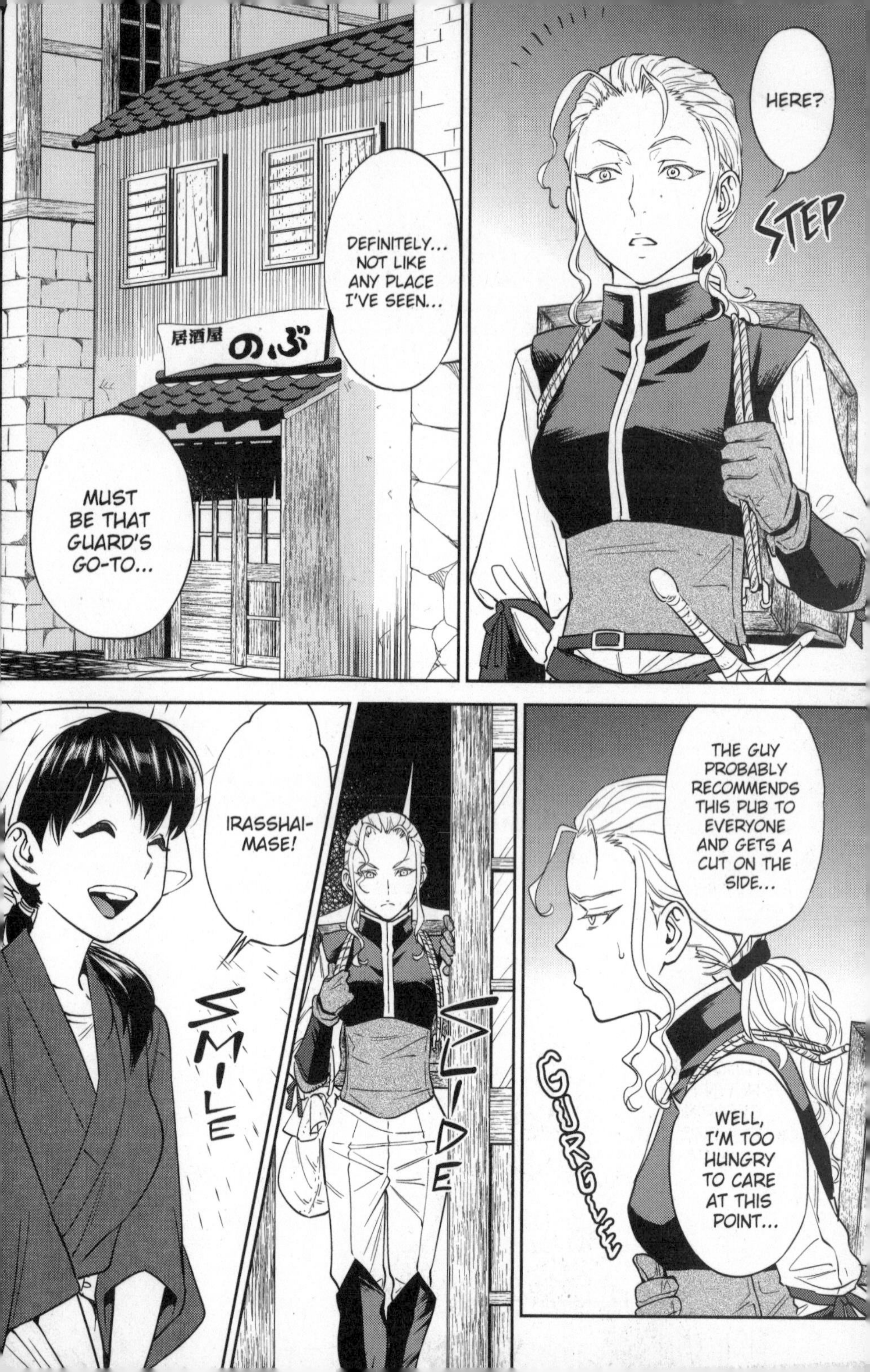
HERE?
STEP
DEFINITELY... NOT LIKE ANY PLACE I'VE SEEN...
居酒屋 のぶ
MUST BE THAT GUARD'S GO-TO...
THE GUY PROBABLY RECOMMENDS THIS PUB TO EVERYONE AND GETS A CUT ON THE SIDE...
GURGLE
WELL, I'M TOO HUNGRY TO CARE AT THIS POINT...
SLIDE
IRASSHAI-MASE!
SMILE

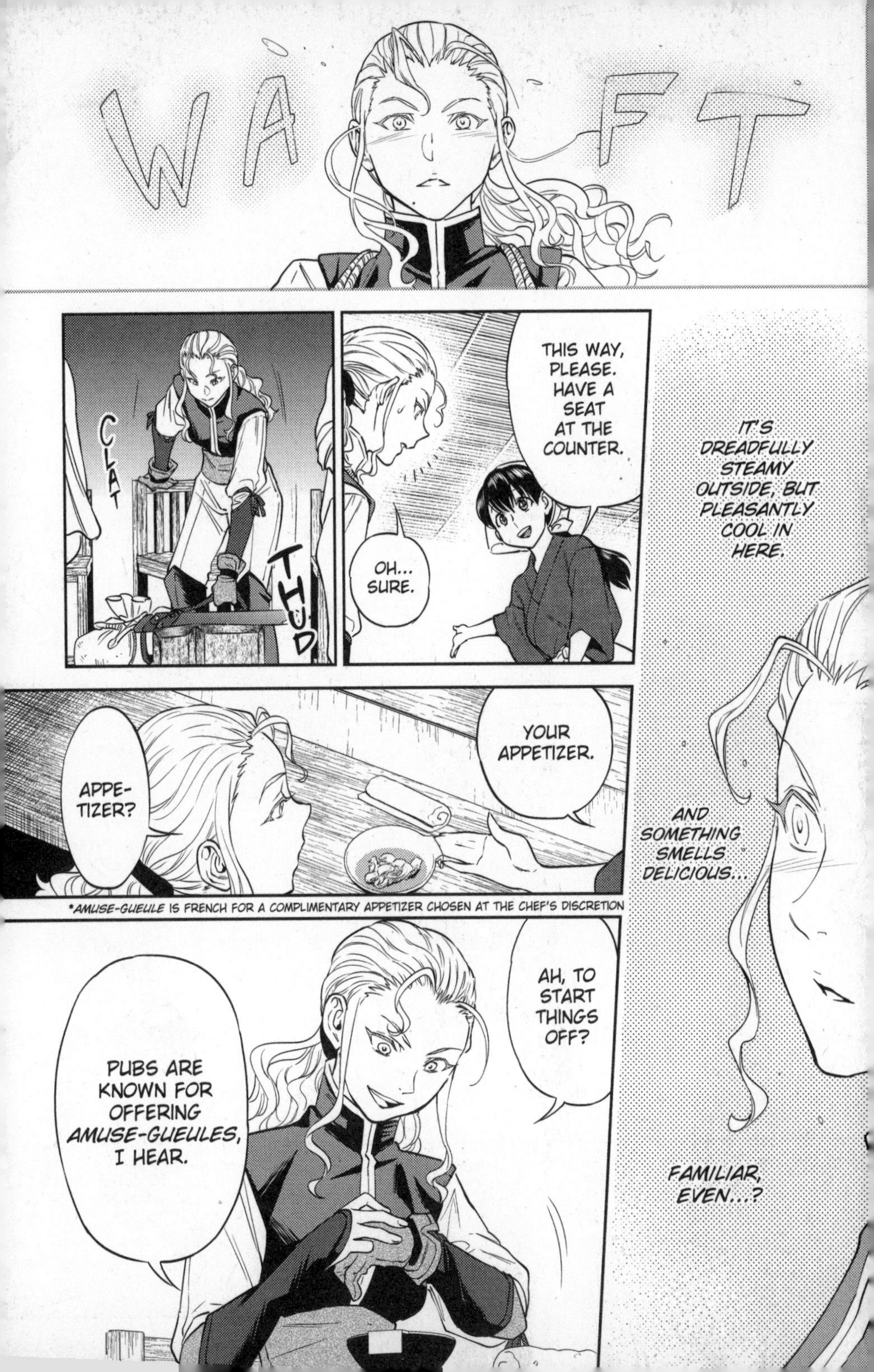
WAFT
IT'S DREADFULLY STEAMY OUTSIDE, BUT PLEASANTLY COOL IN HERE.
AND SOMETHING SMELLS DELICIOUS...
FAMILIAR, EVEN...?
THIS WAY, PLEASE. HAVE A SEAT AT THE COUNTER.
OH... SURE.
CLAT
THUD
YOUR APPETIZER.
APPE-TIZER?
*AMUSE-GUEULE IS FRENCH FOR A COMPLIMENTARY APPETIZER CHOSEN AT THE CHEF'S DISCRETION
AH, TO START THINGS OFF?
PUBS ARE KNOWN FOR OFFERING AMUSE-GUEULES, I HEAR.

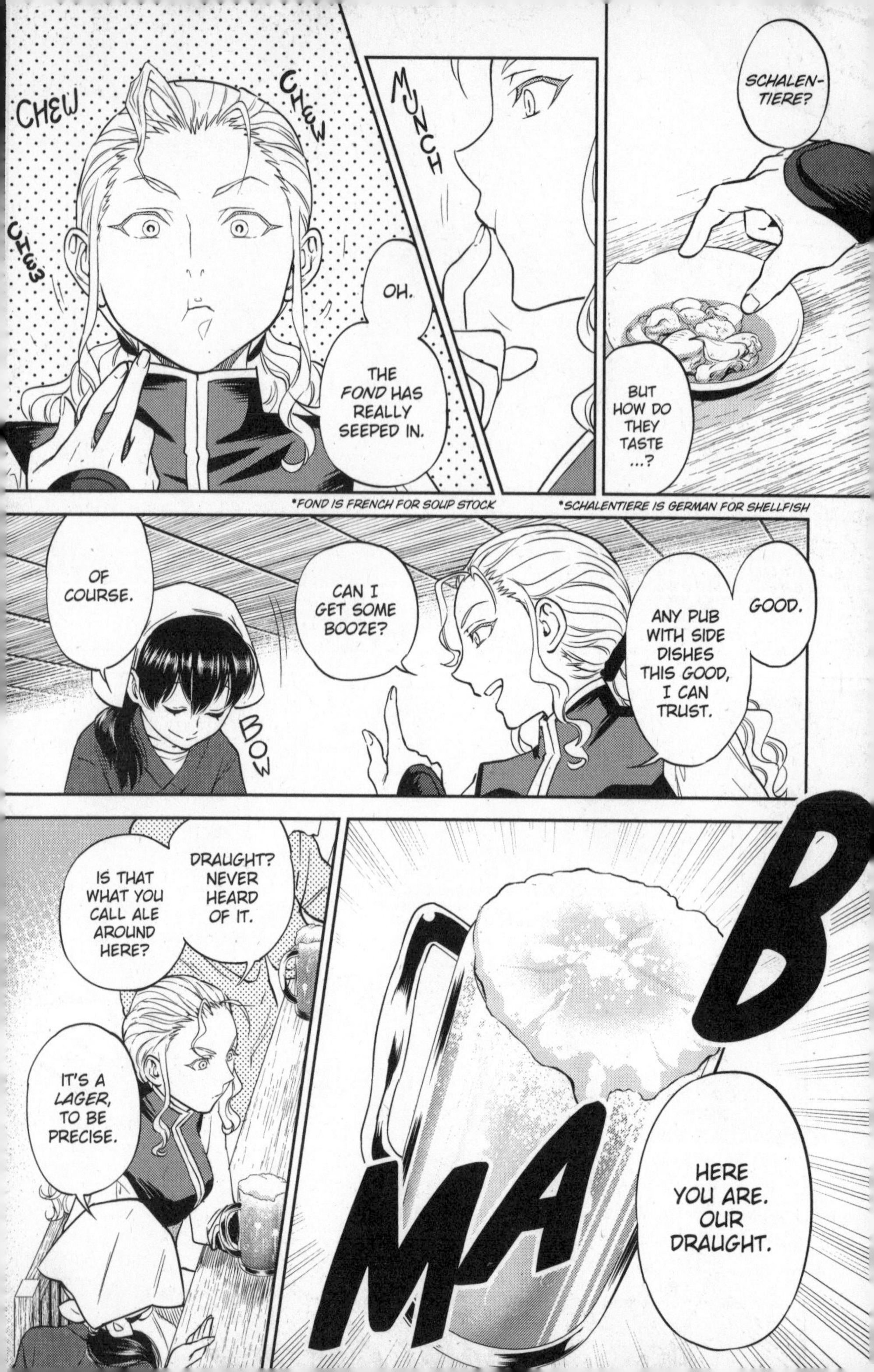
SCHALEN-TIERE?
BUT HOW DO THEY TASTE ...?
MUNCH
OH.
THE FOND HAS REALLY SEEPED IN.
CHEW
CHEW
CHEW
*FOND IS FRENCH FOR SOUP STOCK
*SCHALENTIERE IS GERMAN FOR SHELLFISH
GOOD.
ANY PUB WITH SIDE DISHES THIS GOOD, I CAN TRUST.
CAN I GET SOME BOOZE?
OF COURSE.
BOW
HERE YOU ARE. OUR DRAUGHT.
DRAUGHT? NEVER HEARD OF IT.
IS THAT WHAT YOU CALL ALE AROUND HERE?
IT'S A LAGER, TO BE PRECISE.

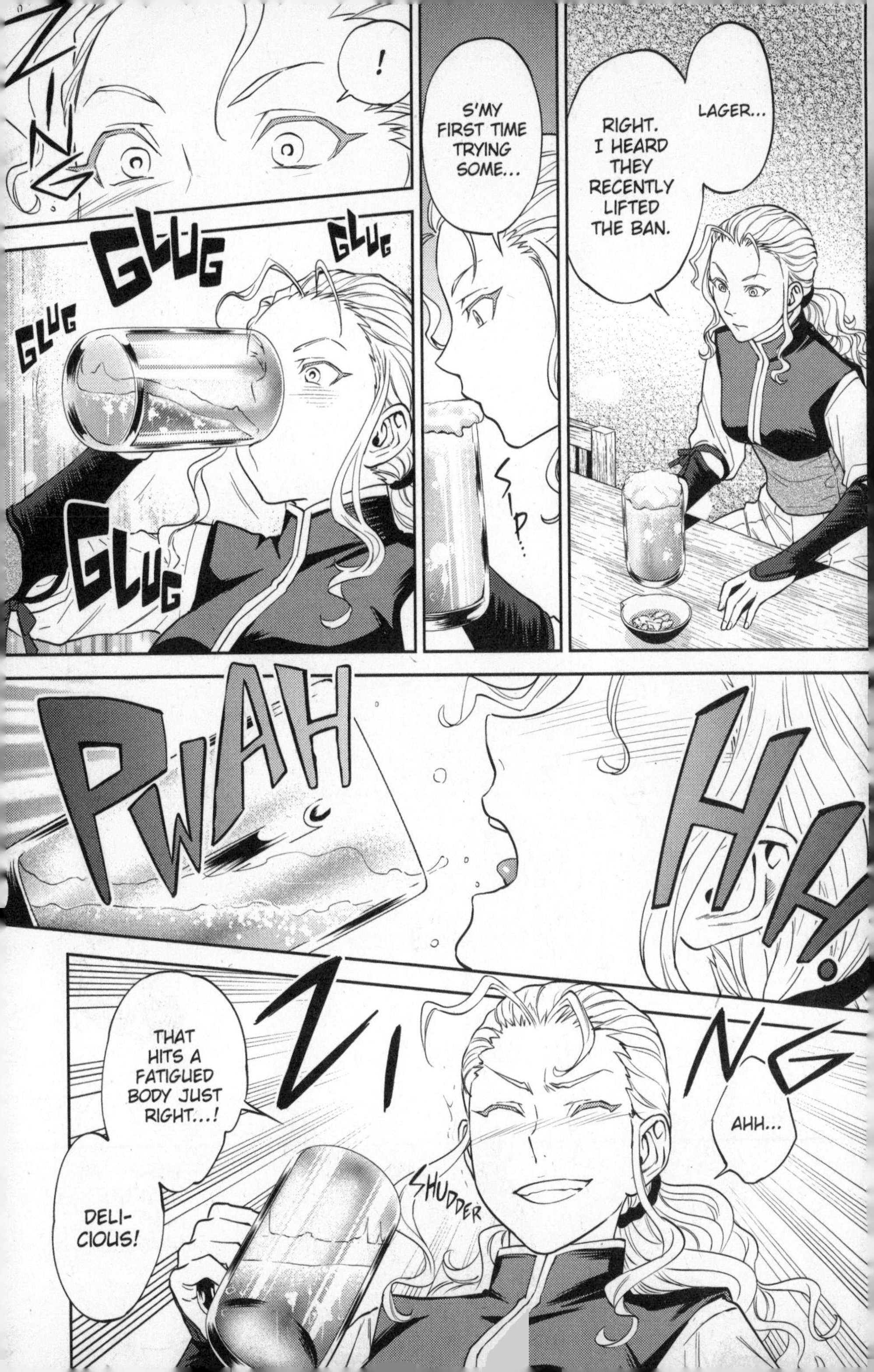
LAGER...
RIGHT. I HEARD THEY RECENTLY LIFTED THE BAN.
S'MY FIRST TIME TRYING SOME...
SIP...
!
ZING
GLUG
GLUG
GLUG
GLUG
HAH!
PWAH
ZING
AHH...
THAT HITS A FATIGUED BODY JUST RIGHT...!
SHUDDER
DELI-
CIOUS!

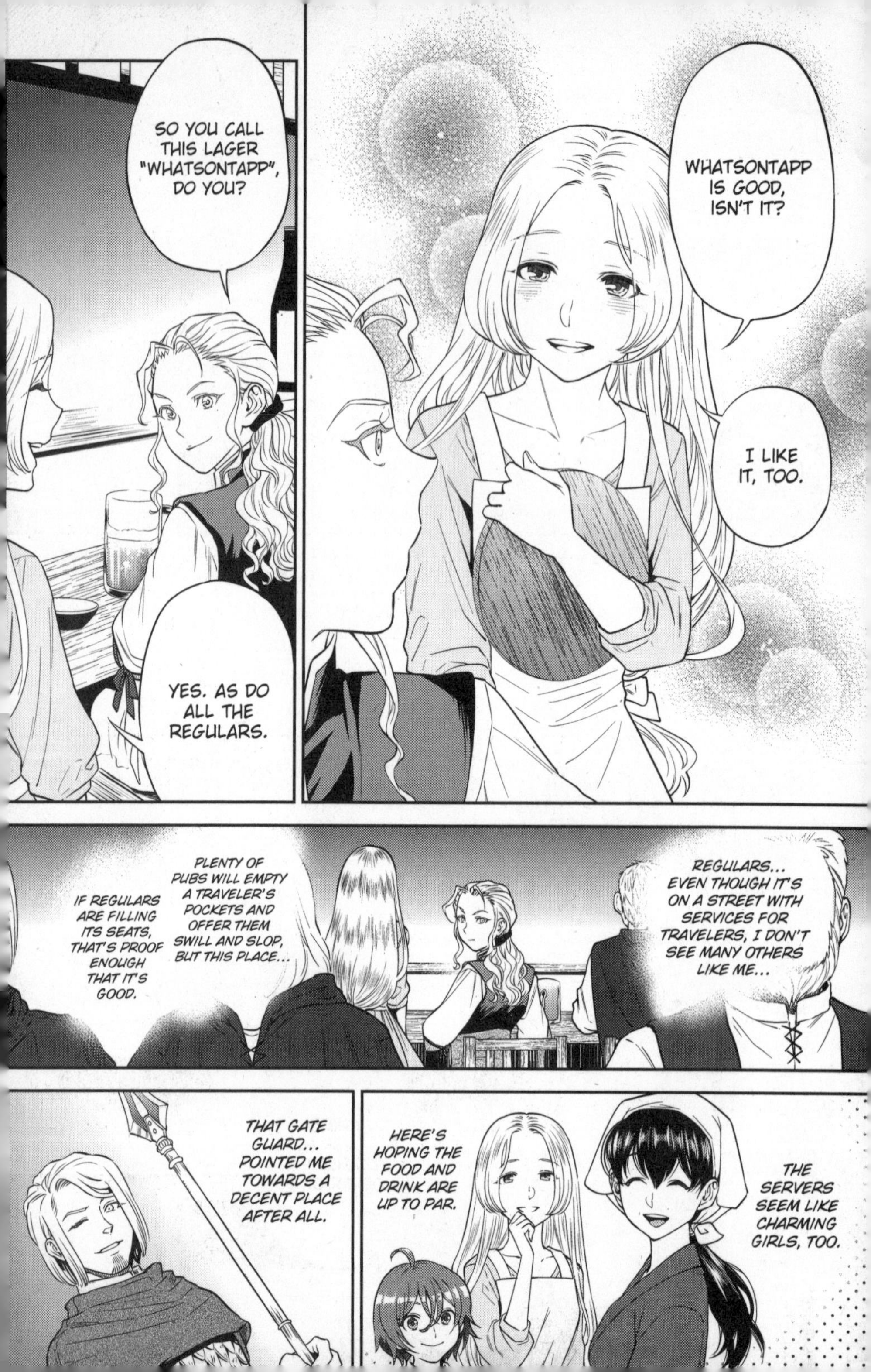
WHATSONTAPP IS GOOD, ISN'T IT?
I LIKE IT, TOO.
SO YOU CALL THIS LAGER "WHATSONTAPP", DO YOU?
YES. AS DO ALL THE REGULARS.
REGULARS... EVEN THOUGH IT'S ON A STREET WITH SERVICES FOR TRAVELERS, I DON'T SEE MANY OTHERS LIKE ME...
PLENTY OF PUBS WILL EMPTY A TRAVELER'S POCKETS AND OFFER THEM SWILL AND SLOP, BUT THIS PLACE...
IF REGULARS ARE FILLING ITS SEATS, THAT'S PROOF ENOUGH THAT IT'S GOOD.
THE SERVERS SEEM LIKE CHARMING GIRLS, TOO.
HERE'S HOPING THE FOOD AND DRINK ARE UP TO PAR.
THAT GATE GUARD... POINTED ME TOWARDS A DECENT PLACE AFTER ALL.

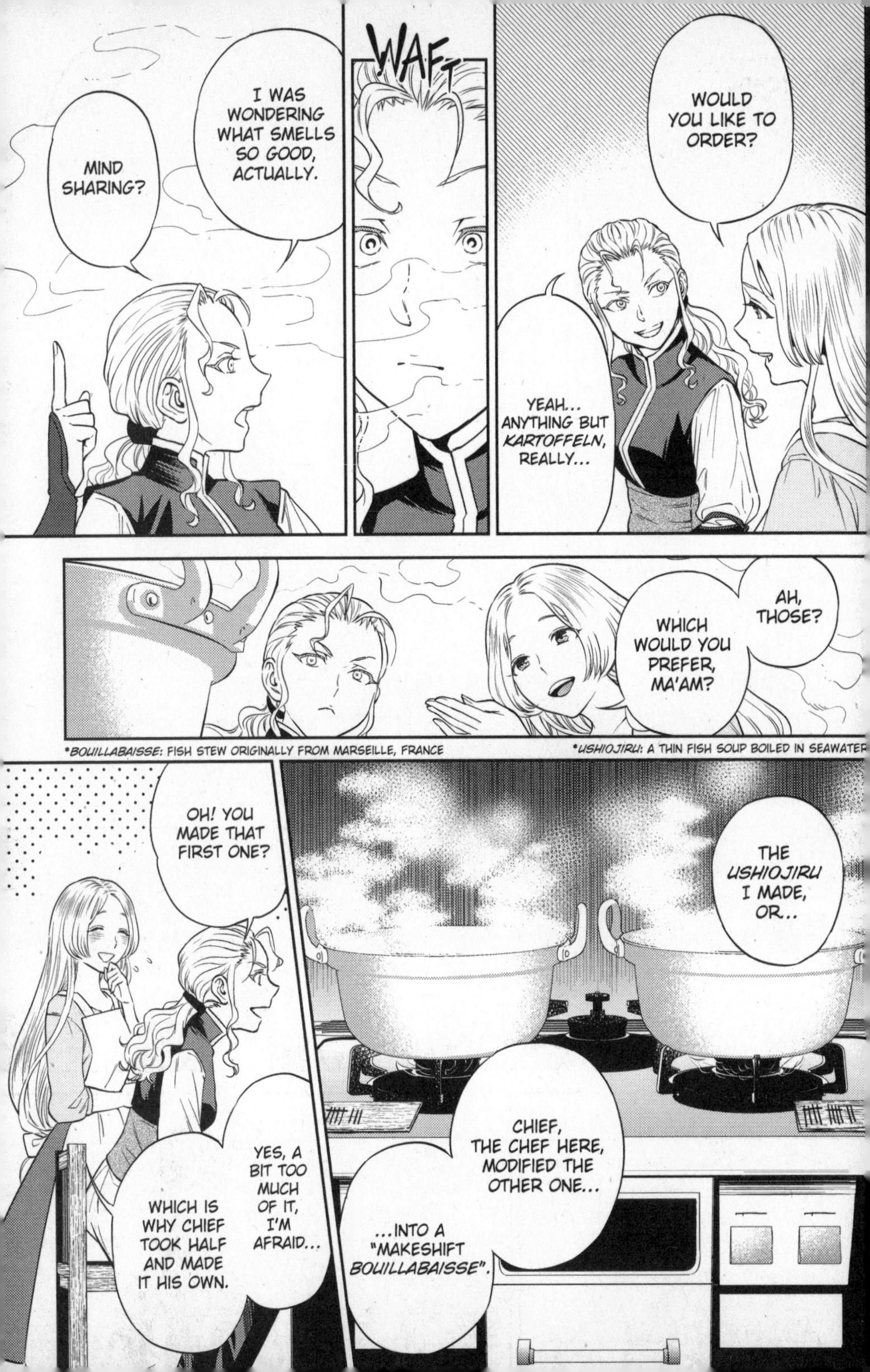
WOULD YOU LIKE TO ORDER?
YEAH... ANYTHING BUT *KARTOFFELN*, REALLY...
WAFT
I WAS WONDERING WHAT SMELLS SO GOOD, ACTUALLY.
MIND SHARING?
AH, THOSE?
WHICH WOULD YOU PREFER, MA'AM?
*USHIOJIRU: A THIN FISH SOUP BOILED IN SEAWATER
*BOUILLABAISSE: FISH STEW ORIGINALLY FROM MARSEILLE, FRANCE
THE *USHIOJIRU* I MADE, OR...
CHIEF, THE CHEF HERE, MODIFIED THE OTHER ONE...
...INTO A "MAKESHIFT *BOUILLABAISSE*".
OH! YOU MADE THAT FIRST ONE?
YES, A BIT TOO MUCH OF IT, I'M AFRAID...
WHICH IS WHY CHIEF TOOK HALF AND MADE IT HIS OWN.

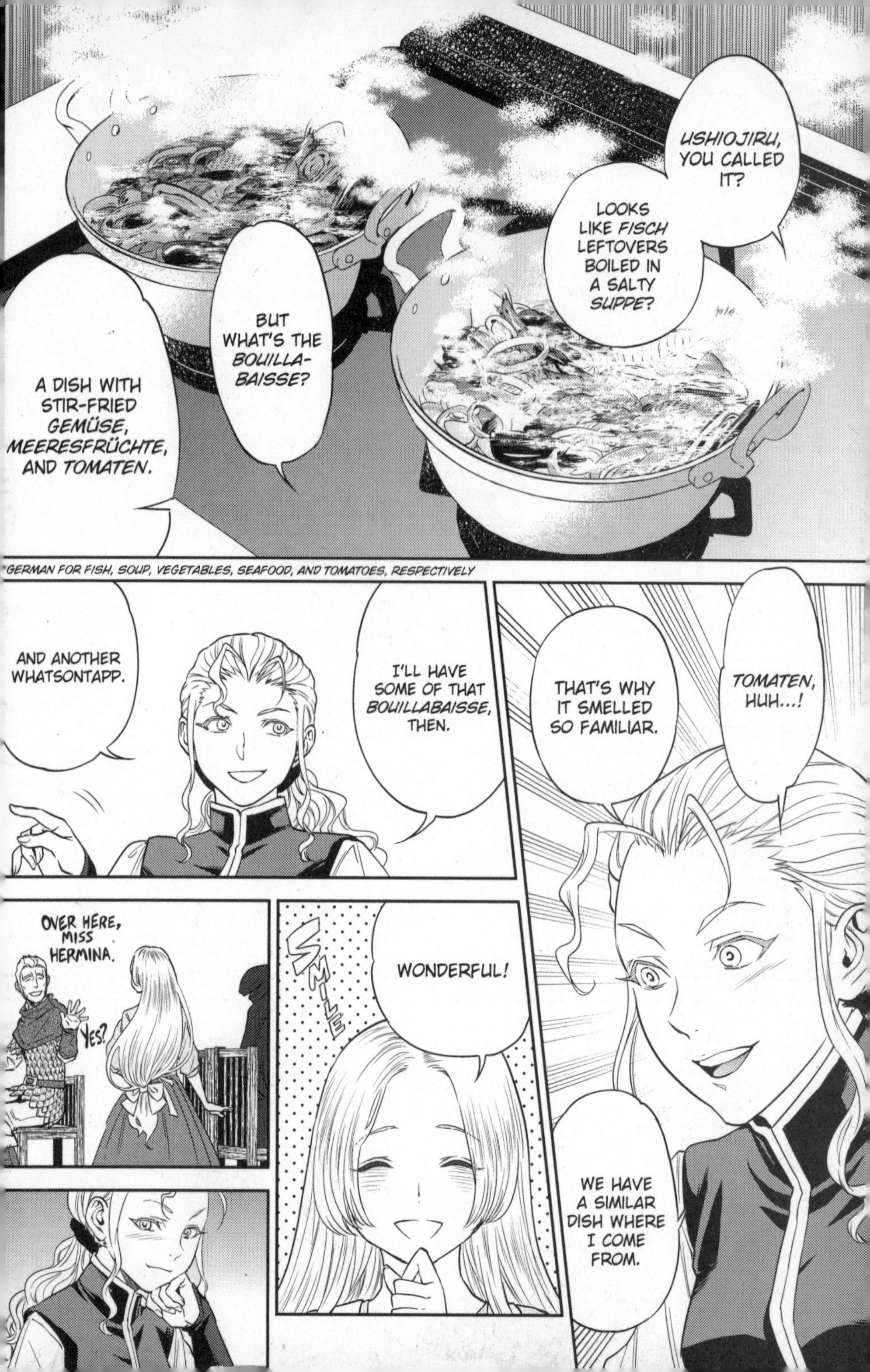
USHIOJIRU, YOU CALLED IT?
LOOKS LIKE FISCH LEFTOVERS BOILED IN A SALTY SUPPE?
BUT WHAT'S THE BOUILLA-BAISSE?
A DISH WITH STIR-FRIED GEMÜSE, MEERESFRÜCHTE, AND TOMATEN.
TOMATEN, HUH...!
THAT'S WHY IT SMELLED SO FAMILIAR.
WE HAVE A SIMILAR DISH WHERE I COME FROM.
I'LL HAVE SOME OF THAT BOUILLABAISSE, THEN.
AND ANOTHER WHATSONTAPP.
SMILE
WONDERFUL!
OVER HERE, MISS HERMINA.
YES?

*GERMAN FOR FISH, SOUP, VEGETABLES, SEAFOOD, AND TOMATOES, RESPECTIVELY

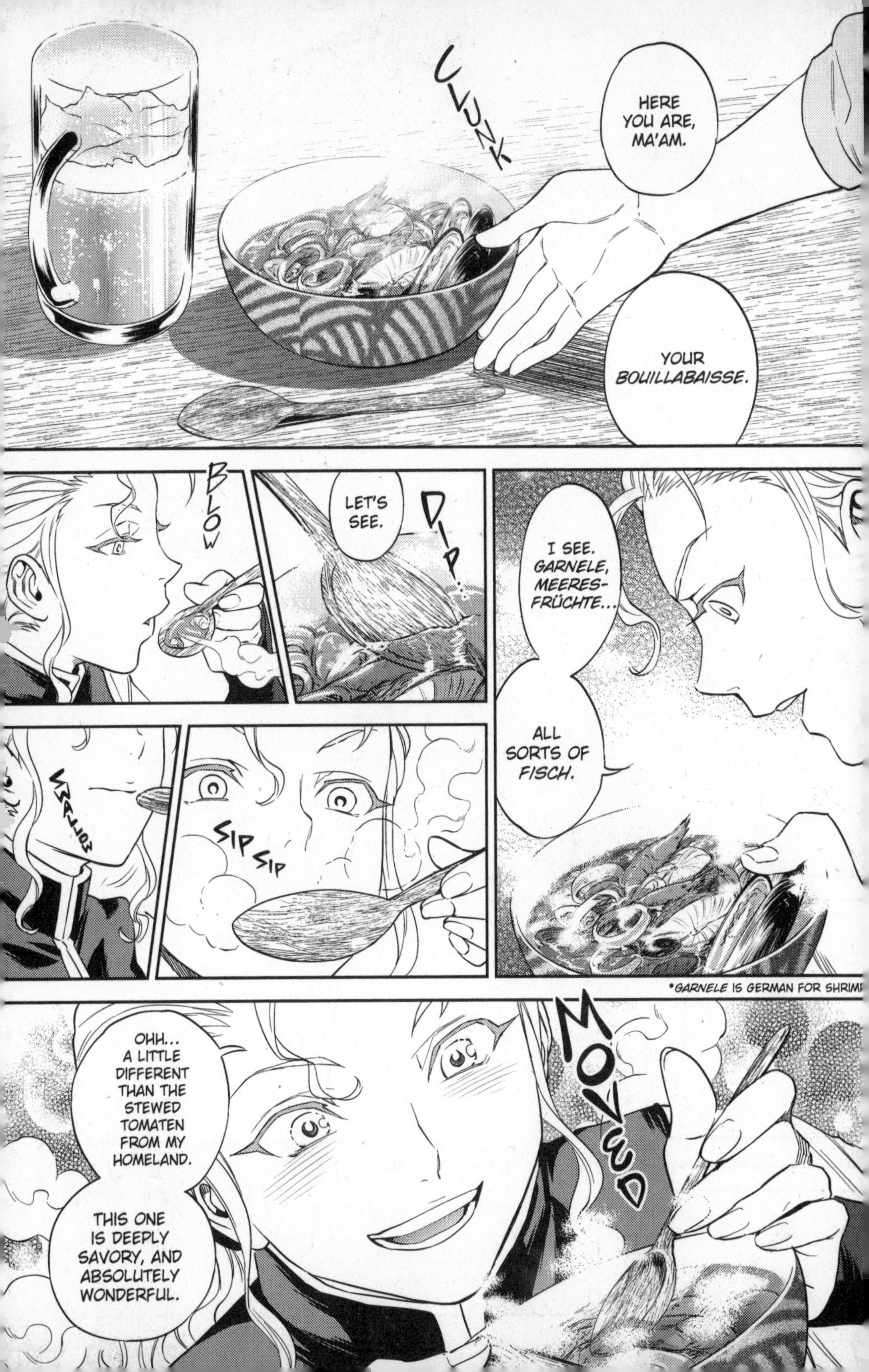
CLUNK
HERE YOU ARE, MA'AM.
YOUR BOUILLABAISSE.
I SEE. GARNELE, MEERES-FRÜCHTE...
ALL SORTS OF FISCH.
LET'S SEE.
DIP...
BLOW
SIP SIP
SWALLOW
*GARNELE IS GERMAN FOR SHRIMP
MOVED
OHH... A LITTLE DIFFERENT THAN THE STEWED TOMATEN FROM MY HOMELAND.
THIS ONE IS DEEPLY SAVORY, AND ABSOLUTELY WONDERFUL.

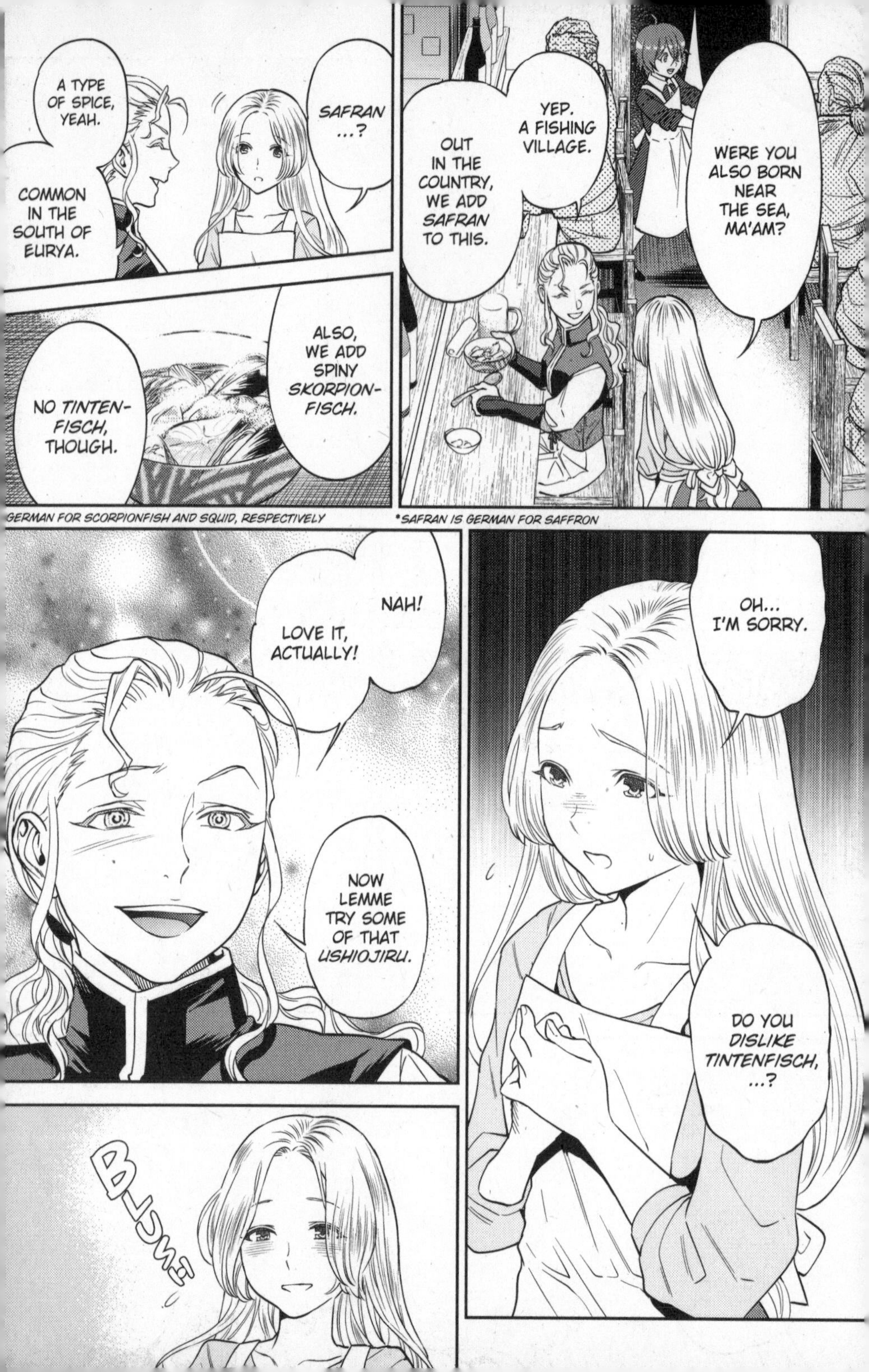
WERE YOU ALSO BORN NEAR THE SEA, MA'AM?
YEP. A FISHING VILLAGE.
OUT IN THE COUNTRY, WE ADD SAFRAN TO THIS.
*SAFRAN IS GERMAN FOR SAFFRON
SAFRAN ...?
A TYPE OF SPICE, YEAH.
COMMON IN THE SOUTH OF EURYA.
ALSO, WE ADD SPINY SKORPIONFISCH.
NO TINTENFISCH, THOUGH.
GERMAN FOR SCORPIONFISH AND SQUID, RESPECTIVELY
OH... I'M SORRY.
DO YOU DISLIKE TINTENFISCH, ...?
NAH!
LOVE IT, ACTUALLY!
NOW LEMME TRY SOME OF THAT USHIOJIRU.
BLUSH

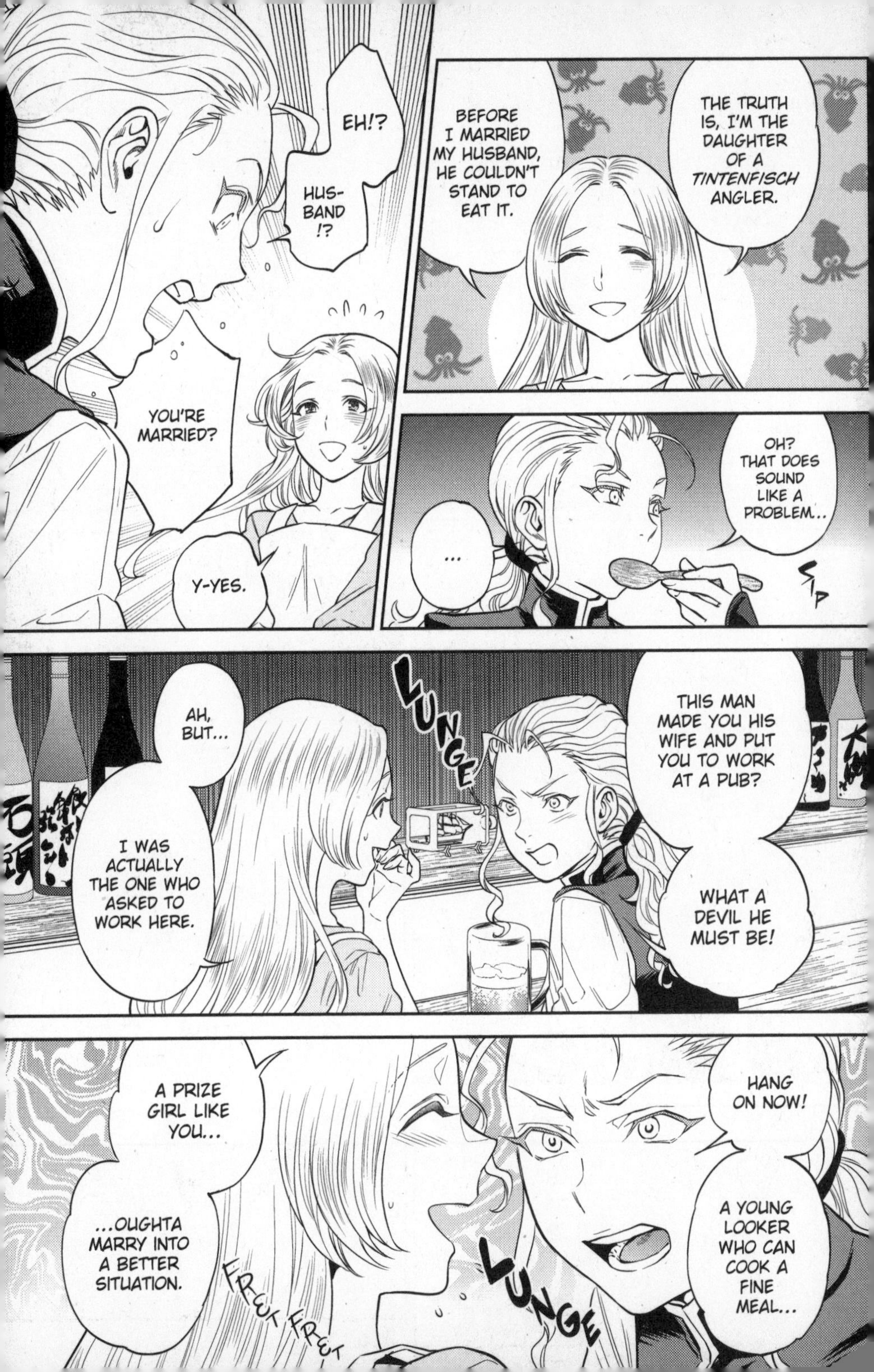
THE TRUTH IS, I'M THE DAUGHTER OF A *TINTENFISCH* ANGLER.
BEFORE I MARRIED MY HUSBAND, HE COULDN'T STAND TO EAT IT.
OH? THAT DOES SOUND LIKE A PROBLEM...
SIP
...
EH!?
HUS-BAND!?
YOU'RE MARRIED?
Y-YES.
THIS MAN MADE YOU HIS WIFE AND PUT YOU TO WORK AT A PUB?
WHAT A DEVIL HE MUST BE!
LUNGE
AH, BUT...
I WAS ACTUALLY THE ONE WHO ASKED TO WORK HERE.
HANG ON NOW!
A YOUNG LOOKER WHO CAN COOK A FINE MEAL...
LUNGE
A PRIZE GIRL LIKE YOU...
...OUGHTA MARRY INTO A BETTER SITUATION.
FRET FRET

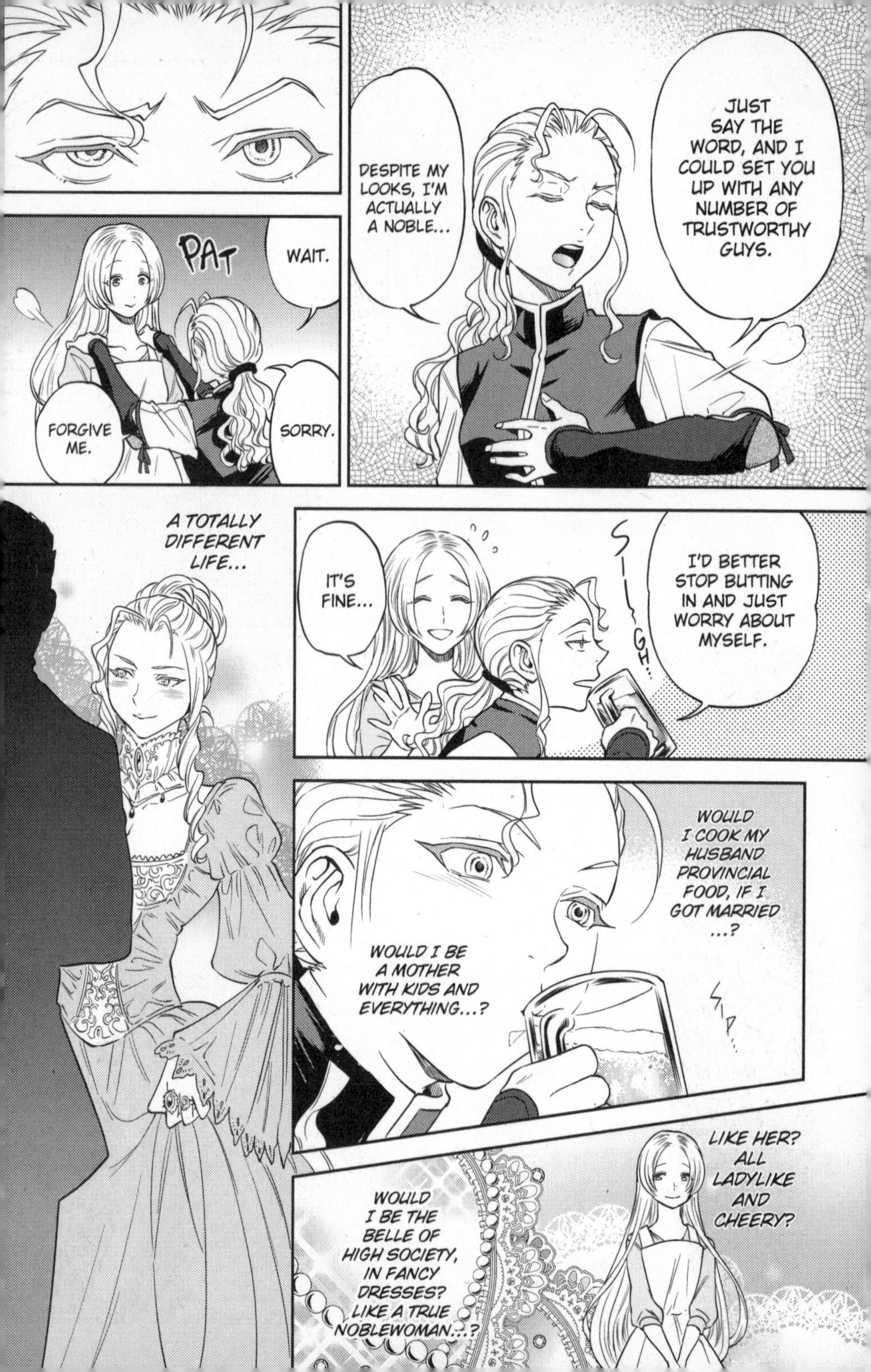
JUST SAY THE WORD, AND I COULD SET YOU UP WITH ANY NUMBER OF TRUSTWORTHY GUYS.
DESPITE MY LOOKS, I'M ACTUALLY A NOBLE...
WAIT.
PAT
SORRY.
FORGIVE ME.
I'D BETTER STOP BUTTING IN AND JUST WORRY ABOUT MYSELF.
SIGH...
IT'S FINE...
WOULD I COOK MY HUSBAND PROVINCIAL FOOD, IF I GOT MARRIED ...?
SIP...
WOULD I BE A MOTHER WITH KIDS AND EVERYTHING...?
LIKE HER? ALL LADYLIKE AND CHEERY?
WOULD I BE THE BELLE OF HIGH SOCIETY, IN FANCY DRESSES? LIKE A TRUE NOBLEWOMAN...?
A TOTALLY DIFFERENT LIFE...

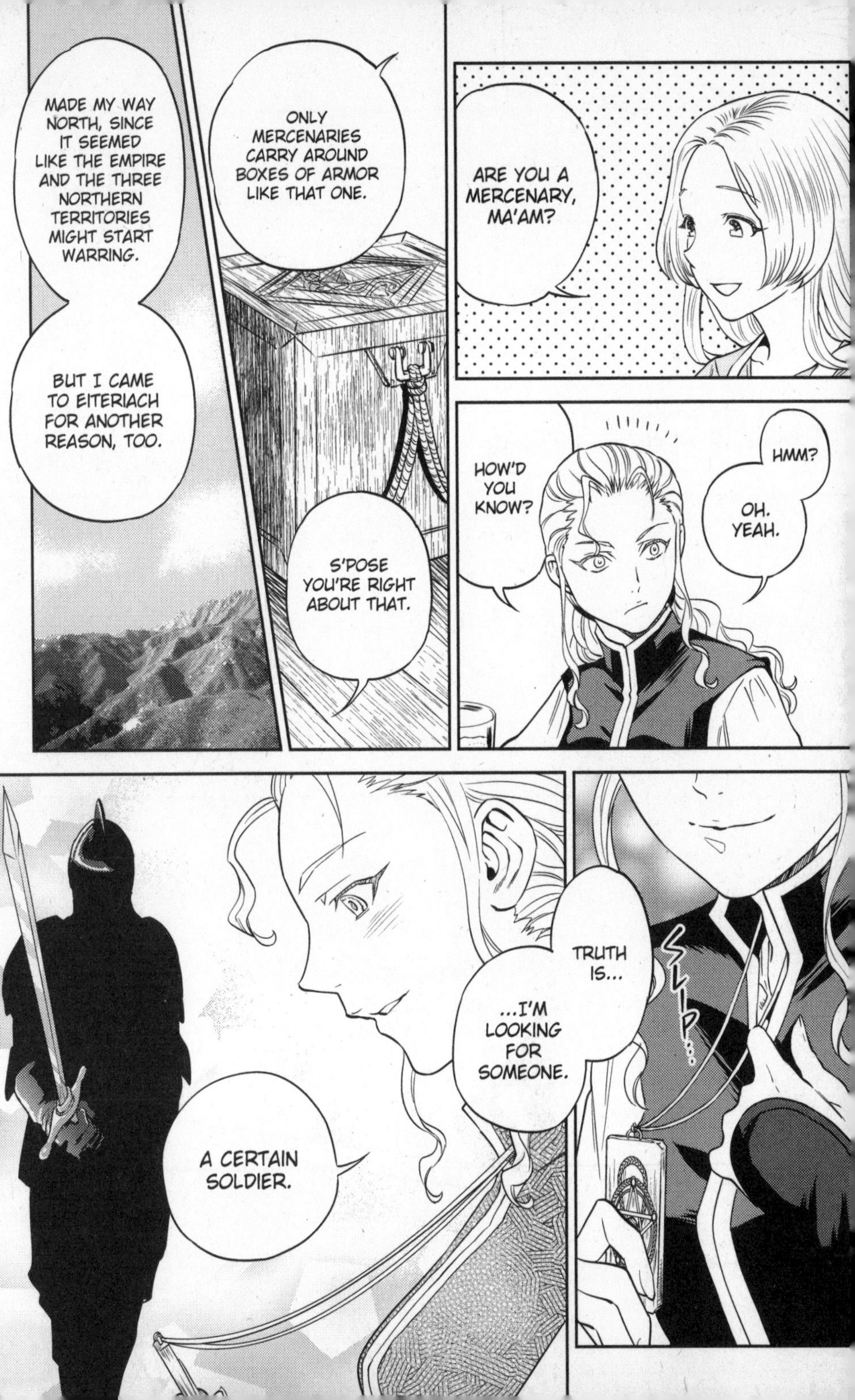
ARE YOU A MERCENARY, MA'AM?
HMM?
OH. YEAH.
HOW'D YOU KNOW?
ONLY MERCENARIES CARRY AROUND BOXES OF ARMOR LIKE THAT ONE.
S'POSE YOU'RE RIGHT ABOUT THAT.
MADE MY WAY NORTH, SINCE IT SEEMED LIKE THE EMPIRE AND THE THREE NORTHERN TERRITORIES MIGHT START WARRING.
BUT I CAME TO EITERIACH FOR ANOTHER REASON, TOO.
TRUTH IS...
...I'M LOOKING FOR SOMEONE.
A CERTAIN SOLDIER.

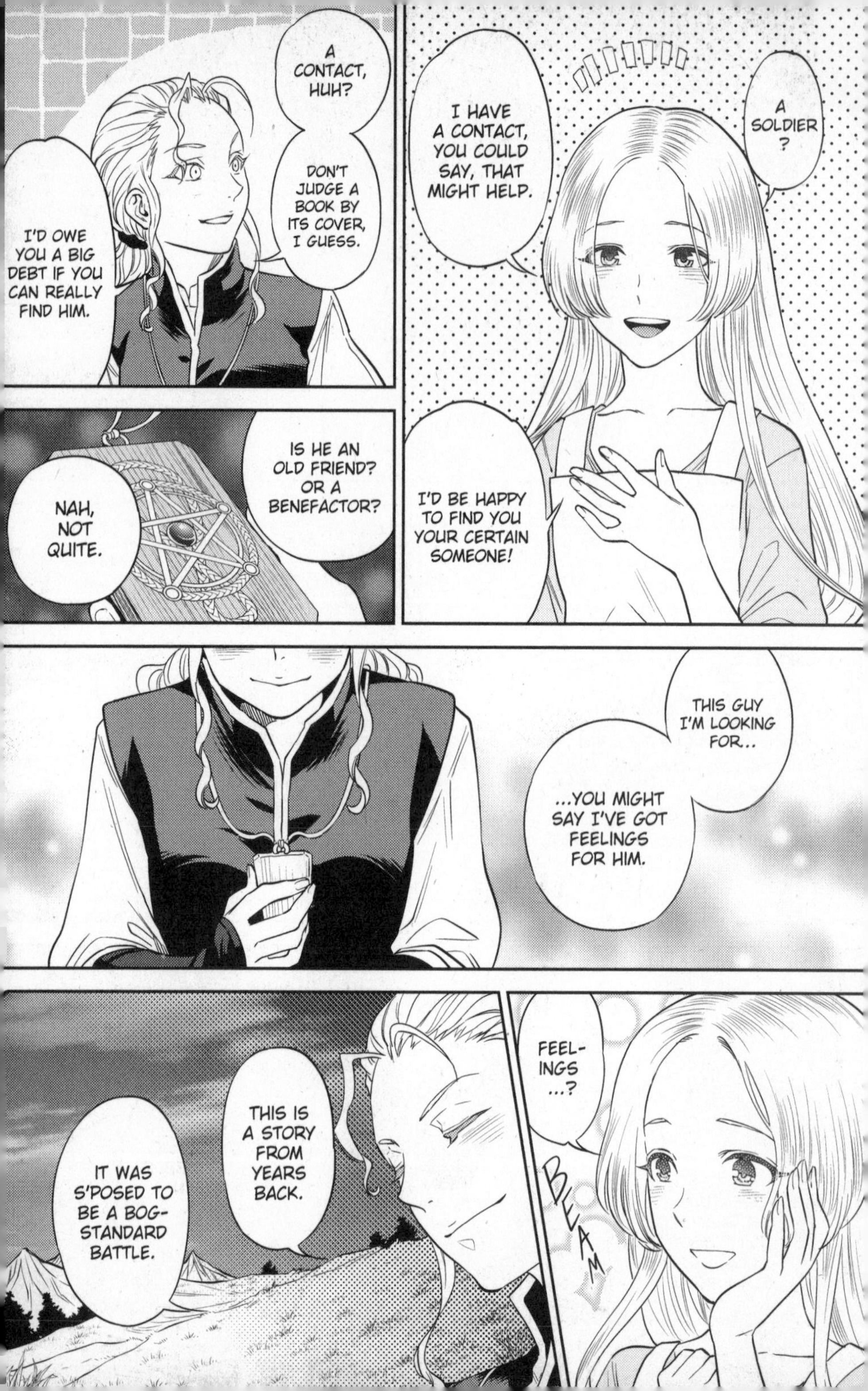
A SOLDIER?
I HAVE A CONTACT, YOU COULD SAY, THAT MIGHT HELP.
I'D BE HAPPY TO FIND YOU YOUR CERTAIN SOMEONE!
A CONTACT, HUH?
DON'T JUDGE A BOOK BY ITS COVER, I GUESS.
I'D OWE YOU A BIG DEBT IF YOU CAN REALLY FIND HIM.
IS HE AN OLD FRIEND? OR A BENEFACTOR?
NAH, NOT QUITE.
THIS GUY I'M LOOKING FOR...
...YOU MIGHT SAY I'VE GOT FEELINGS FOR HIM.
FEEL-INGS ...?
BEAM
THIS IS A STORY FROM YEARS BACK.
IT WAS S'POSED TO BE A BOG-STANDARD BATTLE.

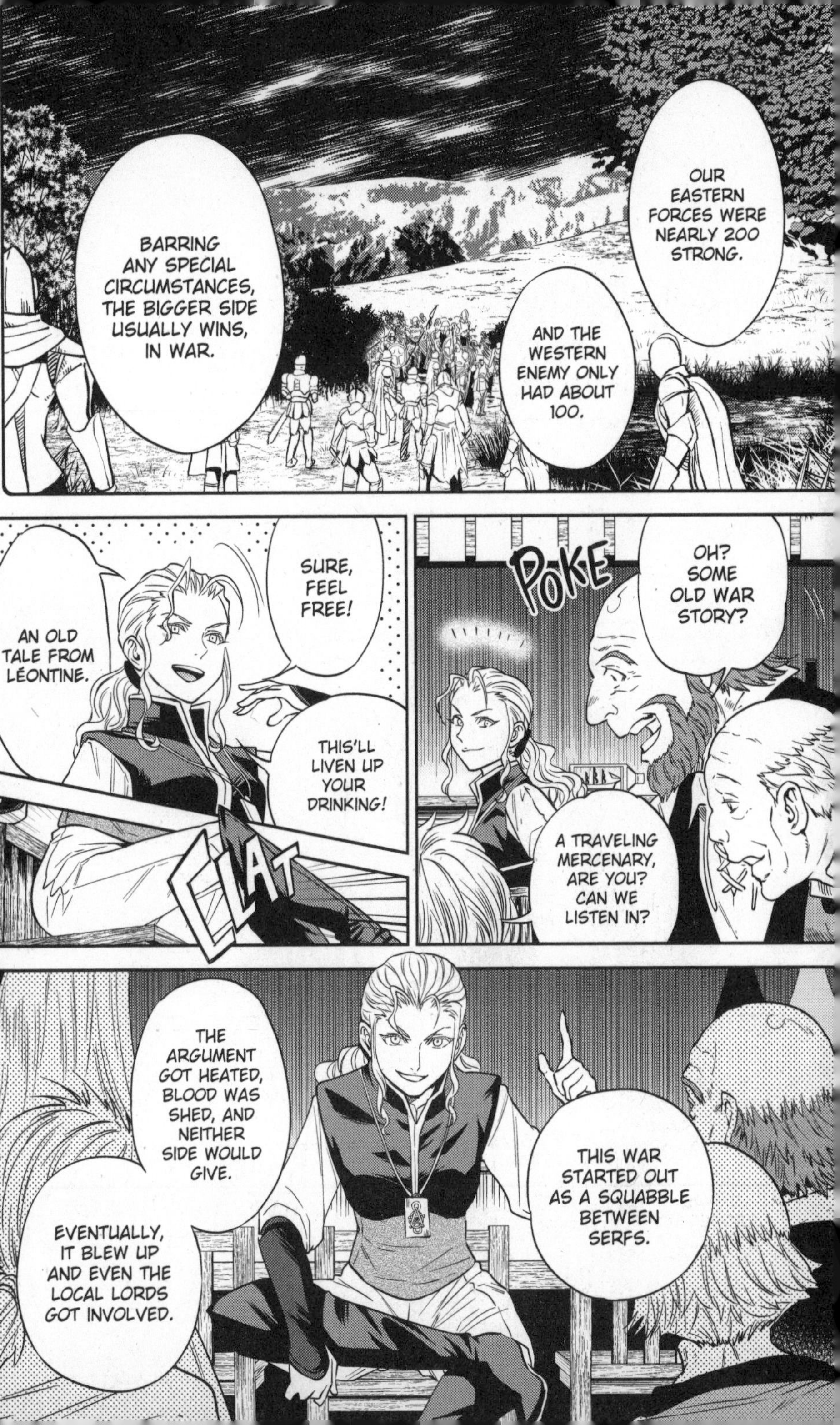
OUR EASTERN FORCES WERE NEARLY 200 STRONG.
AND THE WESTERN ENEMY ONLY HAD ABOUT 100.
BARRING ANY SPECIAL CIRCUMSTANCES, THE BIGGER SIDE USUALLY WINS, IN WAR.
POKE
OH? SOME OLD WAR STORY?
A TRAVELING MERCENARY, ARE YOU? CAN WE LISTEN IN?
SURE, FEEL FREE!
THIS'LL LIVEN UP YOUR DRINKING!
AN OLD TALE FROM LÉONTINE.
CLAT
THIS WAR STARTED OUT AS A SQUABBLE BETWEEN SERFS.
THE ARGUMENT GOT HEATED, BLOOD WAS SHED, AND NEITHER SIDE WOULD GIVE.
EVENTUALLY, IT BLEW UP AND EVEN THE LOCAL LORDS GOT INVOLVED.

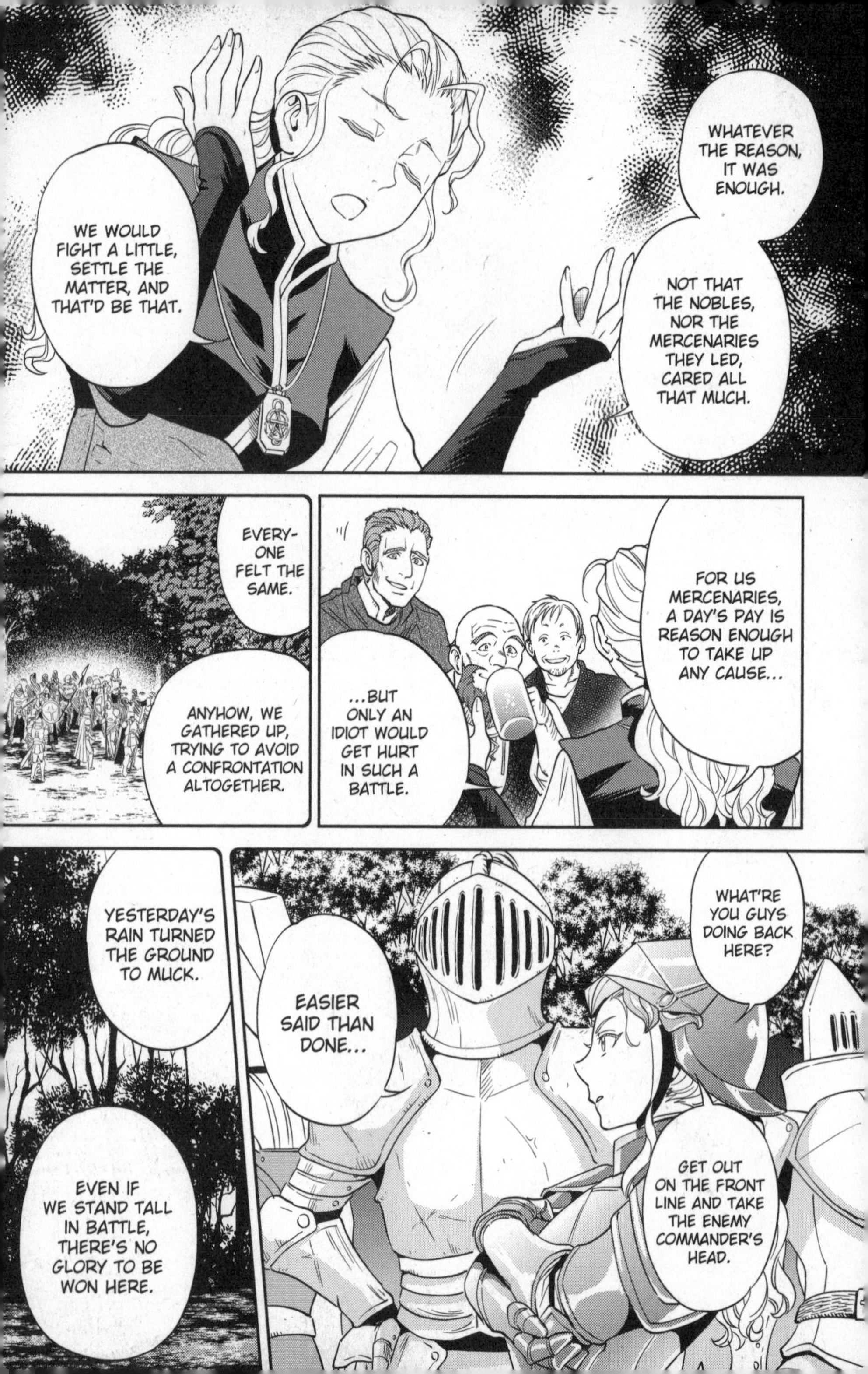
WHATEVER THE REASON, IT WAS ENOUGH.
NOT THAT THE NOBLES, NOR THE MERCENARIES THEY LED, CARED ALL THAT MUCH.
WE WOULD FIGHT A LITTLE, SETTLE THE MATTER, AND THAT'D BE THAT.
FOR US MERCENARIES, A DAY'S PAY IS REASON ENOUGH TO TAKE UP ANY CAUSE...
...BUT ONLY AN IDIOT WOULD GET HURT IN SUCH A BATTLE.
EVERY-ONE FELT THE SAME.
ANYHOW, WE GATHERED UP, TRYING TO AVOID A CONFRONTATION ALTOGETHER.
WHAT'RE YOU GUYS DOING BACK HERE?
GET OUT ON THE FRONT LINE AND TAKE THE ENEMY COMMANDER'S HEAD.
EASIER SAID THAN DONE...
YESTERDAY'S RAIN TURNED THE GROUND TO MUCK.
EVEN IF WE STAND TALL IN BATTLE, THERE'S NO GLORY TO BE WON HERE.

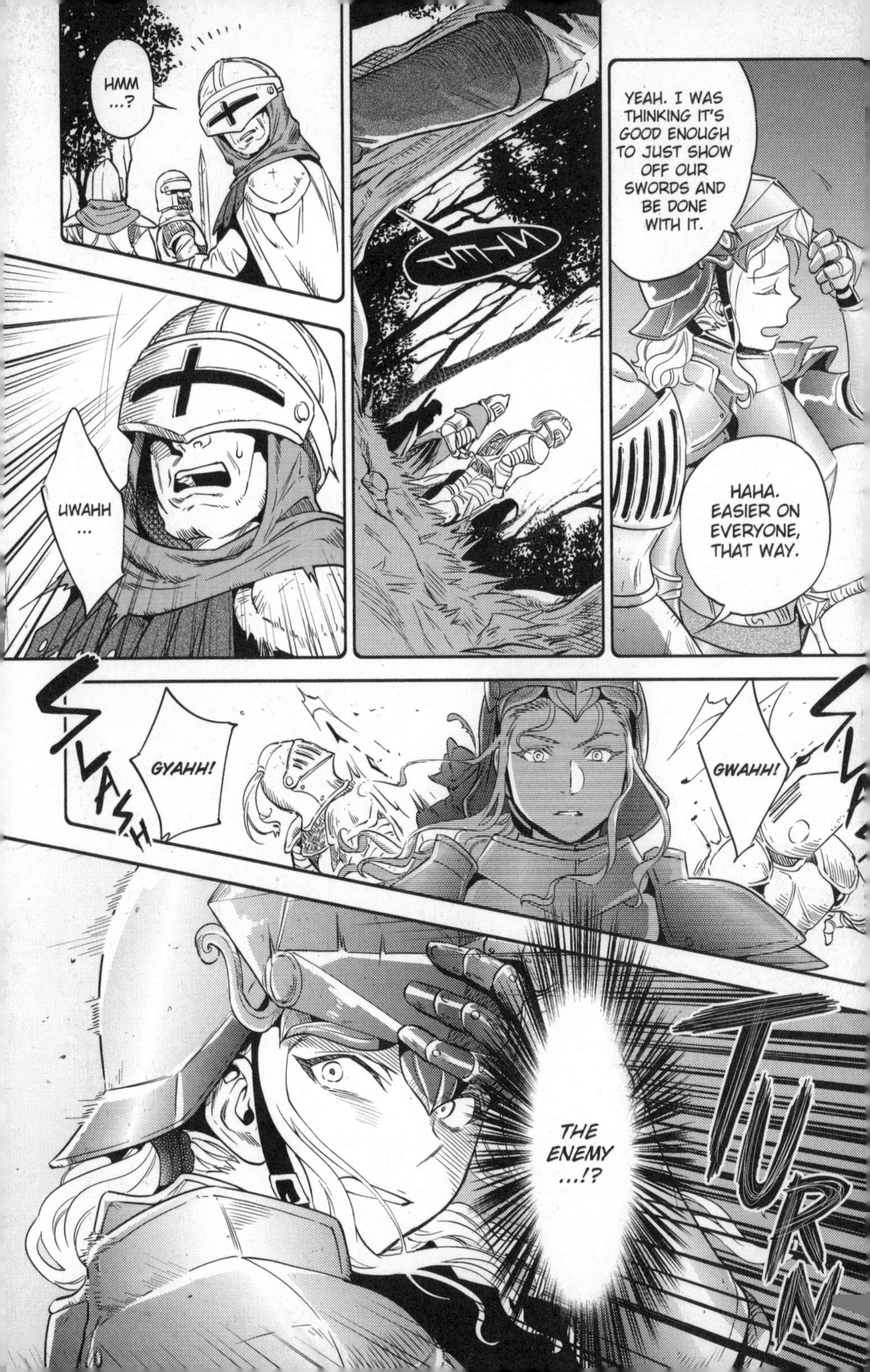
YEAH. I WAS THINKING IT'S GOOD ENOUGH TO JUST SHOW OFF OUR SWORDS AND BE DONE WITH IT.
HAHA. EASIER ON EVERYONE, THAT WAY.
HMM ...?
UWAHH ...
GWAHH!
SLASH
GYAHH!
SLASH
TURN
THE ENEMY ...!?

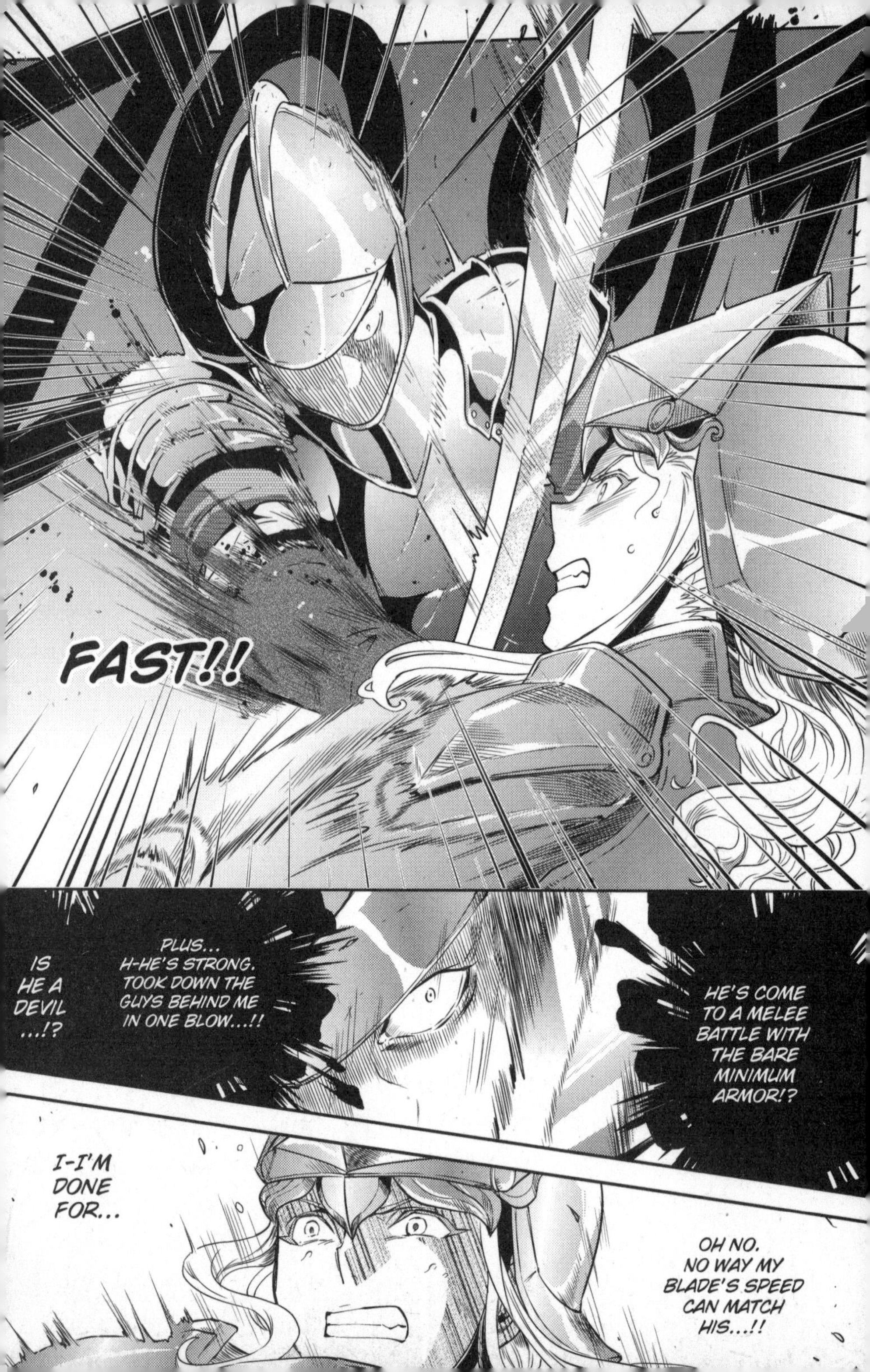
FAST!!
HE'S COME TO A MELEE BATTLE WITH THE BARE MINIMUM ARMOR!?
PLUS... H-HE'S STRONG. TOOK DOWN THE GUYS BEHIND ME IN ONE BLOW...!!
IS HE A DEVIL ...!?
OH NO. NO WAY MY BLADE'S SPEED CAN MATCH HIS...!!
I-I'M DONE FOR...

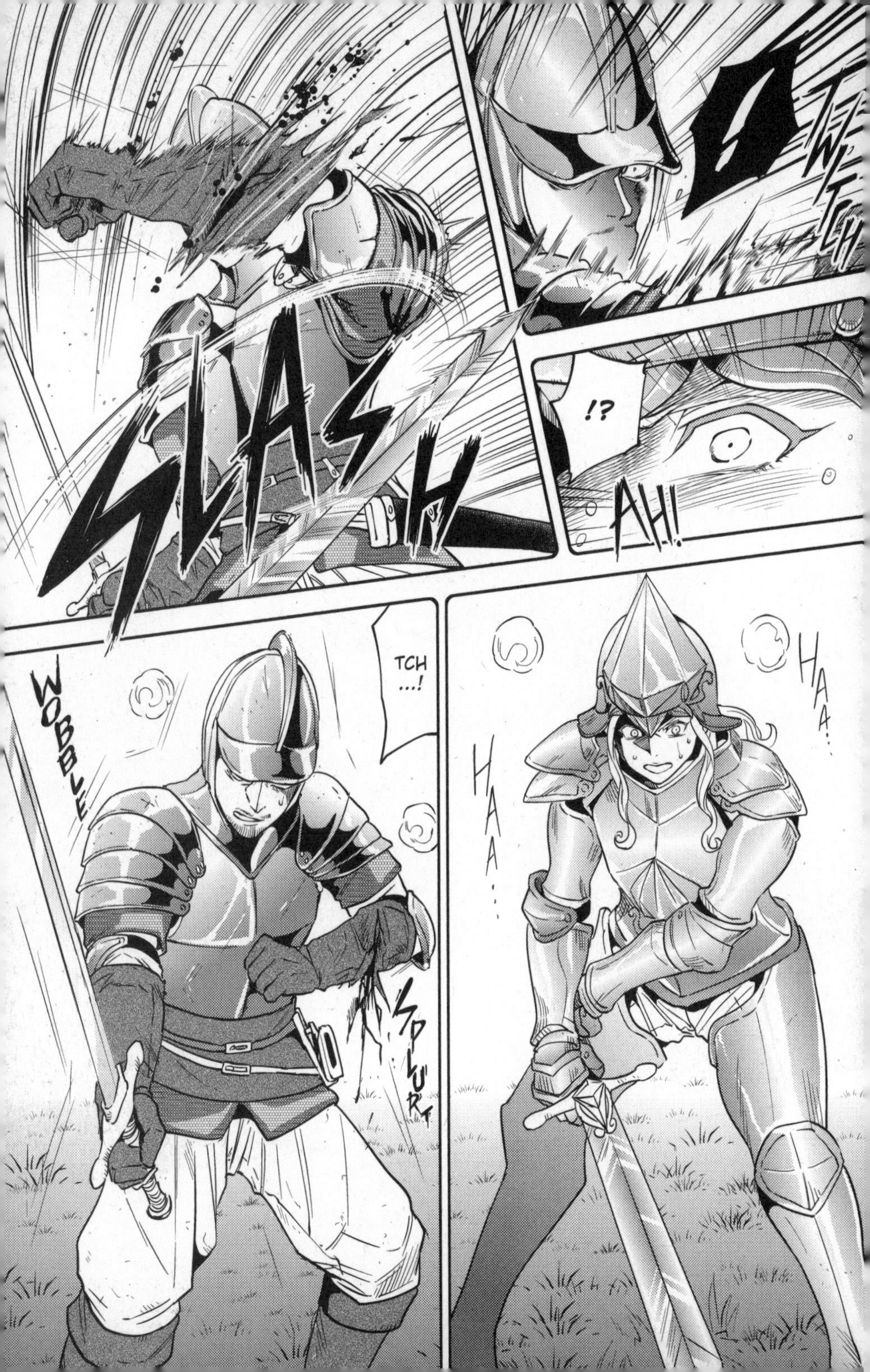

!
TWITCH
!?
AH!
SLASH
HAAA...
HAA...
TCH ...!
WOBBLE
SPLURT

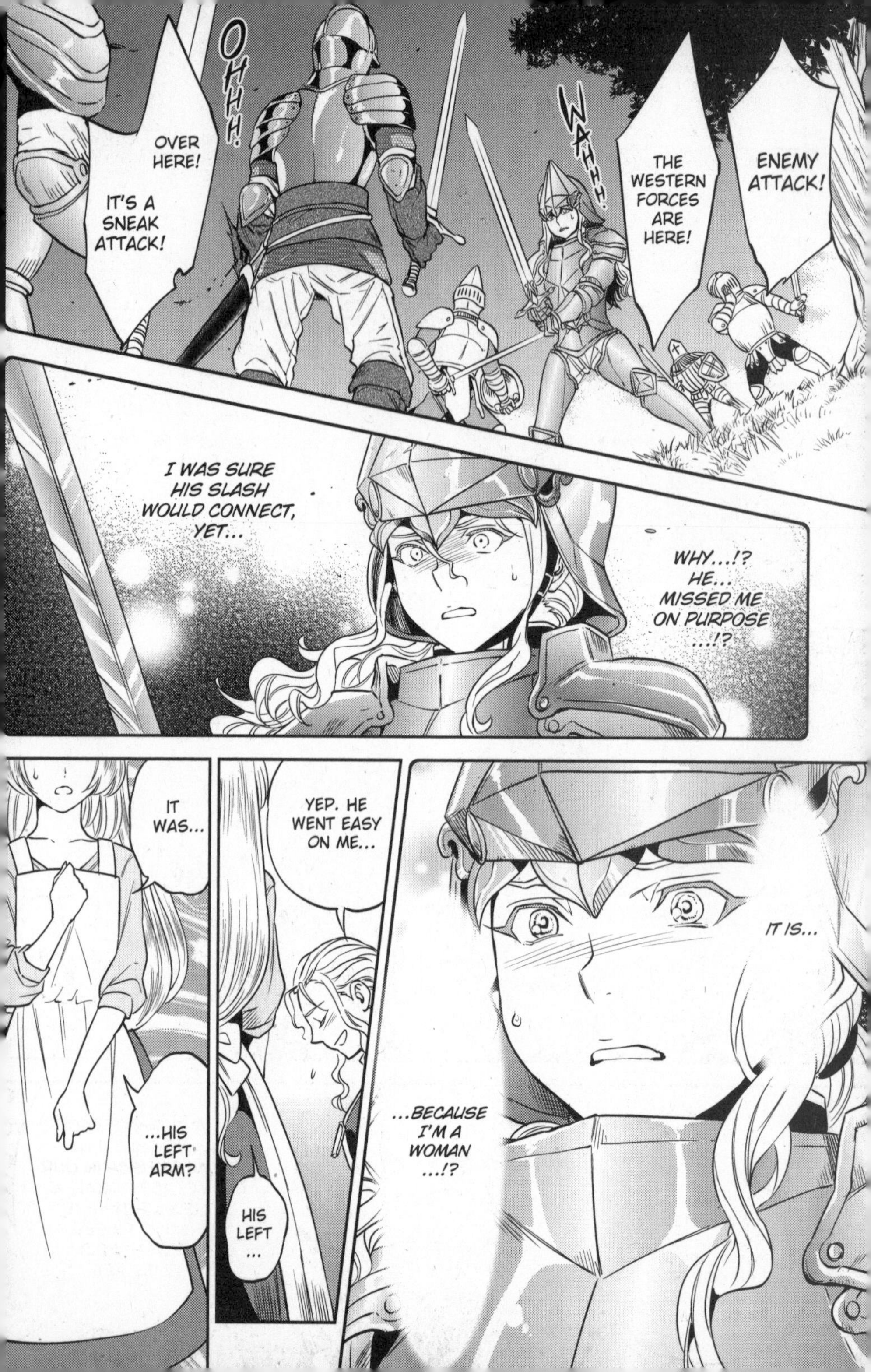
ENEMY ATTACK!
THE WESTERN FORCES ARE HERE!
WAHHH!
OHHH!
OVER HERE!
IT'S A SNEAK ATTACK!
I WAS SURE HIS SLASH WOULD CONNECT, YET...
WHY...!? HE... MISSED ME ON PURPOSE ...!?
IT IS...
...BECAUSE I'M A WOMAN ...!?
YEP. HE WENT EASY ON ME...
HIS LEFT ...
IT WAS...
...HIS LEFT ARM?

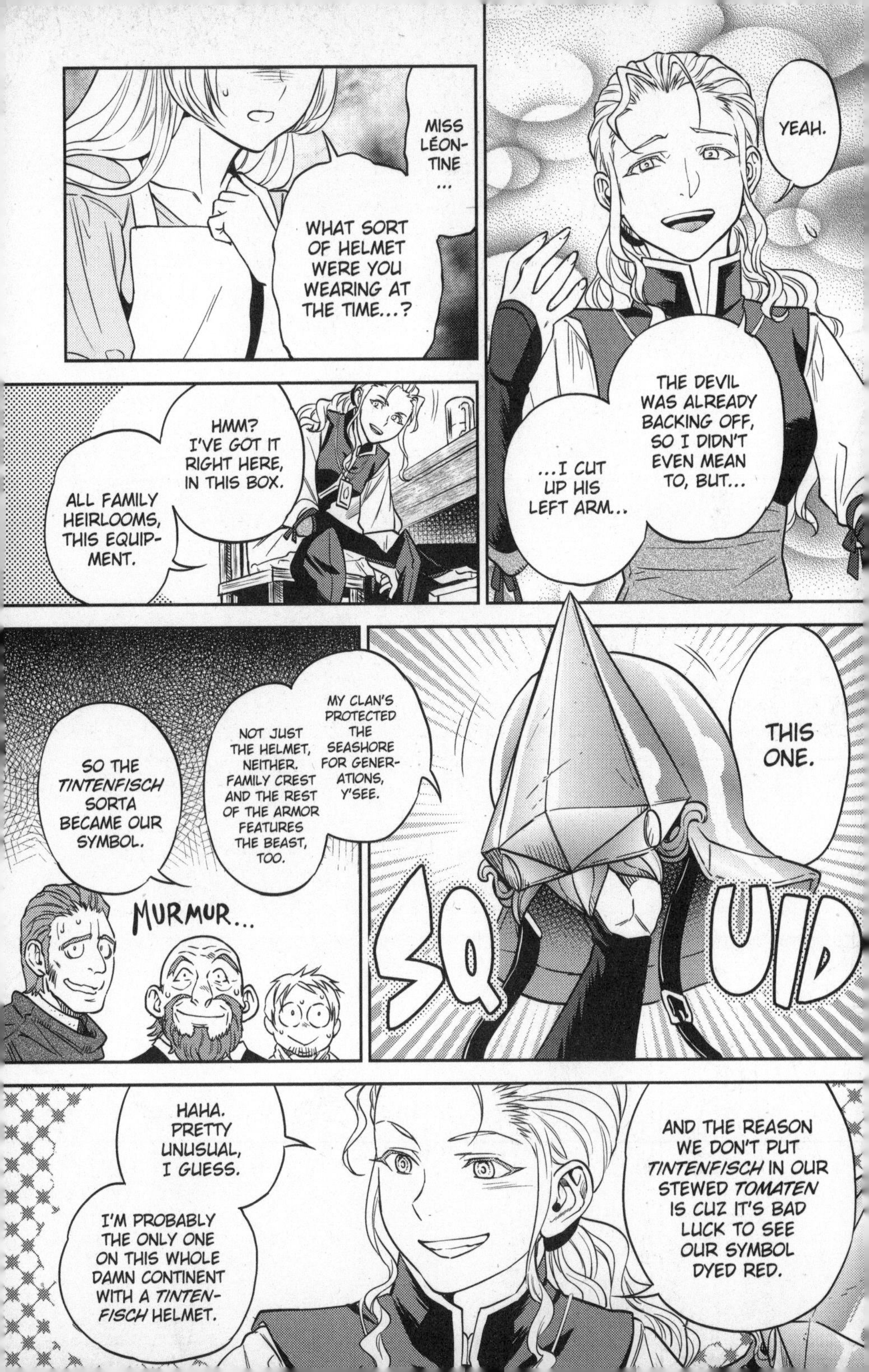
YEAH.
THE DEVIL WAS ALREADY BACKING OFF, SO I DIDN'T EVEN MEAN TO, BUT...
...I CUT UP HIS LEFT ARM...
MISS LÉON-TINE ...
WHAT SORT OF HELMET WERE YOU WEARING AT THE TIME...?
HMM? I'VE GOT IT RIGHT HERE, IN THIS BOX.
ALL FAMILY HEIRLOOMS, THIS EQUIP-MENT.
THIS ONE.
SQUID
MY CLAN'S PROTECTED THE SEASHORE FOR GENER-ATIONS, Y'SEE.
NOT JUST THE HELMET, NEITHER. FAMILY CREST AND THE REST OF THE ARMOR FEATURES THE BEAST, TOO.
SO THE *TINTENFISCH* SORTA BECAME OUR SYMBOL.
MURMUR...
AND THE REASON WE DON'T PUT *TINTENFISCH* IN OUR STEWED *TOMATEN* IS CUZ IT'S BAD LUCK TO SEE OUR SYMBOL DYED RED.
HAHA. PRETTY UNUSUAL, I GUESS.
I'M PROBABLY THE ONLY ONE ON THIS WHOLE DAMN CONTINENT WITH A *TINTEN-FISCH* HELMET.

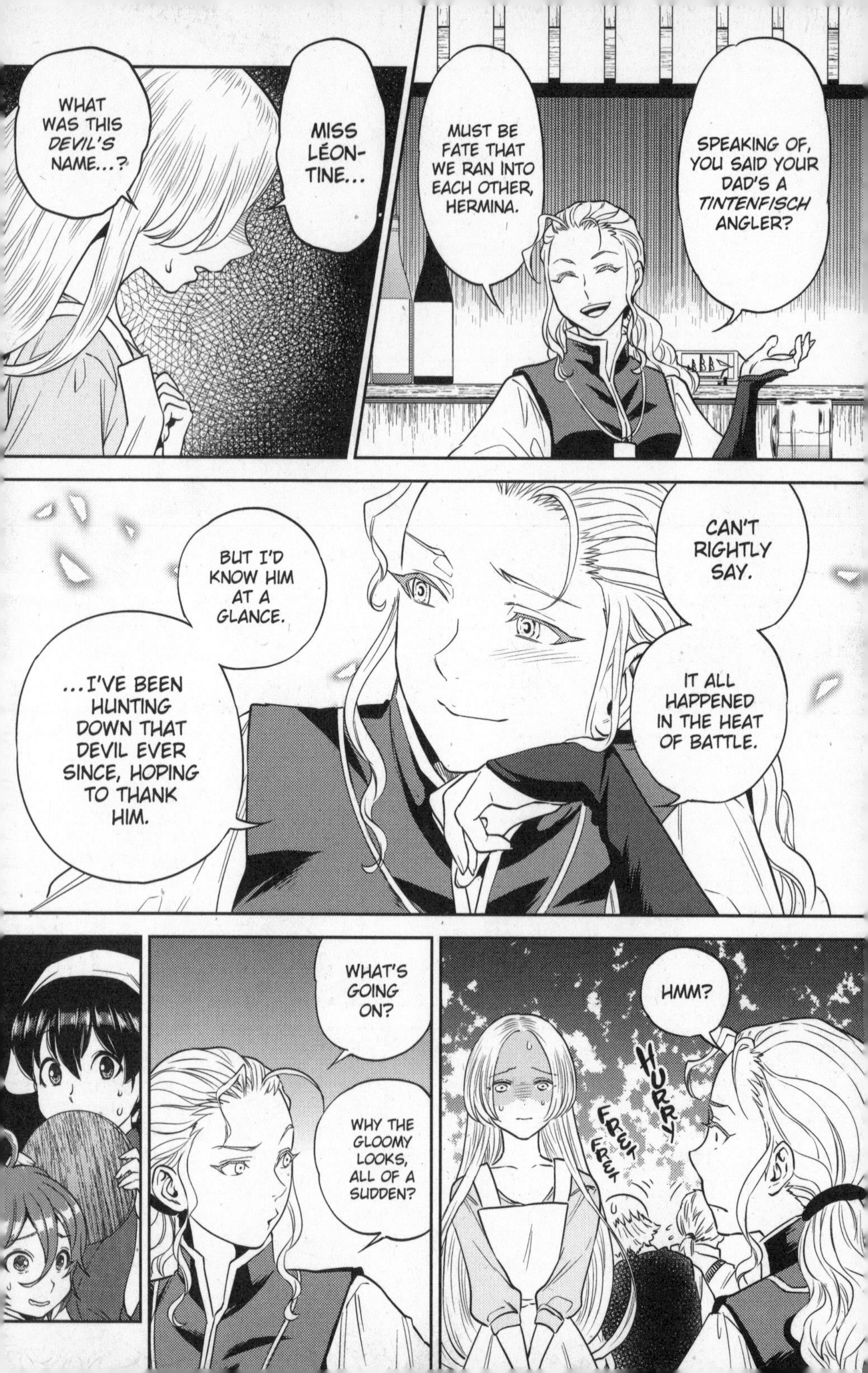
SPEAKING OF, YOU SAID YOUR DAD'S A *TINTENFISCH* ANGLER?
MUST BE FATE THAT WE RAN INTO EACH OTHER, HERMINA.
MISS LÉON-TINE...
WHAT WAS THIS *DEVIL'S* NAME...?
CAN'T RIGHTLY SAY.
IT ALL HAPPENED IN THE HEAT OF BATTLE.
BUT I'D KNOW HIM AT A GLANCE.
...I'VE BEEN HUNTING DOWN THAT DEVIL EVER SINCE, HOPING TO THANK HIM.
HMM?
HURRY
FRET
FRET
WHAT'S GOING ON?
WHY THE GLOOMY LOOKS, ALL OF A SUDDEN?

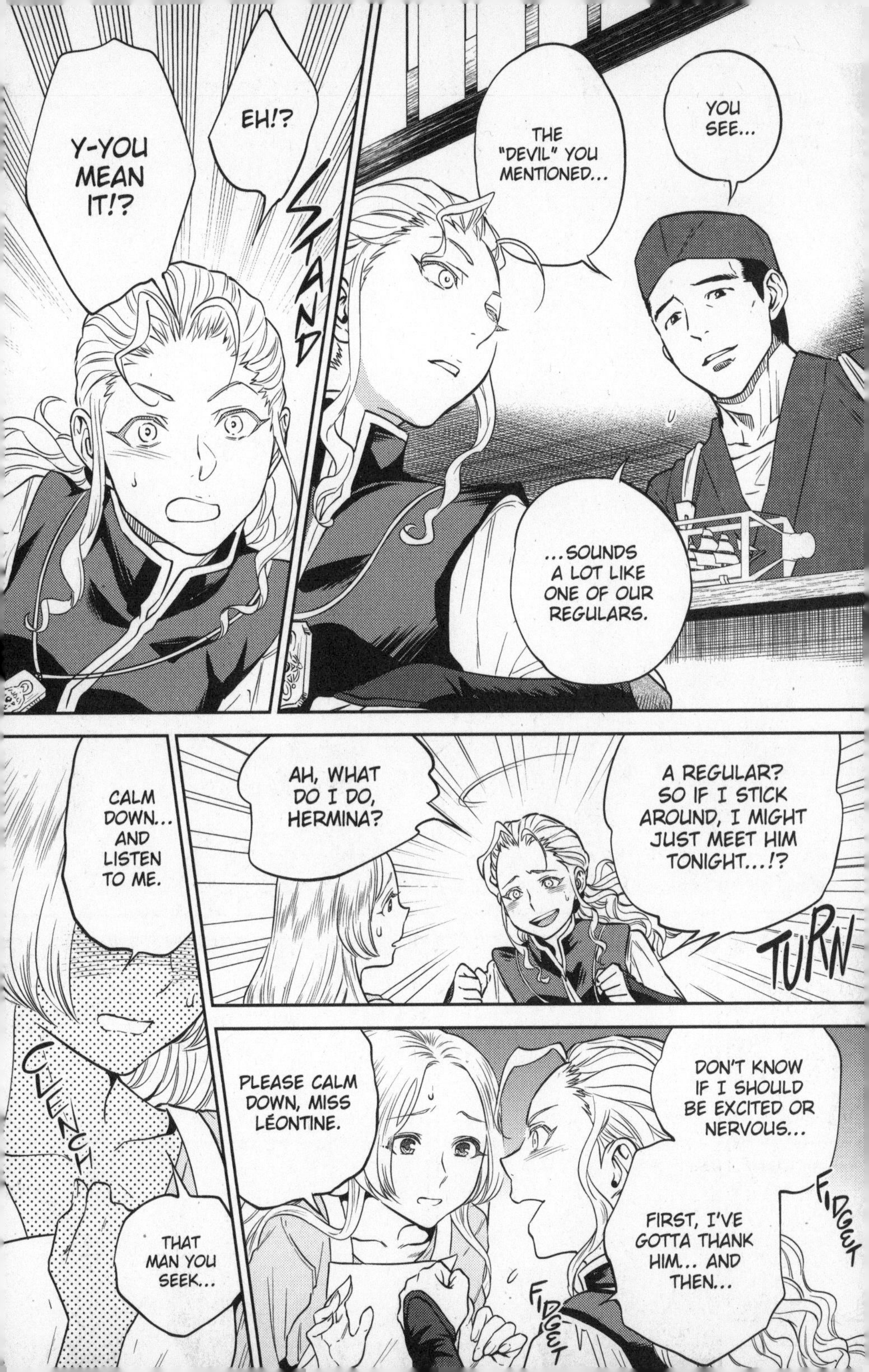
YOU SEE...
THE "DEVIL" YOU MENTIONED...
...SOUNDS A LOT LIKE ONE OF OUR REGULARS.
STAND
EH!?
Y-YOU MEAN IT!?
A REGULAR? SO IF I STICK AROUND, I MIGHT JUST MEET HIM TONIGHT...!?
TURN
AH, WHAT DO I DO, HERMINA?
DON'T KNOW IF I SHOULD BE EXCITED OR NERVOUS...
PLEASE CALM DOWN, MISS LÉONTINE.
FIDGET
FIRST, I'VE GOTTA THANK HIM... AND THEN...
FIDGET
CALM DOWN... AND LISTEN TO ME.
CLENCH
THAT MAN YOU SEEK...

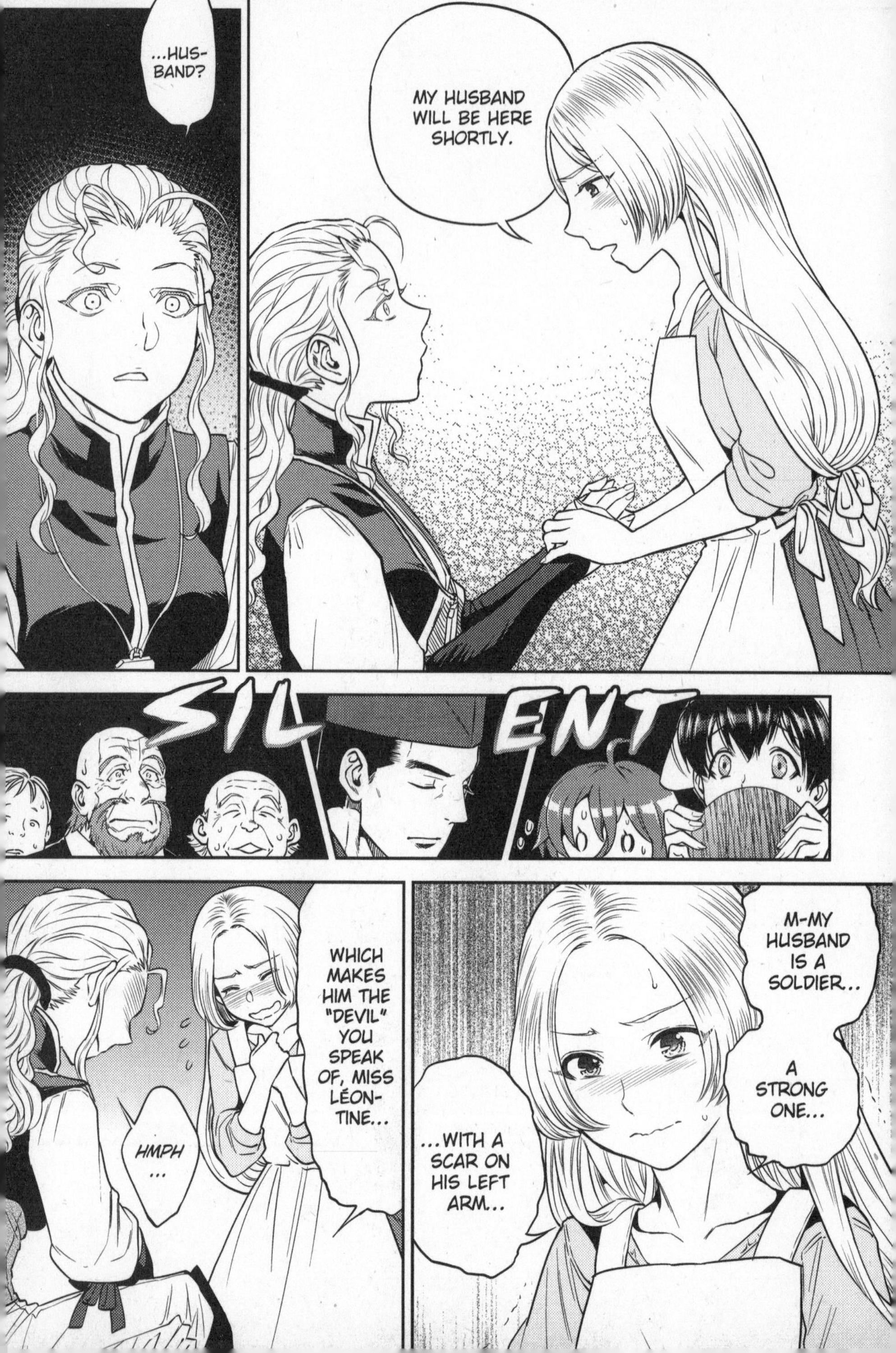
MY HUSBAND WILL BE HERE SHORTLY.
...HUS-BAND?
SILENT
M-MY HUSBAND IS A SOLDIER...
A STRONG ONE...
...WITH A SCAR ON HIS LEFT ARM...
WHICH MAKES HIM THE "DEVIL" YOU SPEAK OF, MISS LÉON-TINE...
HMPH ...

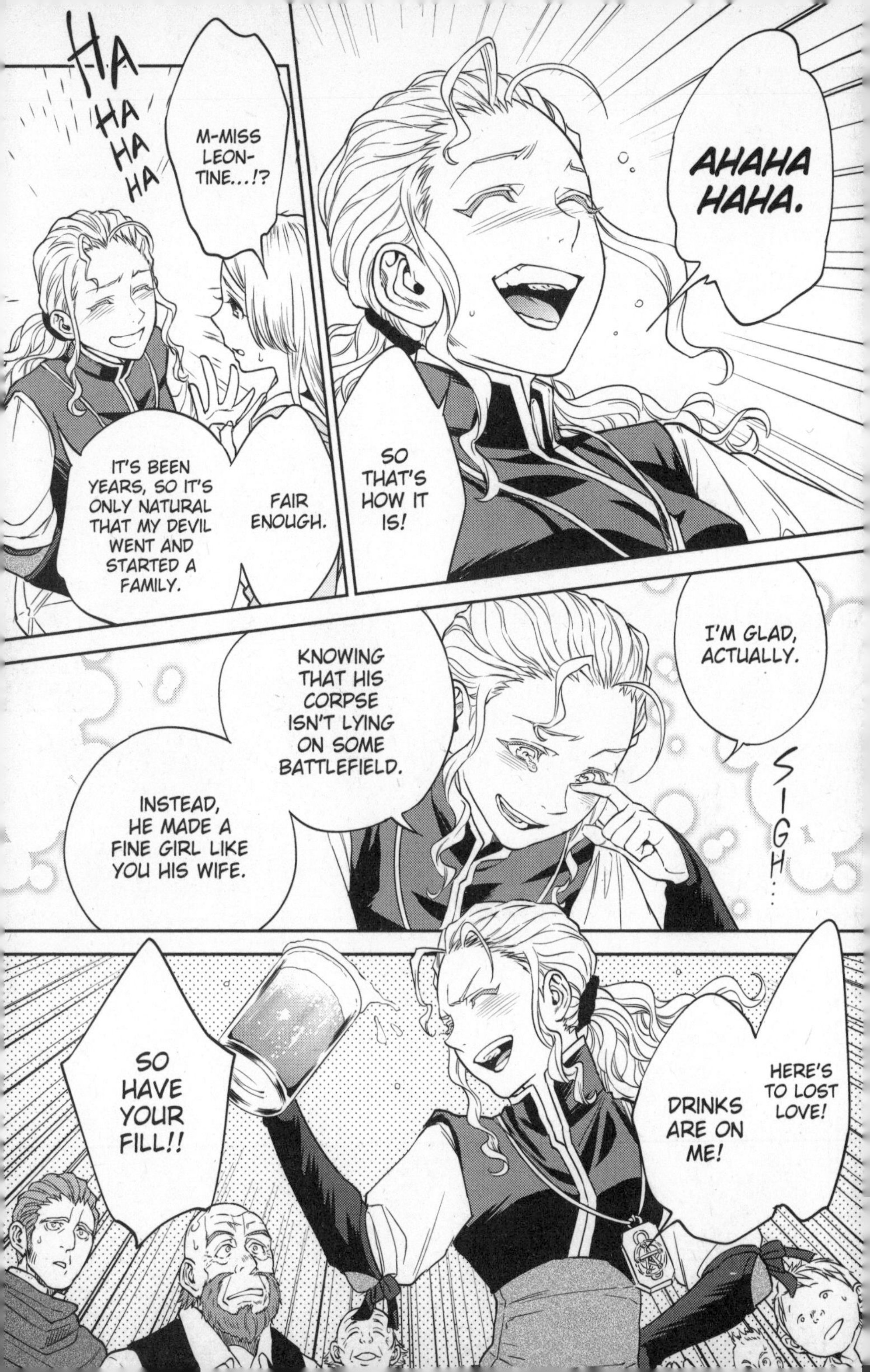
AHAHA HAHA.
SO THAT'S HOW IT IS!
M-MISS LEONTINE...!?
HA HA HA HA HA
FAIR ENOUGH.
IT'S BEEN YEARS, SO IT'S ONLY NATURAL THAT MY DEVIL WENT AND STARTED A FAMILY.
I'M GLAD, ACTUALLY.
KNOWING THAT HIS CORPSE ISN'T LYING ON SOME BATTLEFIELD.
SIGH...
INSTEAD, HE MADE A FINE GIRL LIKE YOU HIS WIFE.
HERE'S TO LOST LOVE!
DRINKS ARE ON ME!
SO HAVE YOUR FILL!!

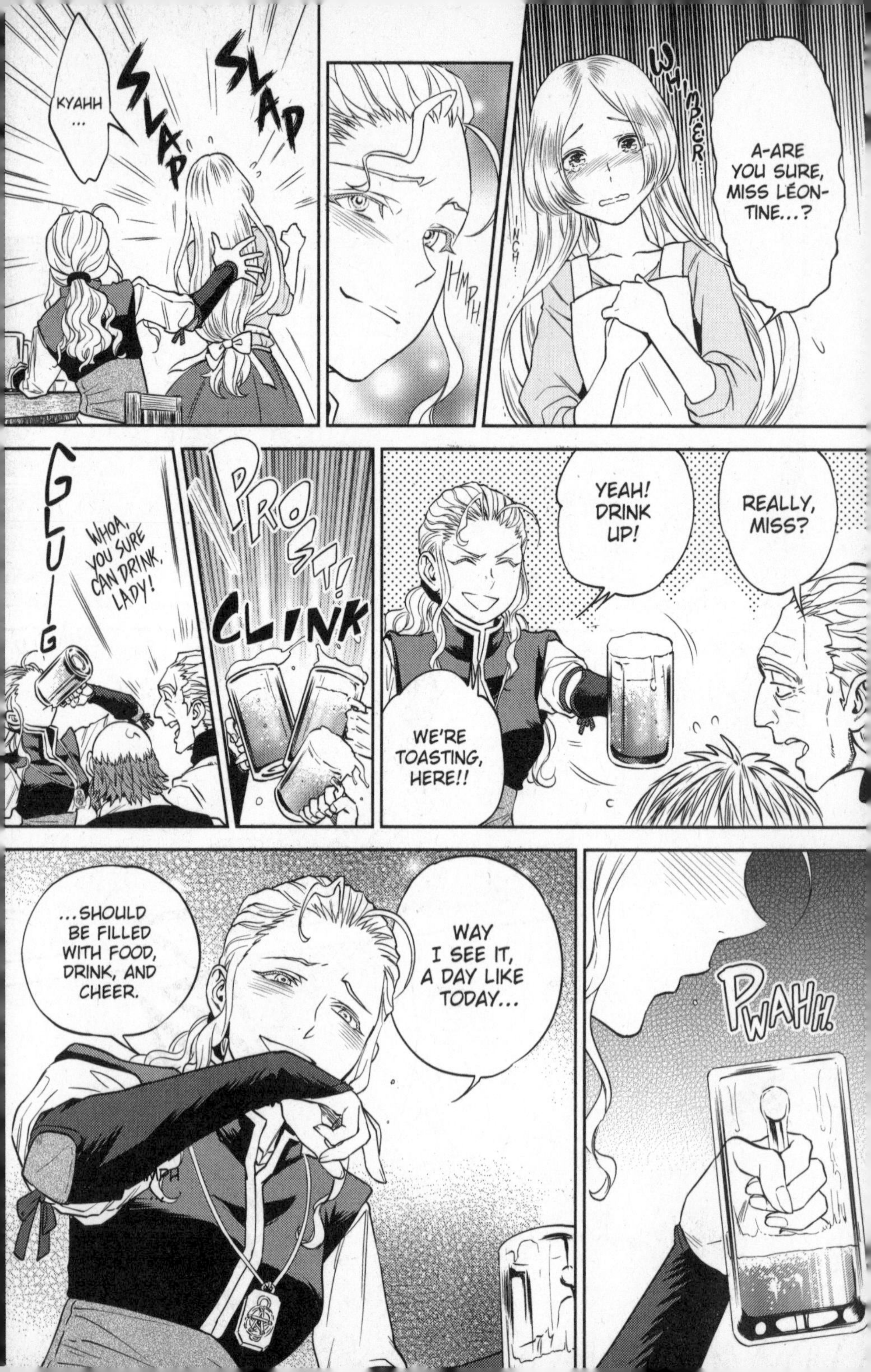
WHIMPER...
A-ARE YOU SURE, MISS LÉONTINE...?
HMPH
KYAHH...
SLAP
SLAP
REALLY, MISS?
YEAH! DRINK UP!
WE'RE TOASTING, HERE!!
PROST!
CLINK
WHOA, YOU SURE CAN DRINK, LADY!
GLUG
PWAHH.
WAY I SEE IT, A DAY LIKE TODAY...
...SHOULD BE FILLED WITH FOOD, DRINK, AND CHEER.

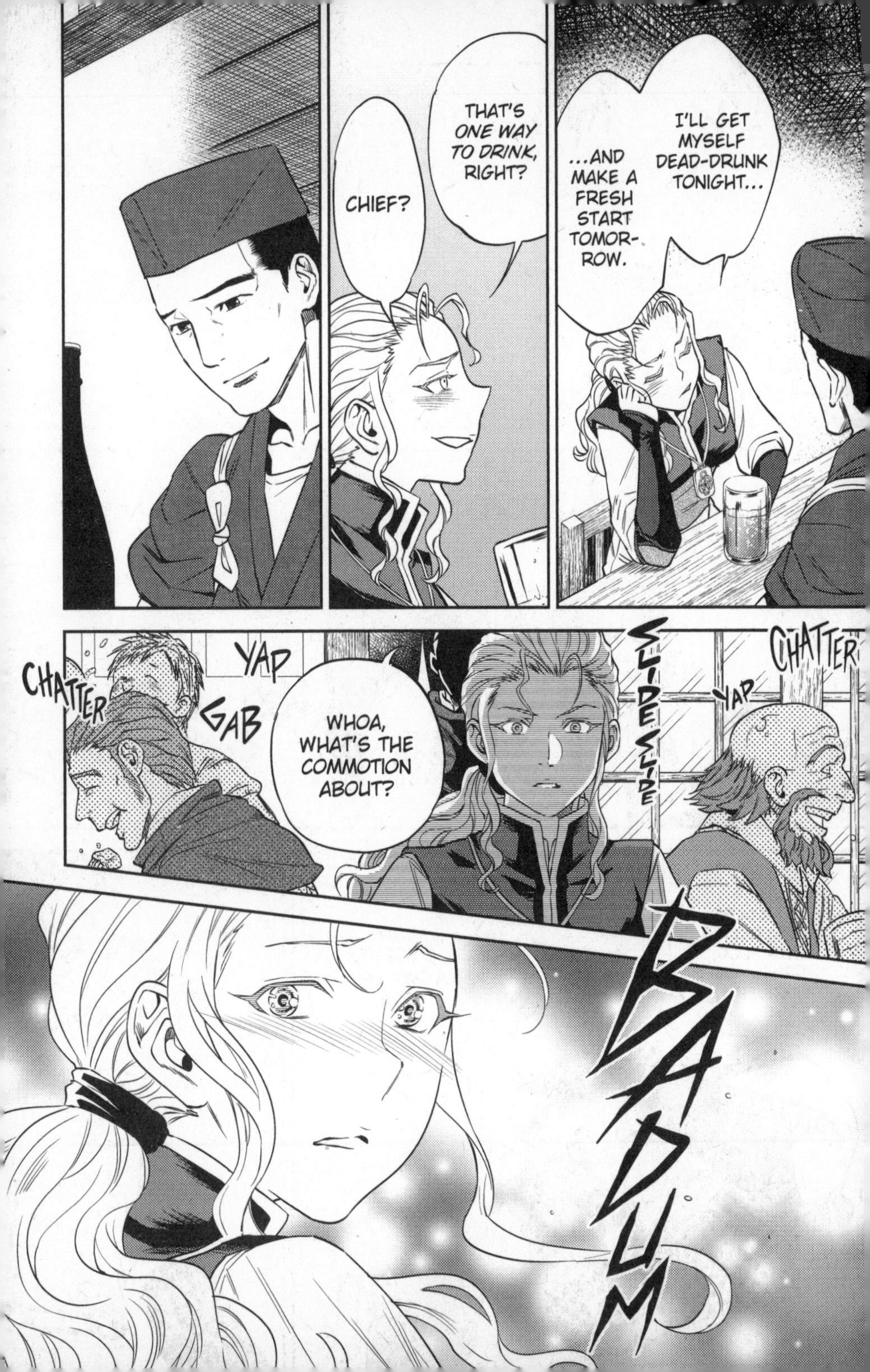
I'LL GET MYSELF DEAD-DRUNK TONIGHT...
...AND MAKE A FRESH START TOMOR-ROW.
THAT'S ONE WAY TO DRINK, RIGHT?
CHIEF?
CHATTER
YAP
SLIDE SLIDE
WHOA, WHAT'S THE COMMOTION ABOUT?
YAP
GAB
CHATTER
BADUM

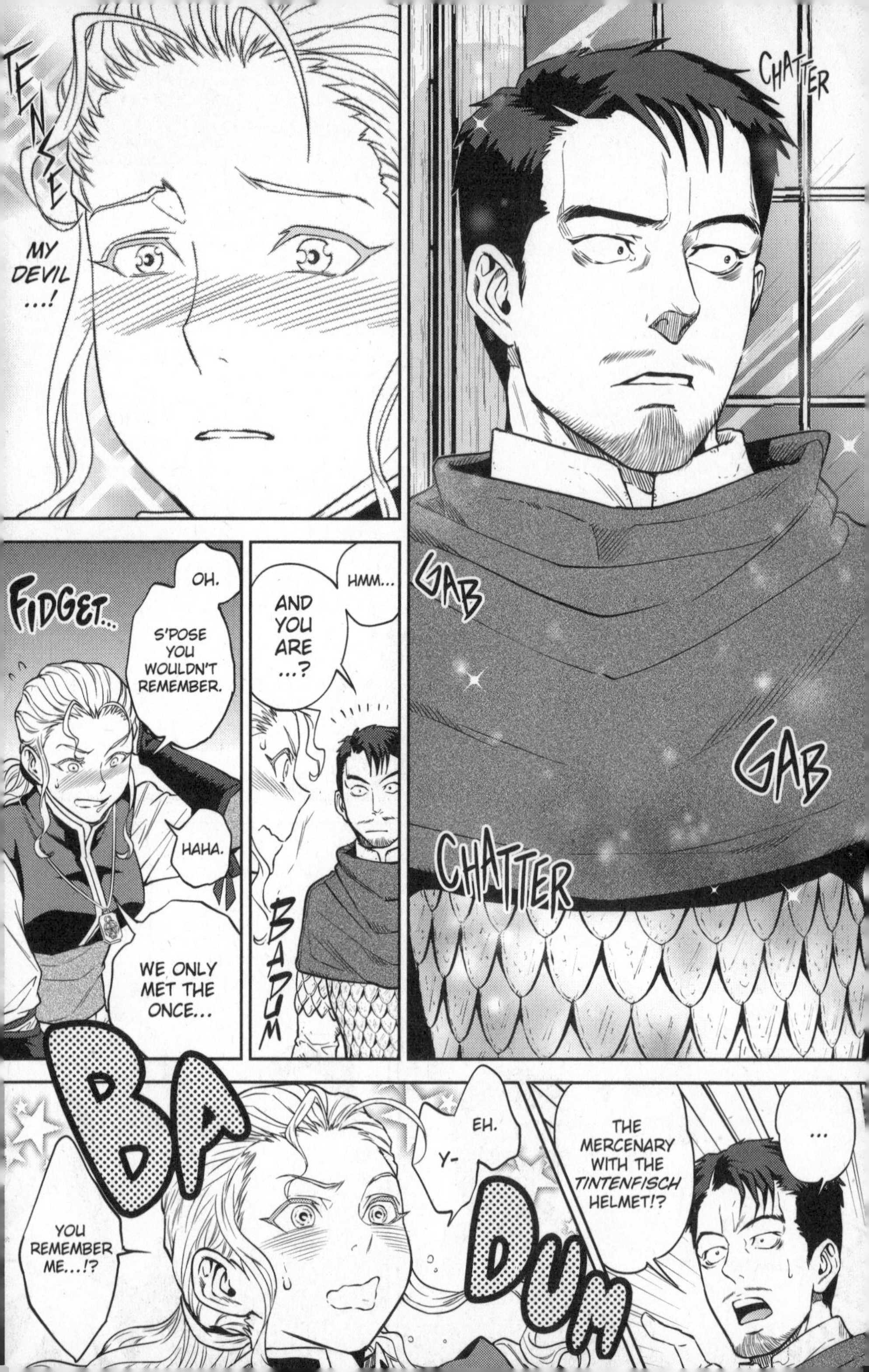
CHATTER
GAB
GAB
CHATTER
TENSE
MY DEVIL ...!
HMM...
AND YOU ARE ...?
BADUM
OH.
FIDGET...
S'POSE YOU WOULDN'T REMEMBER.
HAHA.
WE ONLY MET THE ONCE...
...
THE MERCENARY WITH THE *TINTENFISCH* HELMET!?
EH.
Y-
BADUM
YOU REMEMBER ME...!?

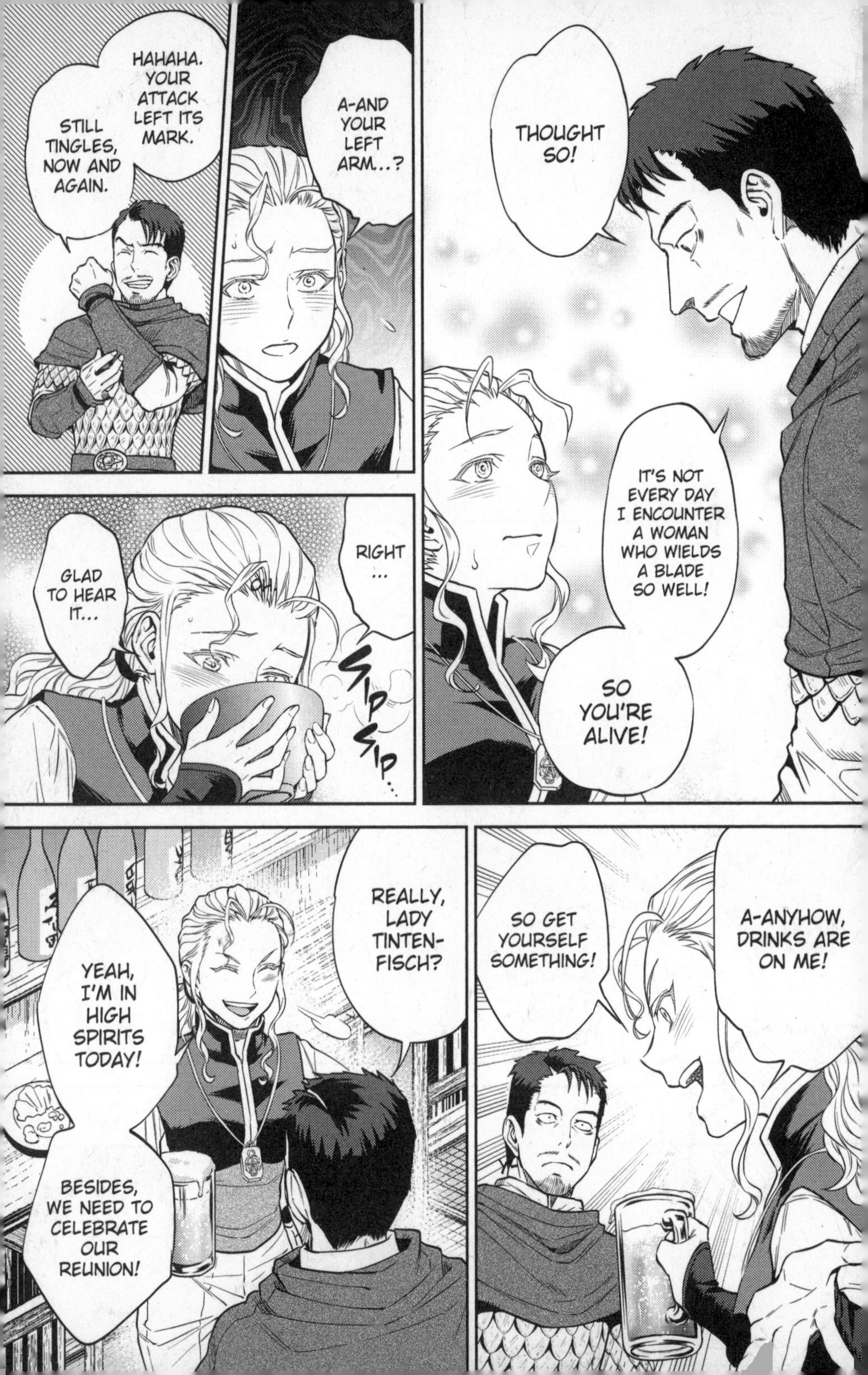
THOUGHT SO!
IT'S NOT EVERY DAY I ENCOUNTER A WOMAN WHO WIELDS A BLADE SO WELL!
SO YOU'RE ALIVE!
A-AND YOUR LEFT ARM...?
HAHAHA. YOUR ATTACK LEFT ITS MARK.
STILL TINGLES, NOW AND AGAIN.
RIGHT ...
OH...
GLAD TO HEAR IT...
SIP SIP...
A-ANYHOW, DRINKS ARE ON ME!
SO GET YOURSELF SOMETHING!
REALLY, LADY TINTEN-FISCH?
YEAH, I'M IN HIGH SPIRITS TODAY!
BESIDES, WE NEED TO CELEBRATE OUR REUNION!

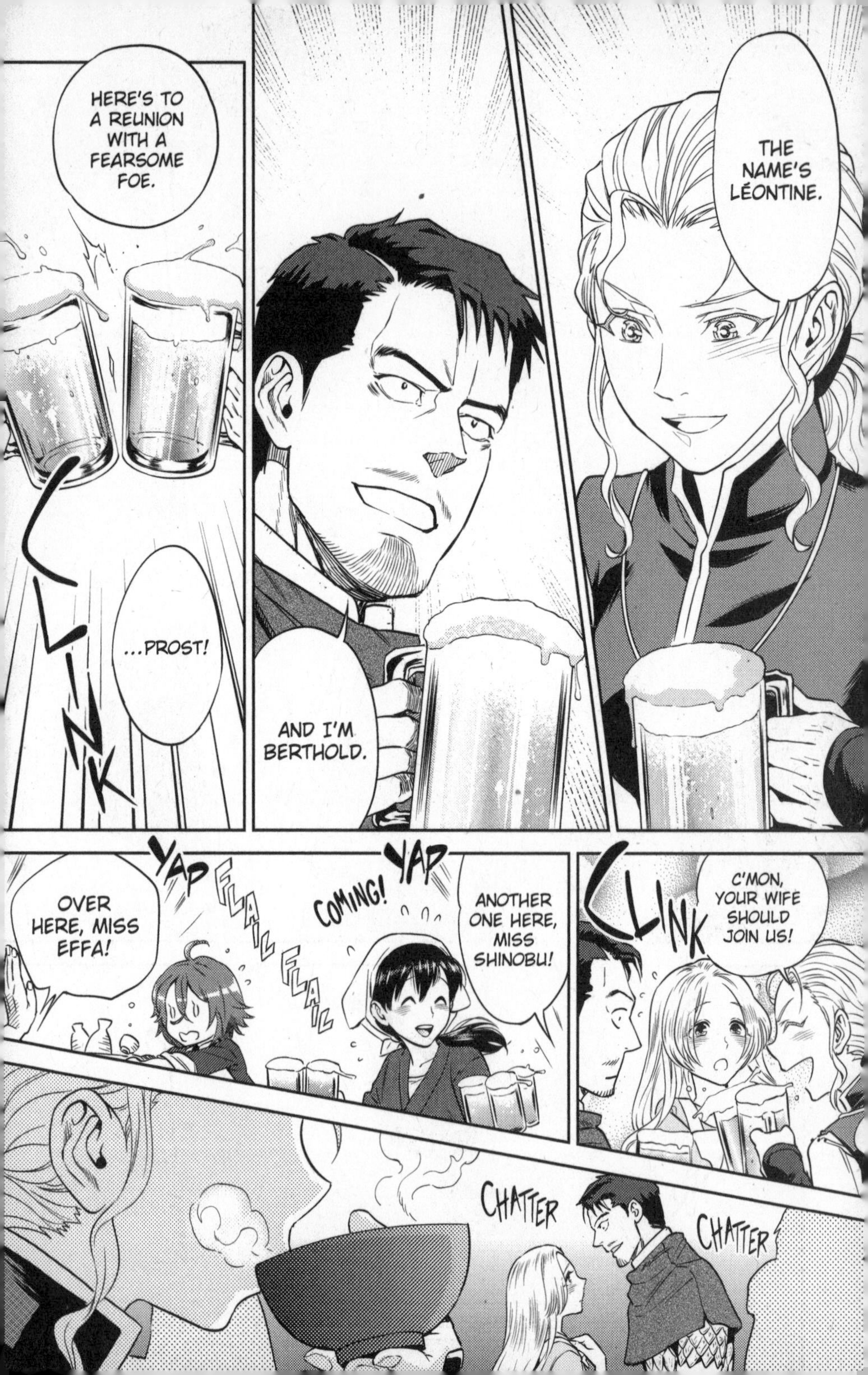
THE NAME'S LÉONTINE.
AND I'M BERTHOLD.
HERE'S TO A REUNION WITH A FEARSOME FOE.
...PROST!
CLINK
CLINK
C'MON, YOUR WIFE SHOULD JOIN US!
YAP
ANOTHER ONE HERE, MISS SHINOBU!
COMING!
FLAIL FLAIL
YAP
OVER HERE, MISS EFFA!
CHATTER
CHATTER

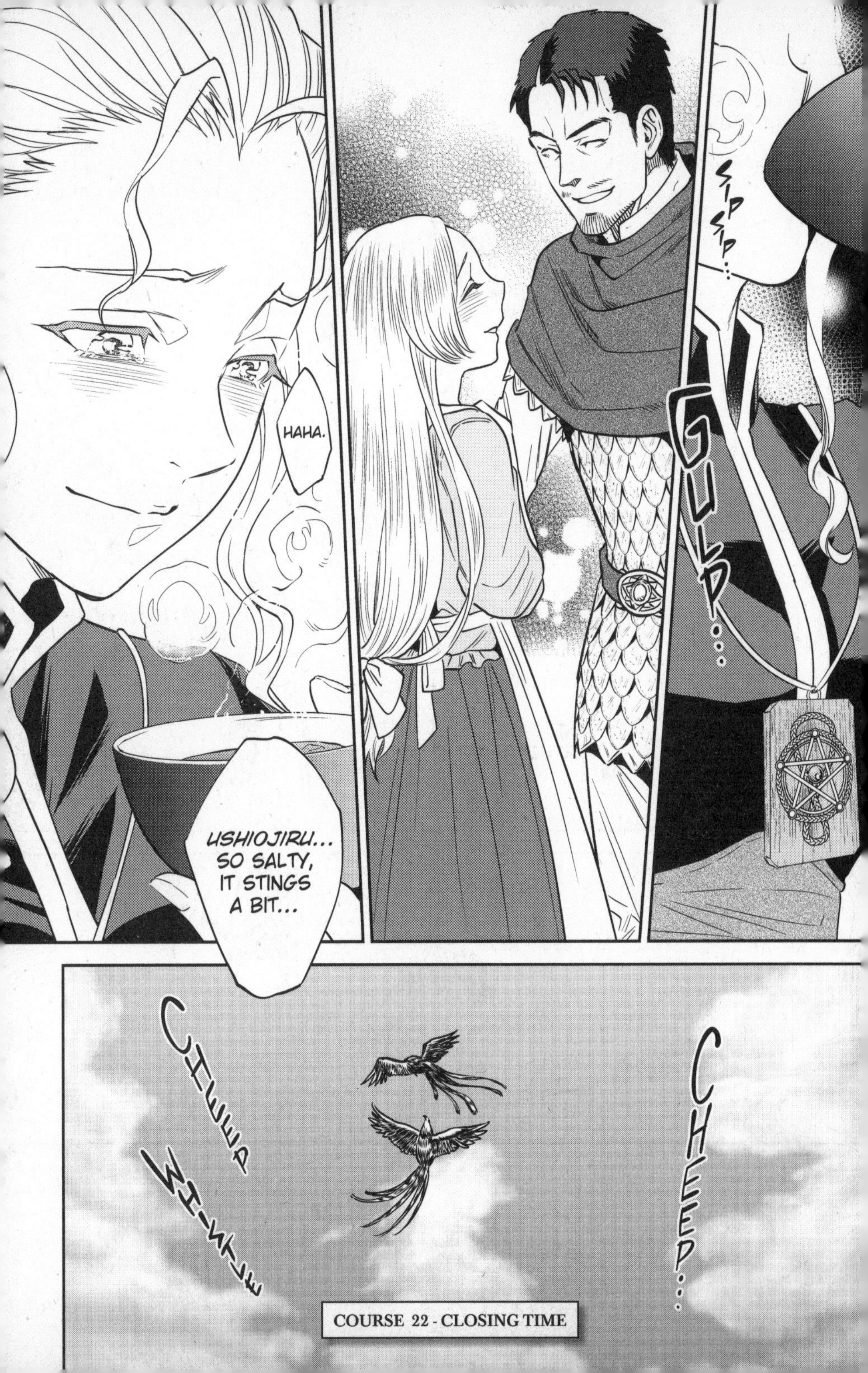
SIP SIP...
GULP...
HAHA.
USHIOJIRU... SO SALTY, IT STINGS A BIT...
CHEEP...
CHWEEP
WHI-WHIW
COURSE 22 - CLOSING TIME

Bouillabaisse

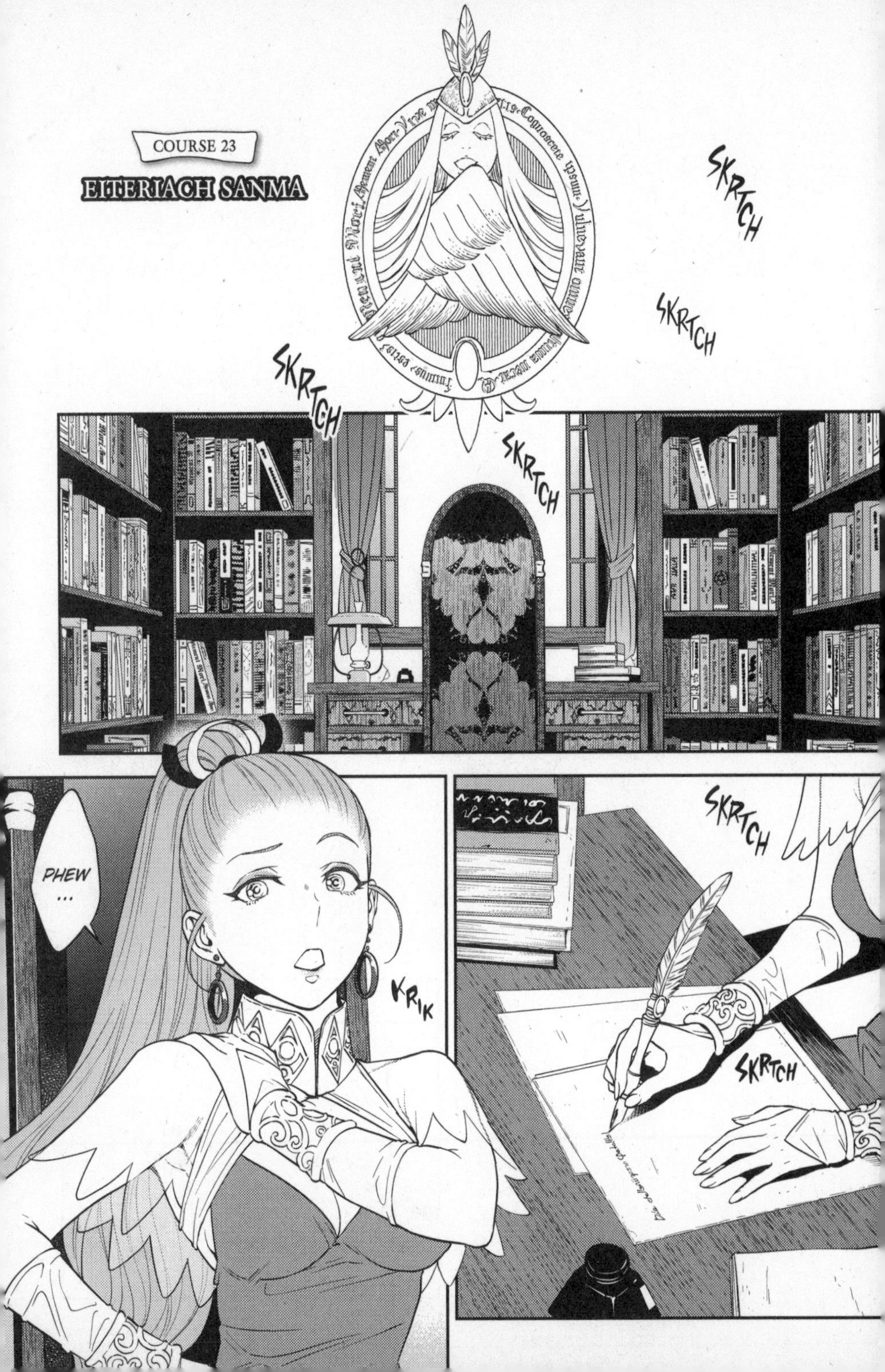
COURSE 23
EITERIACH SANMA
SKRTCH
SKRTCH
SKRTCH
SKRTCH
SKRTCH
SKRTCH
PHEW ...
KRIK

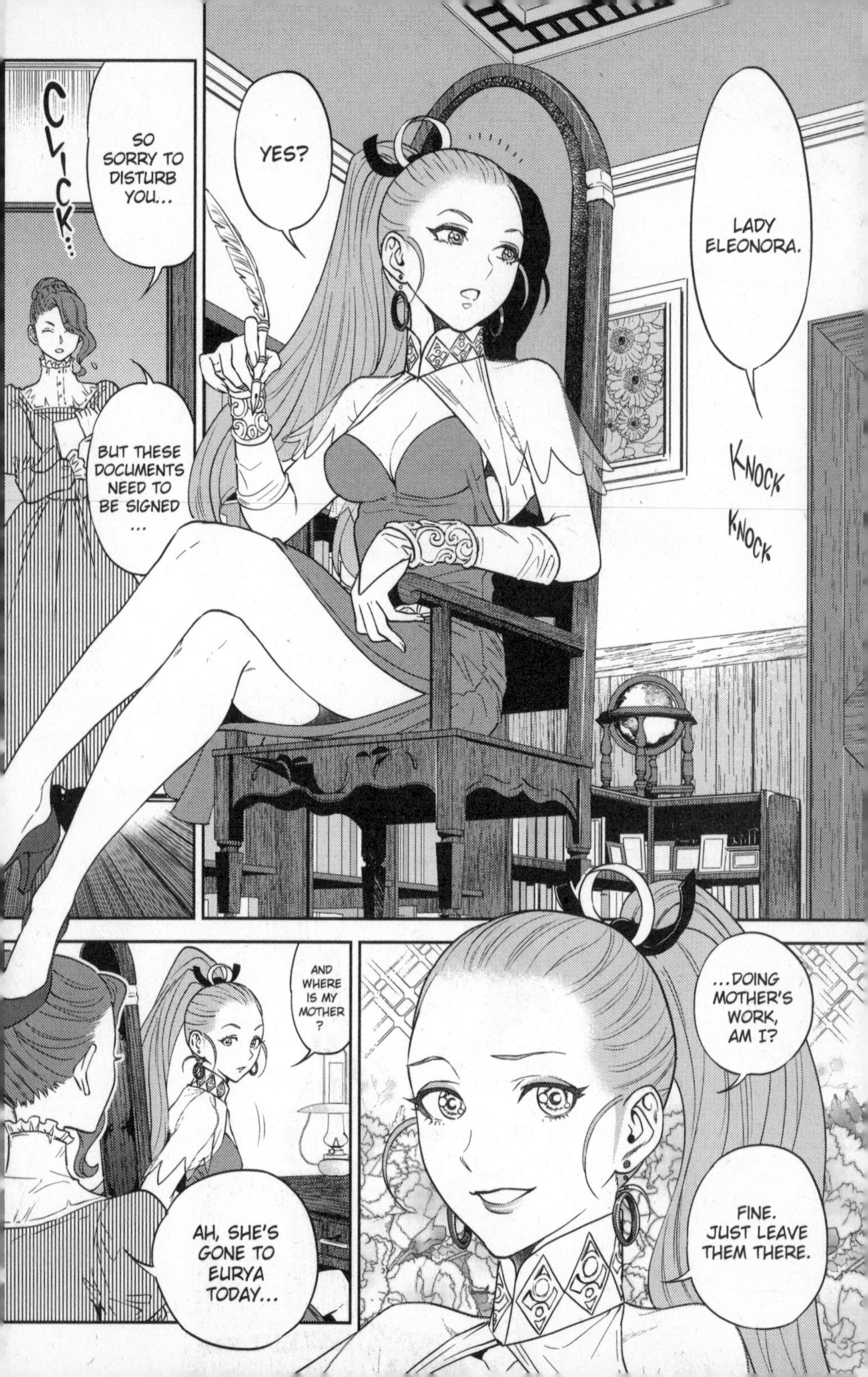
LADY ELEONORA.
KNOCK
KNOCK
YES?
CLICK...
SO SORRY TO DISTURB YOU...
BUT THESE DOCUMENTS NEED TO BE SIGNED ...
...DOING MOTHER'S WORK, AM I?
FINE. JUST LEAVE THEM THERE.
AND WHERE IS MY MOTHER ?
AH, SHE'S GONE TO EURYA TODAY...

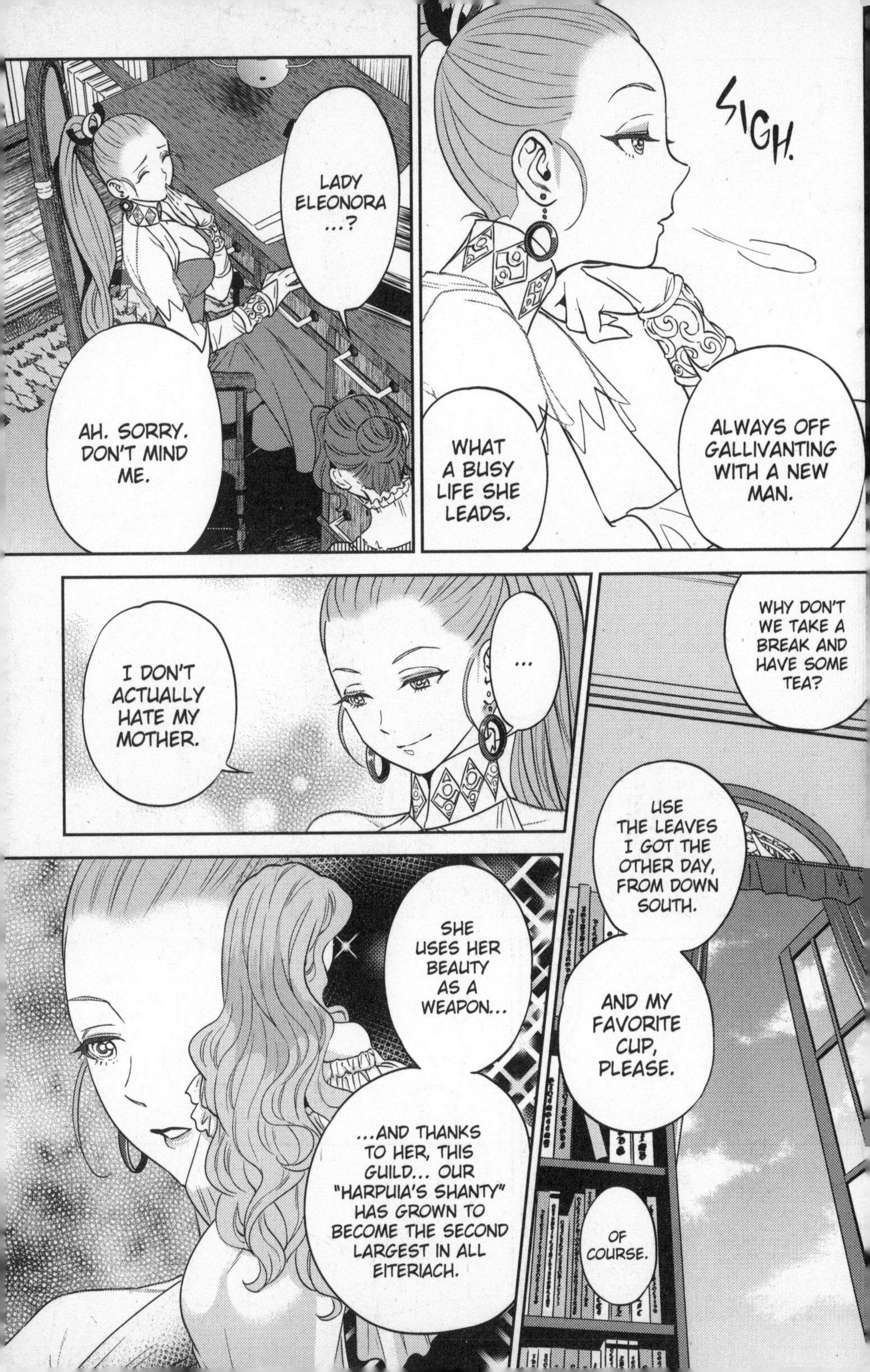
SIGH.
ALWAYS OFF GALLIVANTING WITH A NEW MAN.
WHAT A BUSY LIFE SHE LEADS.
LADY ELEONORA ...?
AH. SORRY. DON'T MIND ME.
WHY DON'T WE TAKE A BREAK AND HAVE SOME TEA?
USE THE LEAVES I GOT THE OTHER DAY, FROM DOWN SOUTH.
AND MY FAVORITE CUP, PLEASE.
OF COURSE.
...
I DON'T ACTUALLY HATE MY MOTHER.
SHE USES HER BEAUTY AS A WEAPON...
...AND THANKS TO HER, THIS GUILD... OUR "HARPUIA'S SHANTY" HAS GROWN TO BECOME THE SECOND LARGEST IN ALL EITERIACH.

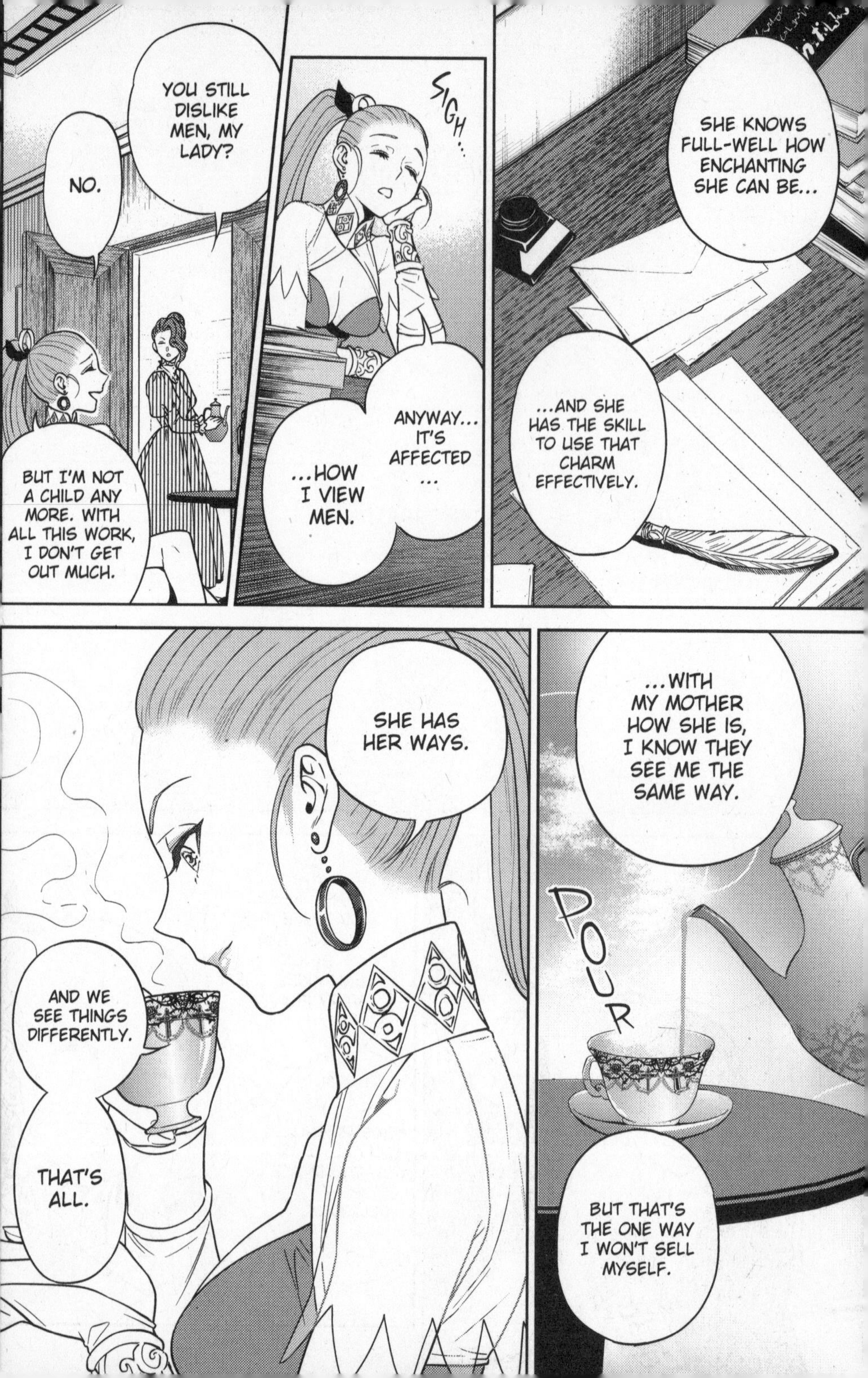
SHE KNOWS FULL-WELL HOW ENCHANTING SHE CAN BE...
...AND SHE HAS THE SKILL TO USE THAT CHARM EFFECTIVELY.
SIGH...
ANYWAY... IT'S AFFECTED ...
...HOW I VIEW MEN.
YOU STILL DISLIKE MEN, MY LADY?
NO.
BUT I'M NOT A CHILD ANY MORE. WITH ALL THIS WORK, I DON'T GET OUT MUCH.
...WITH MY MOTHER HOW SHE IS, I KNOW THEY SEE ME THE SAME WAY.
POUR
BUT THAT'S THE ONE WAY I WON'T SELL MYSELF.
SHE HAS HER WAYS.
AND WE SEE THINGS DIFFERENTLY.
THAT'S ALL.

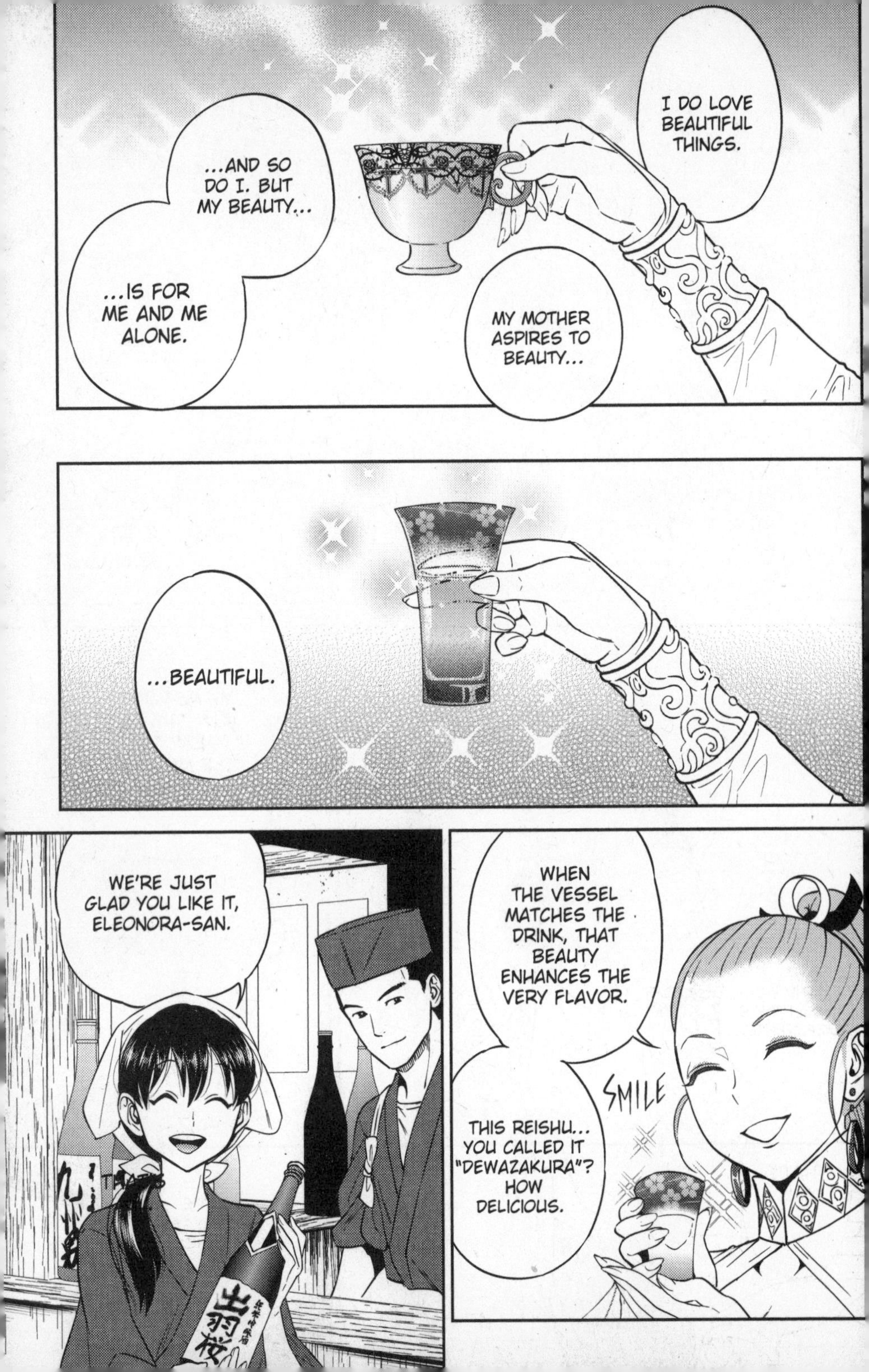
I DO LOVE BEAUTIFUL THINGS.
MY MOTHER ASPIRES TO BEAUTY...
...AND SO DO I. BUT MY BEAUTY...
...IS FOR ME AND ME ALONE.
...BEAUTIFUL.
WHEN THE VESSEL MATCHES THE DRINK, THAT BEAUTY ENHANCES THE VERY FLAVOR.
SMILE
THIS REISHU... YOU CALLED IT "DEWAZAKURA"? HOW DELICIOUS.
WE'RE JUST GLAD YOU LIKE IT, ELEONORA-SAN.

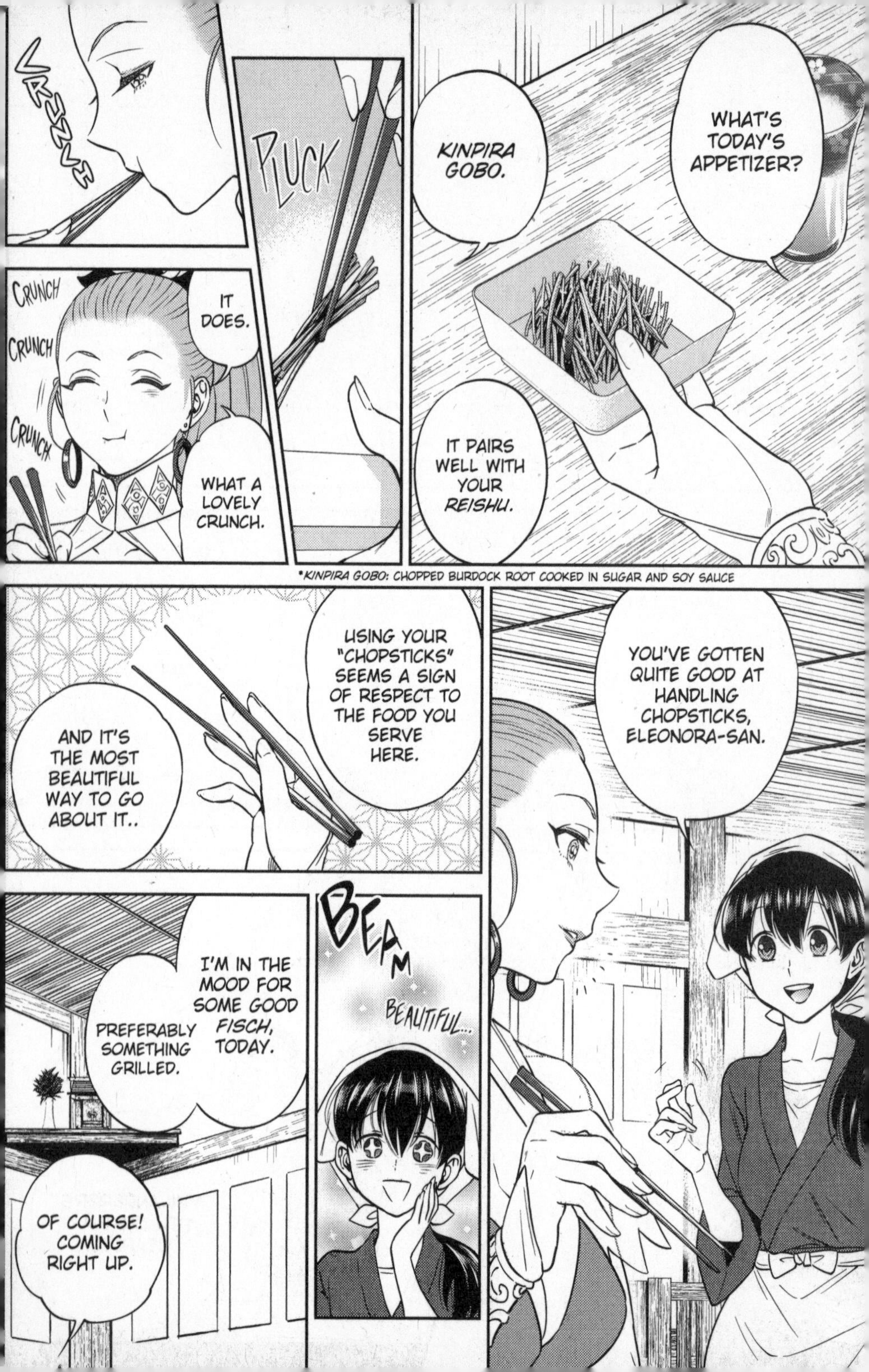

WHAT'S TODAY'S APPETIZER?
KINPIRA GOBO.
IT PAIRS WELL WITH YOUR REISHU.
PLUCK
CRUNCH
IT DOES.
CRUNCH
CRUNCH
CRUNCH
WHAT A LOVELY CRUNCH.
YOU'VE GOTTEN QUITE GOOD AT HANDLING CHOPSTICKS, ELEONORA-SAN.
USING YOUR "CHOPSTICKS" SEEMS A SIGN OF RESPECT TO THE FOOD YOU SERVE HERE.
AND IT'S THE MOST BEAUTIFUL WAY TO GO ABOUT IT..
BEAM
BEAUTIFUL...
I'M IN THE MOOD FOR SOME GOOD FISCH, TODAY.
PREFERABLY SOMETHING GRILLED.
OF COURSE! COMING RIGHT UP.

*KINPIRA GOBO: CHOPPED BURDOCK ROOT COOKED IN SUGAR AND SOY SAUCE

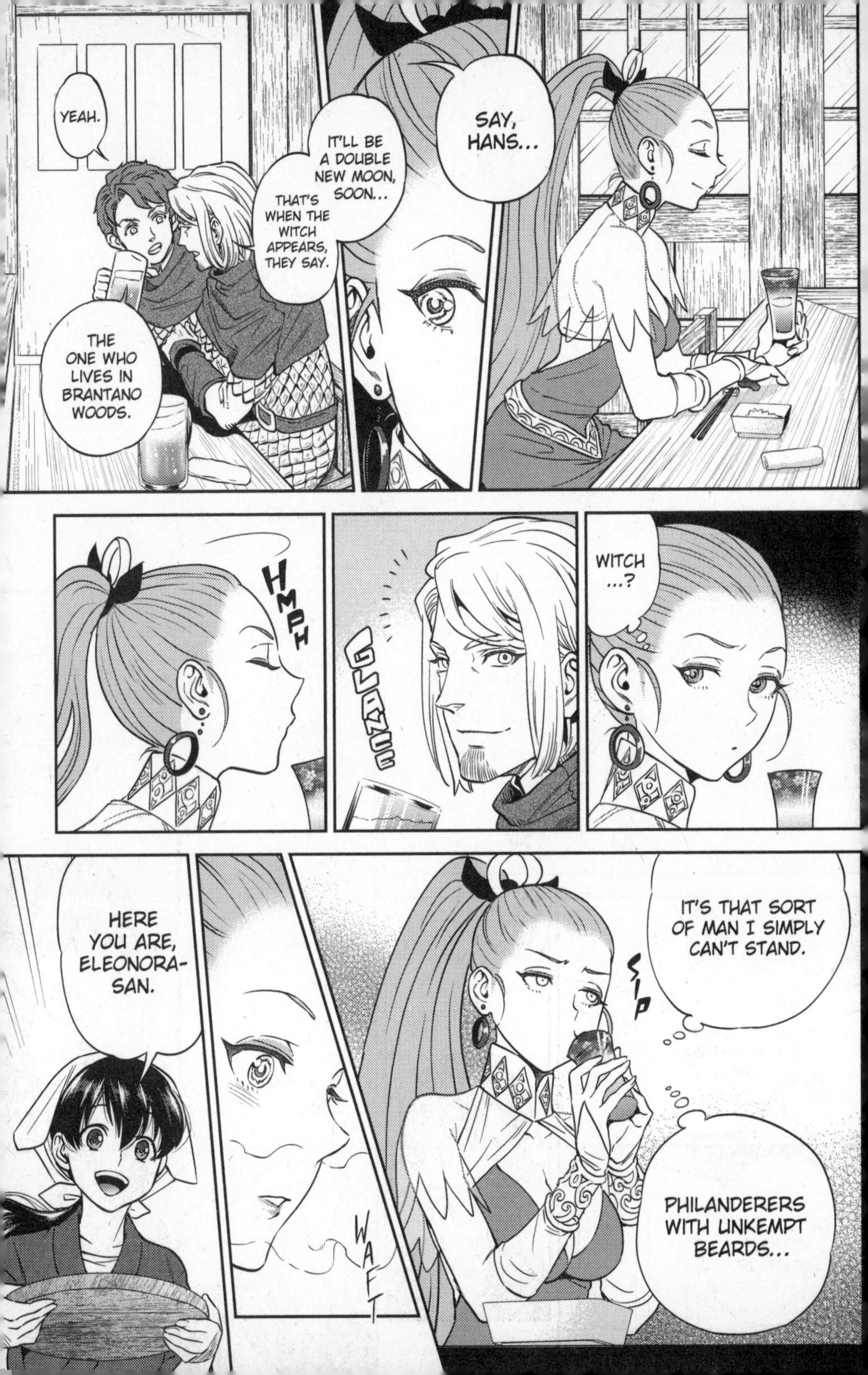
SAY, HANS...
IT'LL BE A DOUBLE NEW MOON, SOON...
THAT'S WHEN THE WITCH APPEARS, THEY SAY.
YEAH.
THE ONE WHO LIVES IN BRANTANO WOODS.
WITCH ...?
GLANCE
HMPH
IT'S THAT SORT OF MAN I SIMPLY CAN'T STAND.
SIP
PHILANDERERS WITH UNKEMPT BEARDS...
WAFT
HERE YOU ARE, ELEONORA-SAN.

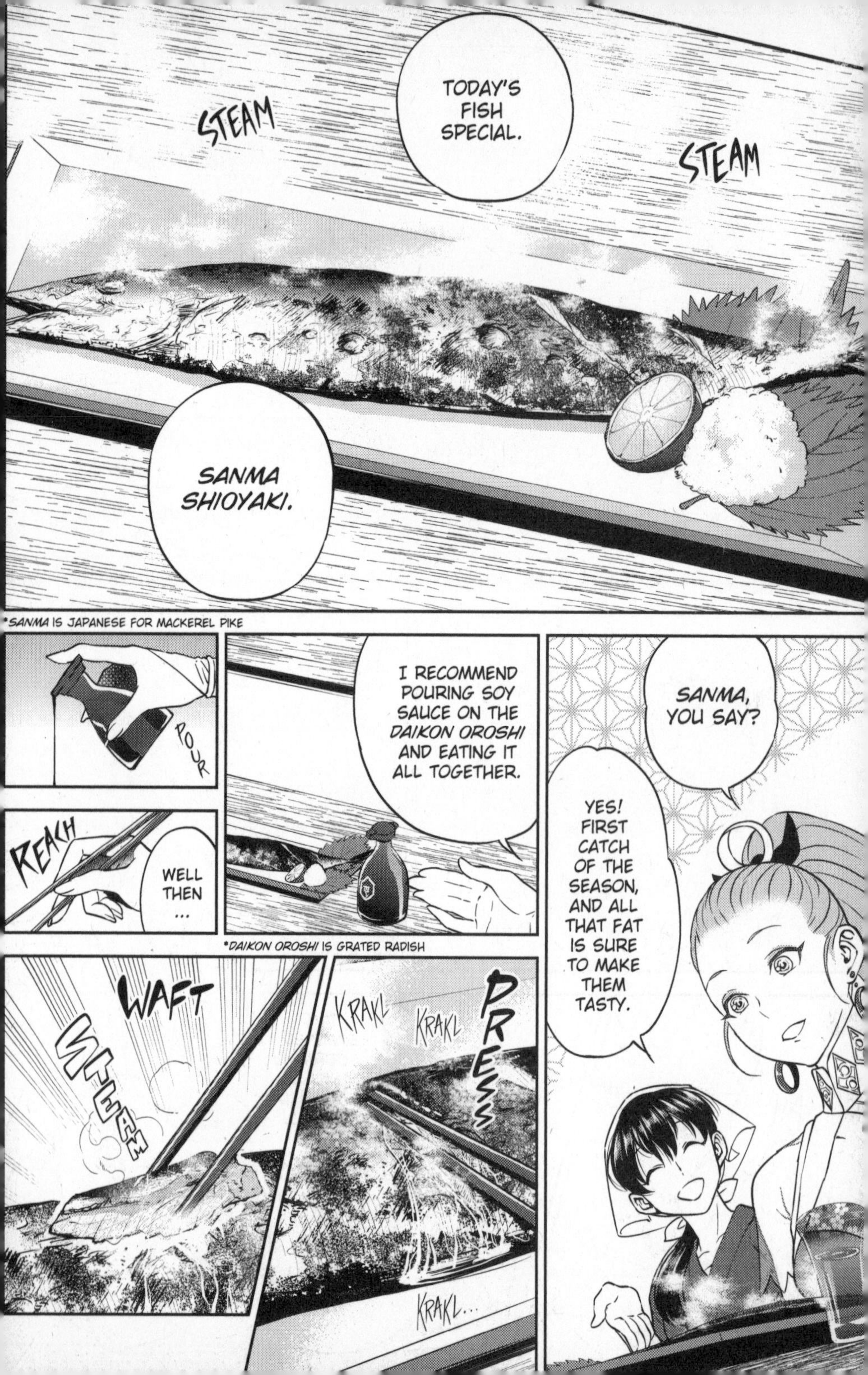
STEAM
TODAY'S FISH SPECIAL.
STEAM
SANMA SHIOYAKI.
*SANMA IS JAPANESE FOR MACKEREL PIKE
SANMA, YOU SAY?
YES! FIRST CATCH OF THE SEASON, AND ALL THAT FAT IS SURE TO MAKE THEM TASTY.
I RECOMMEND POURING SOY SAUCE ON THE DAIKON OROSHI AND EATING IT ALL TOGETHER.
POUR
REACH
WELL THEN ...
*DAIKON OROSHI IS GRATED RADISH
PRESS
KRAKL
KRAKL
KRAKL...
WAFT
STEAM

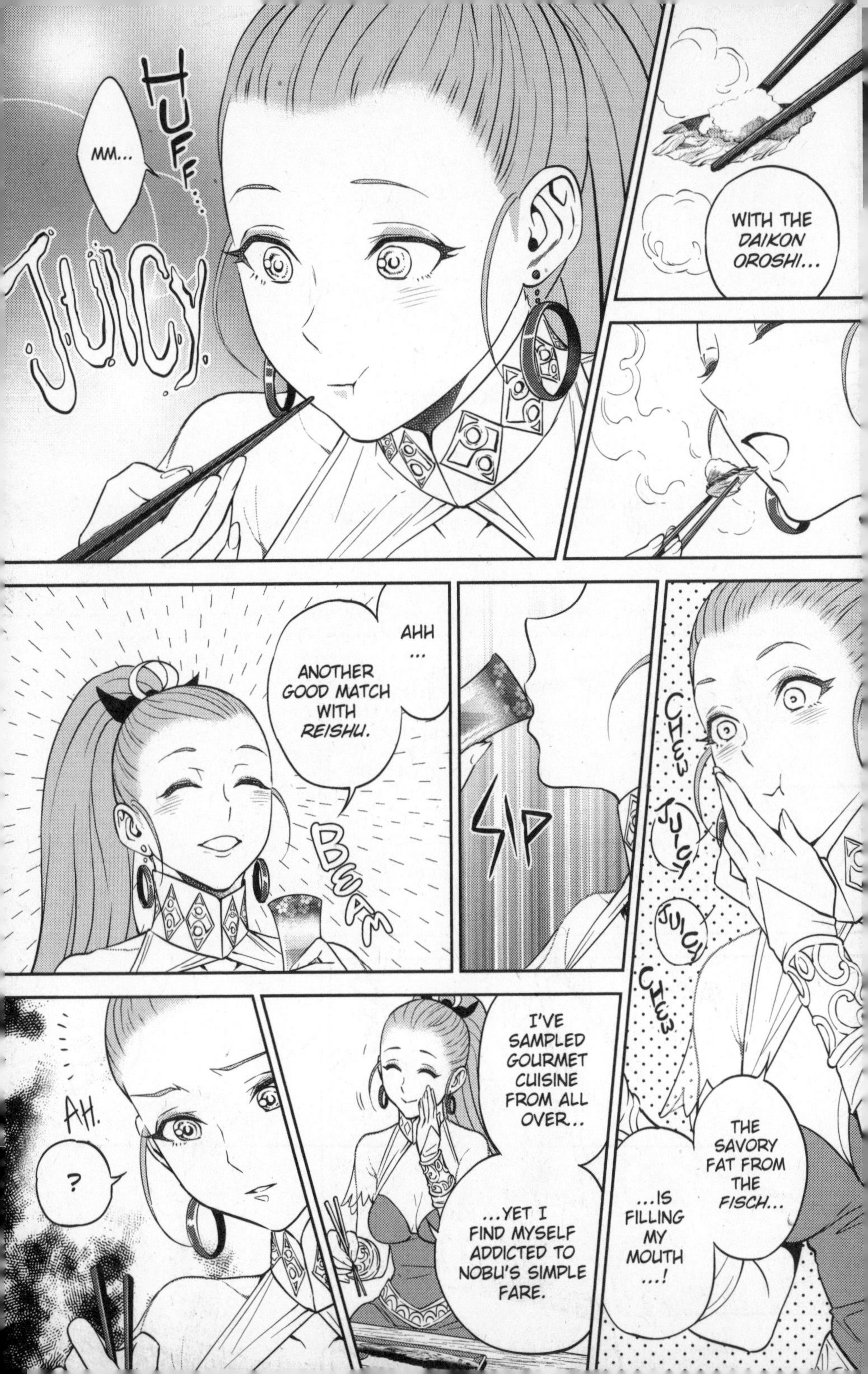
WITH THE DAIKON OROSHI...
HUFF...
MM...
JUICY
CHEW
JUICY
JUICY
CHEW
THE SAVORY FAT FROM THE FISCH...
...IS FILLING MY MOUTH...!
SIP
AHH...
ANOTHER GOOD MATCH WITH REISHU.
BEAM
I'VE SAMPLED GOURMET CUISINE FROM ALL OVER...
...YET I FIND MYSELF ADDICTED TO NOBU'S SIMPLE FARE.
AH.
?

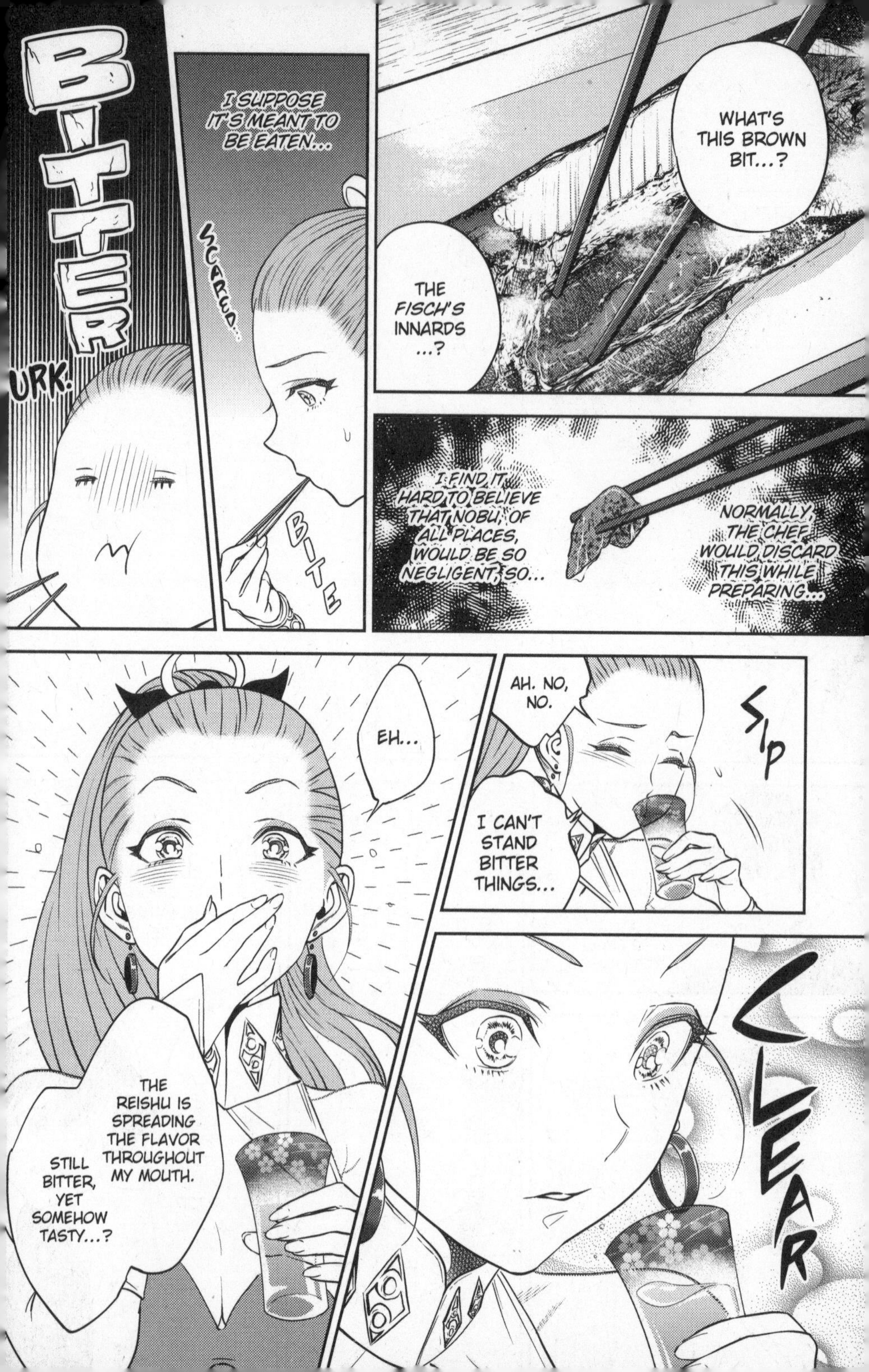
WHAT'S THIS BROWN BIT...?
THE FISCH'S INNARDS ...?
NORMALLY, THE CHEF WOULD DISCARD THIS WHILE PREPARING...
I FIND IT HARD TO BELIEVE THAT NOBU, OF ALL PLACES, WOULD BE SO NEGLIGENT, SO...
I SUPPOSE IT'S MEANT TO BE EATEN...
SCARED...
BITE
BITTER
URK.
SLIP
AH. NO, NO.
I CAN'T STAND BITTER THINGS...
CLEAR
EH...
THE REISHU IS SPREADING THE FLAVOR THROUGHOUT MY MOUTH.
STILL BITTER, YET SOMEHOW TASTY...?

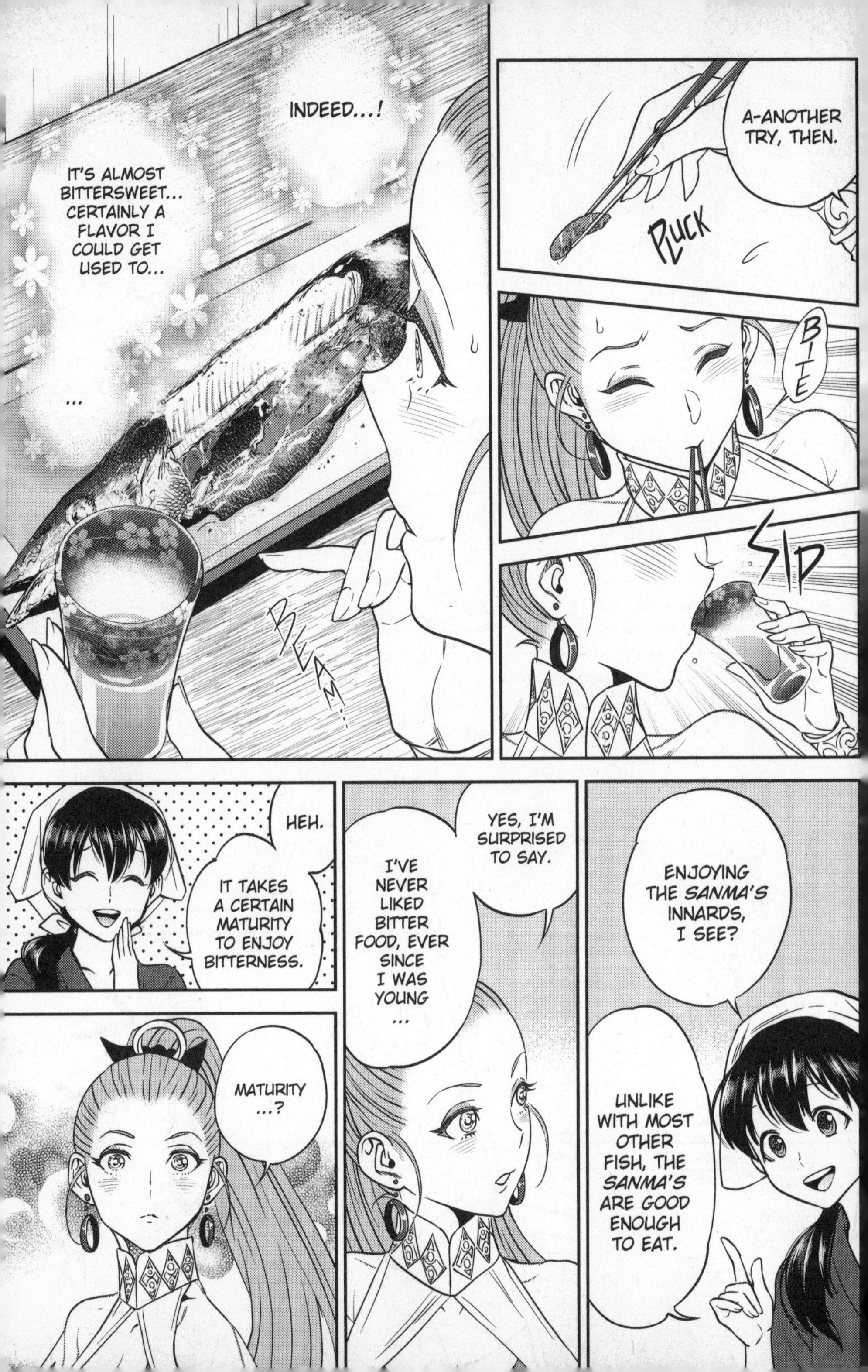
A-ANOTHER TRY, THEN.
PLUCK
BITE
SIP
INDEED...!
IT'S ALMOST BITTERSWEET... CERTAINLY A FLAVOR I COULD GET USED TO...
...
BLAM!
ENJOYING THE *SANMA'S* INNARDS, I SEE?
UNLIKE WITH MOST OTHER FISH, THE *SANMA'S* ARE GOOD ENOUGH TO EAT.
YES, I'M SURPRISED TO SAY.
I'VE NEVER LIKED BITTER FOOD, EVER SINCE I WAS YOUNG ...
HEH.
IT TAKES A CERTAIN MATURITY TO ENJOY BITTERNESS.
MATURITY ...?

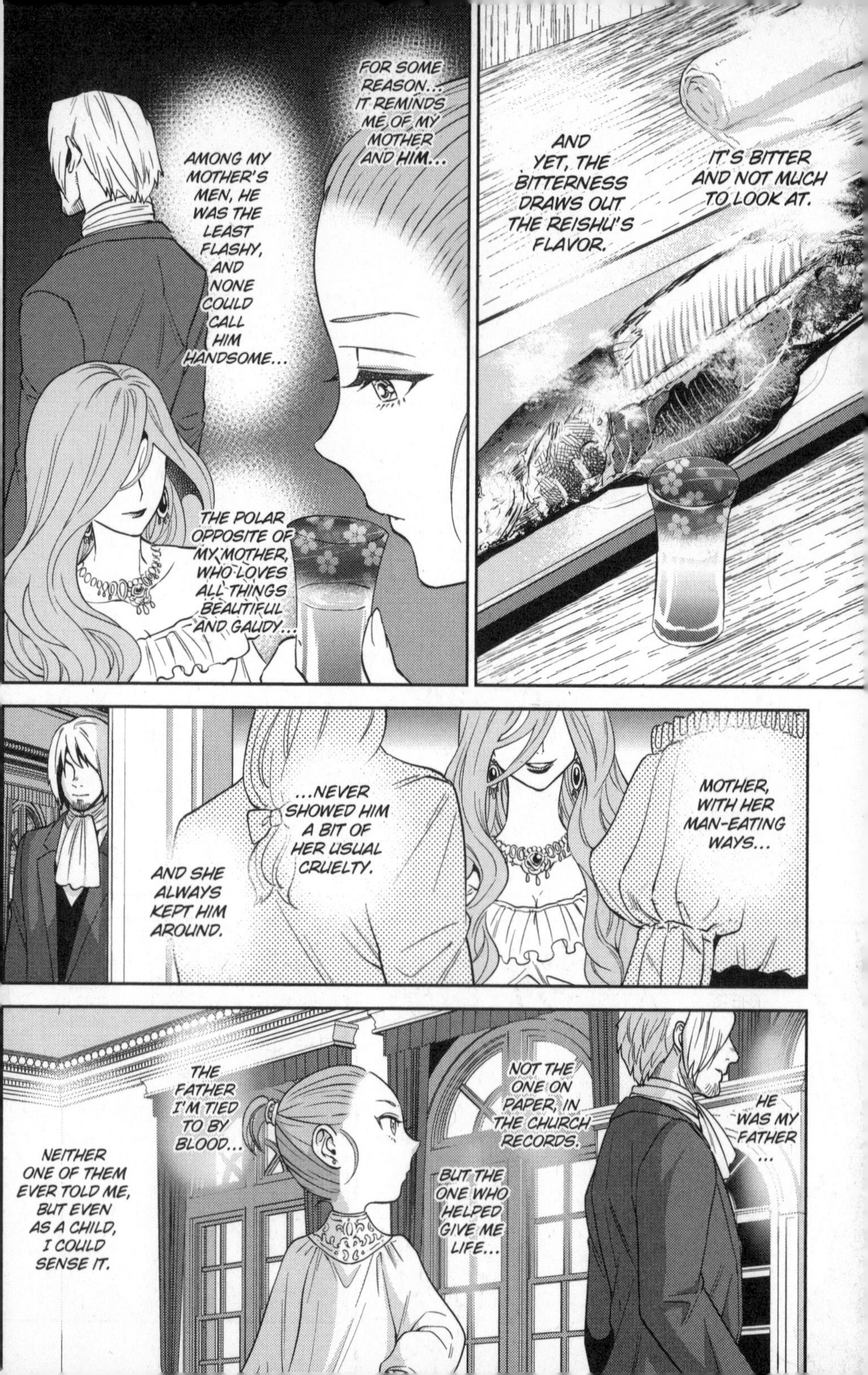
IT'S BITTER AND NOT MUCH TO LOOK AT.
AND YET, THE BITTERNESS DRAWS OUT THE REISHU'S FLAVOR.
FOR SOME REASON... IT REMINDS ME OF MY MOTHER AND HIM...
AMONG MY MOTHER'S MEN, HE WAS THE LEAST FLASHY, AND NONE COULD CALL HIM HANDSOME...
THE POLAR OPPOSITE OF MY MOTHER, WHO LOVES ALL THINGS BEAUTIFUL AND GAUDY...
MOTHER, WITH HER MAN-EATING WAYS...
...NEVER SHOWED HIM A BIT OF HER USUAL CRUELTY.
AND SHE ALWAYS KEPT HIM AROUND.
HE WAS MY FATHER...
NOT THE ONE ON PAPER, IN THE CHURCH RECORDS.
BUT THE ONE WHO HELPED GIVE ME LIFE...
THE FATHER I'M TIED TO BY BLOOD...
NEITHER ONE OF THEM EVER TOLD ME, BUT EVEN AS A CHILD, I COULD SENSE IT.

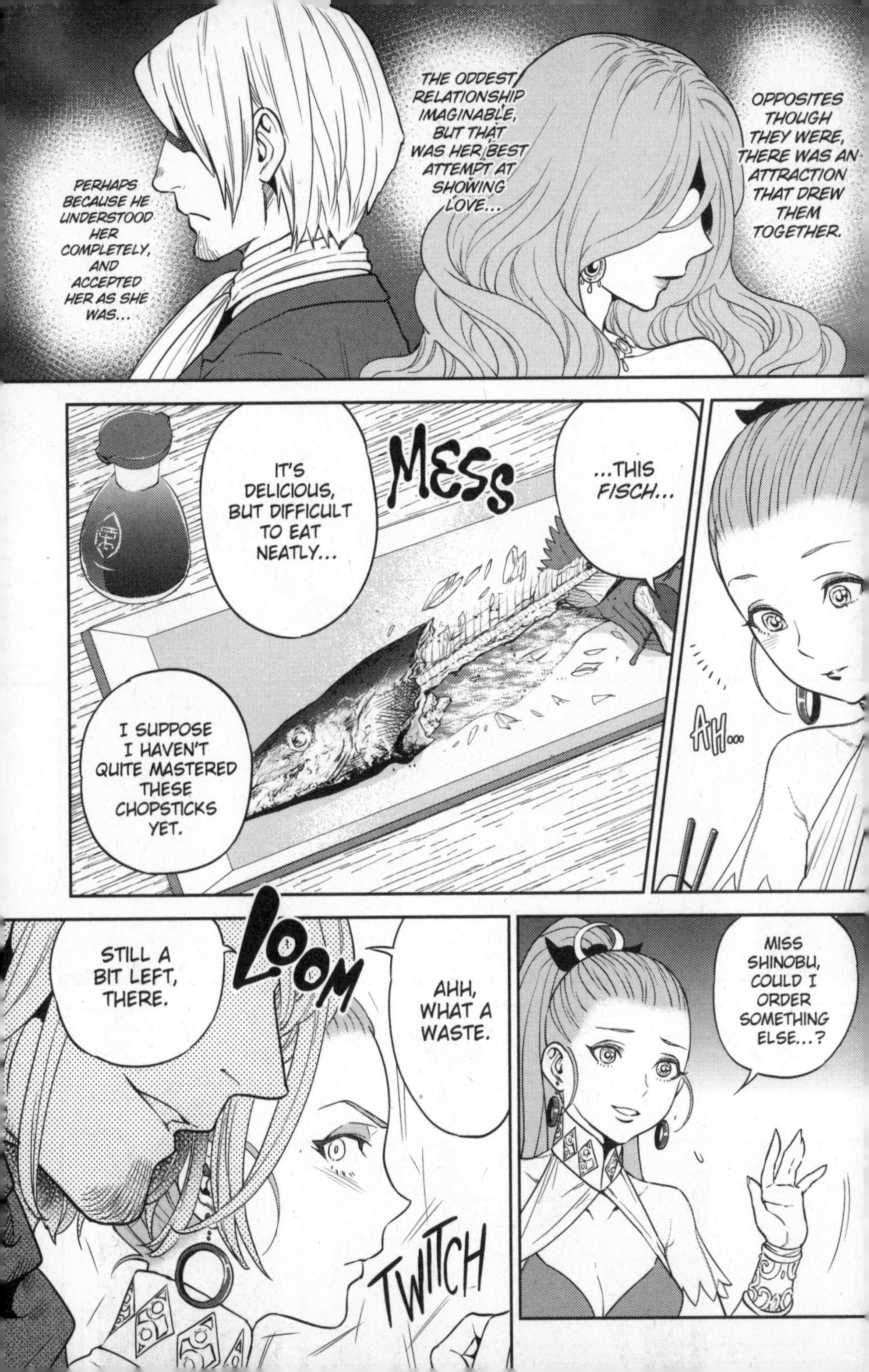
OPPOSITES THOUGH THEY WERE, THERE WAS AN ATTRACTION THAT DREW THEM TOGETHER.
THE ODDEST RELATIONSHIP IMAGINABLE, BUT THAT WAS HER BEST ATTEMPT AT SHOWING LOVE...
PERHAPS BECAUSE HE UNDERSTOOD HER COMPLETELY, AND ACCEPTED HER AS SHE WAS...
AH...
...THIS FISCH...
MESS
IT'S DELICIOUS, BUT DIFFICULT TO EAT NEATLY...
I SUPPOSE I HAVEN'T QUITE MASTERED THESE CHOPSTICKS YET.
MISS SHINOBU, COULD I ORDER SOMETHING ELSE...?
AHH, WHAT A WASTE.
LOOM
STILL A BIT LEFT, THERE.
TWITCH

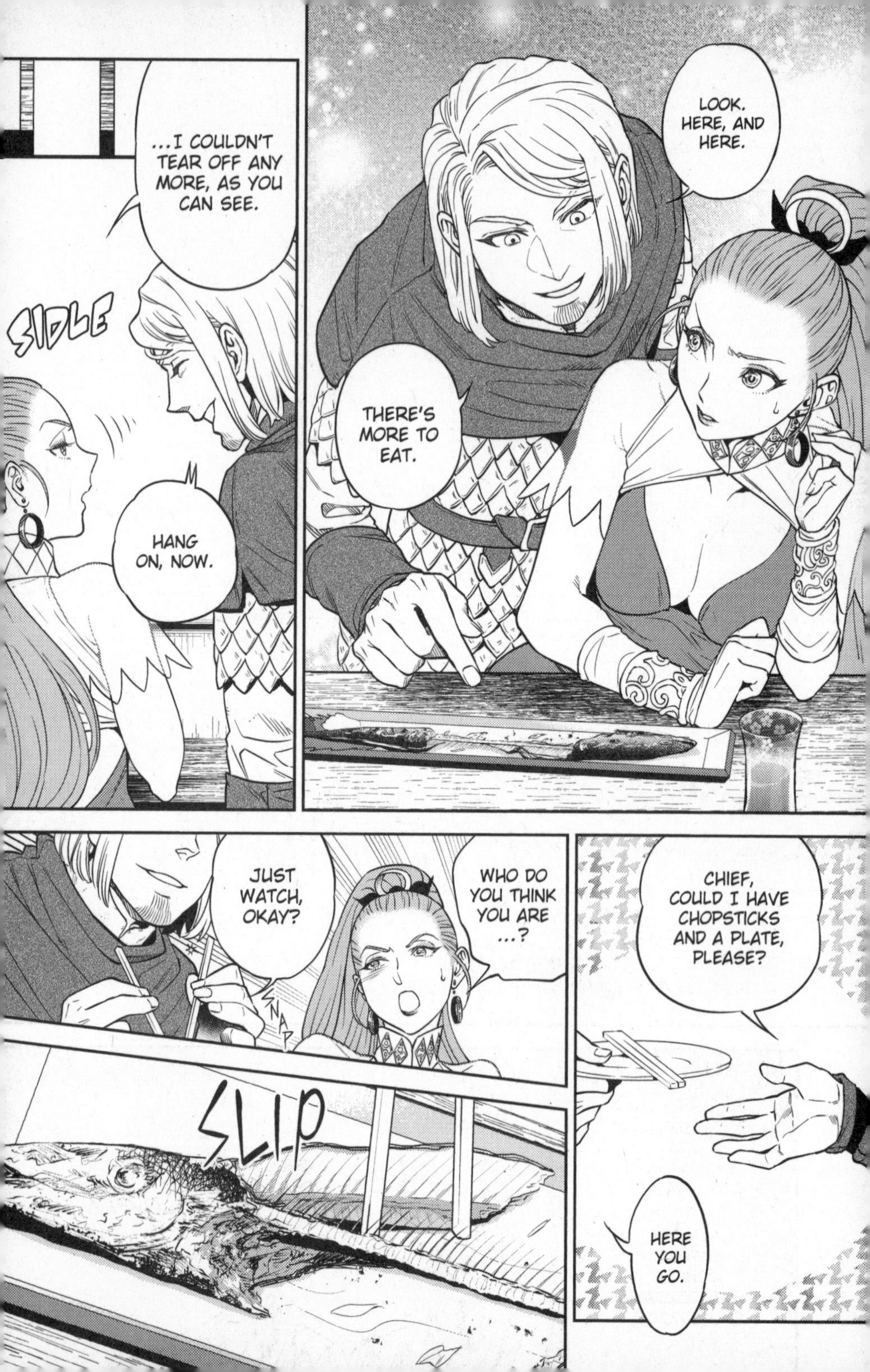
LOOK. HERE, AND HERE.
THERE'S MORE TO EAT.
...I COULDN'T TEAR OFF ANY MORE, AS YOU CAN SEE.
SIDLE
HANG ON, NOW.
CHIEF, COULD I HAVE CHOPSTICKS AND A PLATE, PLEASE?
HERE YOU GO.
WHO DO YOU THINK YOU ARE ...?
JUST WATCH, OKAY?
SNAP
SLIP

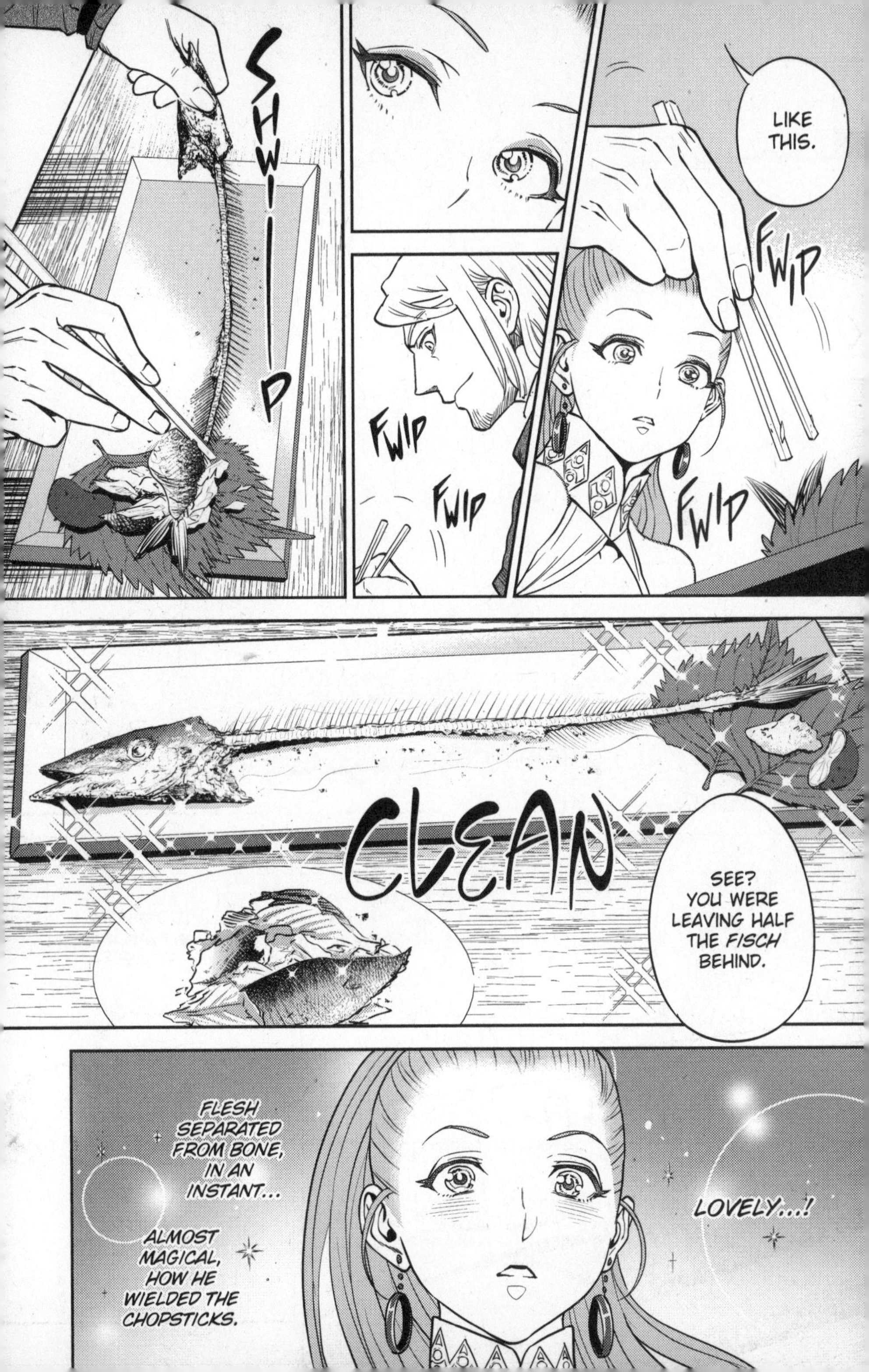
LIKE THIS.
FWIP
FWIP
FWIP
FWIP
SHWIIIP
SEE? YOU WERE LEAVING HALF THE *FISCH* BEHIND.
CLEAN
LOVELY...!
FLESH SEPARATED FROM BONE, IN AN INSTANT...
ALMOST MAGICAL, HOW HE WIELDED THE CHOPSTICKS.

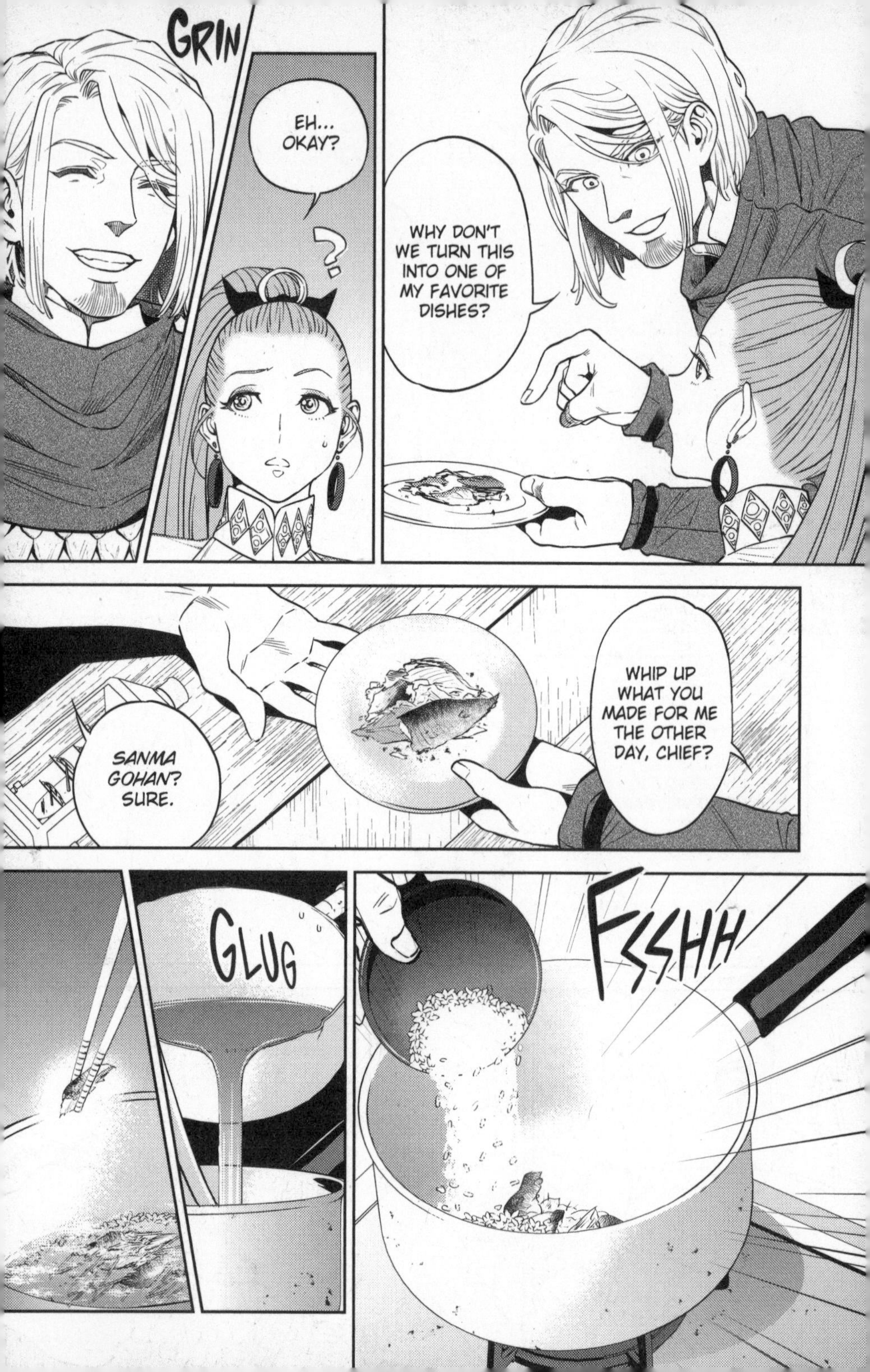
WHY DON'T WE TURN THIS INTO ONE OF MY FAVORITE DISHES?
EH... OKAY?
?
GRIN
WHIP UP WHAT YOU MADE FOR ME THE OTHER DAY, CHIEF?
SANMA GOHAN? SURE.
FSSHH
GLUG

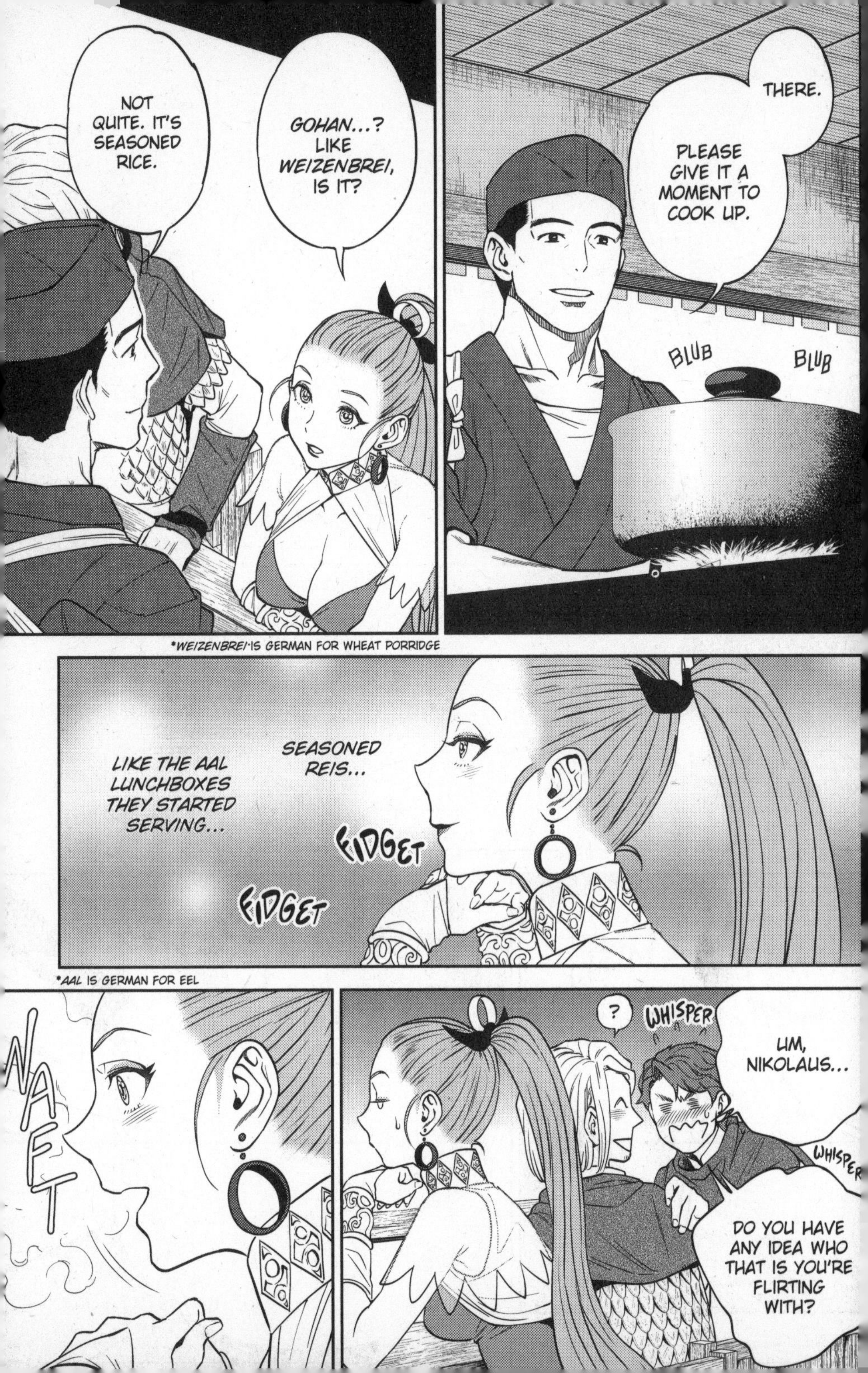
THERE.
PLEASE GIVE IT A MOMENT TO COOK UP.
BLUB
BLUB
GOHAN...? LIKE WEIZENBREI, IS IT?
NOT QUITE. IT'S SEASONED RICE.
*WEIZENBREI IS GERMAN FOR WHEAT PORRIDGE
SEASONED REIS...
LIKE THE AAL LUNCHBOXES THEY STARTED SERVING...
FIDGET
FIDGET
*AAL IS GERMAN FOR EEL
UM, NIKOLAUS...
WHISPER
?
WHISPER
DO YOU HAVE ANY IDEA WHO THAT IS YOU'RE FLIRTING WITH?
NAAET

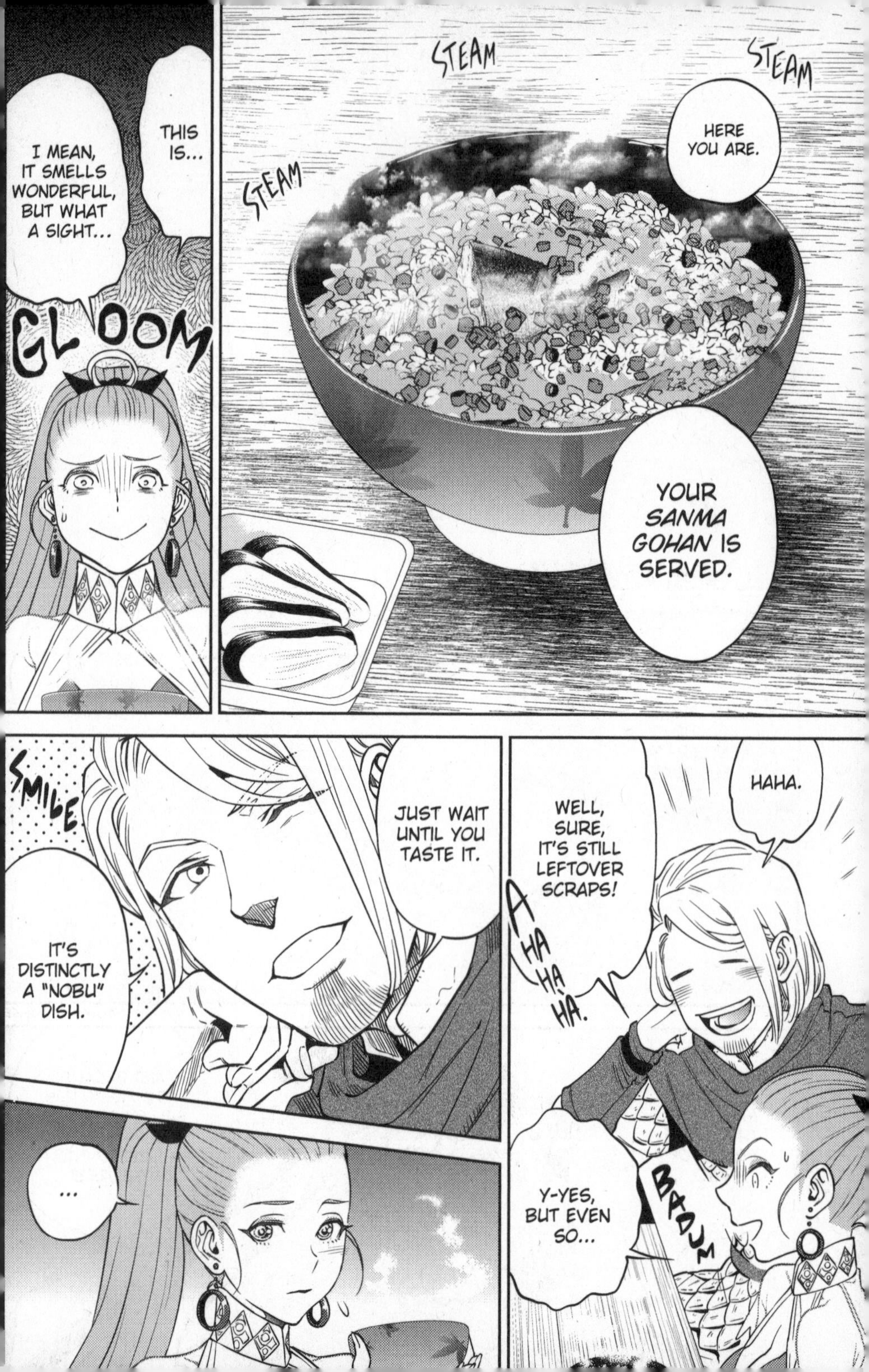
STEAM
STEAM
HERE YOU ARE.
STEAM
YOUR *SANMA GOHAN* IS SERVED.
THIS IS...
I MEAN, IT SMELLS WONDERFUL, BUT WHAT A SIGHT...
GLOOM
HAHA.
WELL, SURE, IT'S STILL LEFTOVER SCRAPS!
AHAHAHA.
Y-YES, BUT EVEN SO...
BADUM
JUST WAIT UNTIL YOU TASTE IT.
SMILE
IT'S DISTINCTLY A "NOBU" DISH.
...

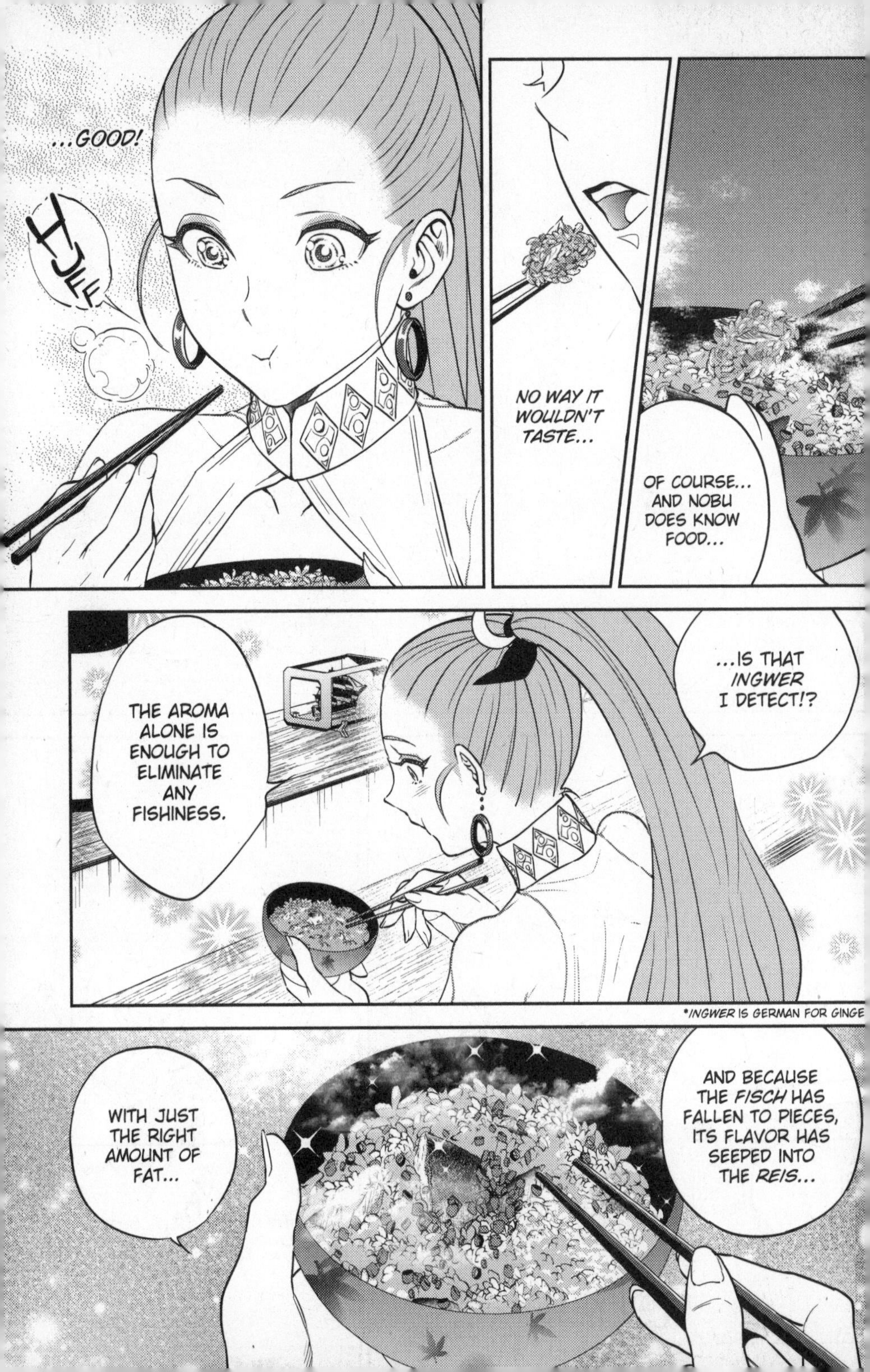
OF COURSE... AND NOBU DOES KNOW FOOD...
NO WAY IT WOULDN'T TASTE...
...GOOD!
HJUFF
...IS THAT *INGWER* I DETECT!?
THE AROMA ALONE IS ENOUGH TO ELIMINATE ANY FISHINESS.
**INGWER* IS GERMAN FOR GINGE
AND BECAUSE THE *FISCH* HAS FALLEN TO PIECES, ITS FLAVOR HAS SEEPED INTO THE *REIS*...
WITH JUST THE RIGHT AMOUNT OF FAT...

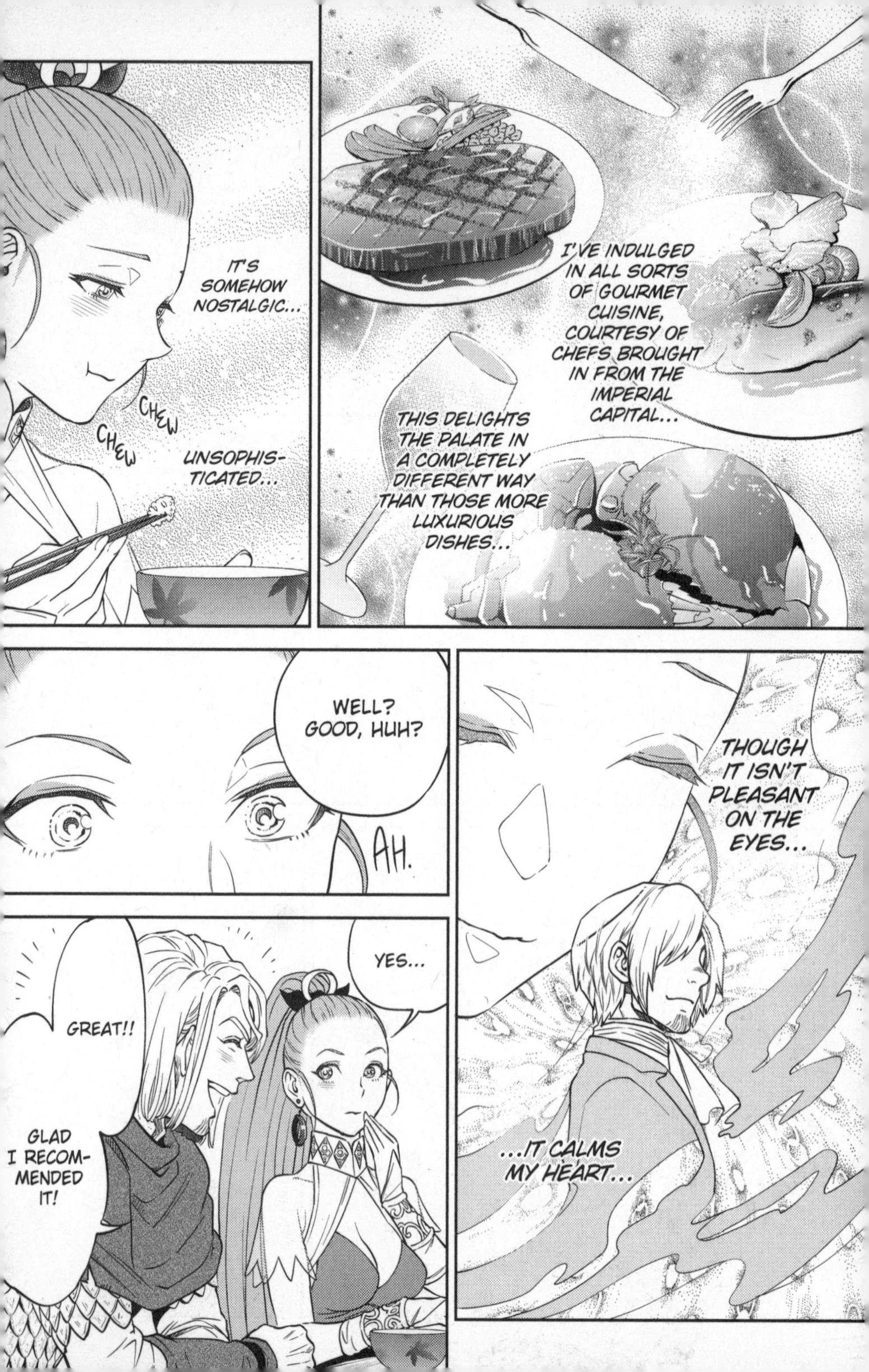

I'VE INDULGED IN ALL SORTS OF GOURMET CUISINE, COURTESY OF CHEFS BROUGHT IN FROM THE IMPERIAL CAPITAL...
THIS DELIGHTS THE PALATE IN A COMPLETELY DIFFERENT WAY THAN THOSE MORE LUXURIOUS DISHES...
IT'S SOMEHOW NOSTALGIC...
CHEW
CHEW
UNSOPHISTICATED...
THOUGH IT ISN'T PLEASANT ON THE EYES...
...IT CALMS MY HEART...
WELL? GOOD, HUH?
AH.
YES...
GREAT!!
GLAD I RECOMMENDED IT!

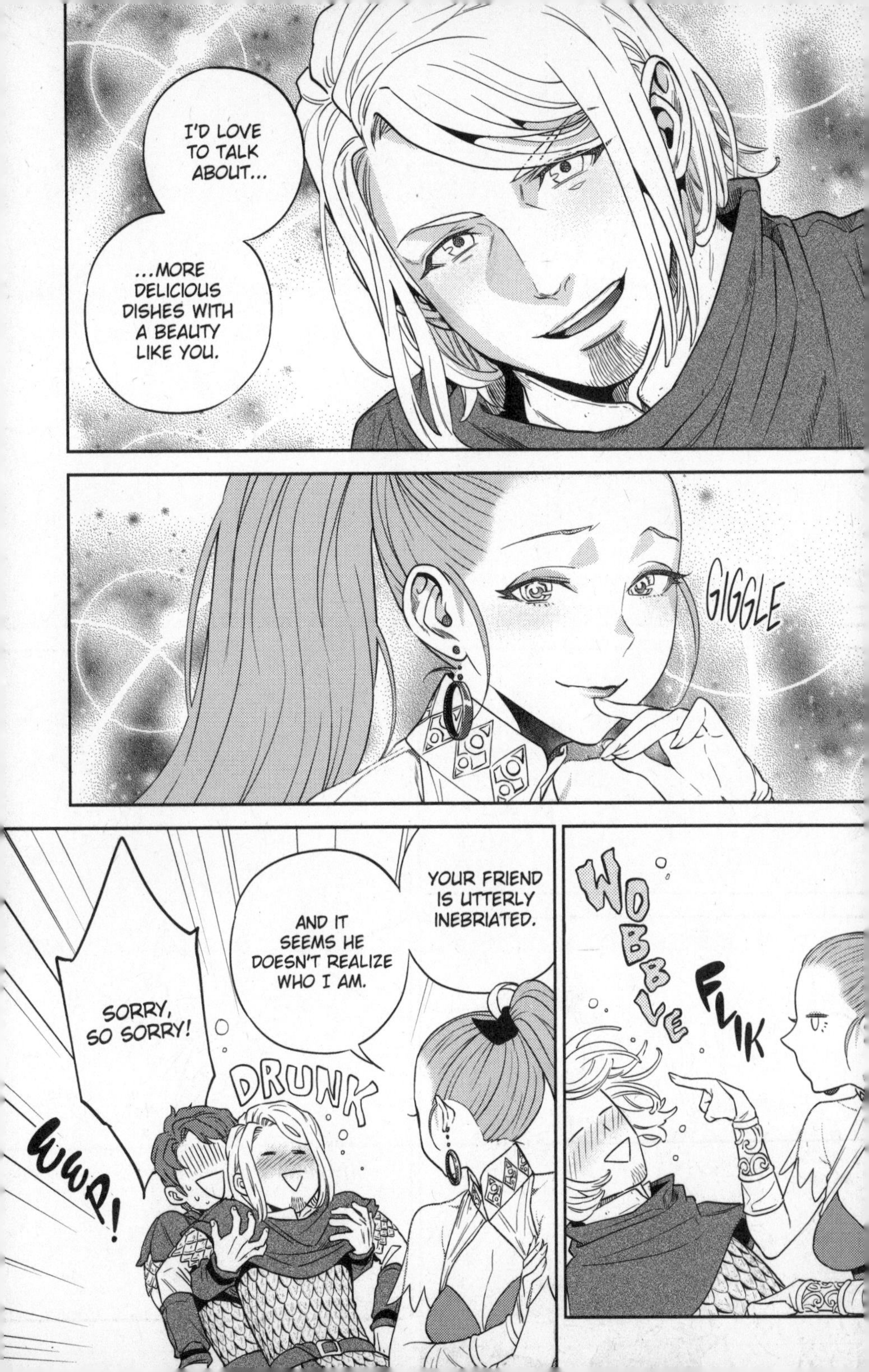
I'D LOVE TO TALK ABOUT...
...MORE DELICIOUS DISHES WITH A BEAUTY LIKE YOU.
GIGGLE
WOBBLE
FLIK
YOUR FRIEND IS UTTERLY INEBRIATED.
AND IT SEEMS HE DOESN'T REALIZE WHO I AM.
DRUNK
SORRY, SO SORRY!
WWP!

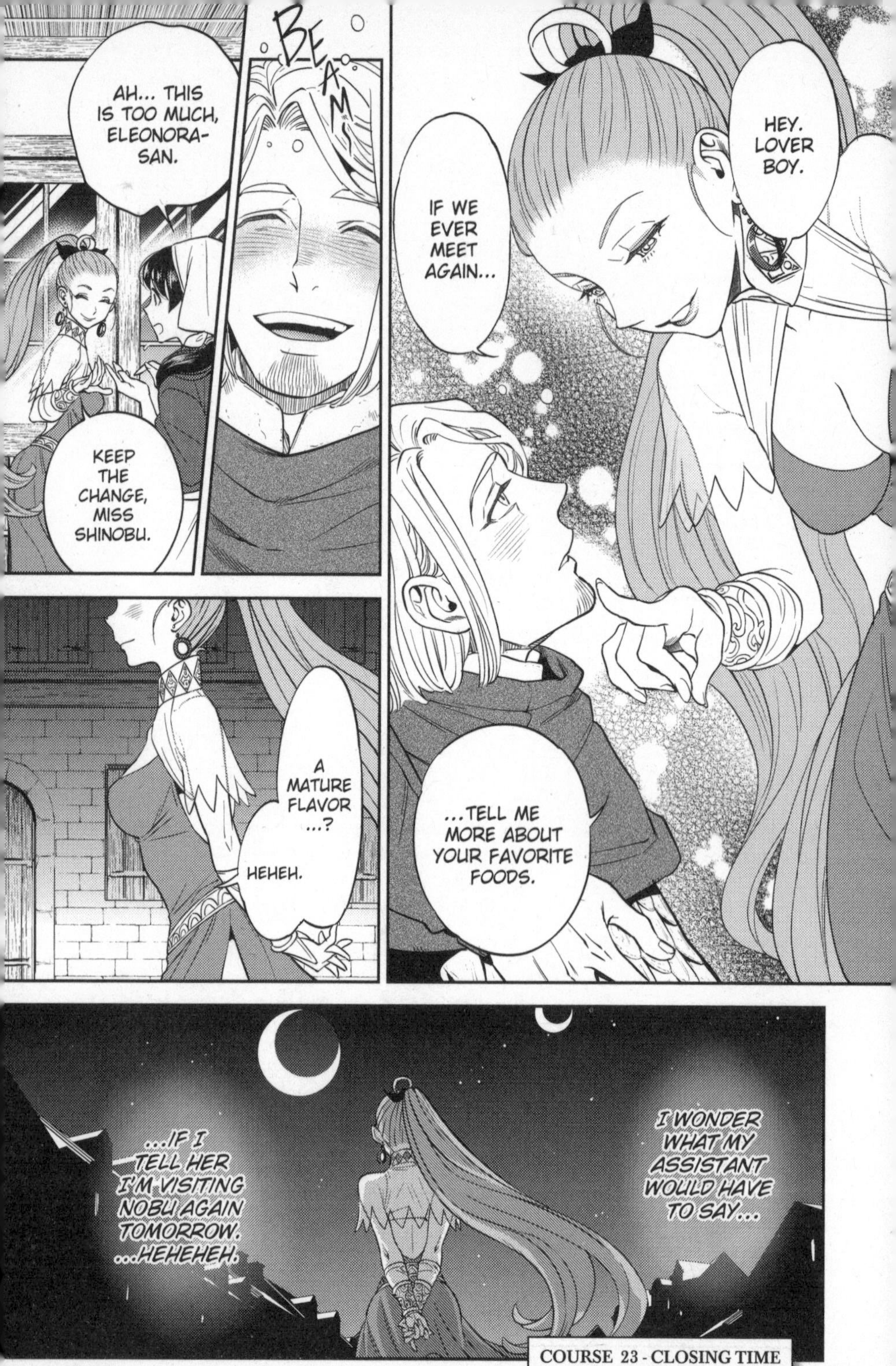
HEY. LOVER BOY.
IF WE EVER MEET AGAIN...
...TELL ME MORE ABOUT YOUR FAVORITE FOODS.
BEAM
AH... THIS IS TOO MUCH, ELEONORA-SAN.
KEEP THE CHANGE, MISS SHINOBU.
A MATURE FLAVOR ...?
HEHEH.
I WONDER WHAT MY ASSISTANT WOULD HAVE TO SAY...
...IF I TELL HER I'M VISITING NOBU AGAIN TOMORROW. ...HEHEHEH.
COURSE 23 - CLOSING TIME

Sanma Shioyaki

OTHERWORLDLY IZAKAYA

NOBU

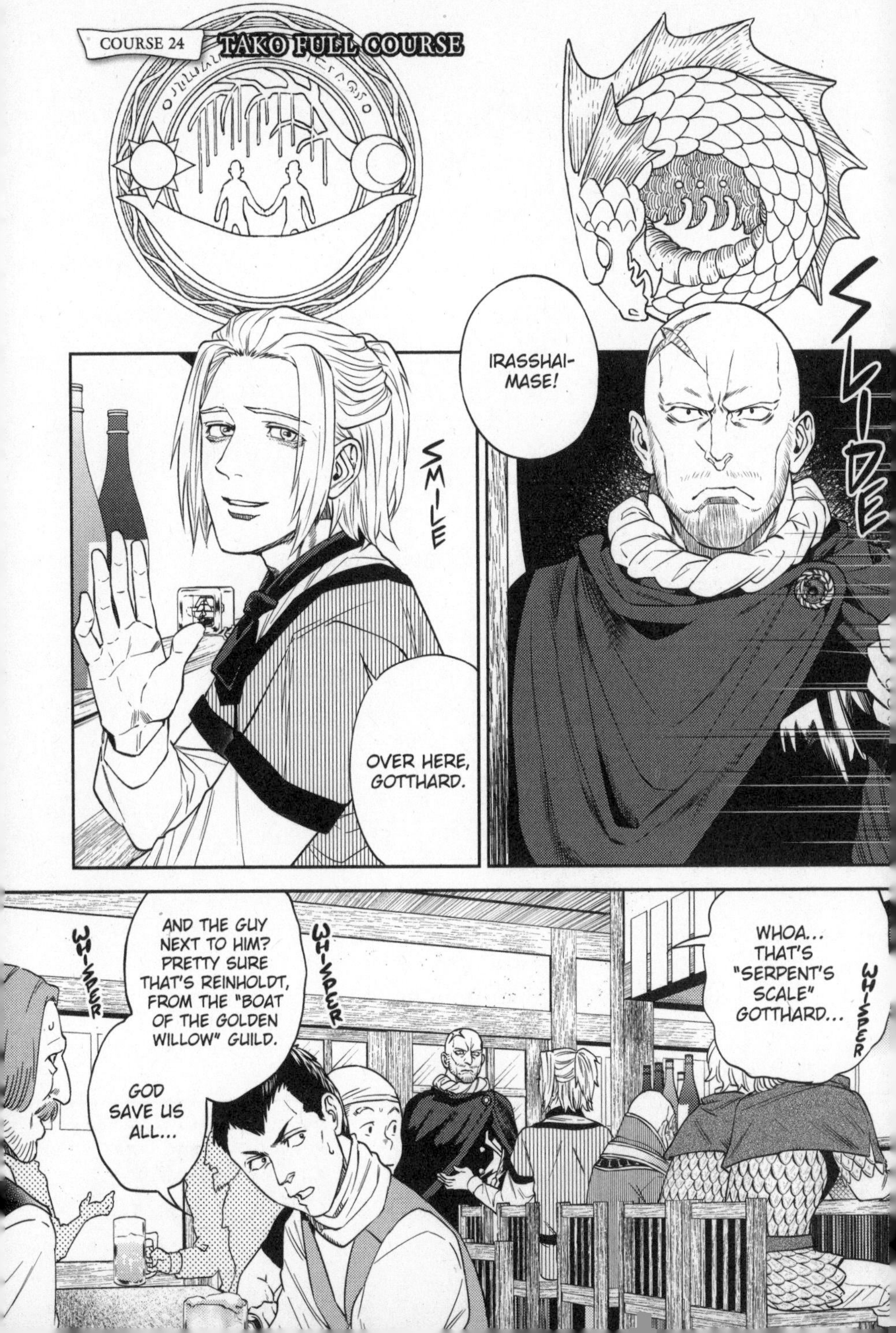
COURSE 24
TAKO FULL COURSE
SLIDE
IRASSHAI-MASE!
SMILE
OVER HERE, GOTTHARD.
WHISPER
WHOA... THAT'S "SERPENT'S SCALE" GOTTHARD...
WHISPER
AND THE GUY NEXT TO HIM? PRETTY SURE THAT'S REINHOLDT, FROM THE "BOAT OF THE GOLDEN WILLOW" GUILD.
GOD SAVE US ALL...
WHISPER

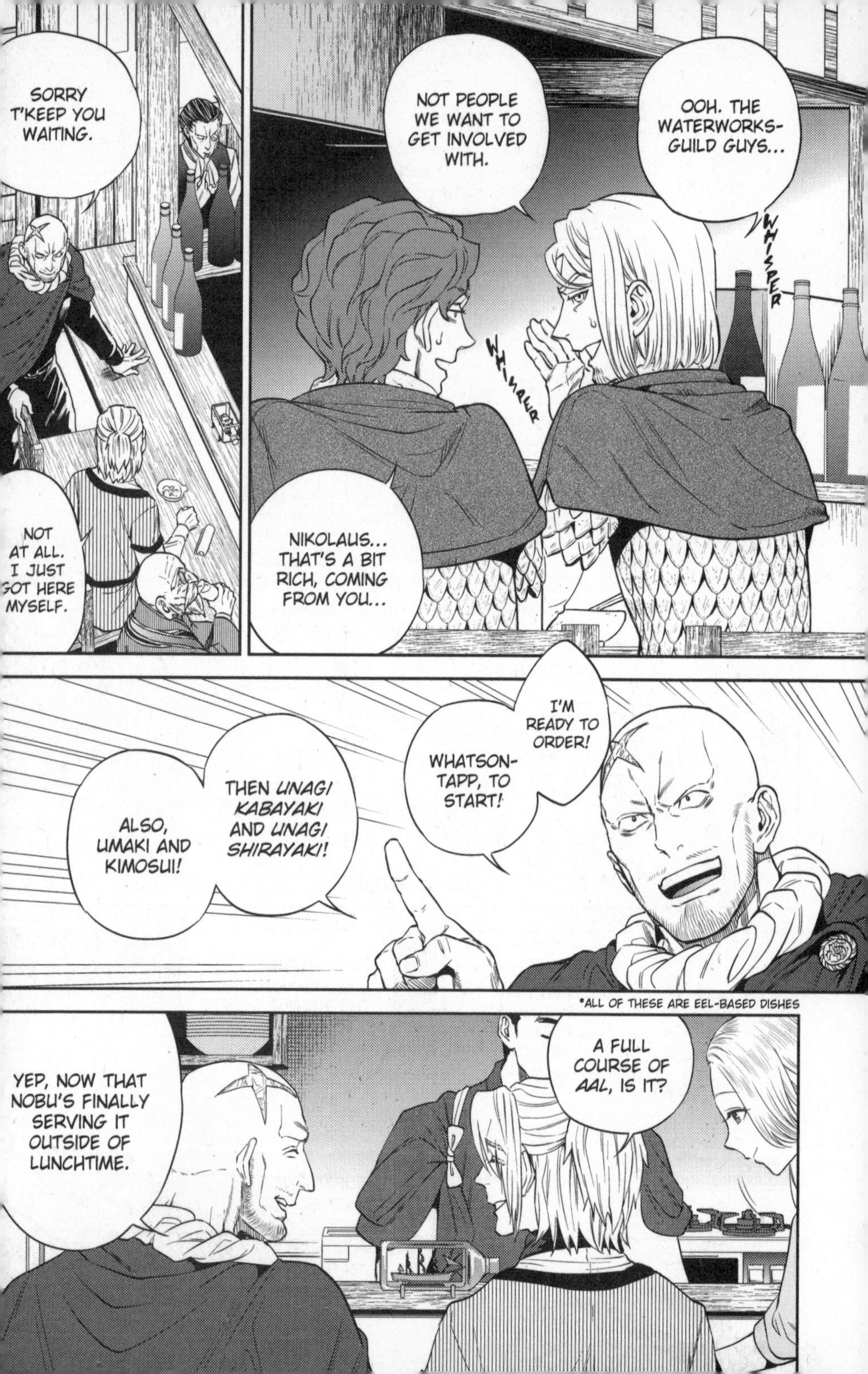
OOH. THE WATERWORKS-GUILD GUYS...
WHISPER
NOT PEOPLE WE WANT TO GET INVOLVED WITH.
WHISPER
NIKOLAUS... THAT'S A BIT RICH, COMING FROM YOU...
SORRY T'KEEP YOU WAITING.
NOT AT ALL. I JUST GOT HERE MYSELF.
I'M READY TO ORDER!
WHATSON-TAPP, TO START!
THEN *UNAGI KABAYAKI* AND *UNAGI SHIRAYAKI*!
ALSO, UMAKI AND KIMOSUI!
A FULL COURSE OF *AAL*, IS IT?
YEP, NOW THAT NOBU'S FINALLY SERVING IT OUTSIDE OF LUNCHTIME.

*ALL OF THESE ARE EEL-BASED DISHES

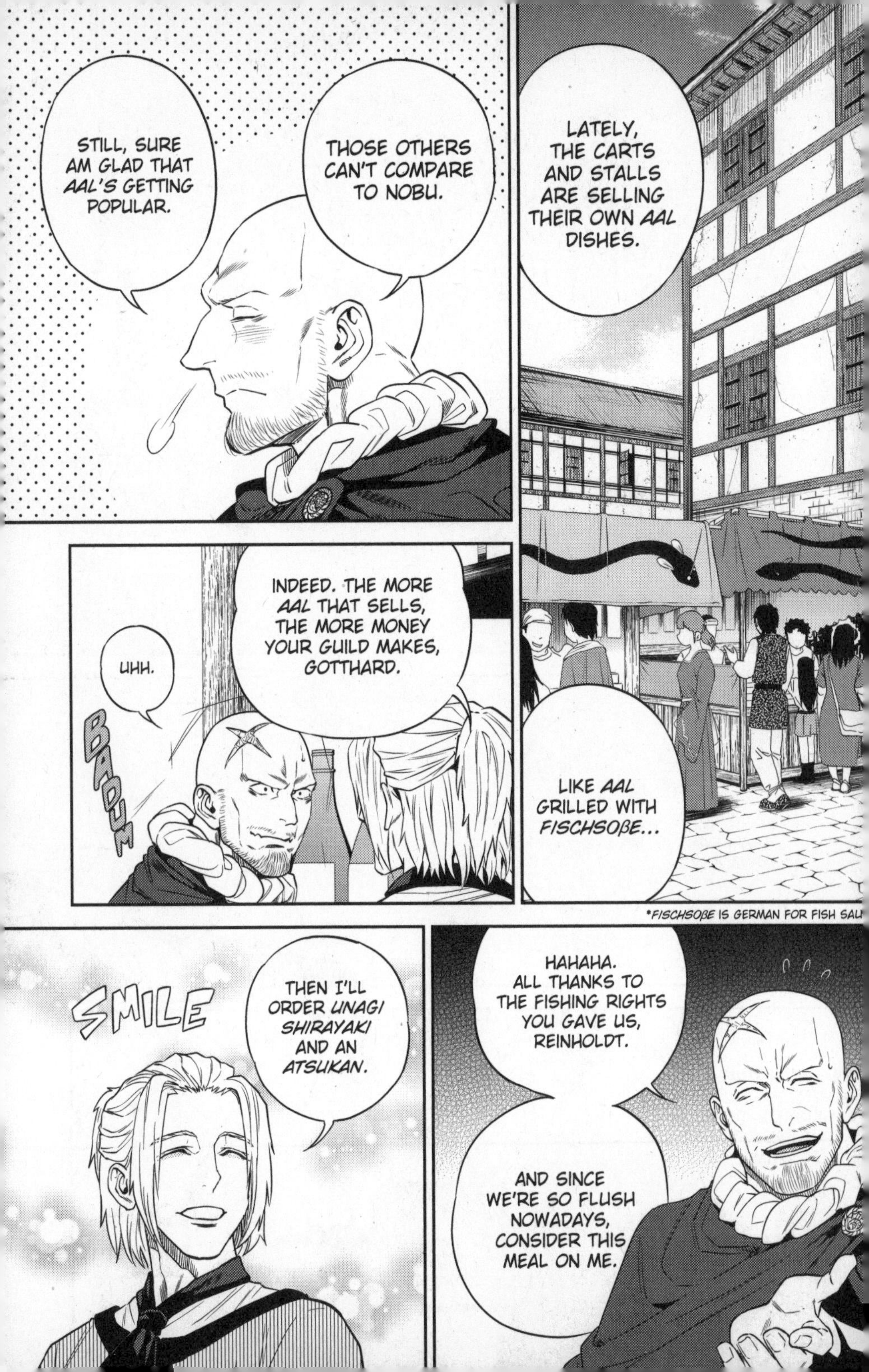
LATELY, THE CARTS AND STALLS ARE SELLING THEIR OWN *AAL* DISHES.
LIKE *AAL* GRILLED WITH *FISCHSOßE*...
THOSE OTHERS CAN'T COMPARE TO NOBU.
STILL, SURE AM GLAD THAT *AAL'S* GETTING POPULAR.
INDEED. THE MORE *AAL* THAT SELLS, THE MORE MONEY YOUR GUILD MAKES, GOTTHARD.
UHH.
BADUM
HAHAHA. ALL THANKS TO THE FISHING RIGHTS YOU GAVE US, REINHOLDT.
AND SINCE WE'RE SO FLUSH NOWADAYS, CONSIDER THIS MEAL ON ME.
THEN I'LL ORDER *UNAGI SHIRAYAKI* AND AN *ATSUKAN*.
SMILE

**FISCHSOßE* IS GERMAN FOR FISH SAU

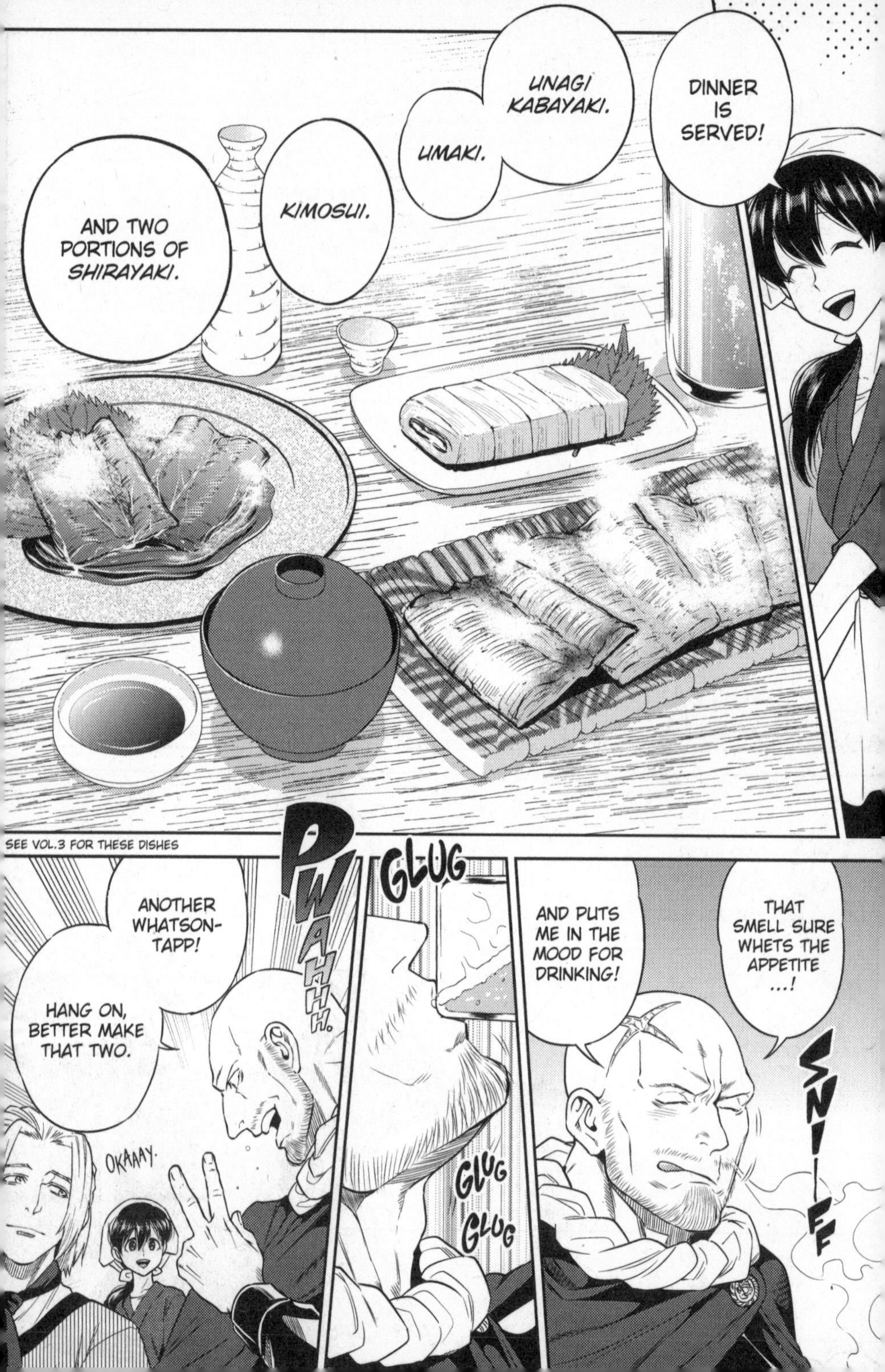
DINNER IS SERVED!
UNAGI KABAYAKI.
UMAKI.
KIMOSUI.
AND TWO PORTIONS OF SHIRAYAKI.
SEE VOL.3 FOR THESE DISHES
THAT SMELL SURE WHETS THE APPETITE ...!
SNIFF
AND PUTS ME IN THE MOOD FOR DRINKING!
GLUG
GLUG
GLUG
PWAHHH.
ANOTHER WHATSON-TAPP!
HANG ON, BETTER MAKE THAT TWO.
OKAAAY.

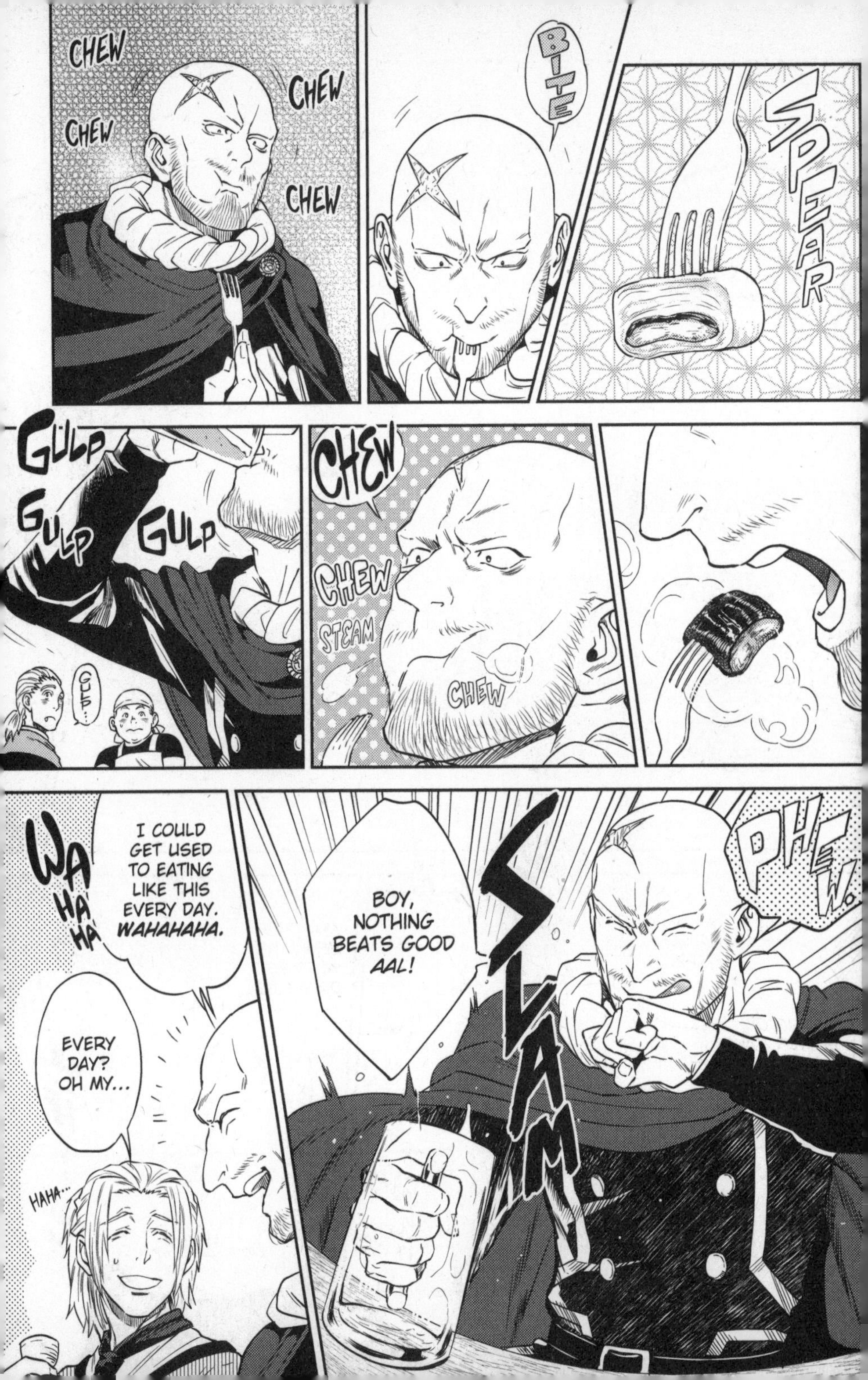
SPEAR
BITE
CHEW
CHEW
CHEW
CHEW
CHEW
CHEW
STEAM
CHEW
GULP
GULP
GULP
GULP...
PHEW.
SLAM
BOY, NOTHING BEATS GOOD AAL!
I COULD GET USED TO EATING LIKE THIS EVERY DAY. WAHAHAHA.
WAHAHA
EVERY DAY? OH MY...
HAHA...

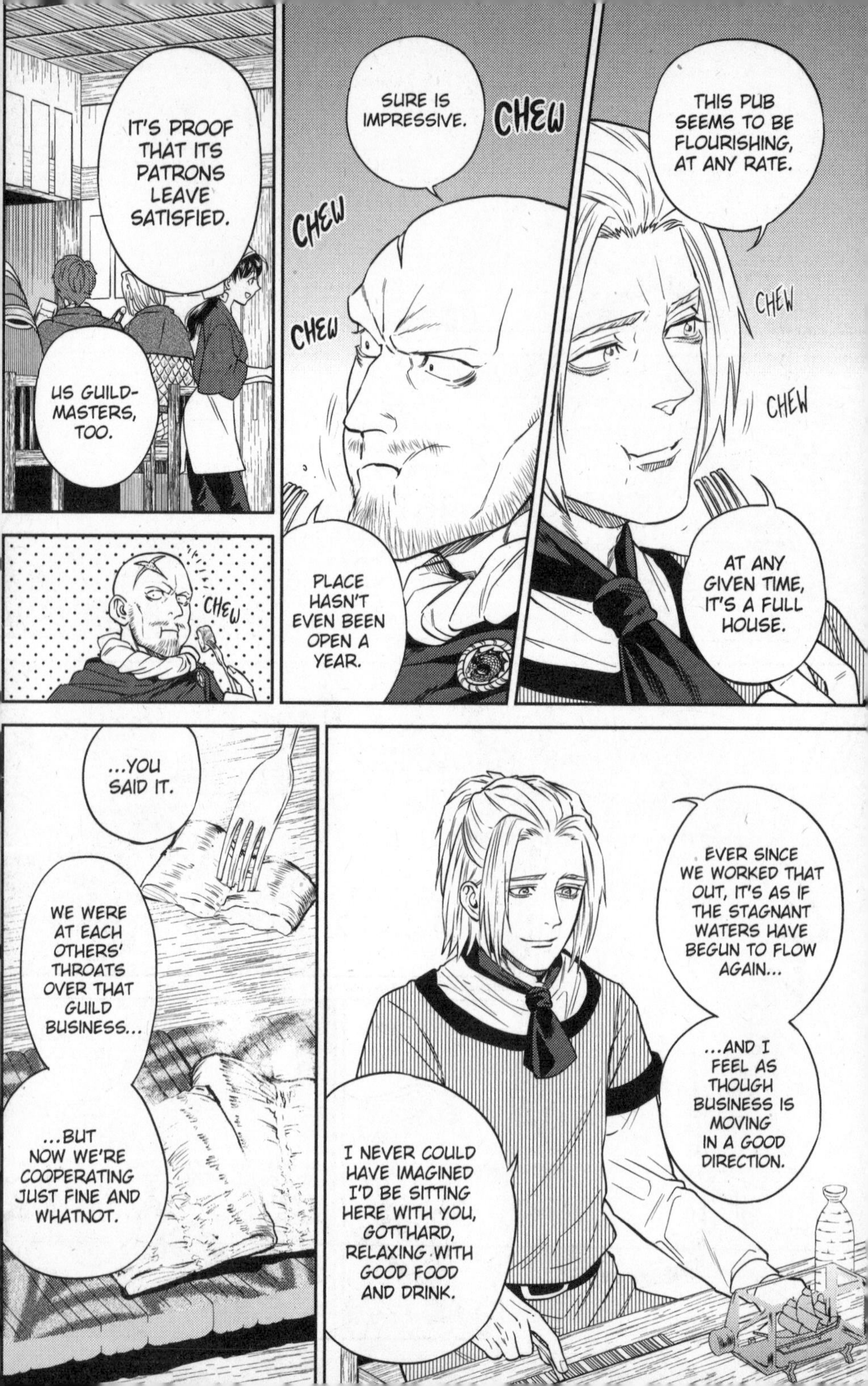
THIS PUB SEEMS TO BE FLOURISHING, AT ANY RATE.
CHEW
CHEW
AT ANY GIVEN TIME, IT'S A FULL HOUSE.
SURE IS IMPRESSIVE.
CHEW
CHEW
CHEW
PLACE HASN'T EVEN BEEN OPEN A YEAR.
IT'S PROOF THAT ITS PATRONS LEAVE SATISFIED.
US GUILD-MASTERS, TOO.
CHEW
EVER SINCE WE WORKED THAT OUT, IT'S AS IF THE STAGNANT WATERS HAVE BEGUN TO FLOW AGAIN...
...AND I FEEL AS THOUGH BUSINESS IS MOVING IN A GOOD DIRECTION.
I NEVER COULD HAVE IMAGINED I'D BE SITTING HERE WITH YOU, GOTTHARD, RELAXING WITH GOOD FOOD AND DRINK.
...YOU SAID IT.
WE WERE AT EACH OTHERS' THROATS OVER THAT GUILD BUSINESS...
...BUT NOW WE'RE COOPERATING JUST FINE AND WHATNOT.

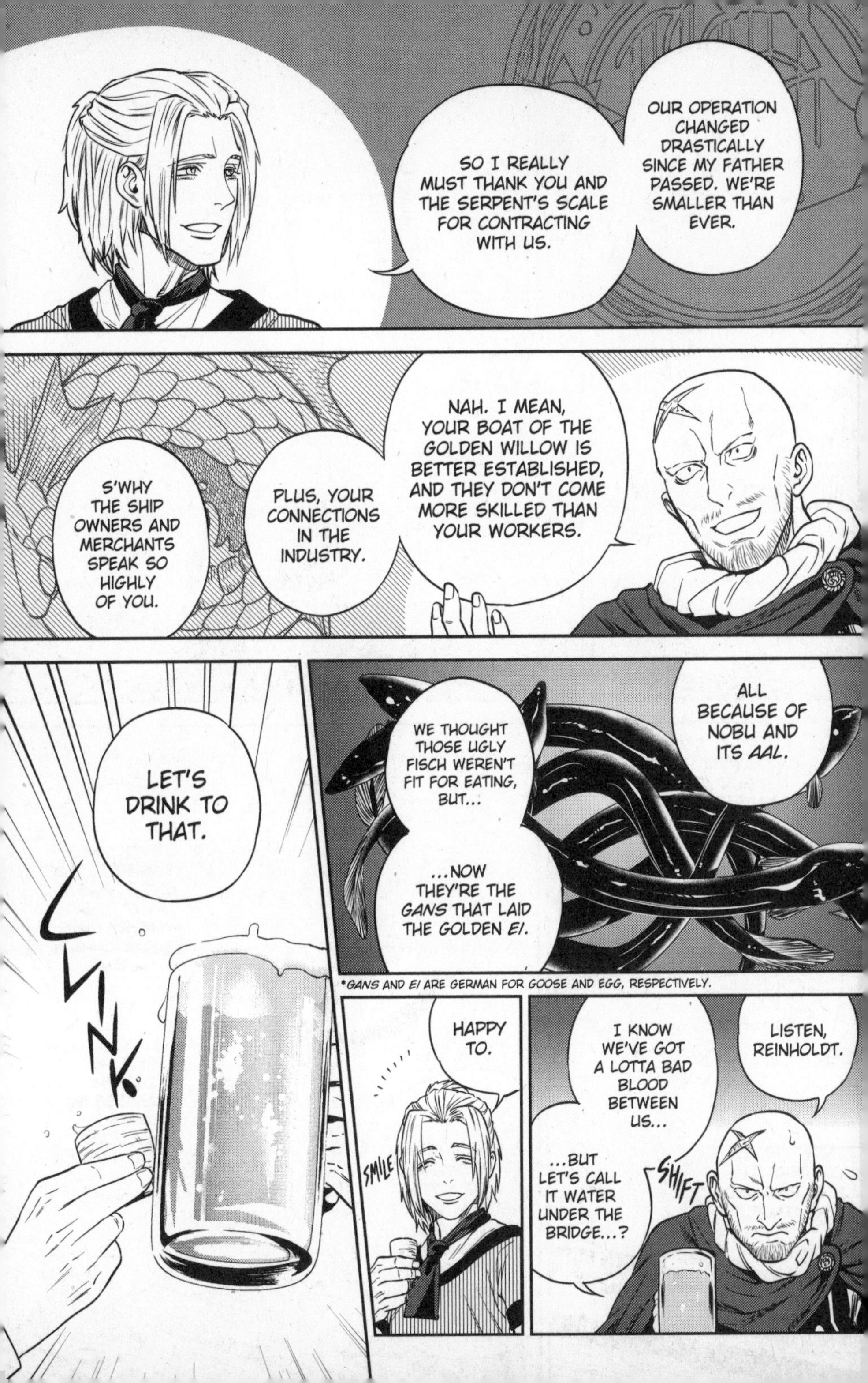
OUR OPERATION CHANGED DRASTICALLY SINCE MY FATHER PASSED. WE'RE SMALLER THAN EVER.
SO I REALLY MUST THANK YOU AND THE SERPENT'S SCALE FOR CONTRACTING WITH US.
NAH. I MEAN, YOUR BOAT OF THE GOLDEN WILLOW IS BETTER ESTABLISHED, AND THEY DON'T COME MORE SKILLED THAN YOUR WORKERS.
PLUS, YOUR CONNECTIONS IN THE INDUSTRY.
S'WHY THE SHIP OWNERS AND MERCHANTS SPEAK SO HIGHLY OF YOU.
ALL BECAUSE OF NOBU AND ITS *AAL*.
WE THOUGHT THOSE UGLY FISCH WEREN'T FIT FOR EATING, BUT...
...NOW THEY'RE THE *GANS* THAT LAID THE GOLDEN *EI*.
**GANS* AND *EI* ARE GERMAN FOR GOOSE AND EGG, RESPECTIVELY.
LISTEN, REINHOLDT.
I KNOW WE'VE GOT A LOTTA BAD BLOOD BETWEEN US...
...BUT LET'S CALL IT WATER UNDER THE BRIDGE...?
SHIFT
HAPPY TO.
SMILE
LET'S DRINK TO THAT.
CLINK

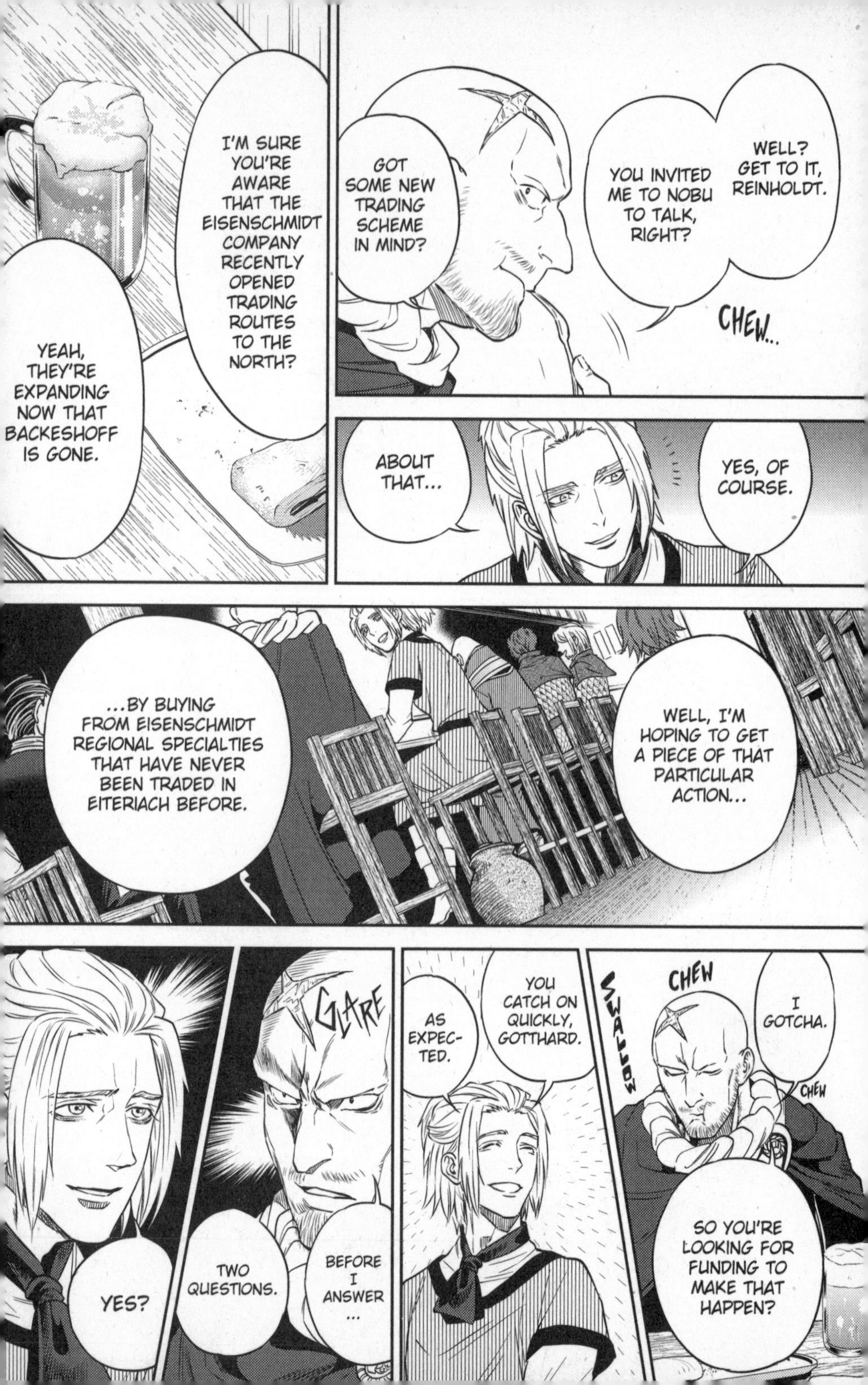
WELL? GET TO IT, REINHOLDT.
YOU INVITED ME TO NOBU TO TALK, RIGHT?
CHEW...
GOT SOME NEW TRADING SCHEME IN MIND?
YES, OF COURSE.
ABOUT THAT...
I'M SURE YOU'RE AWARE THAT THE EISENSCHMIDT COMPANY RECENTLY OPENED TRADING ROUTES TO THE NORTH?
YEAH, THEY'RE EXPANDING NOW THAT BACKESHOFF IS GONE.
WELL, I'M HOPING TO GET A PIECE OF THAT PARTICULAR ACTION...
...BY BUYING FROM EISENSCHMIDT REGIONAL SPECIALTIES THAT HAVE NEVER BEEN TRADED IN EITERIACH BEFORE.
I GOTCHA.
CHEW
SWALLOW
CHEW
SO YOU'RE LOOKING FOR FUNDING TO MAKE THAT HAPPEN?
YOU CATCH ON QUICKLY, GOTTHARD.
AS EXPEC-TED.
GLARE
BEFORE I ANSWER...
TWO QUESTIONS.
YES?

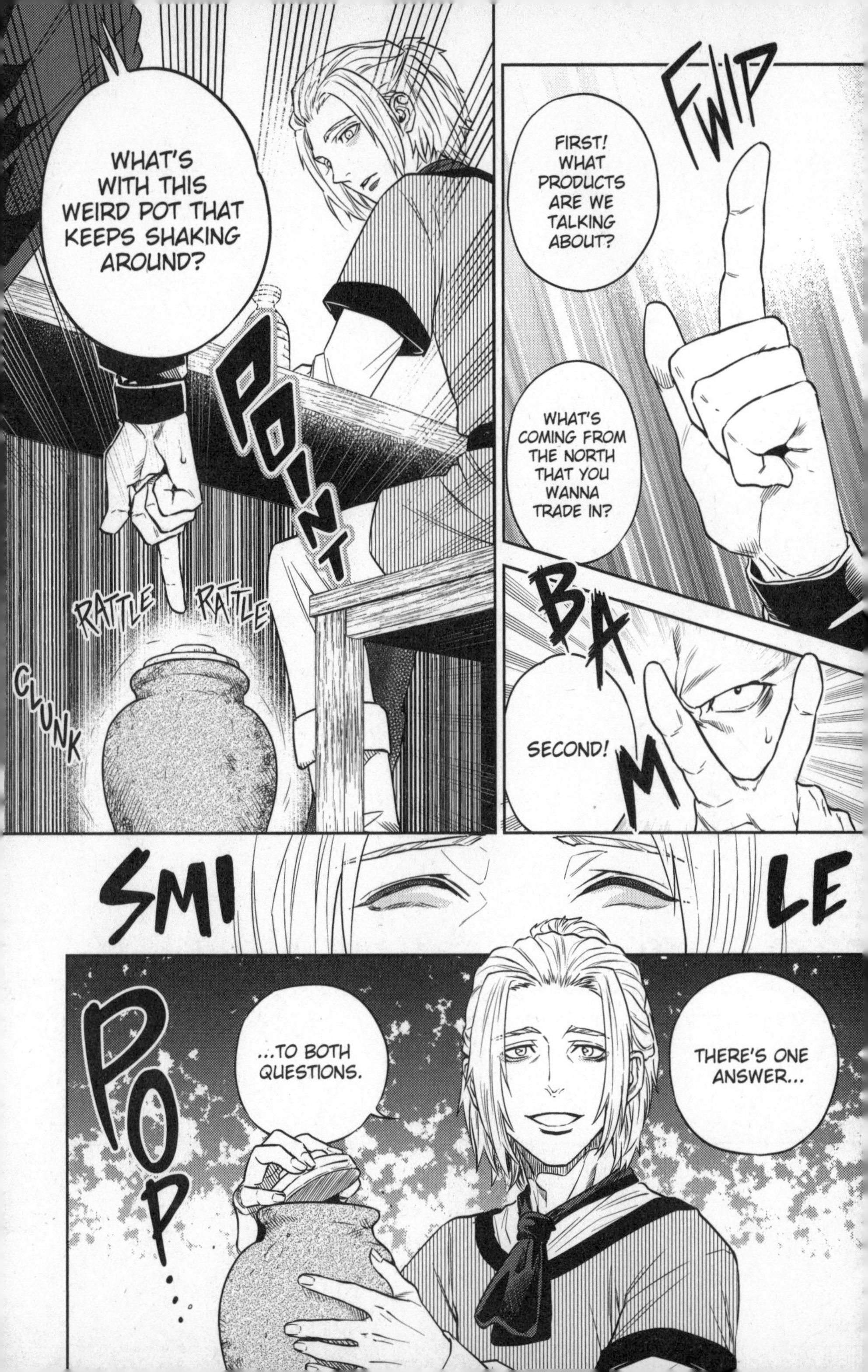
FWIP
FIRST! WHAT PRODUCTS ARE WE TALKING ABOUT?
WHAT'S COMING FROM THE NORTH THAT YOU WANNA TRADE IN?
BAM
SECOND!
WHAT'S WITH THIS WEIRD POT THAT KEEPS SHAKING AROUND?
POINT
RATTLE RATTLE
CLUNK
SMILE
THERE'S ONE ANSWER...
...TO BOTH QUESTIONS.
POP...

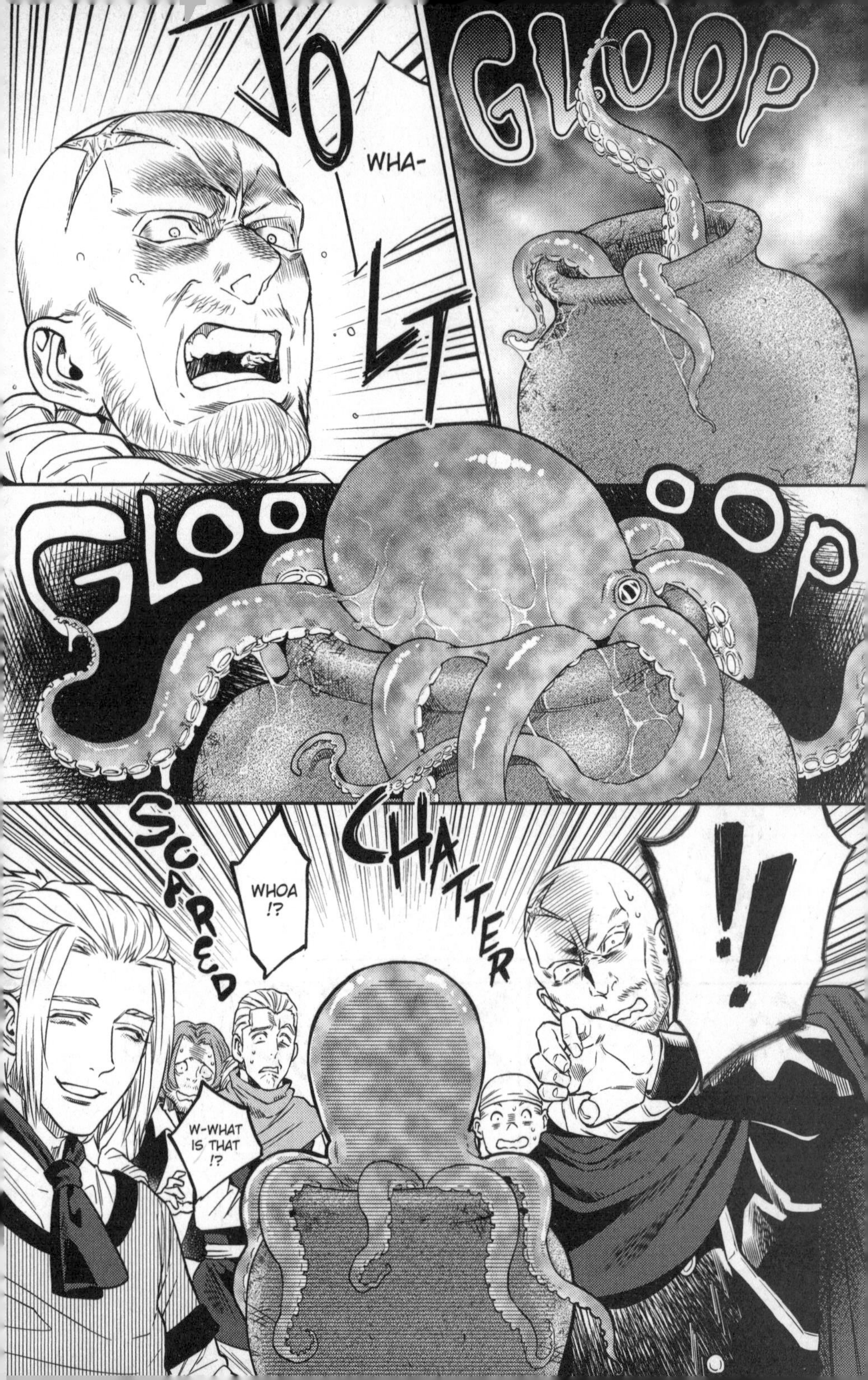

GLOOP
JOLT
WHA-
GLOOOOP
!!
CHATTER
WHOA !?
SCARED
W-WHAT IS THAT !?

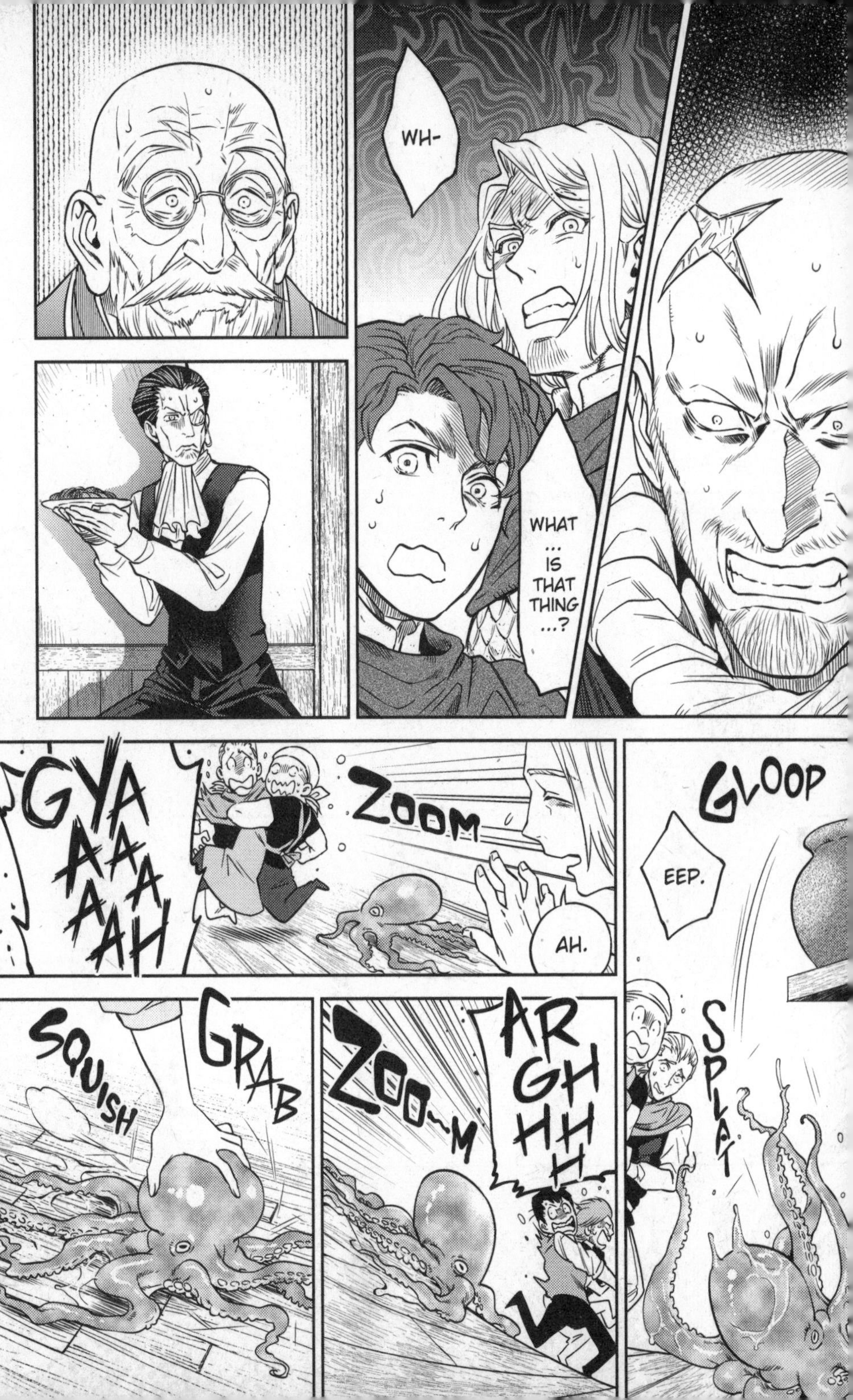
WH-
WHAT ... IS THAT THING ...?
GLOOP
EEP.
ZOOM
AH.
GYAAAAAAH
SPLAT
ARGHHHHHH
ZOO~M
GRAB
SQUISH

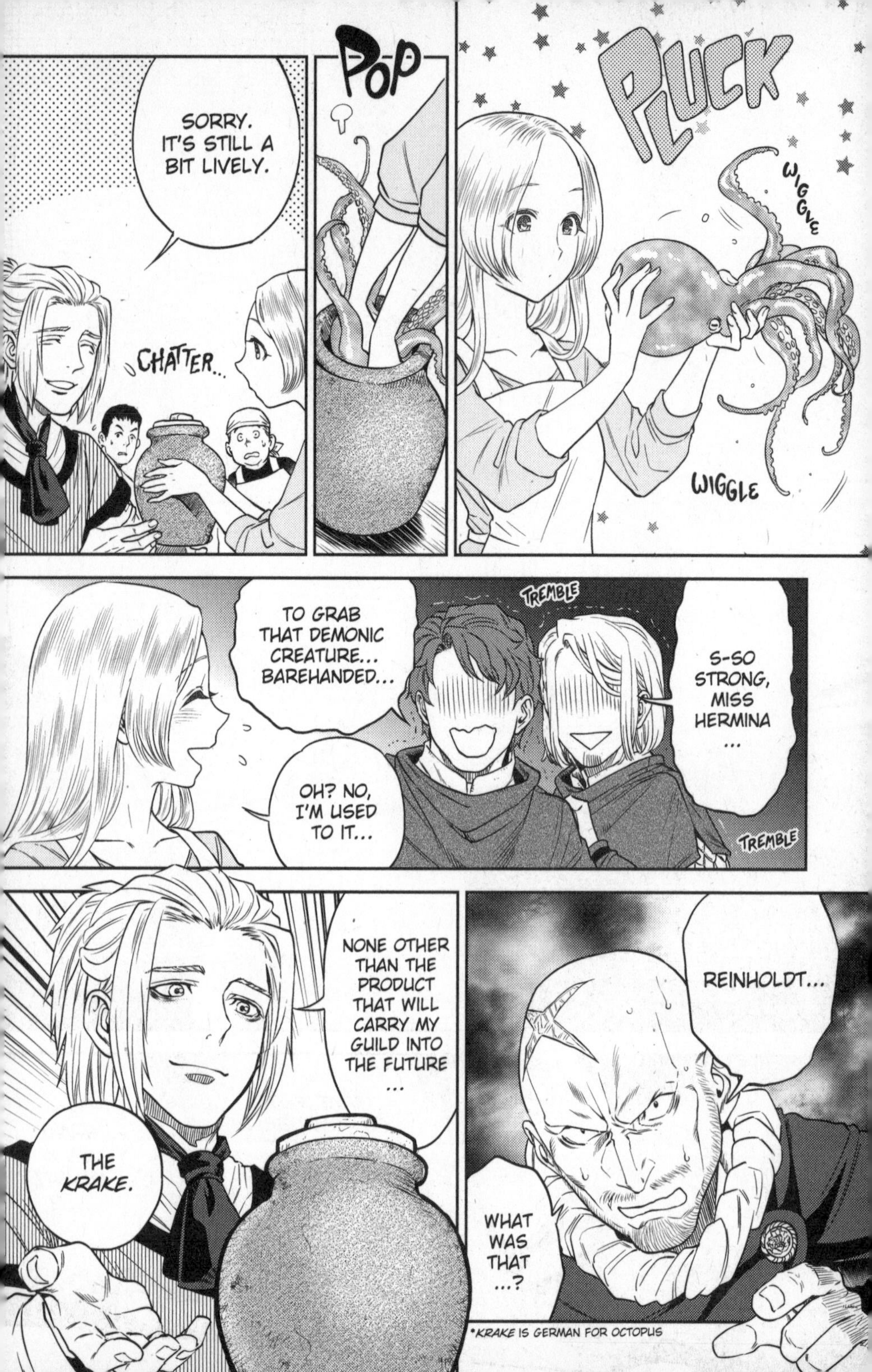
PLUCK
WIGGLE
WIGGLE
POP
SORRY. IT'S STILL A BIT LIVELY.
CHATTER...
TREMBLE
S-SO STRONG, MISS HERMINA ...
TO GRAB THAT DEMONIC CREATURE... BAREHANDED...
OH? NO, I'M USED TO IT...
TREMBLE
REINHOLDT...
WHAT WAS THAT ...?
NONE OTHER THAN THE PRODUCT THAT WILL CARRY MY GUILD INTO THE FUTURE ...
THE *KRAKE*.

**KRAKE* IS GERMAN FOR OCTOPUS

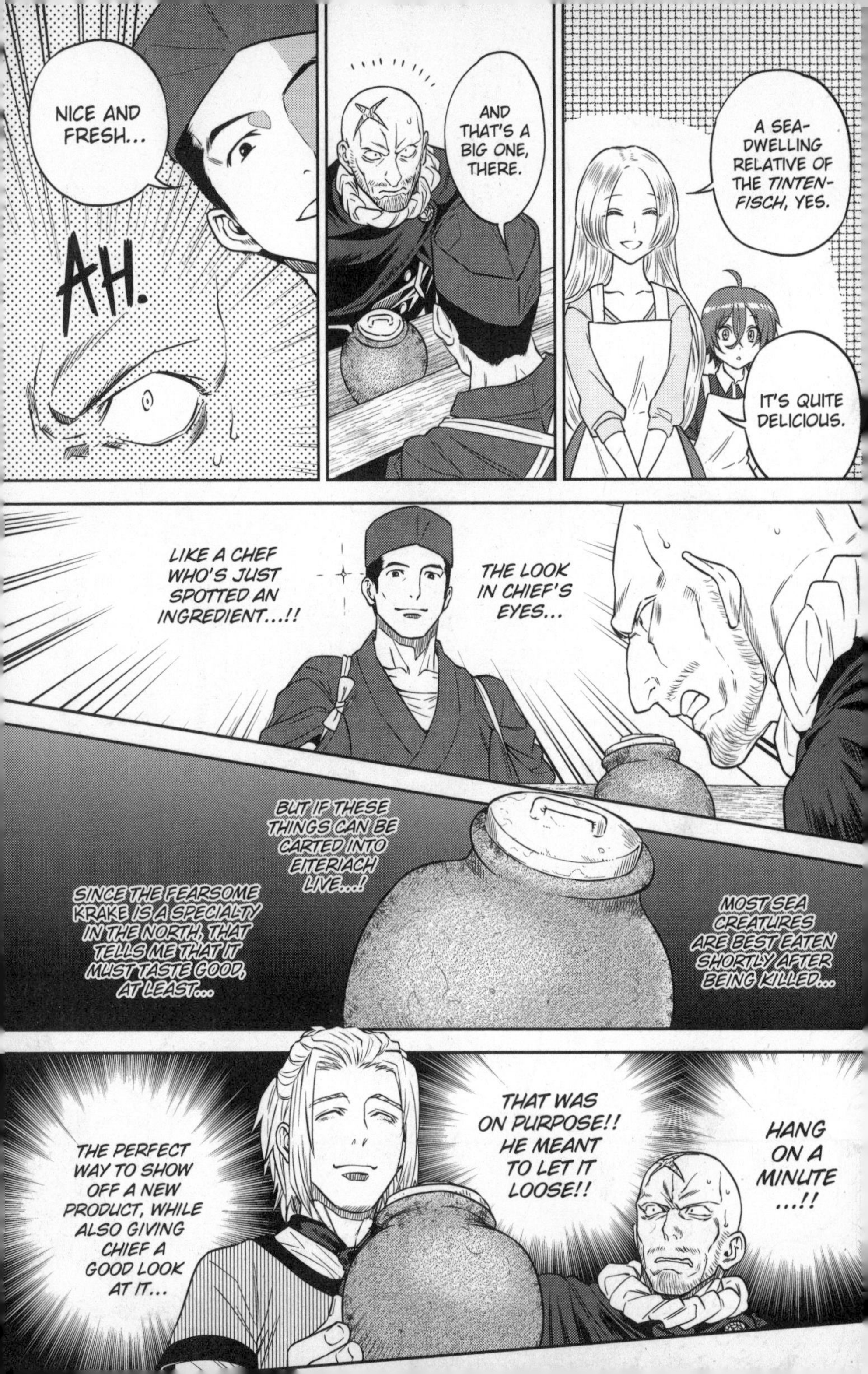
A SEA-DWELLING RELATIVE OF THE *TINTEN-FISCH*, YES.
IT'S QUITE DELICIOUS.
AND THAT'S A BIG ONE, THERE.
NICE AND FRESH...
AH.
THE LOOK IN CHIEF'S EYES...
LIKE A CHEF WHO'S JUST SPOTTED AN INGREDIENT...!!
MOST SEA CREATURES ARE BEST EATEN SHORTLY AFTER BEING KILLED...
BUT IF THESE THINGS CAN BE CARTED INTO EITERIACH LIVE...!
SINCE THE FEARSOME KRAKE IS A SPECIALTY IN THE NORTH, THAT TELLS ME THAT IT MUST TASTE GOOD, AT LEAST...
HANG ON A MINUTE ...!!
THAT WAS ON PURPOSE!! HE MEANT TO LET IT LOOSE!!
THE PERFECT WAY TO SHOW OFF A NEW PRODUCT, WHILE ALSO GIVING CHIEF A GOOD LOOK AT IT...

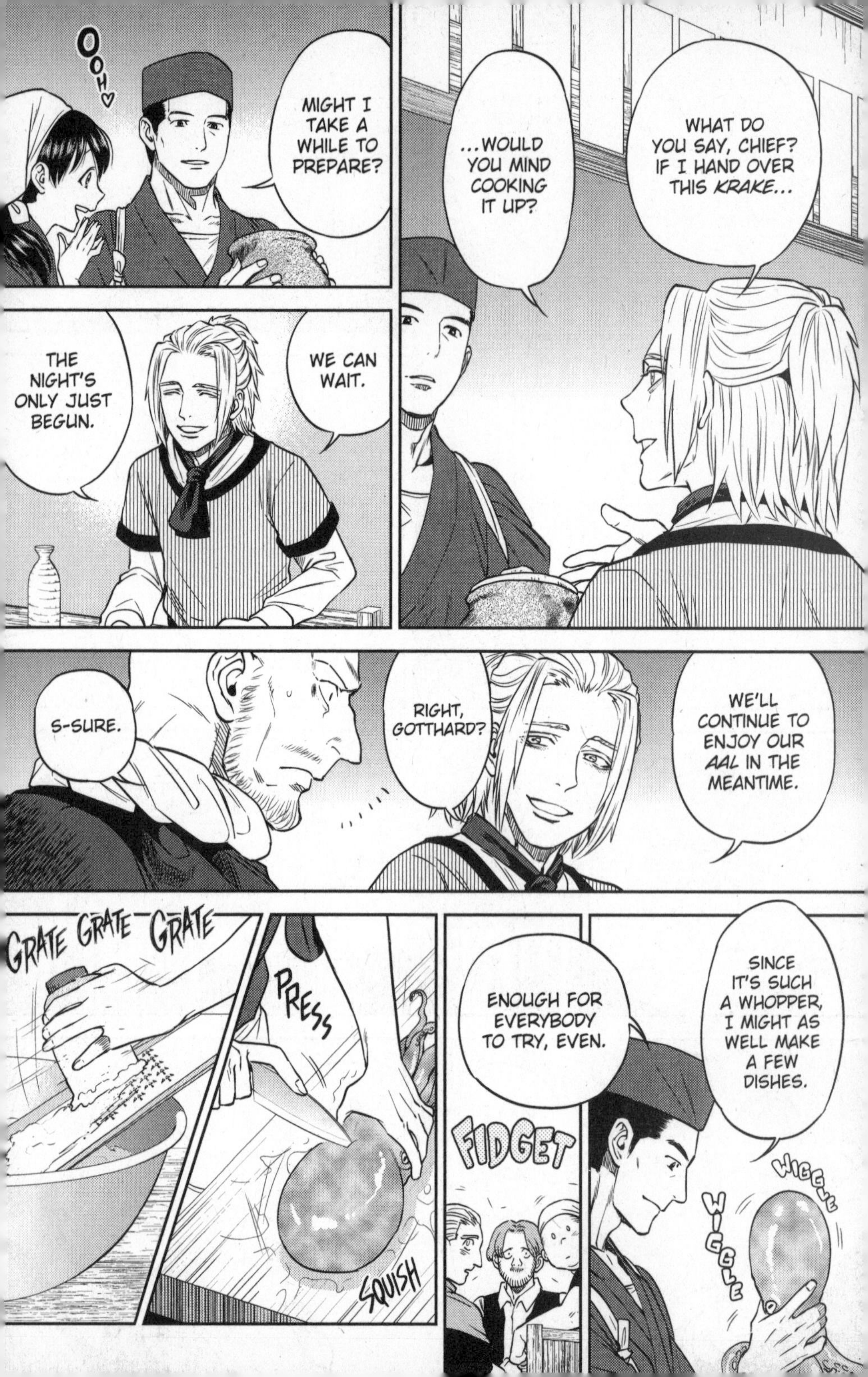
WHAT DO YOU SAY, CHIEF? IF I HAND OVER THIS *KRAKE*...
...WOULD YOU MIND COOKING IT UP?
MIGHT I TAKE A WHILE TO PREPARE?
OOOH♡
WE CAN WAIT.
THE NIGHT'S ONLY JUST BEGUN.
WE'LL CONTINUE TO ENJOY OUR *AAL* IN THE MEANTIME.
RIGHT, GOTTHARD?
S-SURE.
SINCE IT'S SUCH A WHOPPER, I MIGHT AS WELL MAKE A FEW DISHES.
WIGGLE
WIGGLE
ENOUGH FOR EVERYBODY TO TRY, EVEN.
FIDGET
PRESS
SQUISH
GRATE GRATE GRATE

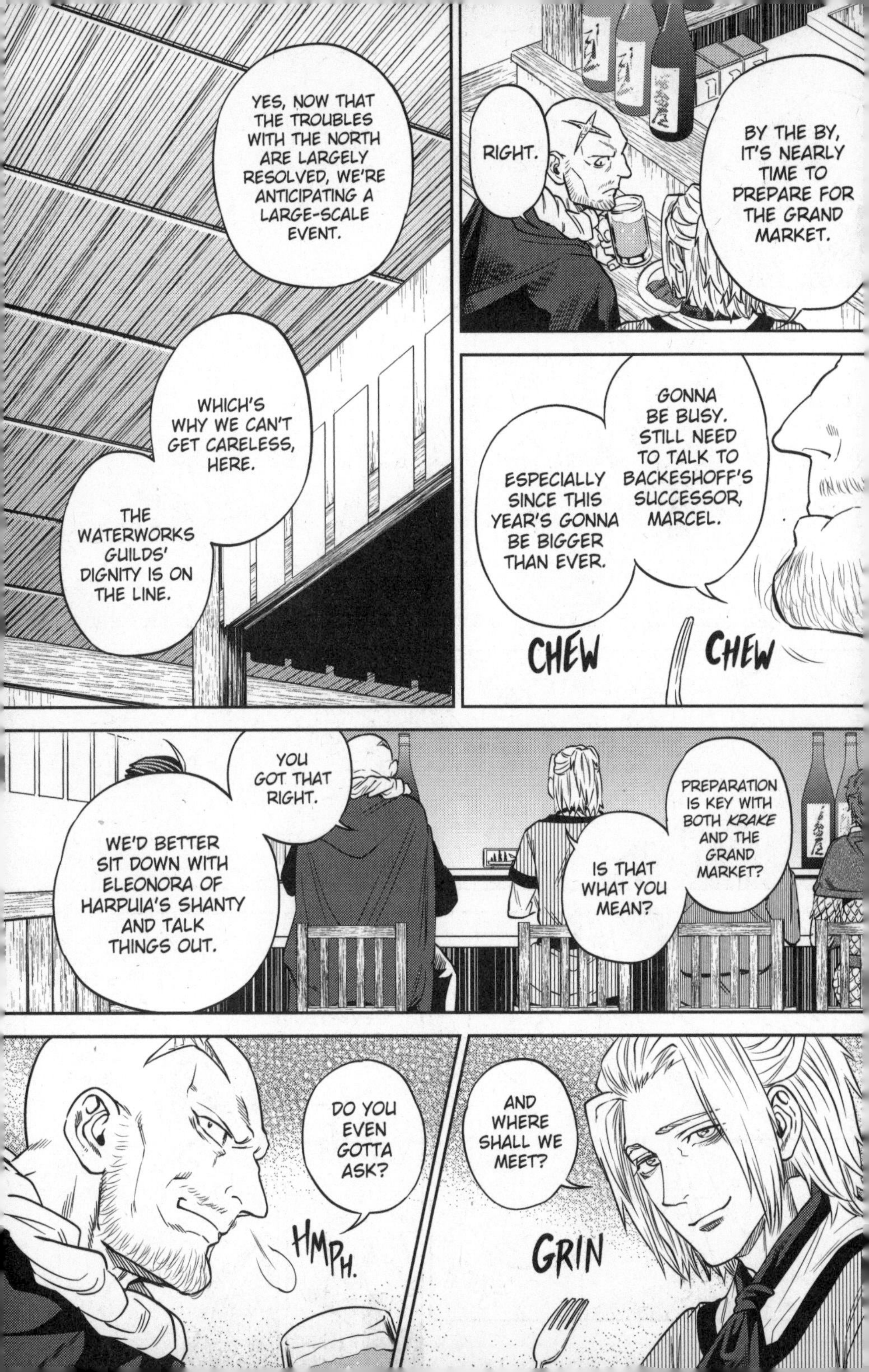
BY THE BY, IT'S NEARLY TIME TO PREPARE FOR THE GRAND MARKET.
RIGHT.
GONNA BE BUSY. STILL NEED TO TALK TO BACKESHOFF'S SUCCESSOR, MARCEL.
ESPECIALLY SINCE THIS YEAR'S GONNA BE BIGGER THAN EVER.
CHEW
CHEW
YES, NOW THAT THE TROUBLES WITH THE NORTH ARE LARGELY RESOLVED, WE'RE ANTICIPATING A LARGE-SCALE EVENT.
WHICH'S WHY WE CAN'T GET CARELESS, HERE.
THE WATERWORKS GUILDS' DIGNITY IS ON THE LINE.
PREPARATION IS KEY WITH BOTH *KRAKE* AND THE GRAND MARKET?
IS THAT WHAT YOU MEAN?
YOU GOT THAT RIGHT.
WE'D BETTER SIT DOWN WITH ELEONORA OF HARPUIA'S SHANTY AND TALK THINGS OUT.
AND WHERE SHALL WE MEET?
GRIN
DO YOU EVEN GOTTA ASK?
HMPH.

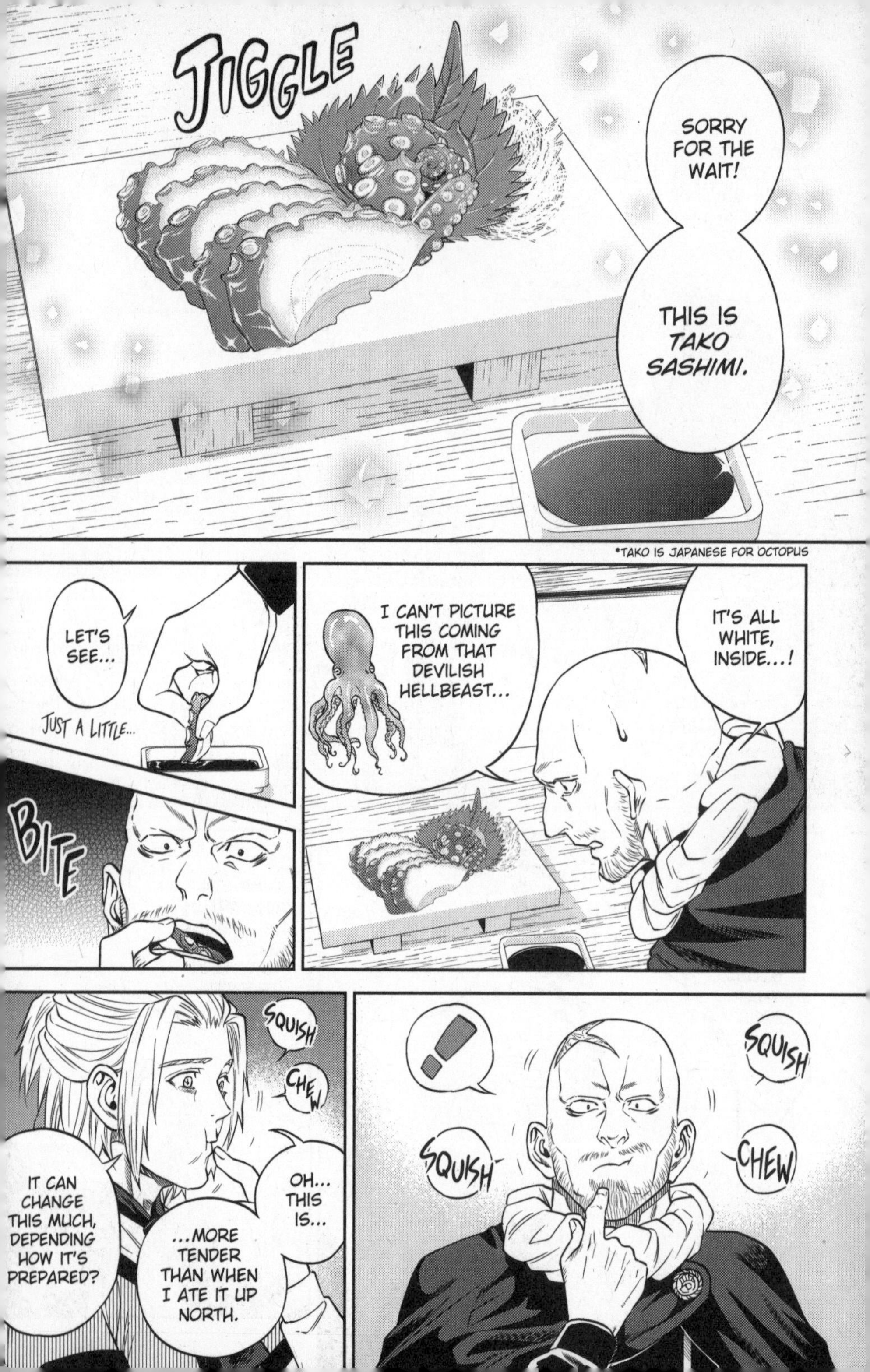
JIGGLE
SORRY FOR THE WAIT!
THIS IS TAKO SASHIMI.
IT'S ALL WHITE, INSIDE...!
I CAN'T PICTURE THIS COMING FROM THAT DEVILISH HELLBEAST...
LET'S SEE...
JUST A LITTLE...
BITE
!
SQUISH
SQUISH
CHEW
CHEW
SQUISH
CHEW
OH... THIS IS...
...MORE TENDER THAN WHEN I ATE IT UP NORTH.
IT CAN CHANGE THIS MUCH, DEPENDING HOW IT'S PREPARED?

*TAKO IS JAPANESE FOR OCTOPUS

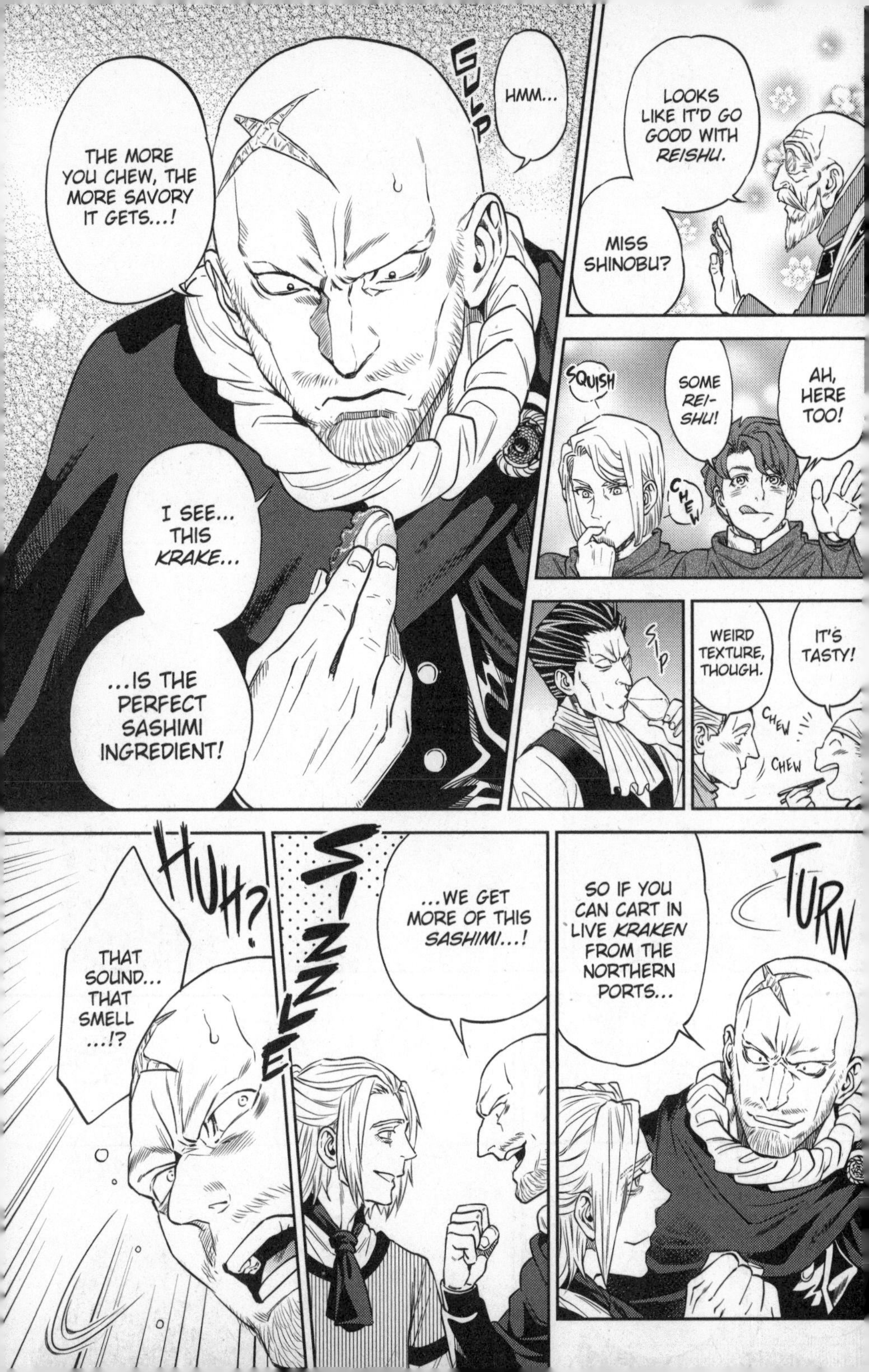
LOOKS LIKE IT'D GO GOOD WITH *REISHU*.
MISS SHINOBU?
AH, HERE TOO!
SOME *REI-SHU*!
SQUISH
CHEW
IT'S TASTY!
WEIRD TEXTURE, THOUGH.
CHEW
CHEW
SIP
GULP
HMM...
THE MORE YOU CHEW, THE MORE SAVORY IT GETS...!
I SEE... THIS *KRAKE*...
...IS THE PERFECT SASHIMI INGREDIENT!
TURN
SO IF YOU CAN CART IN LIVE *KRAKEN* FROM THE NORTHERN PORTS...
...WE GET MORE OF THIS *SASHIMI*...!
SIZZLE
HUH?
THAT SOUND... THAT SMELL ...!?

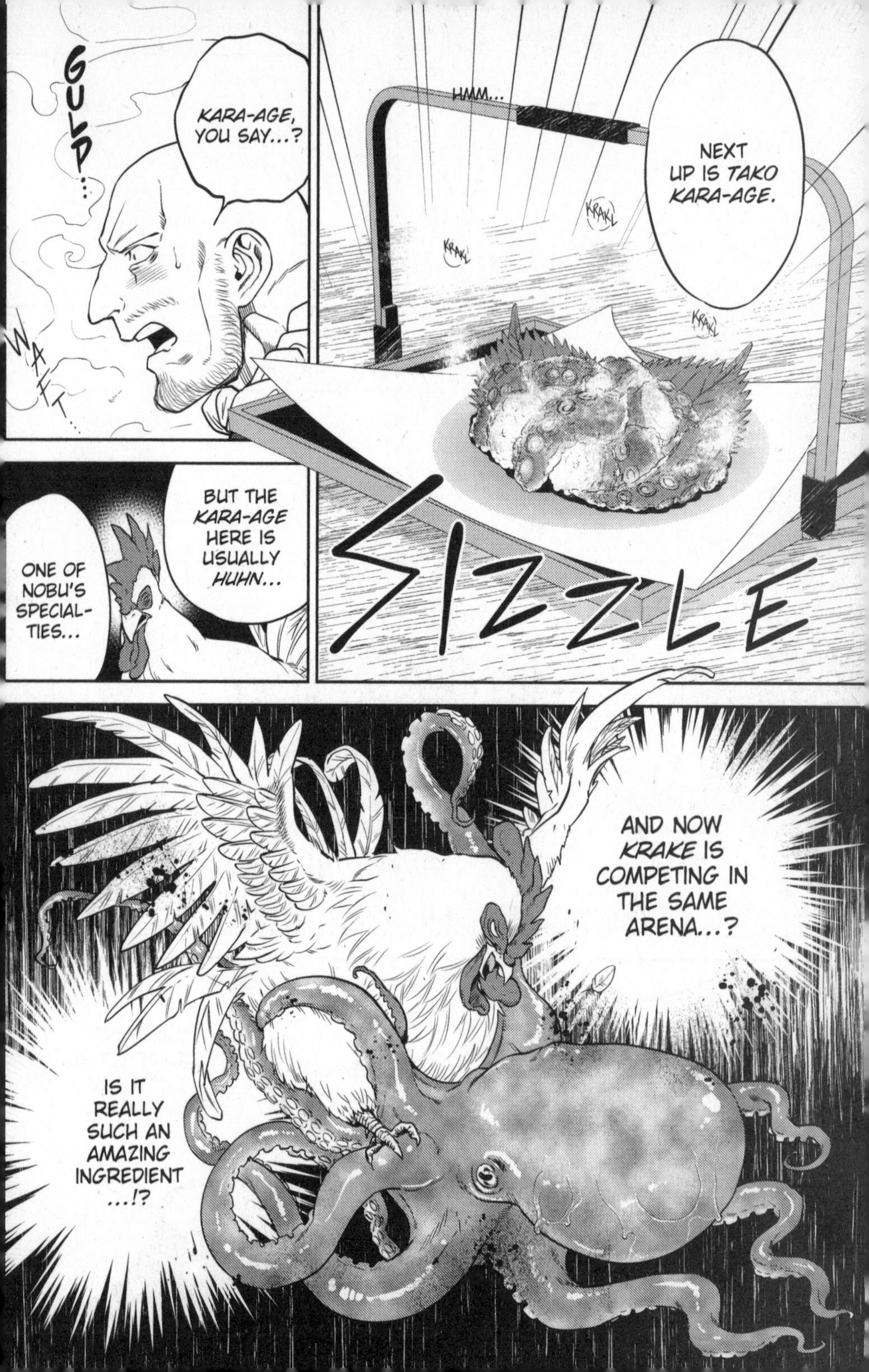
NEXT UP IS TAKO KARA-AGE.
HMM...
KRAKL
KRAKL
KRAKL
SIZZLE
KARA-AGE, YOU SAY...?
GULP...
WAFT...
BUT THE KARA-AGE HERE IS USUALLY HUHN...
ONE OF NOBU'S SPECIAL-TIES...
AND NOW KRAKE IS COMPETING IN THE SAME ARENA...?
IS IT REALLY SUCH AN AMAZING INGREDIENT ...!?

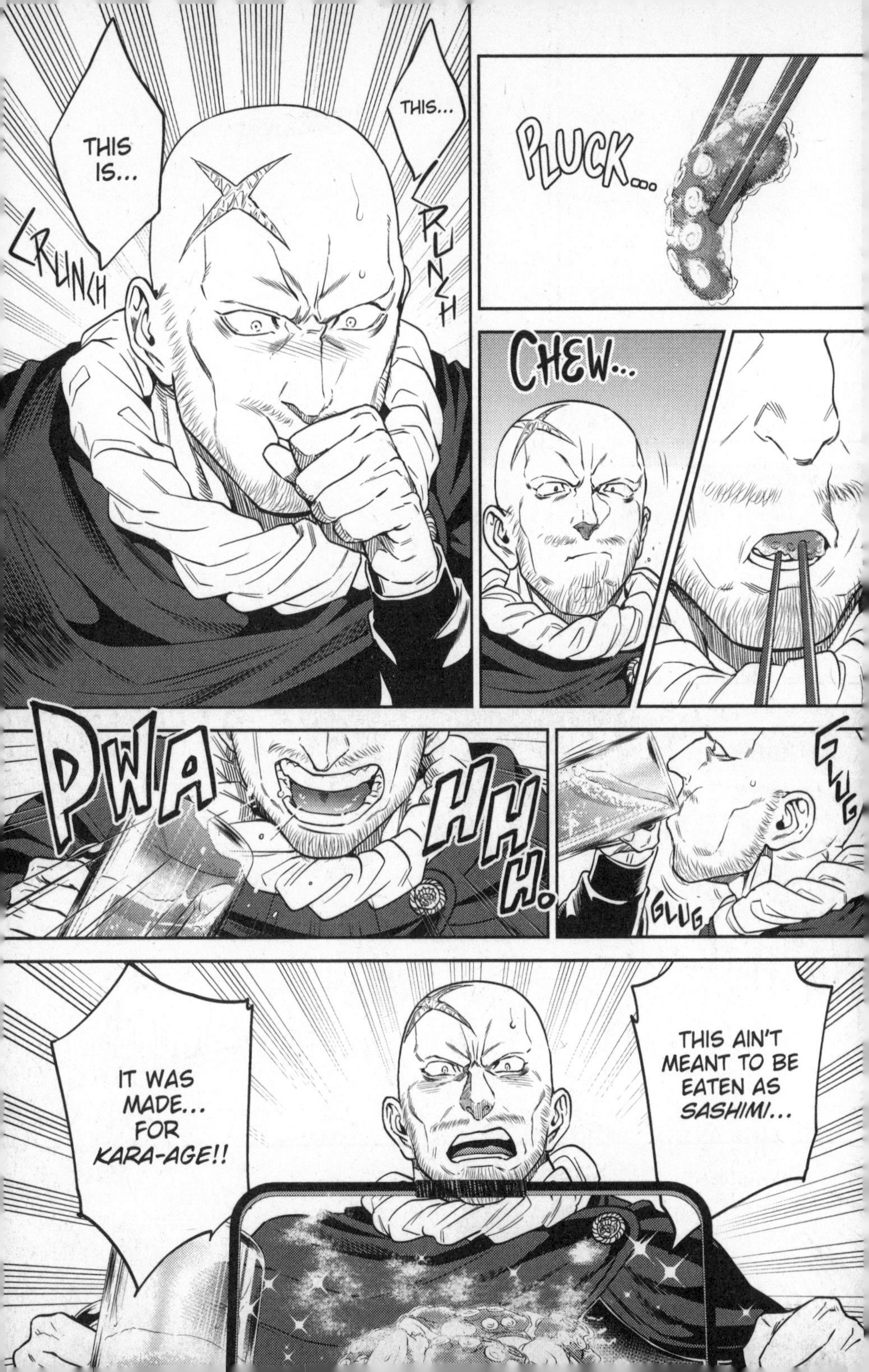
PLUCK...
CHEW...
THIS...
CRUNCH
THIS IS...
CRUNCH
GLUG
GLUG
PWAHHHH.
THIS AIN'T MEANT TO BE EATEN AS *SASHIMI*...
IT WAS MADE... FOR *KARA-AGE*!!

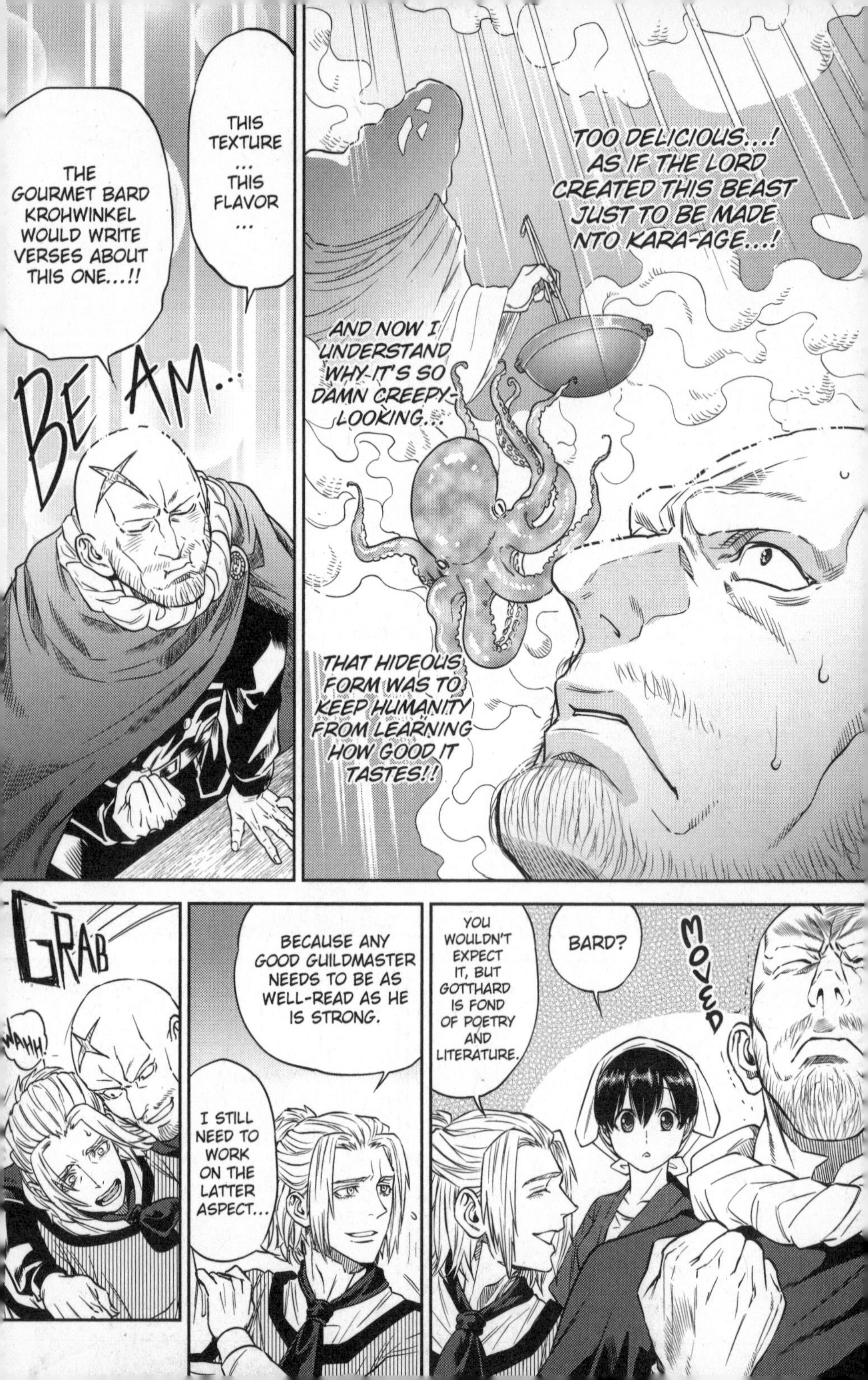
TOO DELICIOUS...! AS IF THE LORD CREATED THIS BEAST JUST TO BE MADE NTO KARA-AGE...!
AND NOW I UNDERSTAND WHY IT'S SO DAMN CREEPY-LOOKING...
THAT HIDEOUS FORM WAS TO KEEP HUMANITY FROM LEARNING HOW GOOD IT TASTES!!
THIS TEXTURE ... THIS FLAVOR ...
THE GOURMET BARD KROHWINKEL WOULD WRITE VERSES ABOUT THIS ONE...!!
BE AM...
MOVED
BARD?
YOU WOULDN'T EXPECT IT, BUT GOTTHARD IS FOND OF POETRY AND LITERATURE.
BECAUSE ANY GOOD GUILDMASTER NEEDS TO BE AS WELL-READ AS HE IS STRONG.
I STILL NEED TO WORK ON THE LATTER ASPECT...
GRAB
WAHH!

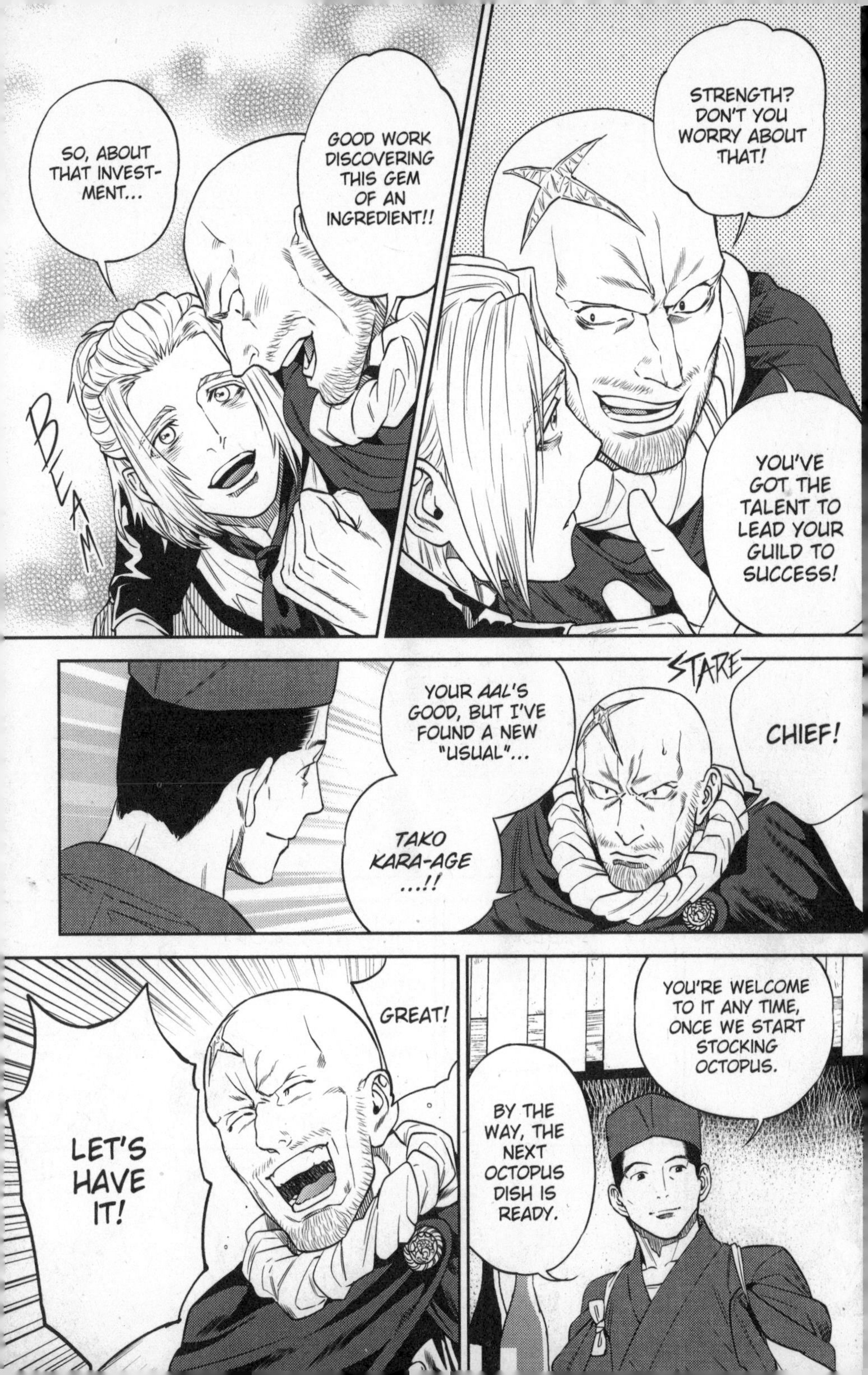
STRENGTH? DON'T YOU WORRY ABOUT THAT!
YOU'VE GOT THE TALENT TO LEAD YOUR GUILD TO SUCCESS!
GOOD WORK DISCOVERING THIS GEM OF AN INGREDIENT!!
SO, ABOUT THAT INVESTMENT...
BEAM
STARE
CHIEF!
YOUR AAL'S GOOD, BUT I'VE FOUND A NEW "USUAL"...
TAKO KARA-AGE ...!!
YOU'RE WELCOME TO IT ANY TIME, ONCE WE START STOCKING OCTOPUS.
BY THE WAY, THE NEXT OCTOPUS DISH IS READY.
GREAT!
LET'S HAVE IT!

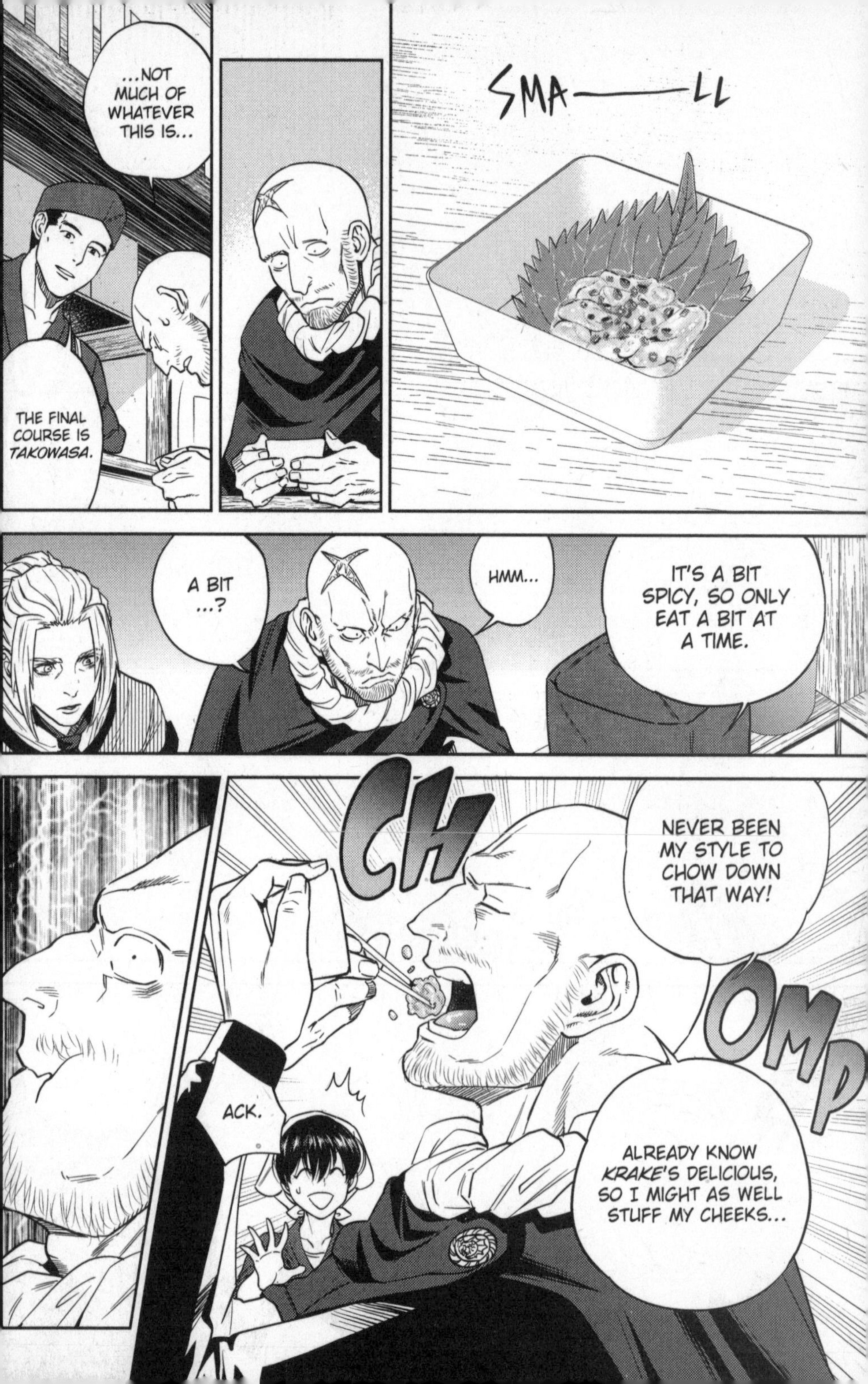
SMA——LL
...NOT MUCH OF WHATEVER THIS IS...
THE FINAL COURSE IS *TAKOWASA*.
IT'S A BIT SPICY, SO ONLY EAT A BIT AT A TIME.
HMM...
A BIT ...?
NEVER BEEN MY STYLE TO CHOW DOWN THAT WAY!
CH
OMP
ALREADY KNOW *KRAKE*'S DELICIOUS, SO I MIGHT AS WELL STUFF MY CHEEKS...
ACK.

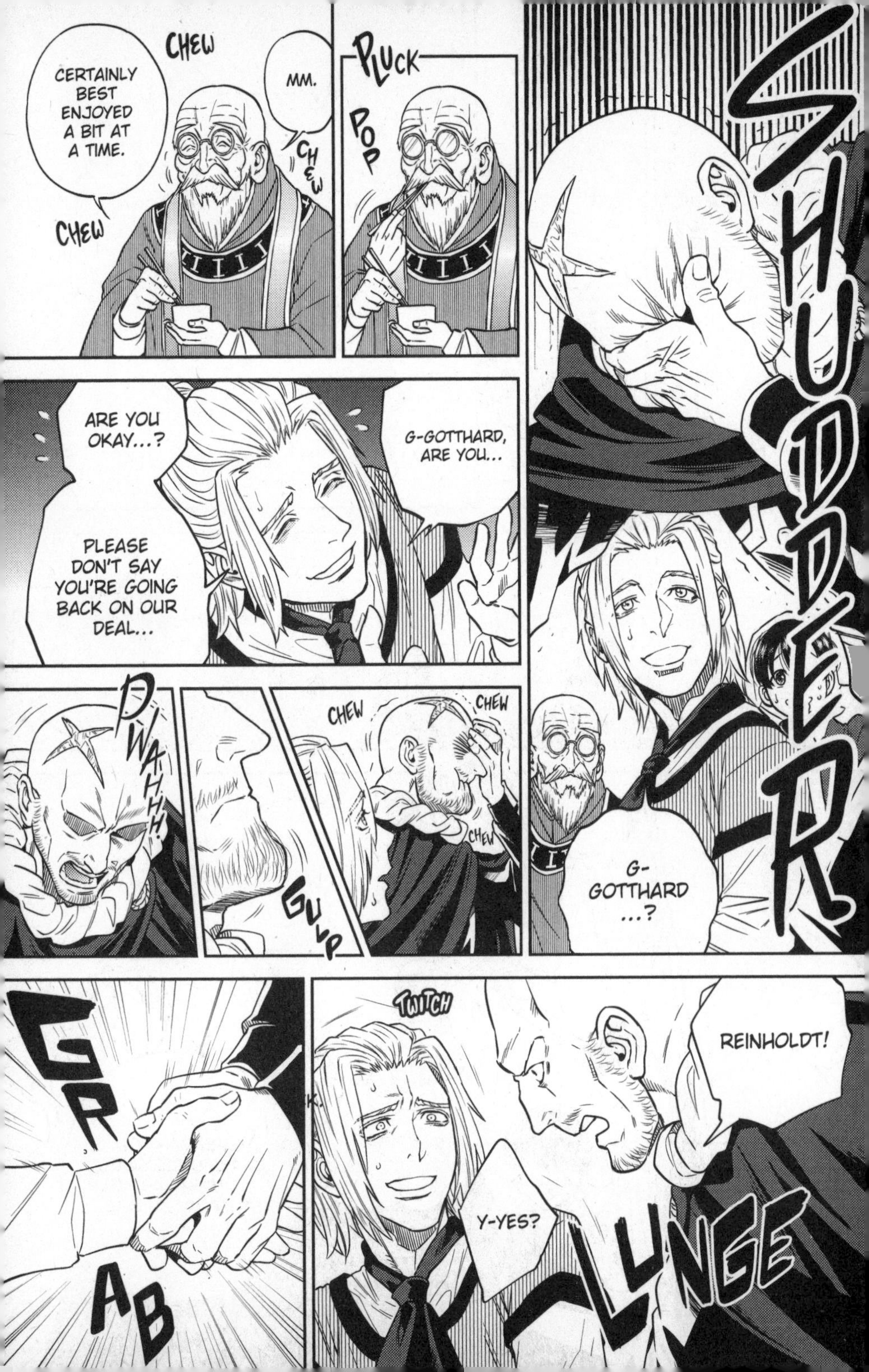
SHUDDER
G-GOTTHARD...?
PLUCK
POP
MM.
CHEW
CHEW
CERTAINLY BEST ENJOYED A BIT AT A TIME.
CHEW
G-GOTTHARD, ARE YOU...
ARE YOU OKAY...?
PLEASE DON'T SAY YOU'RE GOING BACK ON OUR DEAL...
CHEW
CHEW
CHEW
GULP
DWAHHH!
TWITCH
REINHOLDT!
Y-YES?
LUNGE
GRAB

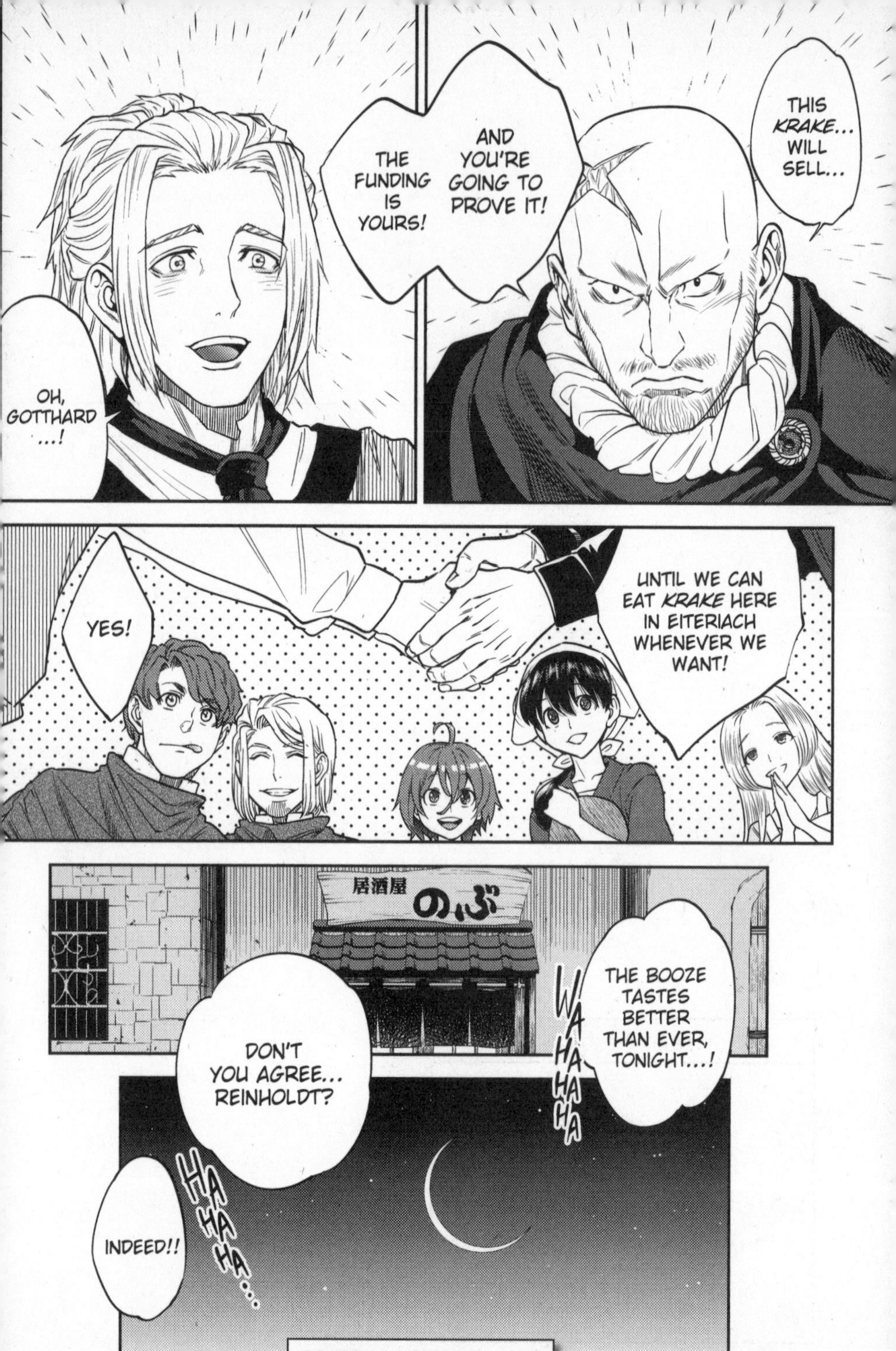
THIS *KRAKE*... WILL SELL...
AND YOU'RE GOING TO PROVE IT!
THE FUNDING IS YOURS!
OH, GOTTHARD ...!
UNTIL WE CAN EAT *KRAKE* HERE IN EITERIACH WHENEVER WE WANT!
YES!
居酒屋
のぶ
THE BOOZE TASTES BETTER THAN EVER, TONIGHT...!
WAHAHAHAHA
DON'T YOU AGREE... REINHOLDT?
HAHAHAHA...
INDEED!!

COURSE 24 - CLOSING TIME

Tako Sashimi

OTHERWORLDLY IZAKAYA

NOBU

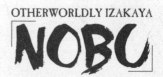

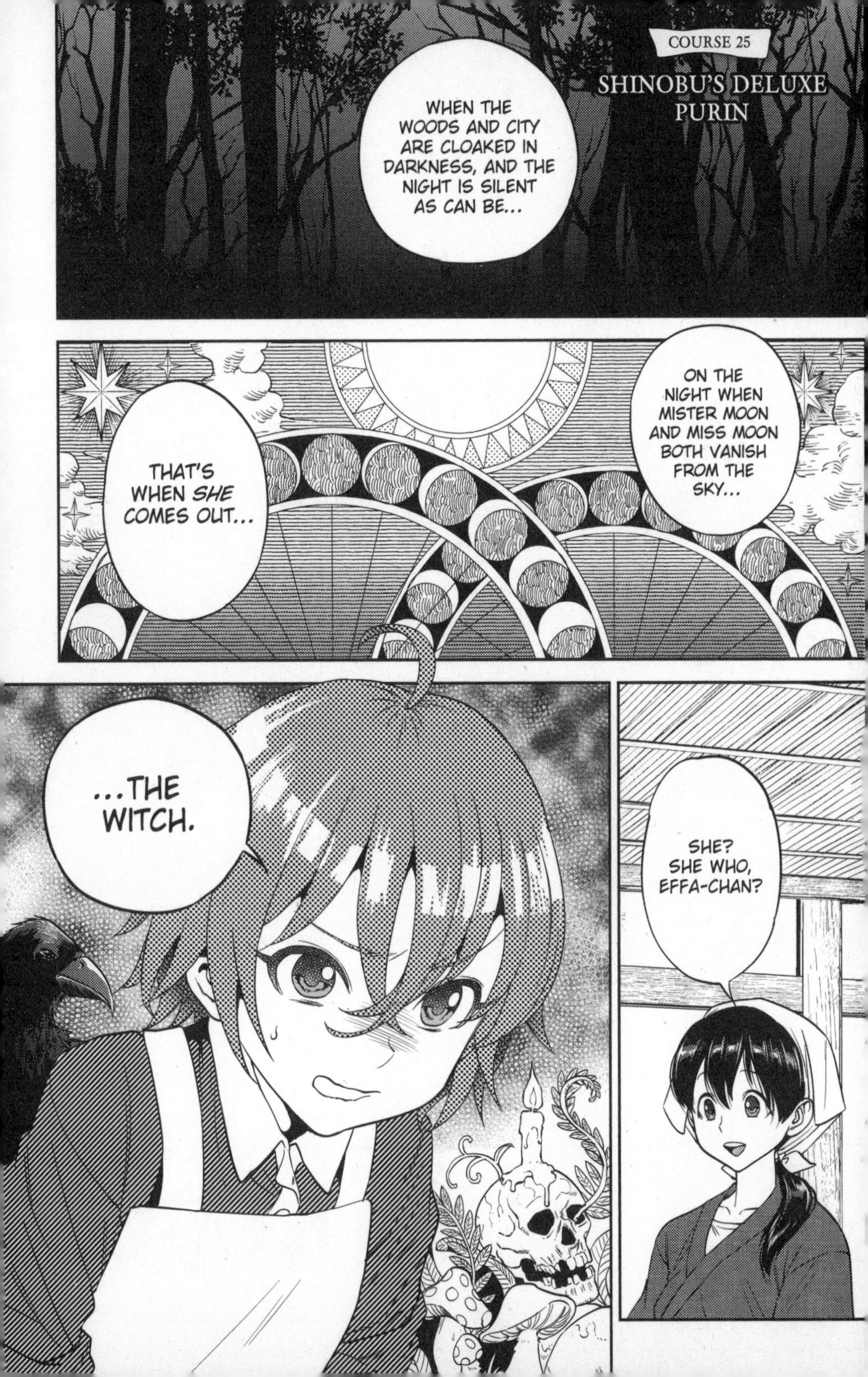
COURSE 25
SHINOBU'S DELUXE PURIN
WHEN THE WOODS AND CITY ARE CLOAKED IN DARKNESS, AND THE NIGHT IS SILENT AS CAN BE...
ON THE NIGHT WHEN MISTER MOON AND MISS MOON BOTH VANISH FROM THE SKY...
THAT'S WHEN *SHE* COMES OUT...
SHE? SHE WHO, EFFA-CHAN?
...THE WITCH.

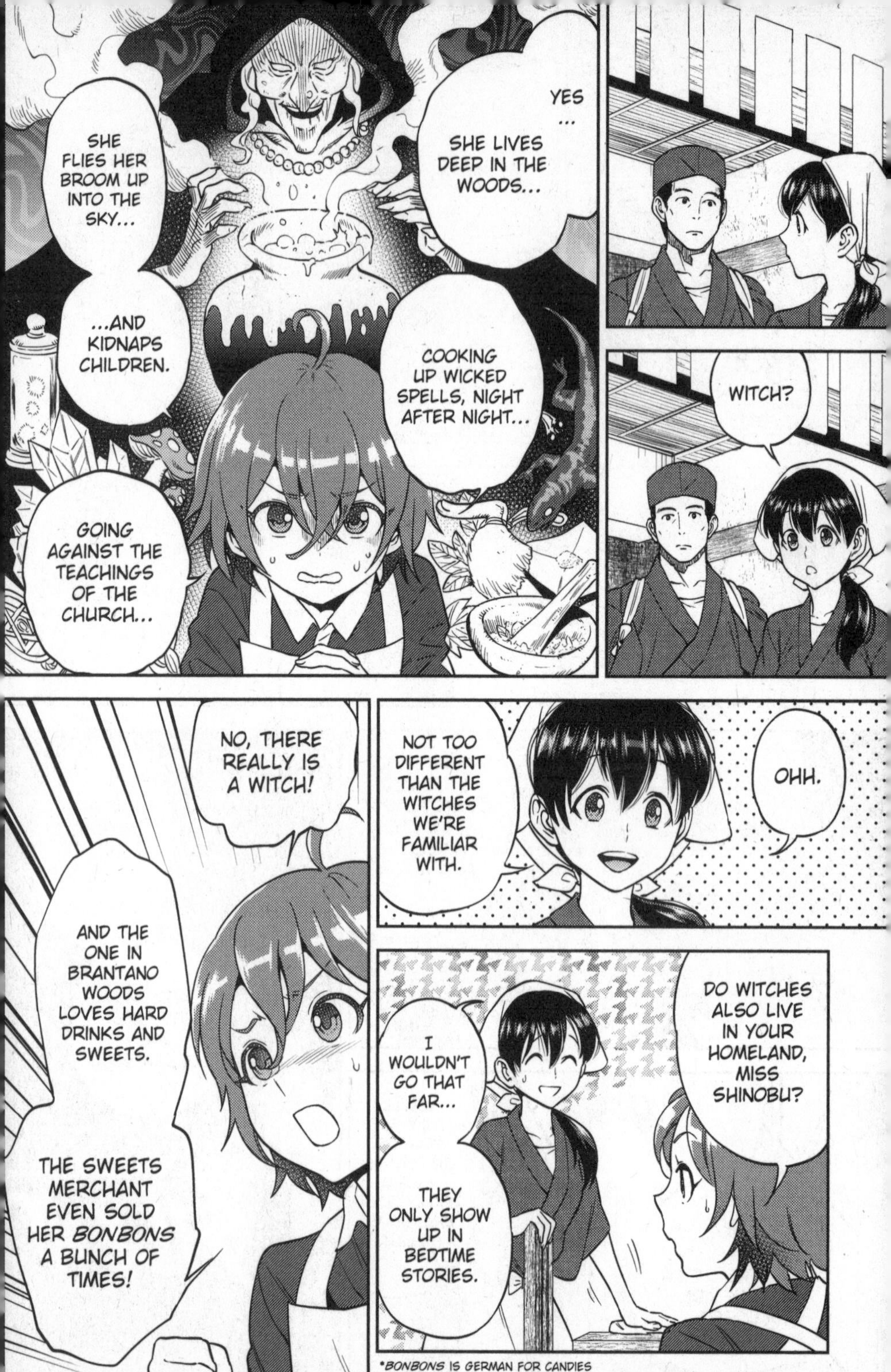
WITCH?
YES ... SHE LIVES DEEP IN THE WOODS...
COOKING UP WICKED SPELLS, NIGHT AFTER NIGHT...
SHE FLIES HER BROOM UP INTO THE SKY...
...AND KIDNAPS CHILDREN.
GOING AGAINST THE TEACHINGS OF THE CHURCH...
OHH.
NOT TOO DIFFERENT THAN THE WITCHES WE'RE FAMILIAR WITH.
DO WITCHES ALSO LIVE IN YOUR HOMELAND, MISS SHINOBU?
I WOULDN'T GO THAT FAR...
THEY ONLY SHOW UP IN BEDTIME STORIES.
NO, THERE REALLY IS A WITCH!
AND THE ONE IN BRANTANO WOODS LOVES HARD DRINKS AND SWEETS.
THE SWEETS MERCHANT EVEN SOLD HER *BONBONS* A BUNCH OF TIMES!

**BONBONS* IS GERMAN FOR CANDIES

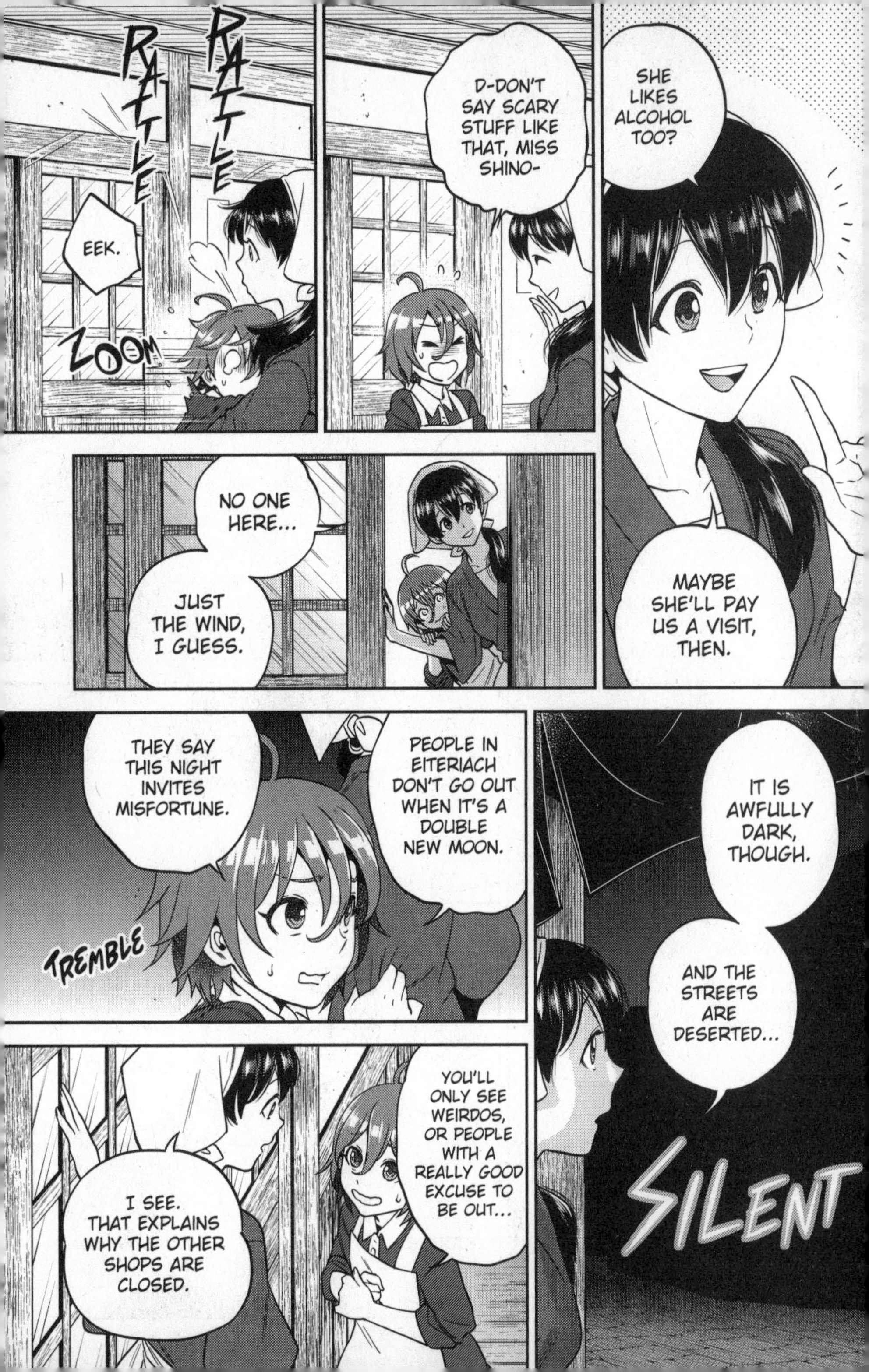
SHE LIKES ALCOHOL TOO?
MAYBE SHE'LL PAY US A VISIT, THEN.
D-DON'T SAY SCARY STUFF LIKE THAT, MISS SHINO-
RATTLE
RATTLE
EEK.
ZOOM
NO ONE HERE...
JUST THE WIND, I GUESS.
IT IS AWFULLY DARK, THOUGH.
AND THE STREETS ARE DESERTED...
SILENT
PEOPLE IN EITERIACH DON'T GO OUT WHEN IT'S A DOUBLE NEW MOON.
THEY SAY THIS NIGHT INVITES MISFORTUNE.
TREMBLE
YOU'LL ONLY SEE WEIRDOS, OR PEOPLE WITH A REALLY GOOD EXCUSE TO BE OUT...
I SEE. THAT EXPLAINS WHY THE OTHER SHOPS ARE CLOSED.

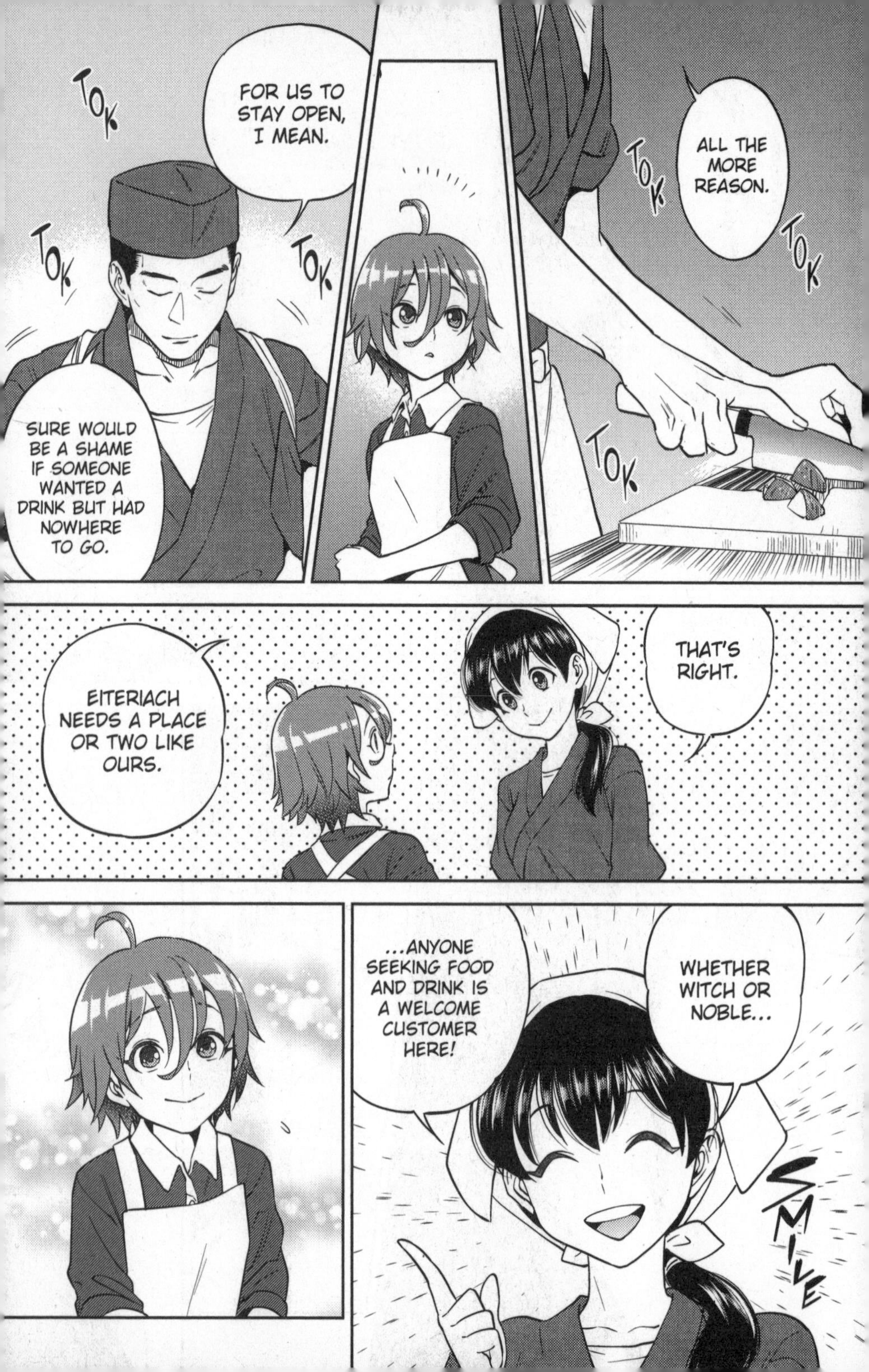
ALL THE MORE REASON.
TOK
TOK
TOK
FOR US TO STAY OPEN, I MEAN.
TOK
TOK
TOK
SURE WOULD BE A SHAME IF SOMEONE WANTED A DRINK BUT HAD NOWHERE TO GO.
THAT'S RIGHT.
EITERIACH NEEDS A PLACE OR TWO LIKE OURS.
WHETHER WITCH OR NOBLE...
...ANYONE SEEKING FOOD AND DRINK IS A WELCOME CUSTOMER HERE!
SMILE

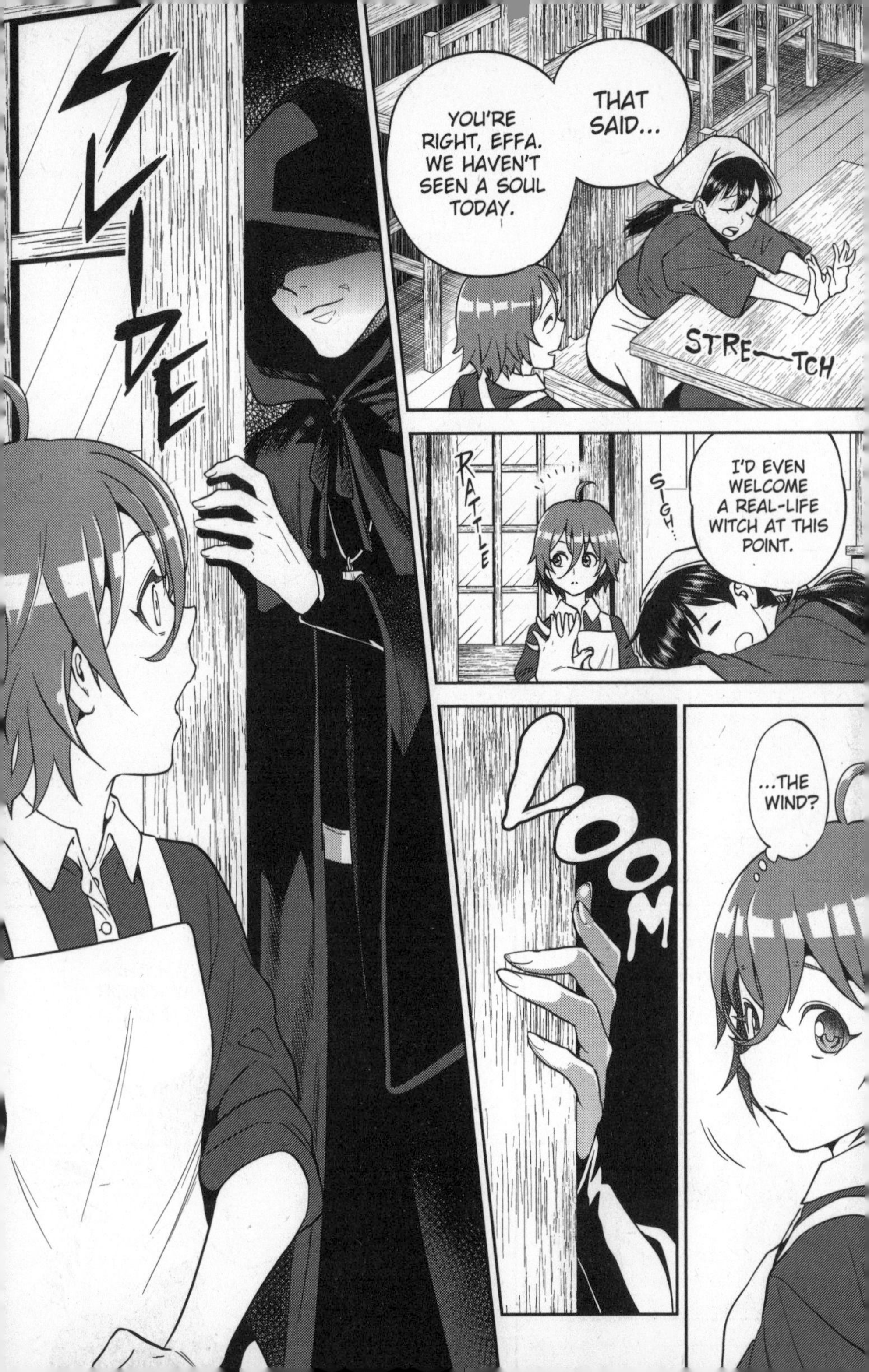
THAT SAID...
YOU'RE RIGHT, EFFA. WE HAVEN'T SEEN A SOUL TODAY.
STRE—TCH
I'D EVEN WELCOME A REAL-LIFE WITCH AT THIS POINT.
SIGH...
RATTLE
...THE WIND?
VOOM
SLIDE

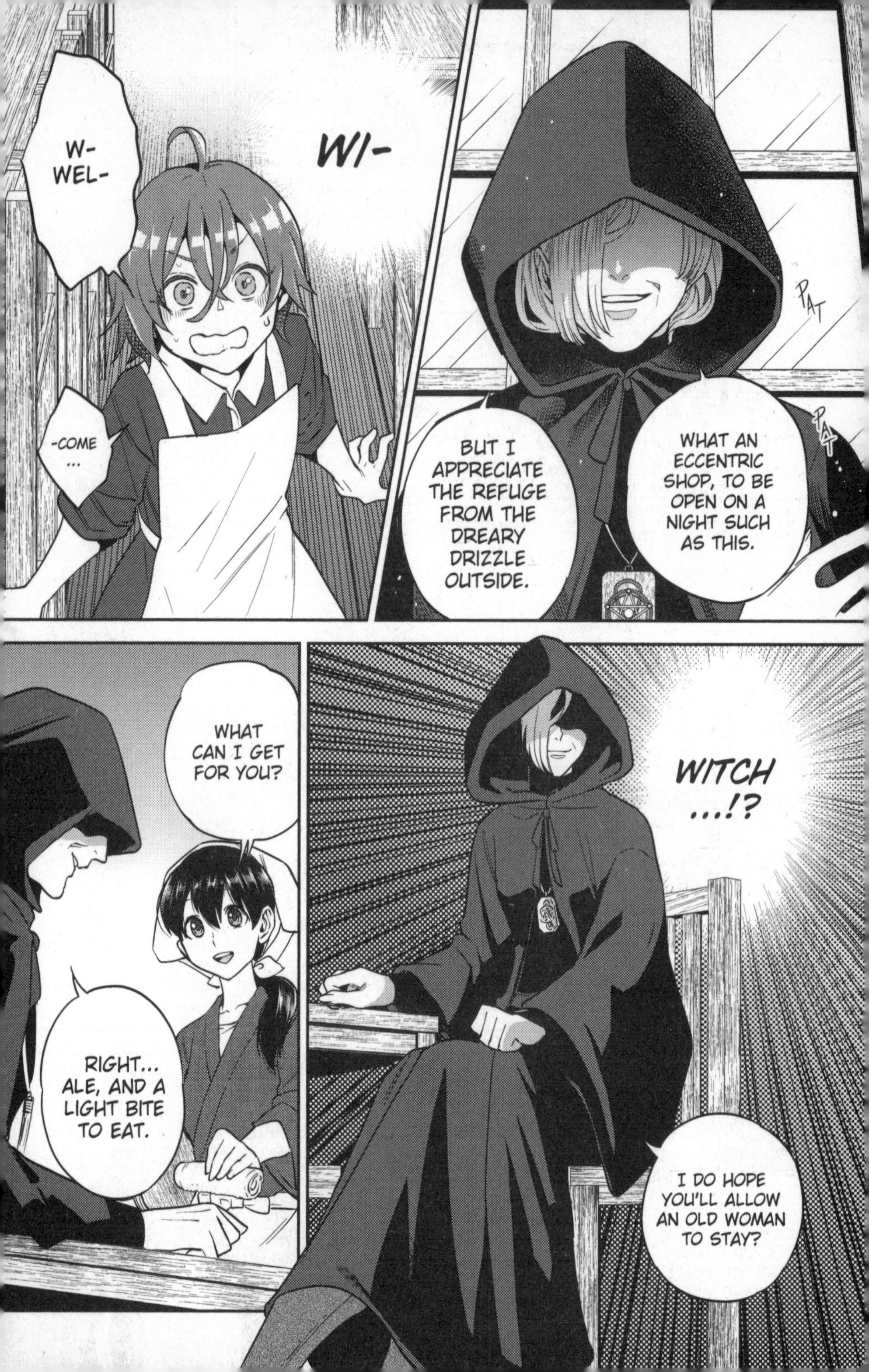
PAT
PAT
WHAT AN ECCENTRIC SHOP, TO BE OPEN ON A NIGHT SUCH AS THIS.
BUT I APPRECIATE THE REFUGE FROM THE DREARY DRIZZLE OUTSIDE.
WI-
W- WEL-
-COME ...
WITCH ...!?
I DO HOPE YOU'LL ALLOW AN OLD WOMAN TO STAY?
WHAT CAN I GET FOR YOU?
RIGHT... ALE, AND A LIGHT BITE TO EAT.

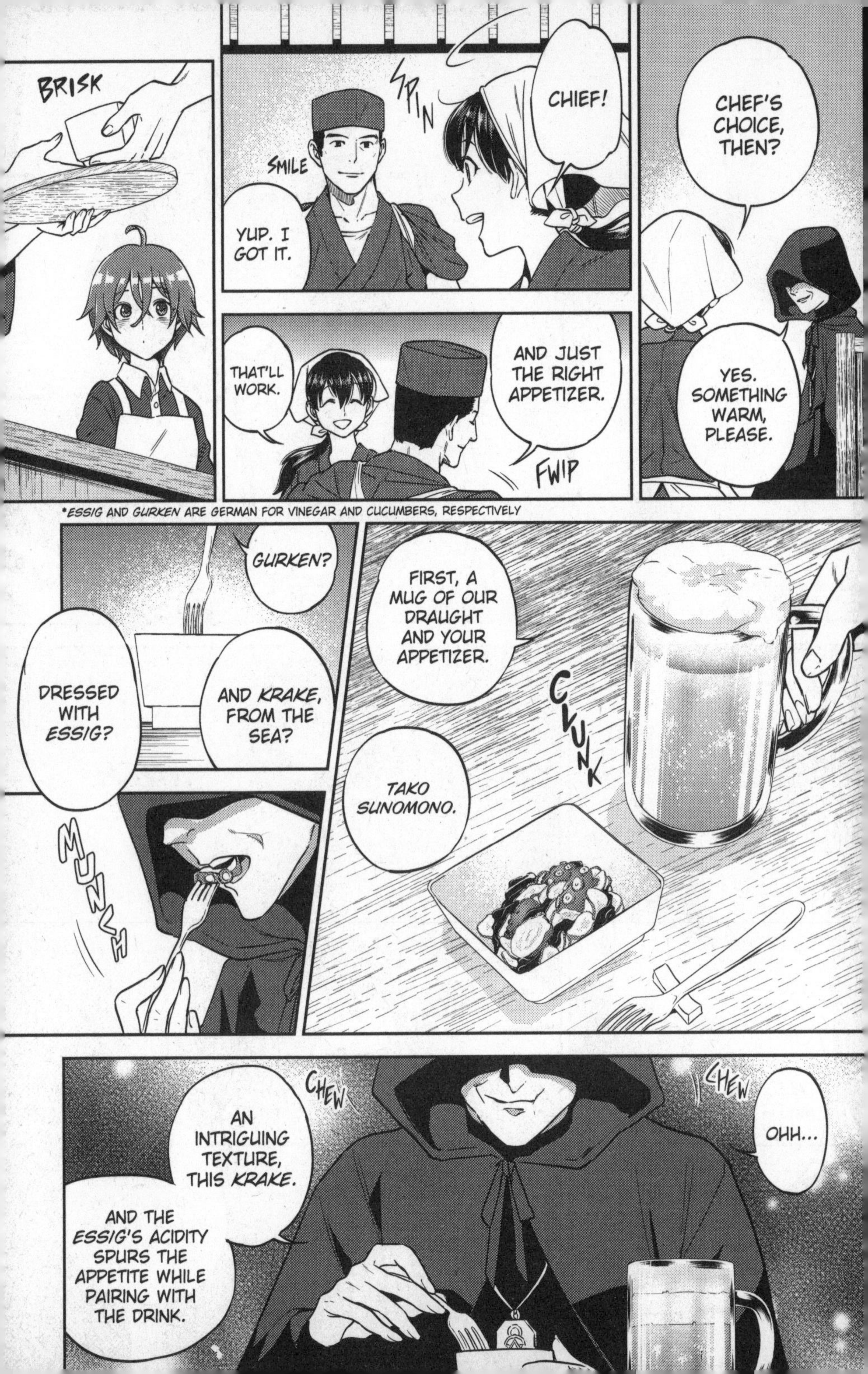
CHEF'S CHOICE, THEN?
YES. SOMETHING WARM, PLEASE.
CHIEF!
SPIN
SMILE
YUP. I GOT IT.
AND JUST THE RIGHT APPETIZER.
FWIP
THAT'LL WORK.
BRISK
FIRST, A MUG OF OUR DRAUGHT AND YOUR APPETIZER.
CLUNK
TAKO SUNOMONO.
GURKEN?
AND KRAKE, FROM THE SEA?
DRESSED WITH ESSIG?
MUNCH
CHEW
OHH...
CHEW
AN INTRIGUING TEXTURE, THIS KRAKE.
AND THE ESSIG'S ACIDITY SPURS THE APPETITE WHILE PAIRING WITH THE DRINK.

*ESSIG AND GURKEN ARE GERMAN FOR VINEGAR AND CUCUMBERS, RESPECTIVELY

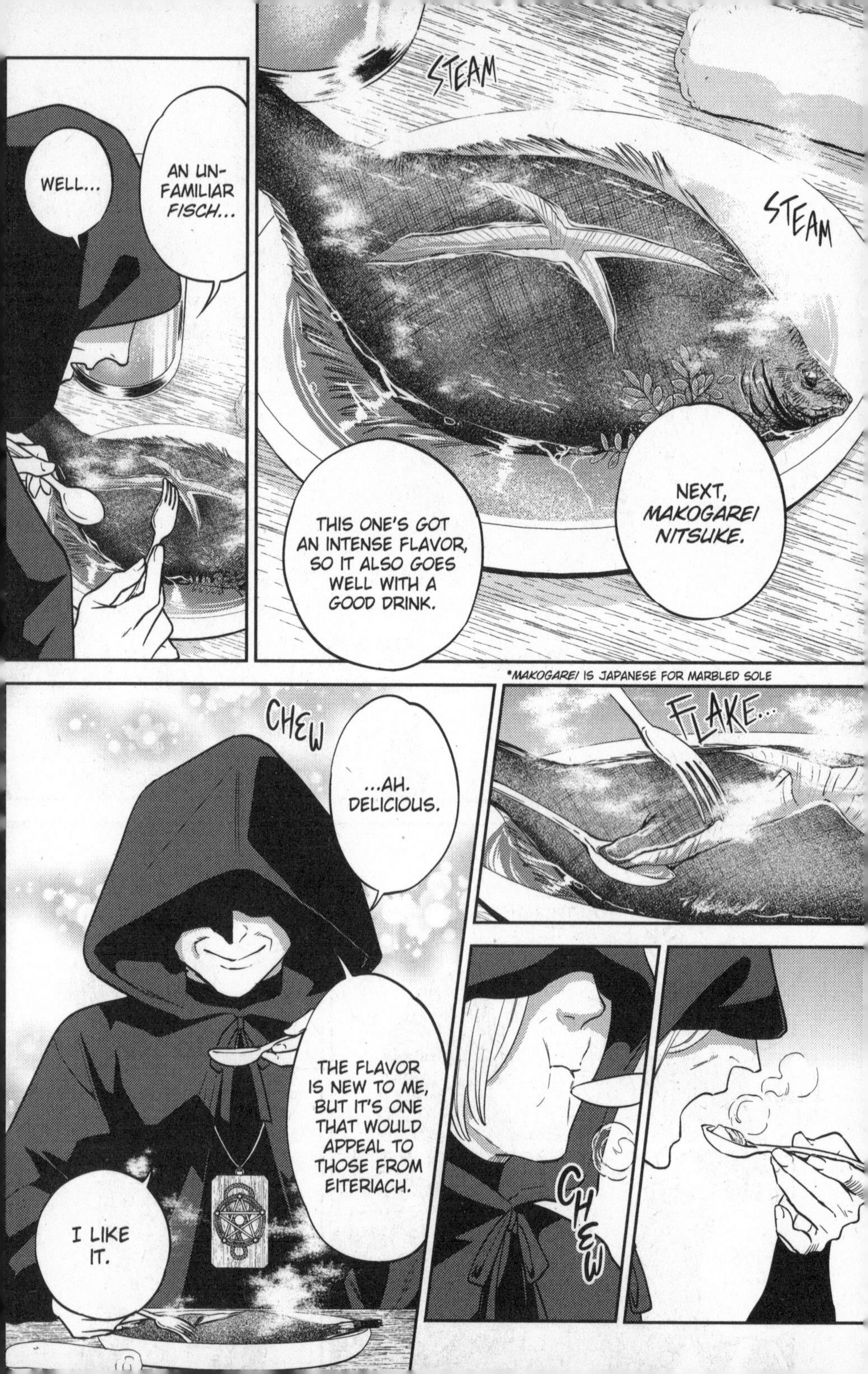
STEAM
STEAM
NEXT, MAKOGAREI NITSUKE.
THIS ONE'S GOT AN INTENSE FLAVOR, SO IT ALSO GOES WELL WITH A GOOD DRINK.
AN UN-FAMILIAR FISCH...
WELL...
FLAKE...
CHEW
CHEW
...AH. DELICIOUS.
THE FLAVOR IS NEW TO ME, BUT IT'S ONE THAT WOULD APPEAL TO THOSE FROM EITERIACH.
I LIKE IT.

*MAKOGAREI IS JAPANESE FOR MARBLED SOLE

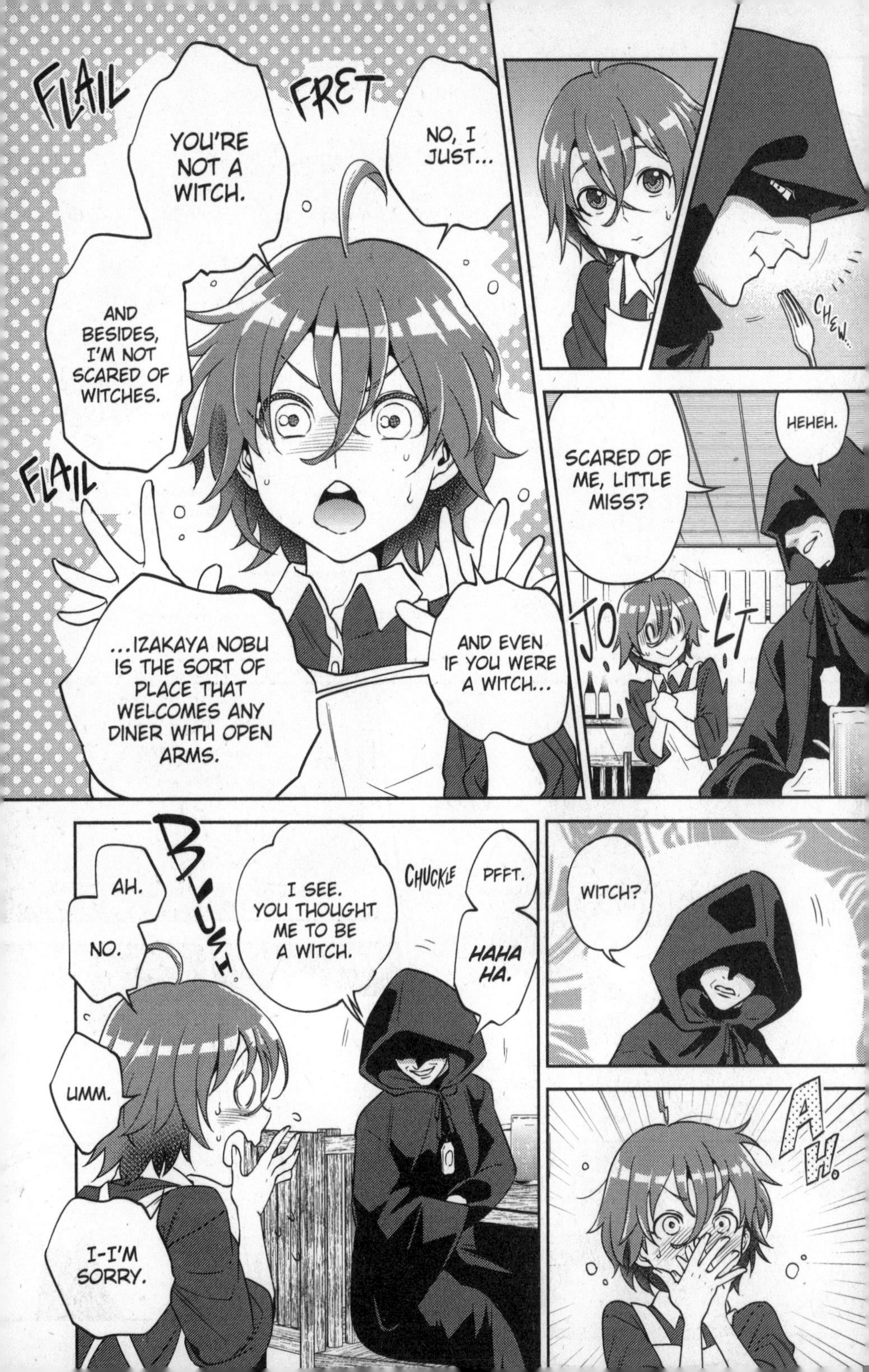

CHEW...
HEHEH.
SCARED OF ME, LITTLE MISS?
JOLT
NO, I JUST...
FRET
YOU'RE NOT A WITCH.
FLAIL
AND BESIDES, I'M NOT SCARED OF WITCHES.
FLAIL
AND EVEN IF YOU WERE A WITCH...
...IZAKAYA NOBU IS THE SORT OF PLACE THAT WELCOMES ANY DINER WITH OPEN ARMS.
WITCH?
AH.
PFFT.
HAHA HA.
CHUCKLE
I SEE. YOU THOUGHT ME TO BE A WITCH.
BLUSH
AH.
NO.
UMM.
I-I'M SORRY.

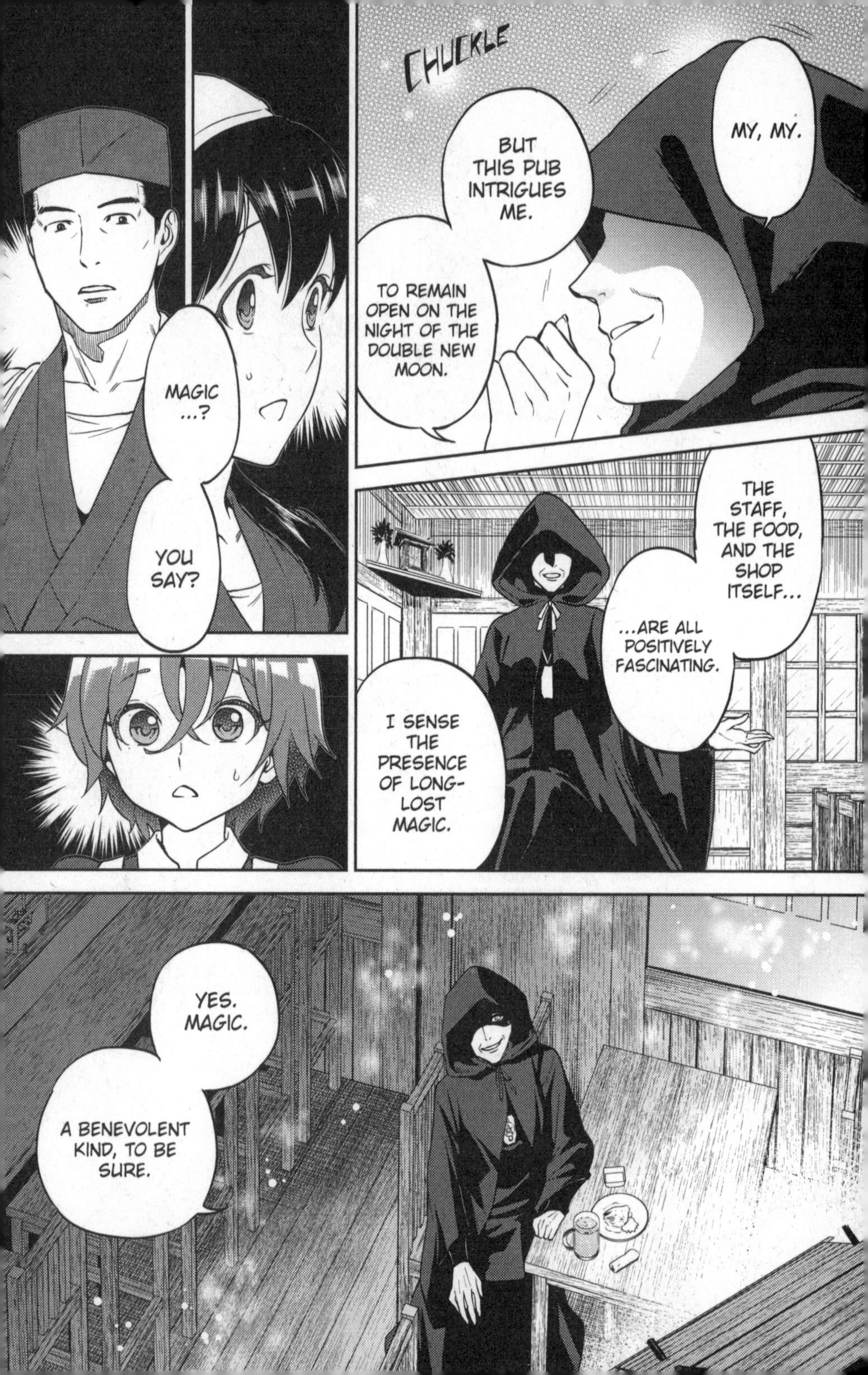
CHUCKLE
MY, MY.
BUT THIS PUB INTRIGUES ME.
TO REMAIN OPEN ON THE NIGHT OF THE DOUBLE NEW MOON.
THE STAFF, THE FOOD, AND THE SHOP ITSELF...
...ARE ALL POSITIVELY FASCINATING.
I SENSE THE PRESENCE OF LONG-LOST MAGIC.
MAGIC ...?
YOU SAY?
YES. MAGIC.
A BENEVOLENT KIND, TO BE SURE.

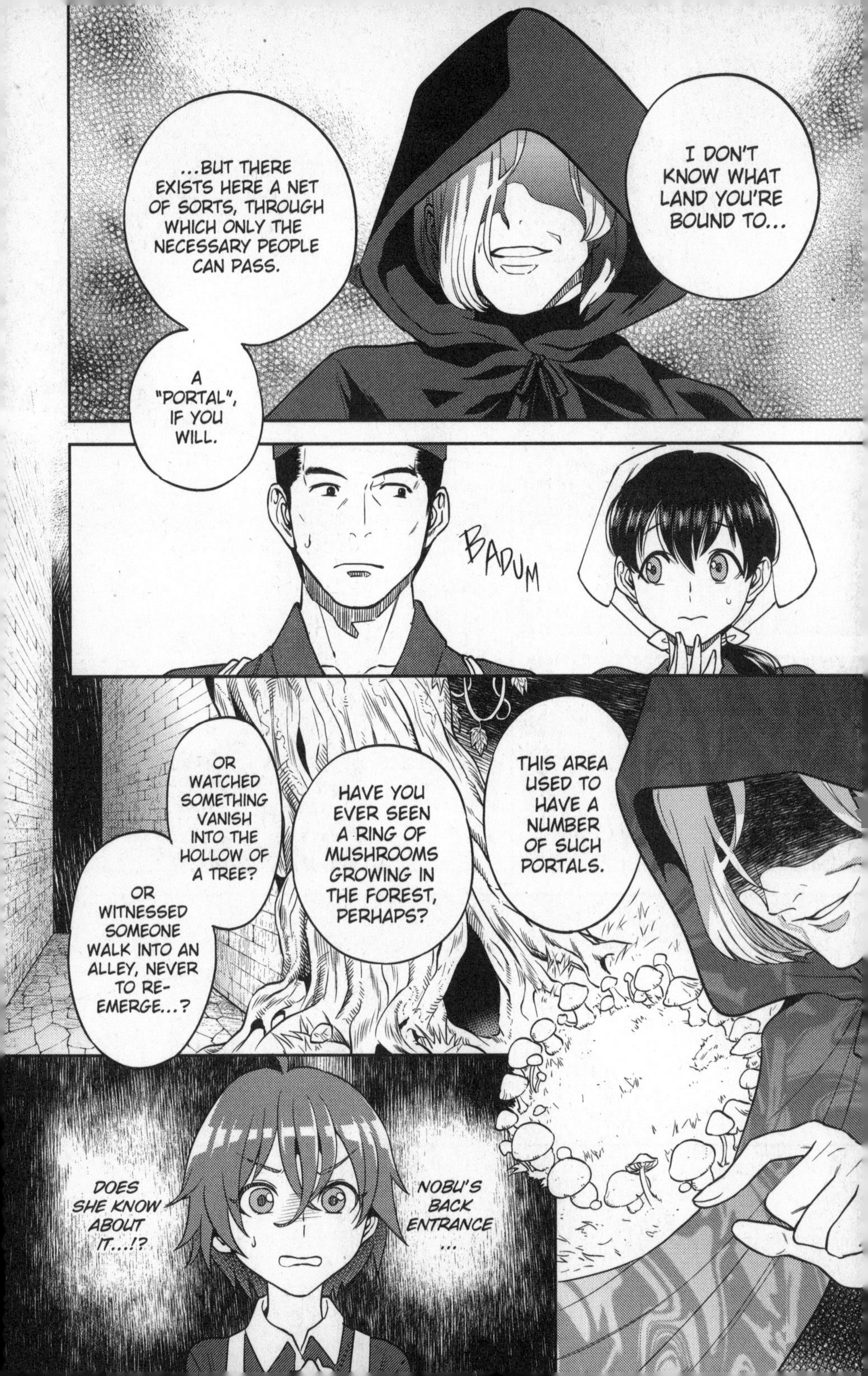
I DON'T KNOW WHAT LAND YOU'RE BOUND TO...
...BUT THERE EXISTS HERE A NET OF SORTS, THROUGH WHICH ONLY THE NECESSARY PEOPLE CAN PASS.
A "PORTAL", IF YOU WILL.
BADUM
THIS AREA USED TO HAVE A NUMBER OF SUCH PORTALS.
HAVE YOU EVER SEEN A RING OF MUSHROOMS GROWING IN THE FOREST, PERHAPS?
OR WATCHED SOMETHING VANISH INTO THE HOLLOW OF A TREE?
OR WITNESSED SOMEONE WALK INTO AN ALLEY, NEVER TO RE-EMERGE...?
NOBU'S BACK ENTRANCE ...
DOES SHE KNOW ABOUT IT...!?

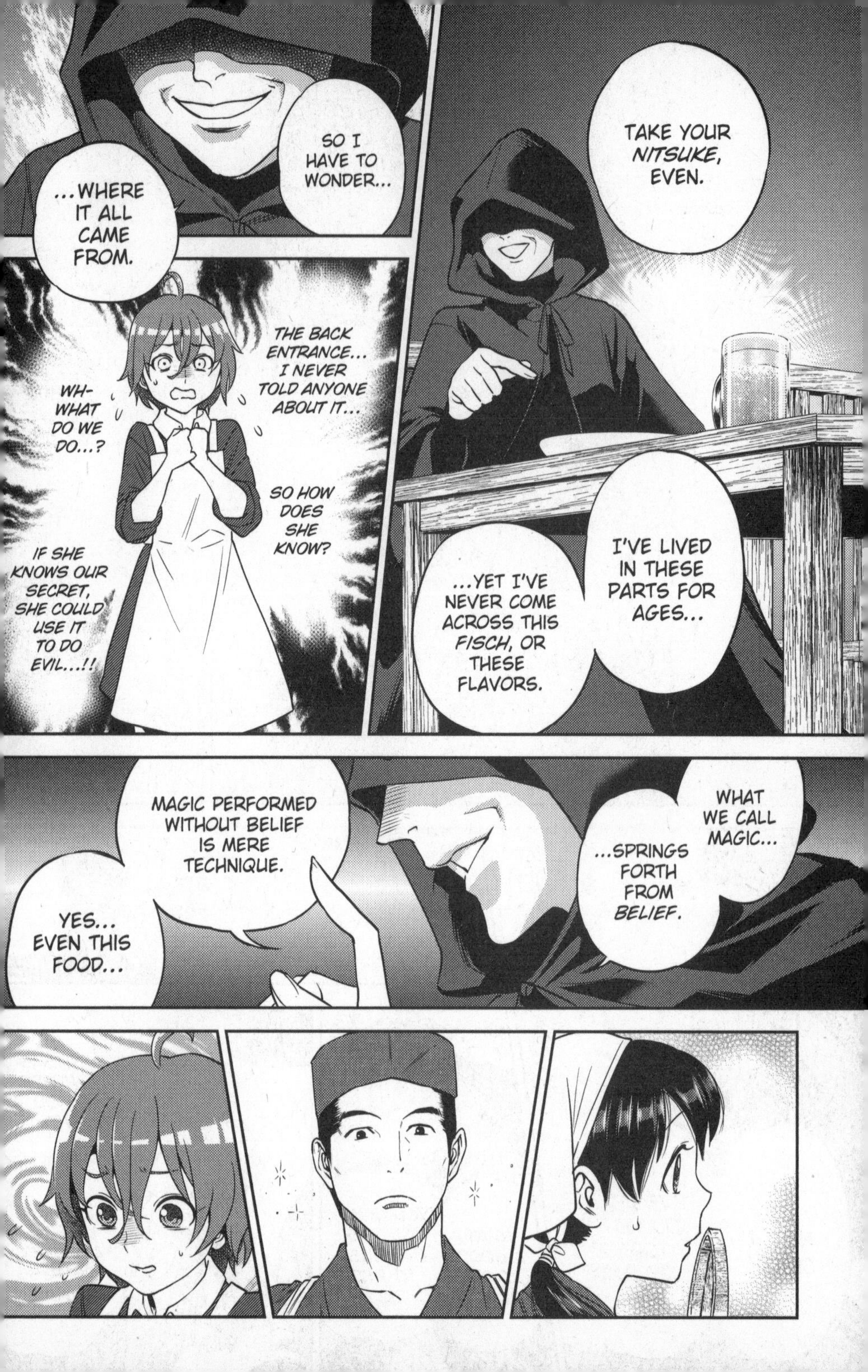
TAKE YOUR *NITSUKE*, EVEN.
I'VE LIVED IN THESE PARTS FOR AGES...
...YET I'VE NEVER COME ACROSS THIS *FISCH*, OR THESE FLAVORS.
SO I HAVE TO WONDER...
...WHERE IT ALL CAME FROM.
THE BACK ENTRANCE... I NEVER TOLD ANYONE ABOUT IT...
SO HOW DOES SHE KNOW?
WH-WHAT DO WE DO...?
IF SHE KNOWS OUR SECRET, SHE COULD USE IT TO DO EVIL...!!
WHAT WE CALL MAGIC...
...SPRINGS FORTH FROM *BELIEF*.
MAGIC PERFORMED WITHOUT BELIEF IS MERE TECHNIQUE.
YES... EVEN THIS FOOD...

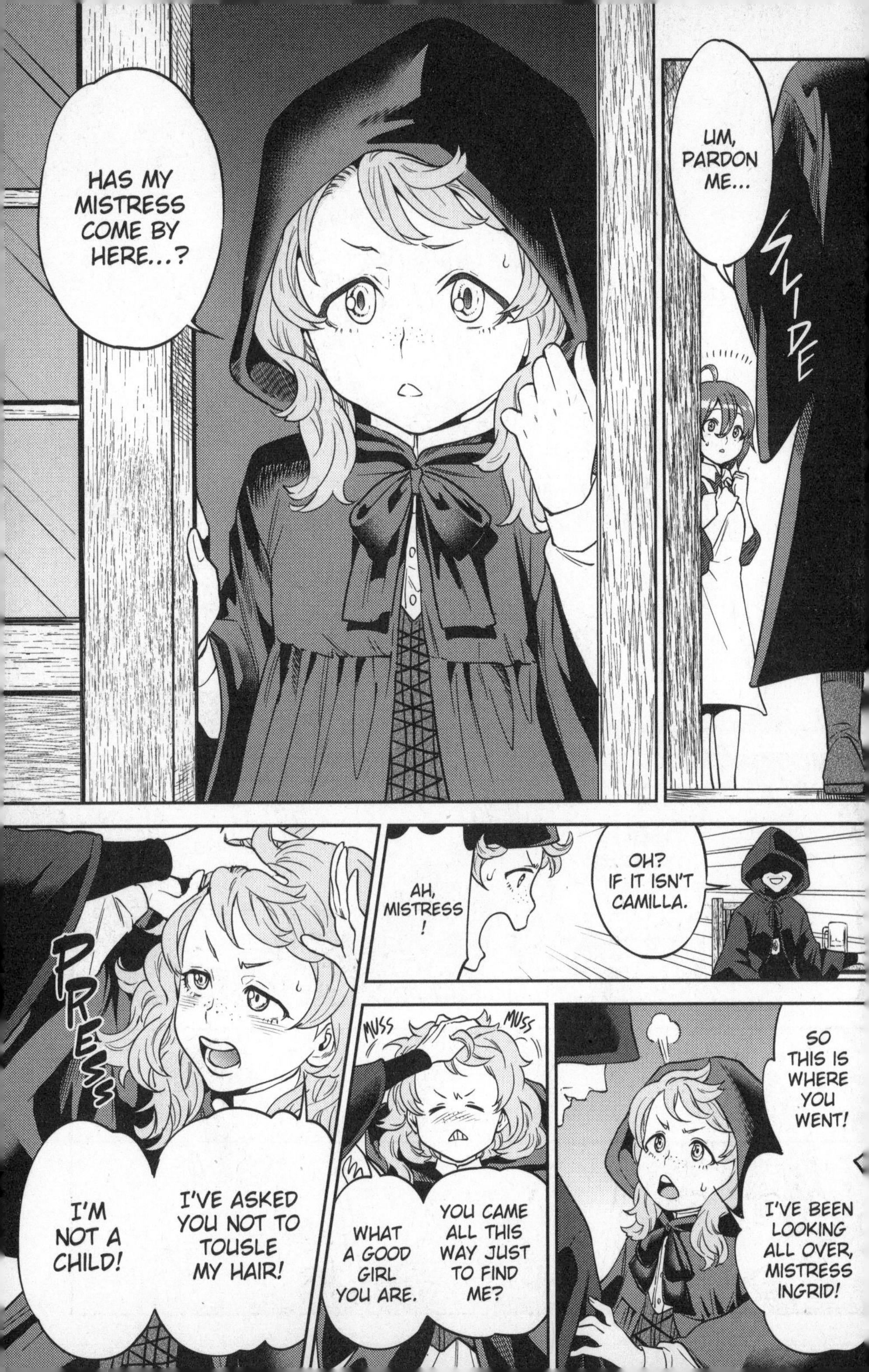
UM, PARDON ME...
SLIDE
HAS MY MISTRESS COME BY HERE...?
OH? IF IT ISN'T CAMILLA.
AH, MISTRESS!
SO THIS IS WHERE YOU WENT!
I'VE BEEN LOOKING ALL OVER, MISTRESS INGRID!
MUSS
MUSS
YOU CAME ALL THIS WAY JUST TO FIND ME?
WHAT A GOOD GIRL YOU ARE.
PRESS
I'VE ASKED YOU NOT TO TOUSLE MY HAIR!
I'M NOT A CHILD!

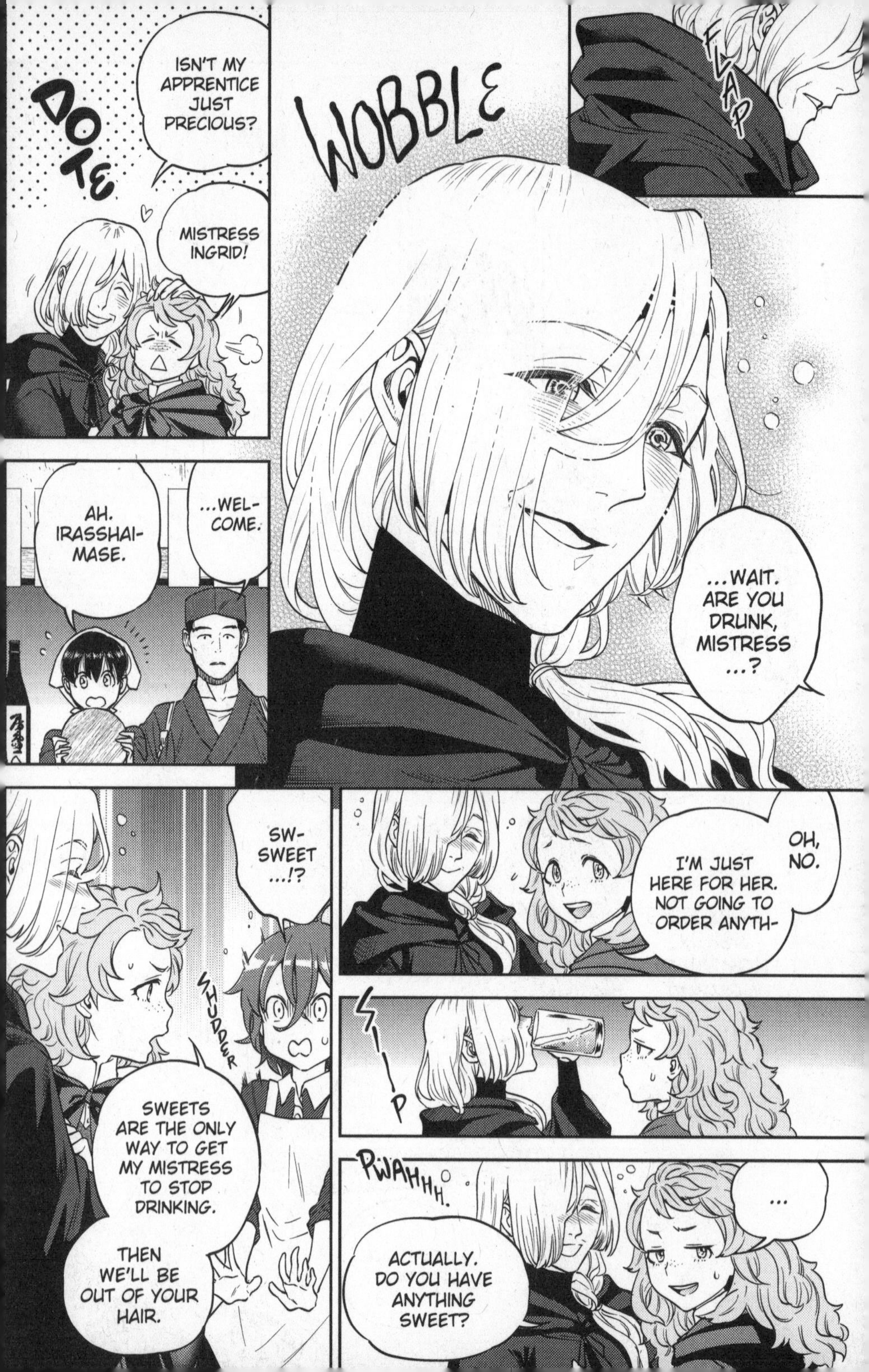
FLAP
WOBBLE
...WAIT. ARE YOU DRUNK, MISTRESS ...?
ISN'T MY APPRENTICE JUST PRECIOUS?
DOTE
MISTRESS INGRID!
...WEL- COME.
AH. IRASSHAI- MASE.
OH, NO.
I'M JUST HERE FOR HER. NOT GOING TO ORDER ANYTH-
SIIIP
...
PWAHHH.
ACTUALLY. DO YOU HAVE ANYTHING SWEET?
SW- SWEET ...!?
SHUDDER
SWEETS ARE THE ONLY WAY TO GET MY MISTRESS TO STOP DRINKING.
THEN WE'LL BE OUT OF YOUR HAIR.

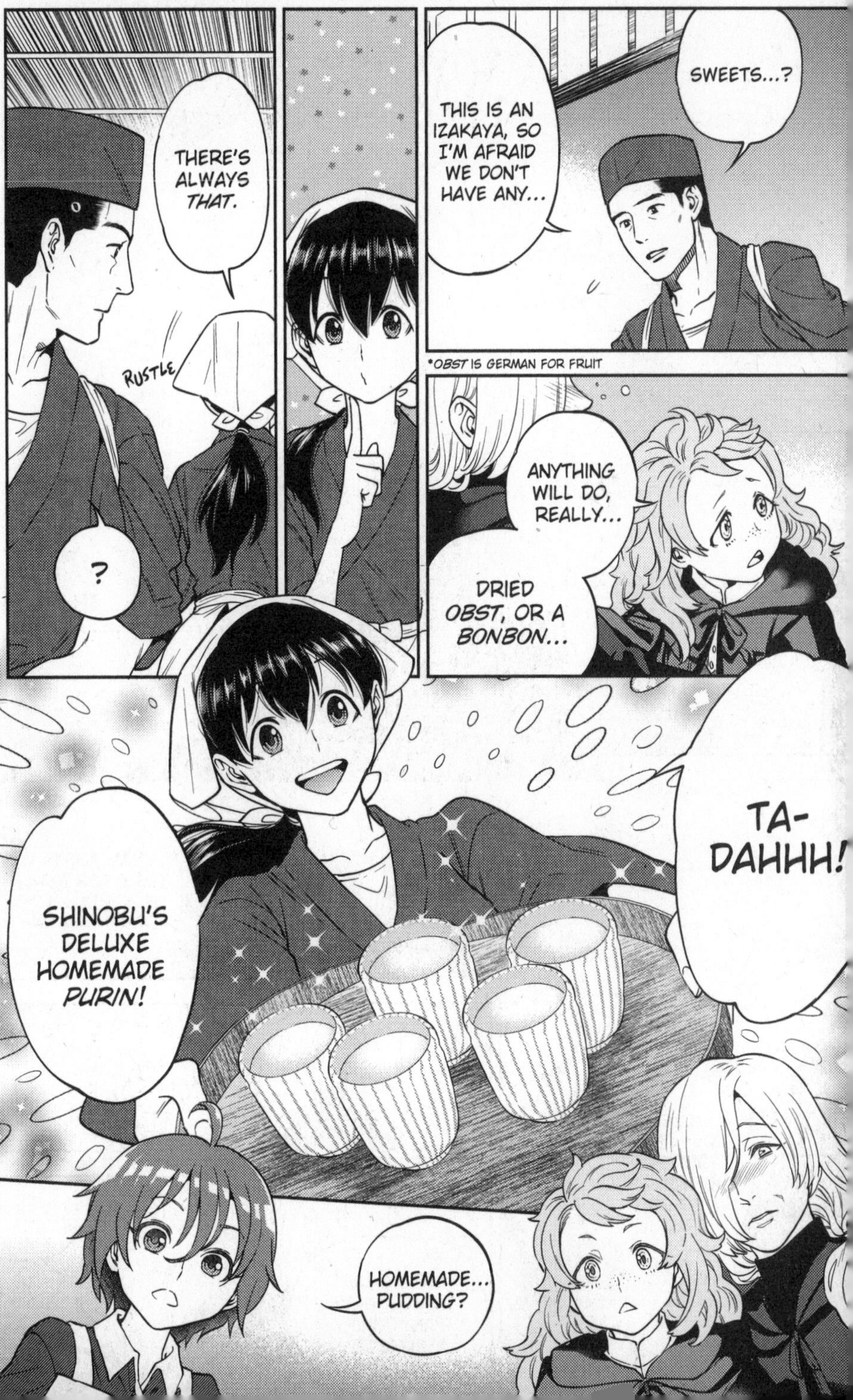
SWEETS...?
THIS IS AN IZAKAYA, SO I'M AFRAID WE DON'T HAVE ANY...
*OBST IS GERMAN FOR FRUIT
ANYTHING WILL DO, REALLY...
DRIED *OBST*, OR A BONBON...
THERE'S ALWAYS *THAT*.
RUSTLE
?
TA-DAHHH!
SHINOBU'S DELUXE HOMEMADE *PURIN*!
HOMEMADE... PUDDING?

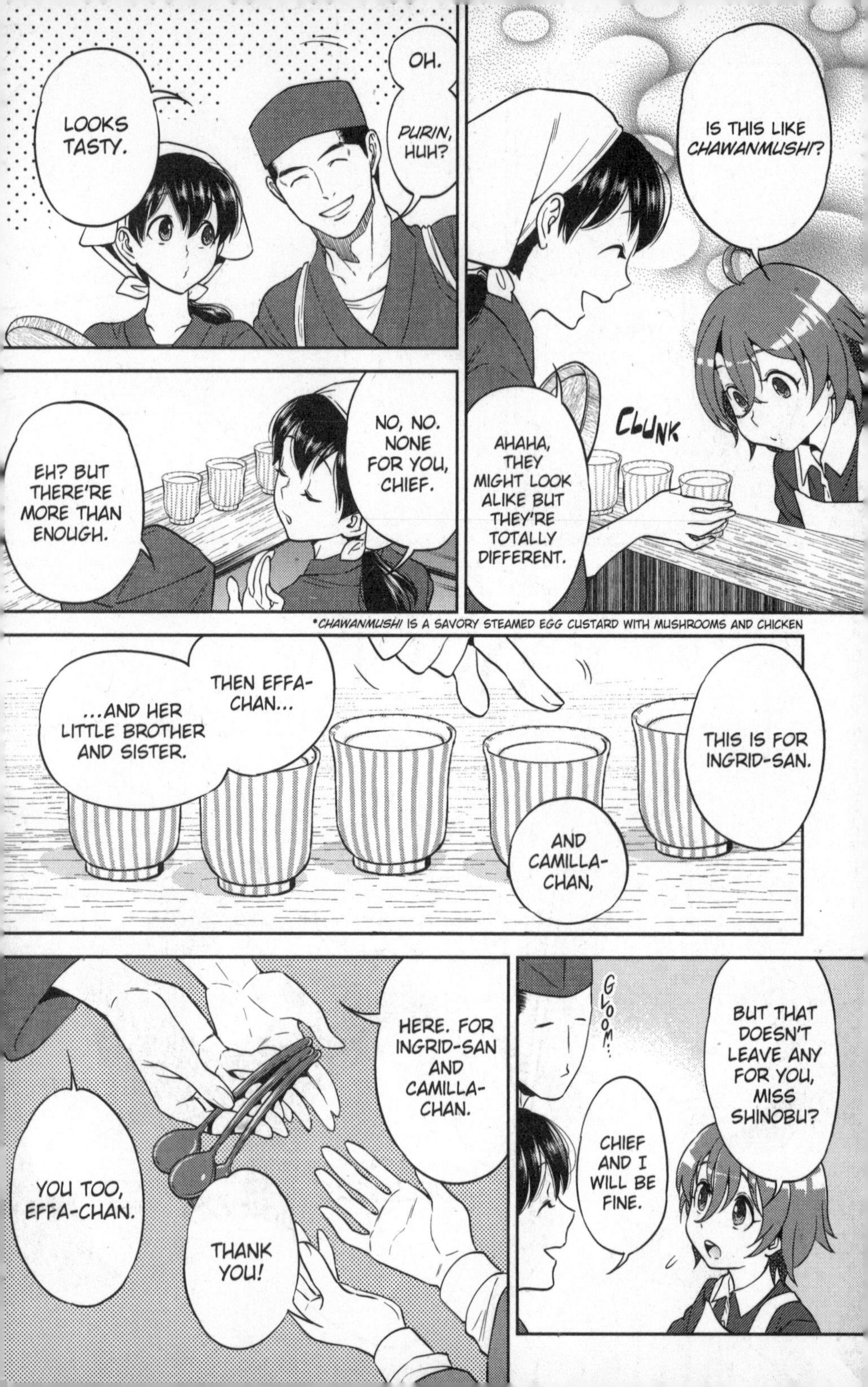
IS THIS LIKE CHAWANMUSHI?
CLUNK
AHAHA, THEY MIGHT LOOK ALIKE BUT THEY'RE TOTALLY DIFFERENT.
OH.
PURIN, HUH?
LOOKS TASTY.
NO, NO. NONE FOR YOU, CHIEF.
EH? BUT THERE'RE MORE THAN ENOUGH.
THIS IS FOR INGRID-SAN.
AND CAMILLA-CHAN,
THEN EFFA-CHAN...
...AND HER LITTLE BROTHER AND SISTER.
BUT THAT DOESN'T LEAVE ANY FOR YOU, MISS SHINOBU?
GLOOM...
CHIEF AND I WILL BE FINE.
HERE. FOR INGRID-SAN AND CAMILLA-CHAN.
YOU TOO, EFFA-CHAN.
THANK YOU!

*CHAWANMUSHI IS A SAVORY STEAMED EGG CUSTARD WITH MUSHROOMS AND CHICKEN

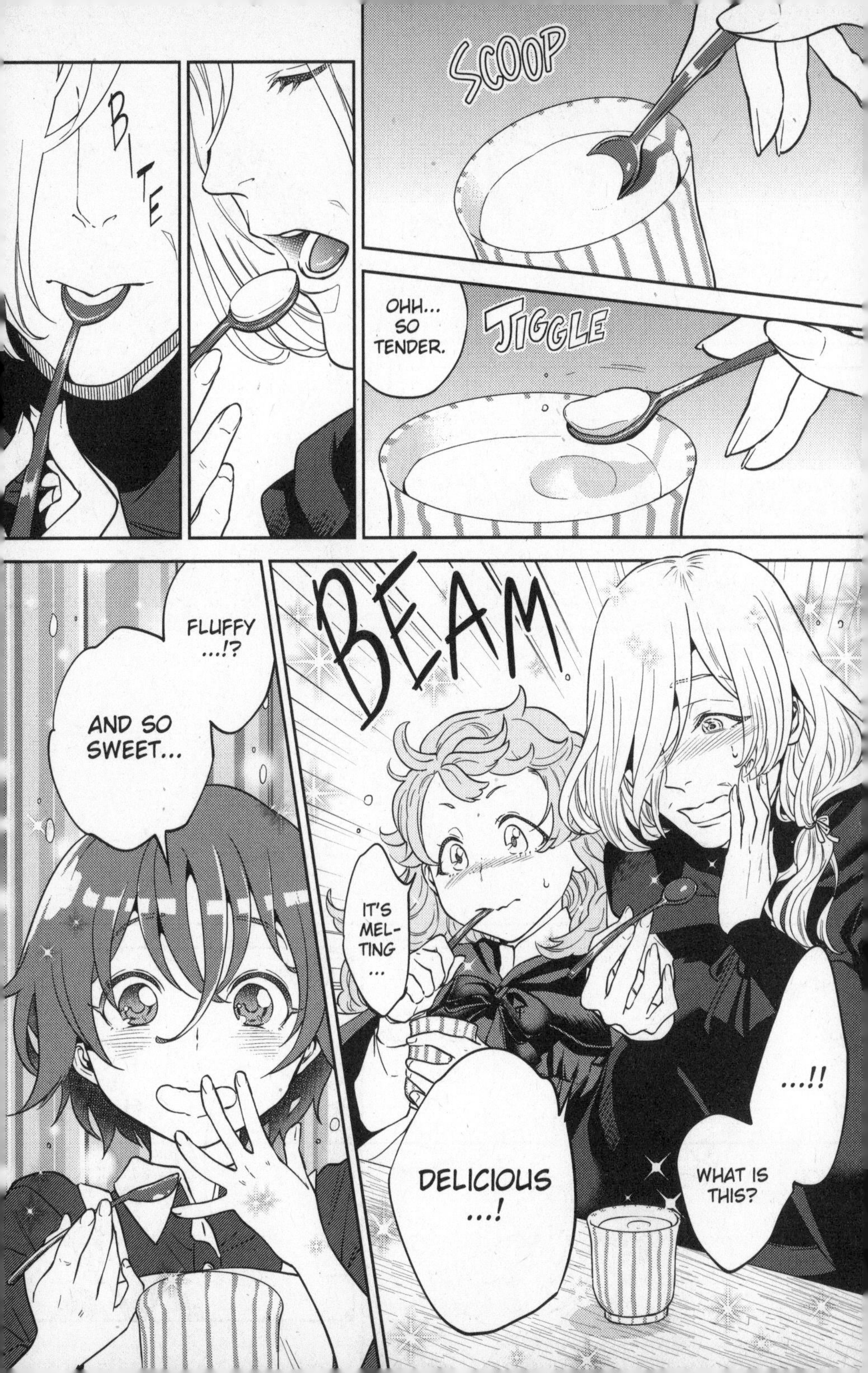
SCOOP
OHH... SO TENDER.
JIGGLE
BITE
BEAM
...!!
WHAT IS THIS?
IT'S MEL-TING...
DELICIOUS...!
FLUFFY...!?
AND SO SWEET...

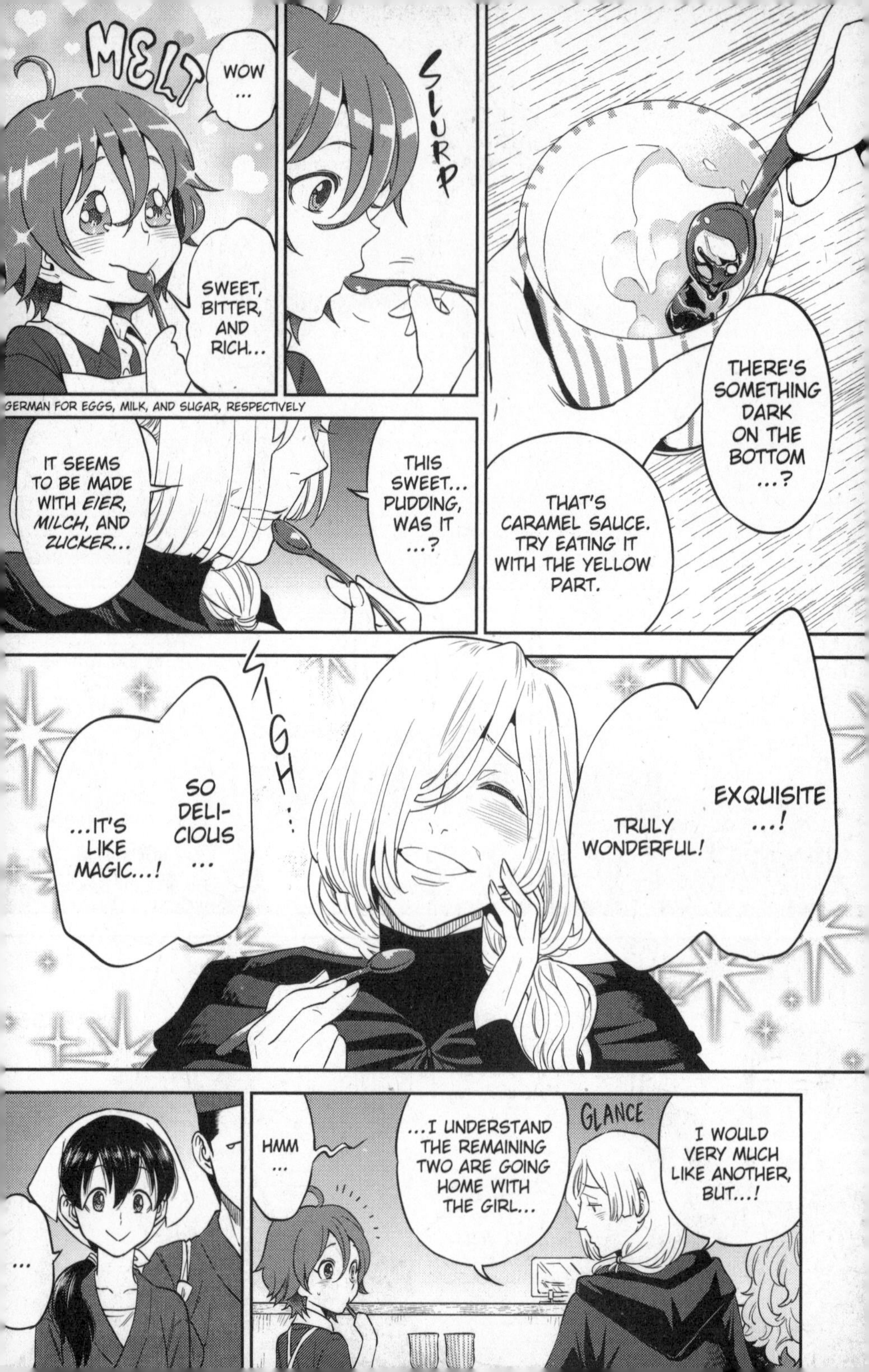
THERE'S SOMETHING DARK ON THE BOTTOM ...?
THAT'S CARAMEL SAUCE. TRY EATING IT WITH THE YELLOW PART.
SLURP
WOW ...
MELT
SWEET, BITTER, AND RICH...
THIS SWEET... PUDDING, WAS IT ...?
IT SEEMS TO BE MADE WITH *EIER*, *MILCH*, AND *ZUCKER*...
GERMAN FOR EGGS, MILK, AND SUGAR, RESPECTIVELY
EXQUISITE ...!
TRULY WONDERFUL!
SIGH...
SO DELICIOUS ...
...IT'S LIKE MAGIC...!
GLANCE
I WOULD VERY MUCH LIKE ANOTHER, BUT...!
...I UNDERSTAND THE REMAINING TWO ARE GOING HOME WITH THE GIRL...
HMM ...
...

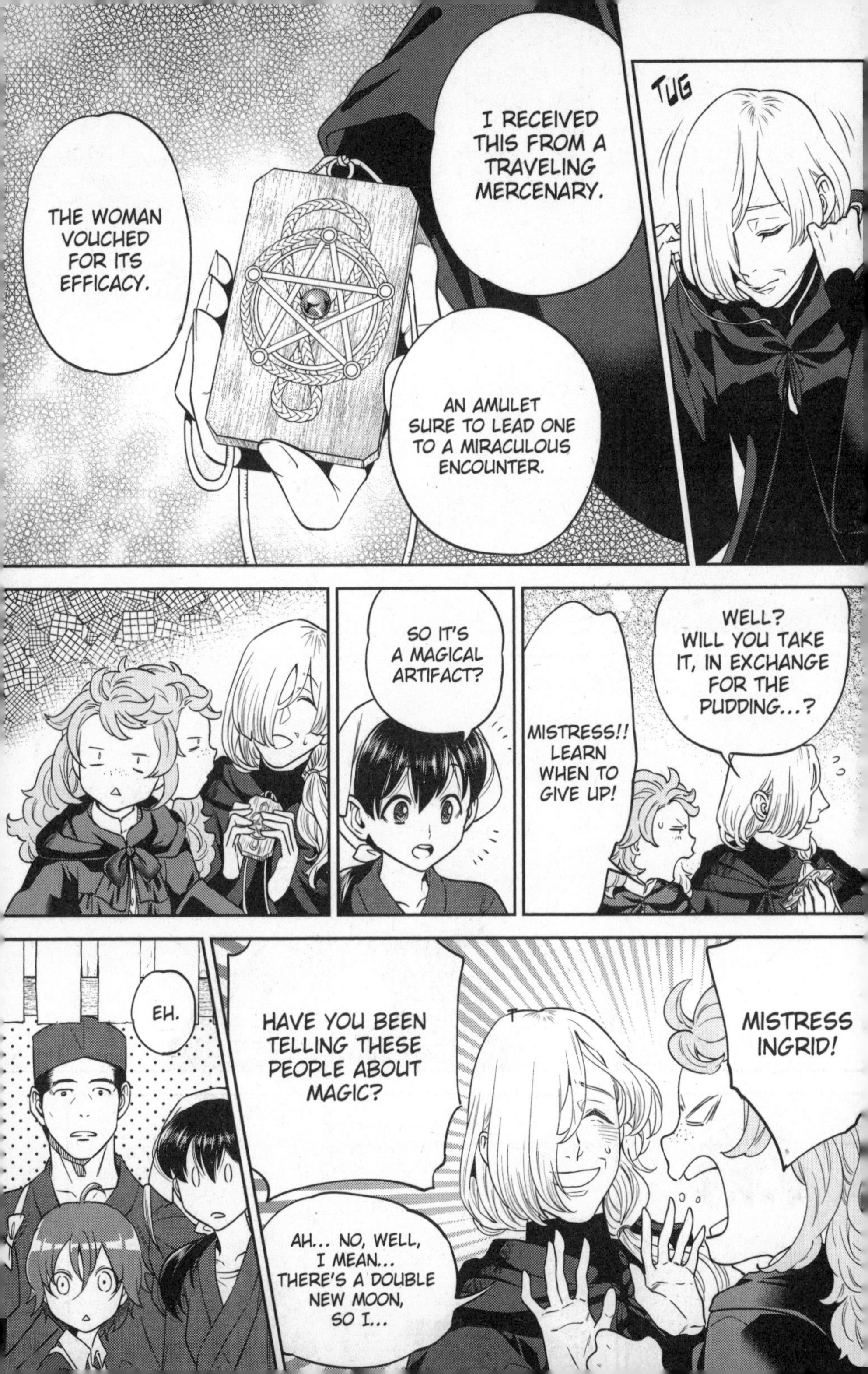
TUG
I RECEIVED THIS FROM A TRAVELING MERCENARY.
AN AMULET SURE TO LEAD ONE TO A MIRACULOUS ENCOUNTER.
THE WOMAN VOUCHED FOR ITS EFFICACY.
WELL? WILL YOU TAKE IT, IN EXCHANGE FOR THE PUDDING...?
MISTRESS!! LEARN WHEN TO GIVE UP!
SO IT'S A MAGICAL ARTIFACT?
MISTRESS INGRID!
HAVE YOU BEEN TELLING THESE PEOPLE ABOUT MAGIC?
AH... NO, WELL, I MEAN... THERE'S A DOUBLE NEW MOON, SO I...
EH.

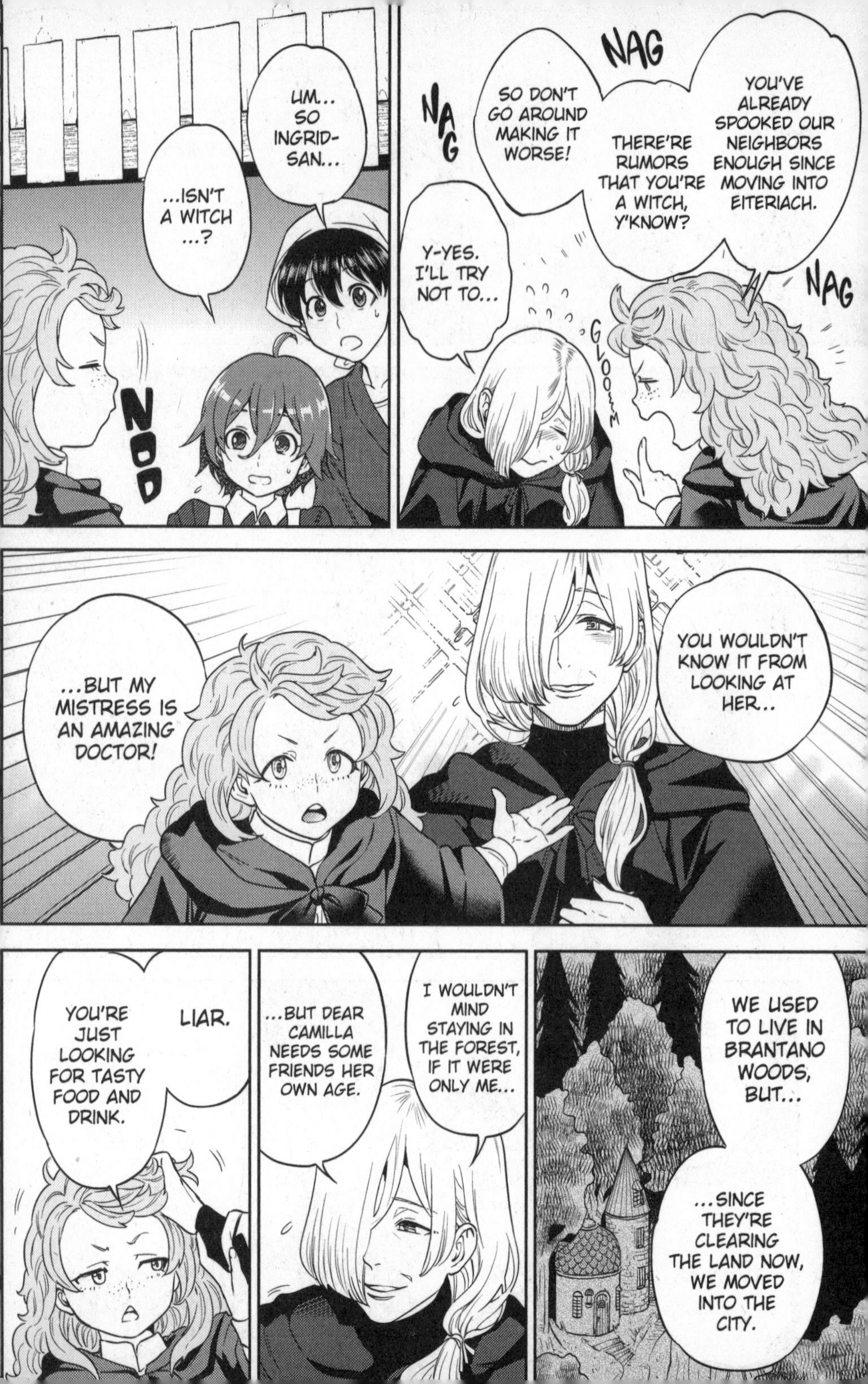
YOU'VE ALREADY SPOOKED OUR NEIGHBORS ENOUGH SINCE MOVING INTO EITERIACH.
NAG
THERE'RE RUMORS THAT YOU'RE A WITCH, Y'KNOW?
SO DON'T GO AROUND MAKING IT WORSE!
NAG
NAG
Y-YES. I'LL TRY NOT TO...
GLOOOM
UM... SO INGRID-SAN...
...ISN'T A WITCH ...?
NOD
YOU WOULDN'T KNOW IT FROM LOOKING AT HER...
...BUT MY MISTRESS IS AN AMAZING DOCTOR!
WE USED TO LIVE IN BRANTANO WOODS, BUT...
...SINCE THEY'RE CLEARING THE LAND NOW, WE MOVED INTO THE CITY.
I WOULDN'T MIND STAYING IN THE FOREST, IF IT WERE ONLY ME...
...BUT DEAR CAMILLA NEEDS SOME FRIENDS HER OWN AGE.
LIAR.
YOU'RE JUST LOOKING FOR TASTY FOOD AND DRINK.

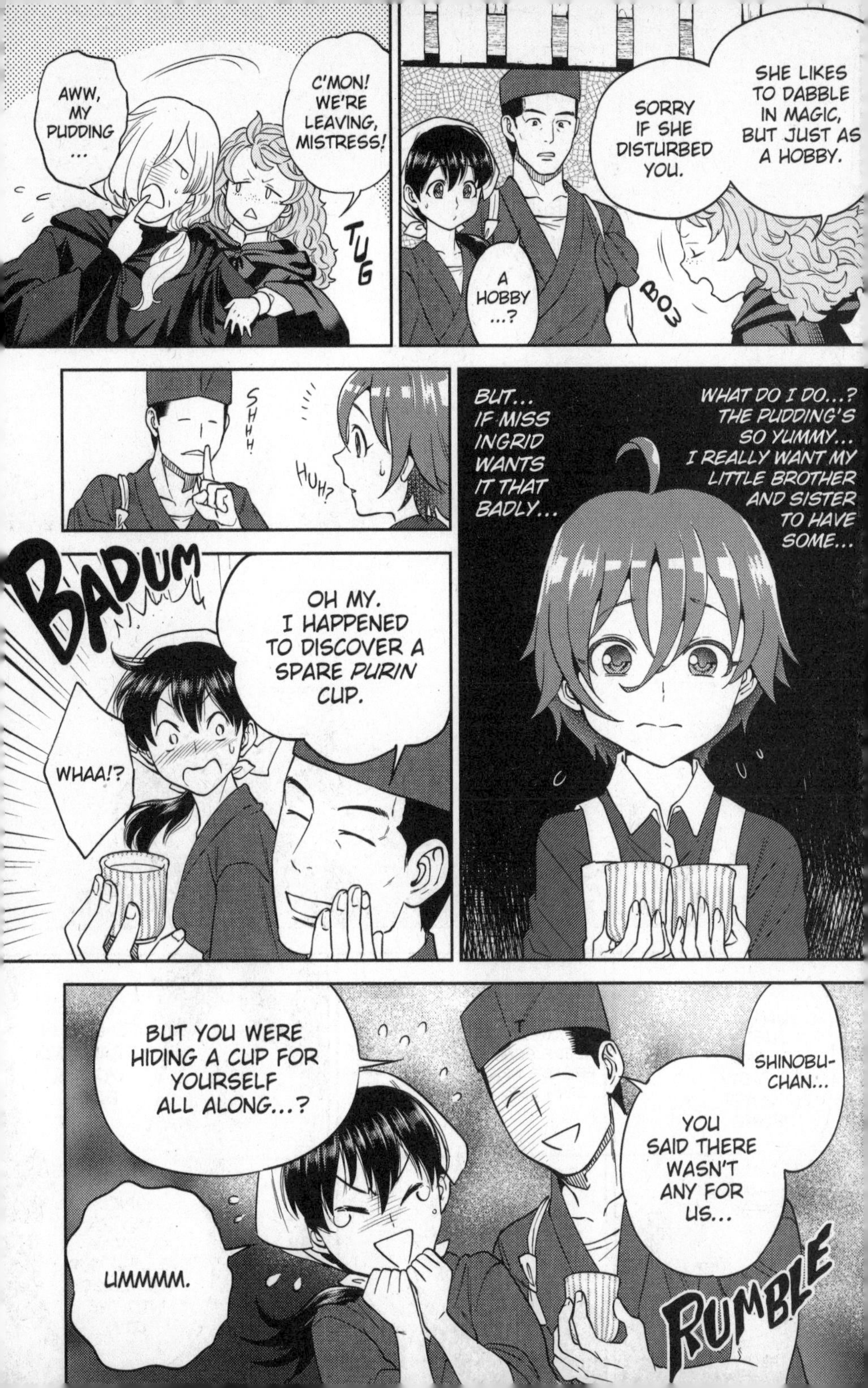
SHE LIKES TO DABBLE IN MAGIC, BUT JUST AS A HOBBY.
SORRY IF SHE DISTURBED YOU.
A HOBBY ...?
C'MON! WE'RE LEAVING, MISTRESS!
TUG
AWW, MY PUDDING ...
WHAT DO I DO...? THE PUDDING'S SO YUMMY... I REALLY WANT MY LITTLE BROTHER AND SISTER TO HAVE SOME...
BUT... IF MISS INGRID WANTS IT THAT BADLY...
SHHH
HUH?
BADUM
OH MY. I HAPPENED TO DISCOVER A SPARE *PURIN* CUP.
WHAA!?
SHINOBU-CHAN...
YOU SAID THERE WASN'T ANY FOR US...
BUT YOU WERE HIDING A CUP FOR YOURSELF ALL ALONG...?
RUMBLE
UMMMM.

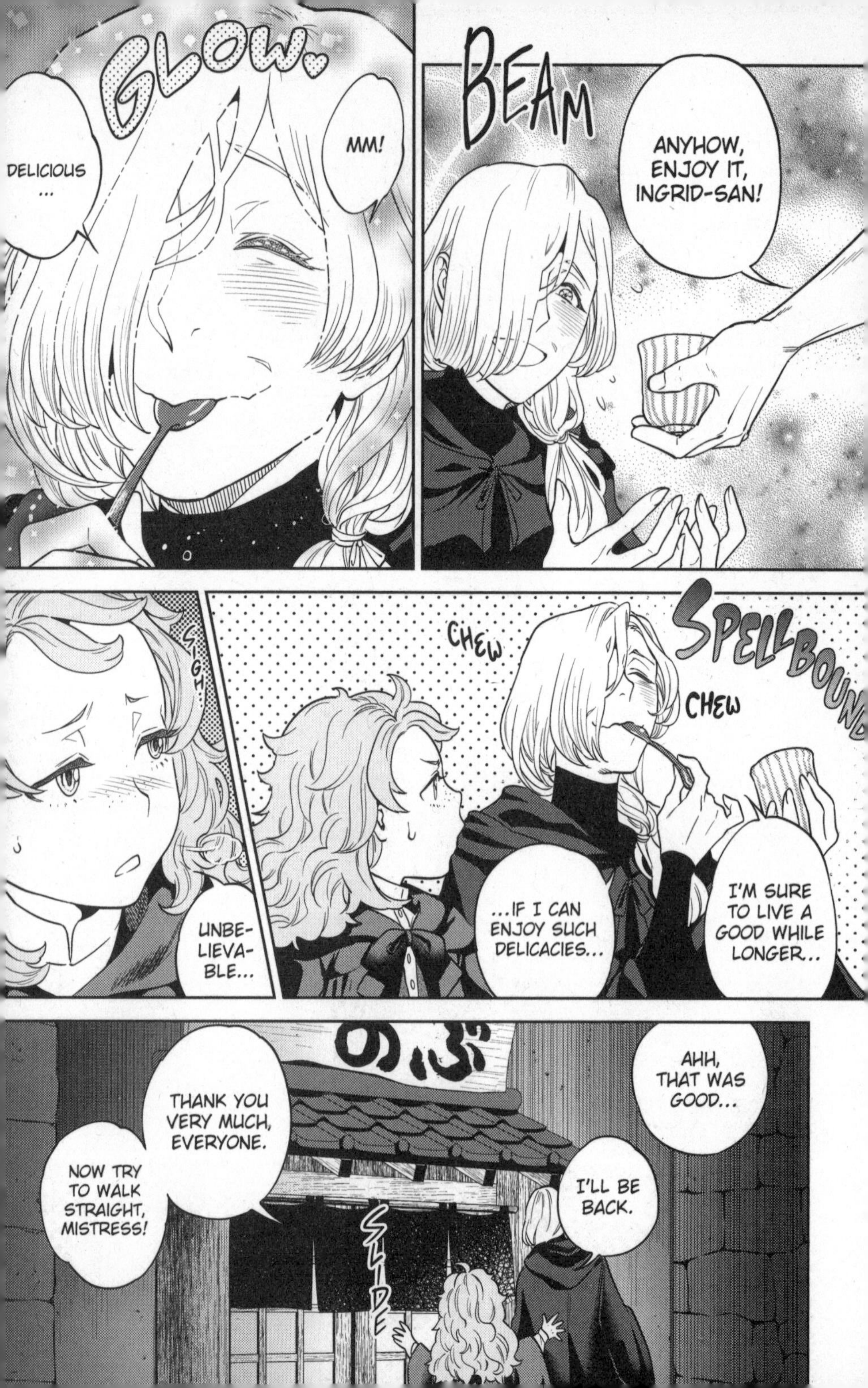
BEAM
ANYHOW, ENJOY IT, INGRID-SAN!
GLOW
MM!
DELICIOUS ...
SPELLBOUND
CHEW
CHEW
I'M SURE TO LIVE A GOOD WHILE LONGER...
...IF I CAN ENJOY SUCH DELICACIES...
UNBE-LIEVA-BLE...
SIGH...
のぶ
AHH, THAT WAS GOOD...
I'LL BE BACK.
THANK YOU VERY MUCH, EVERYONE.
NOW TRY TO WALK STRAIGHT, MISTRESS!
SLIDE

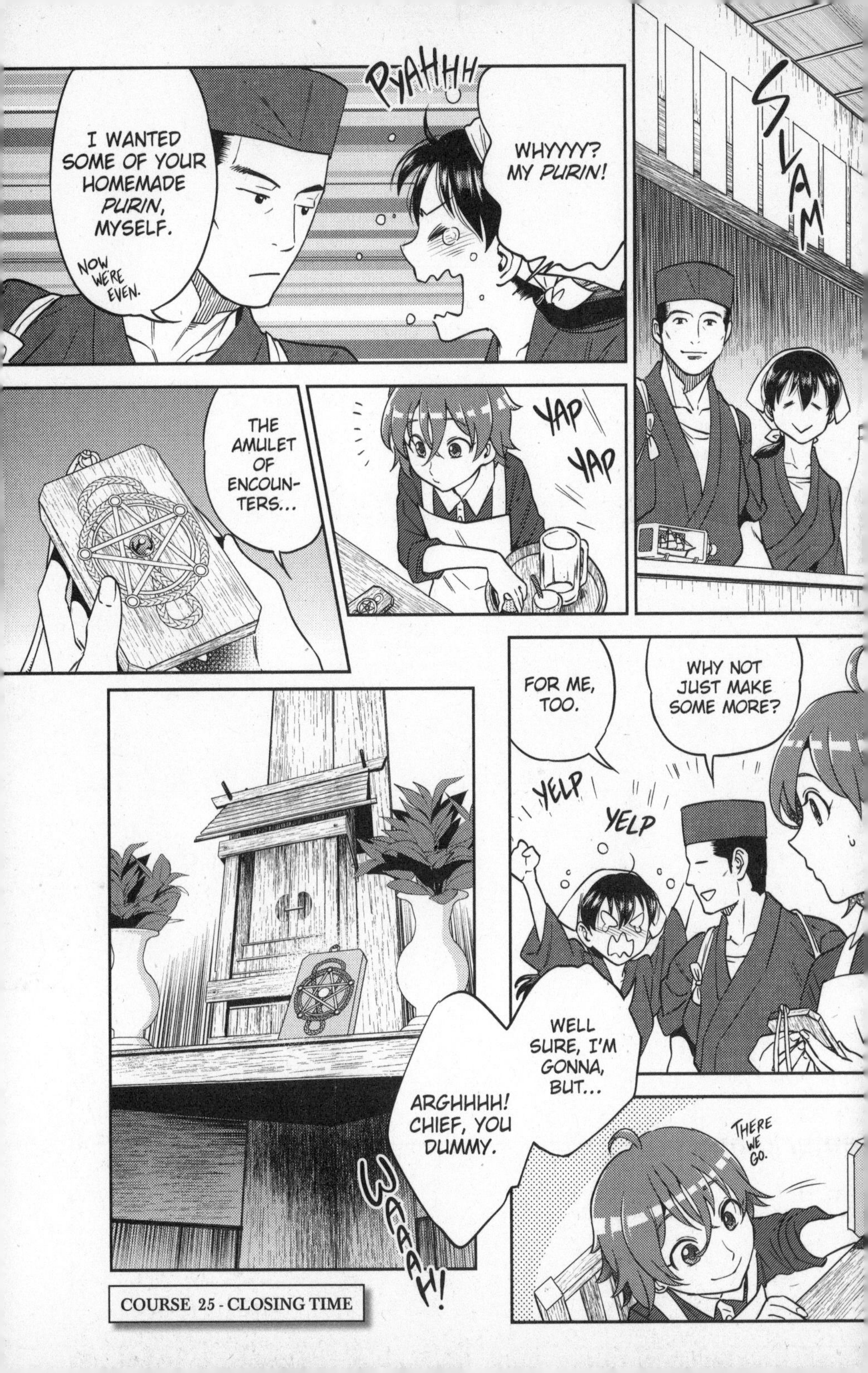
SLAM
PYAHHH
WHYYYY? MY PURIN!
I WANTED SOME OF YOUR HOMEMADE PURIN, MYSELF.
NOW WE'RE EVEN.
YAP
YAP
THE AMULET OF ENCOUN-TERS...
WHY NOT JUST MAKE SOME MORE?
FOR ME, TOO.
YELP
YELP
WELL SURE, I'M GONNA, BUT...
ARGHHHH! CHIEF, YOU DUMMY.
THERE WE GO.
WAAAAH!

COURSE 25 - CLOSING TIME

Shinobu's Deluxe Homemade Purin

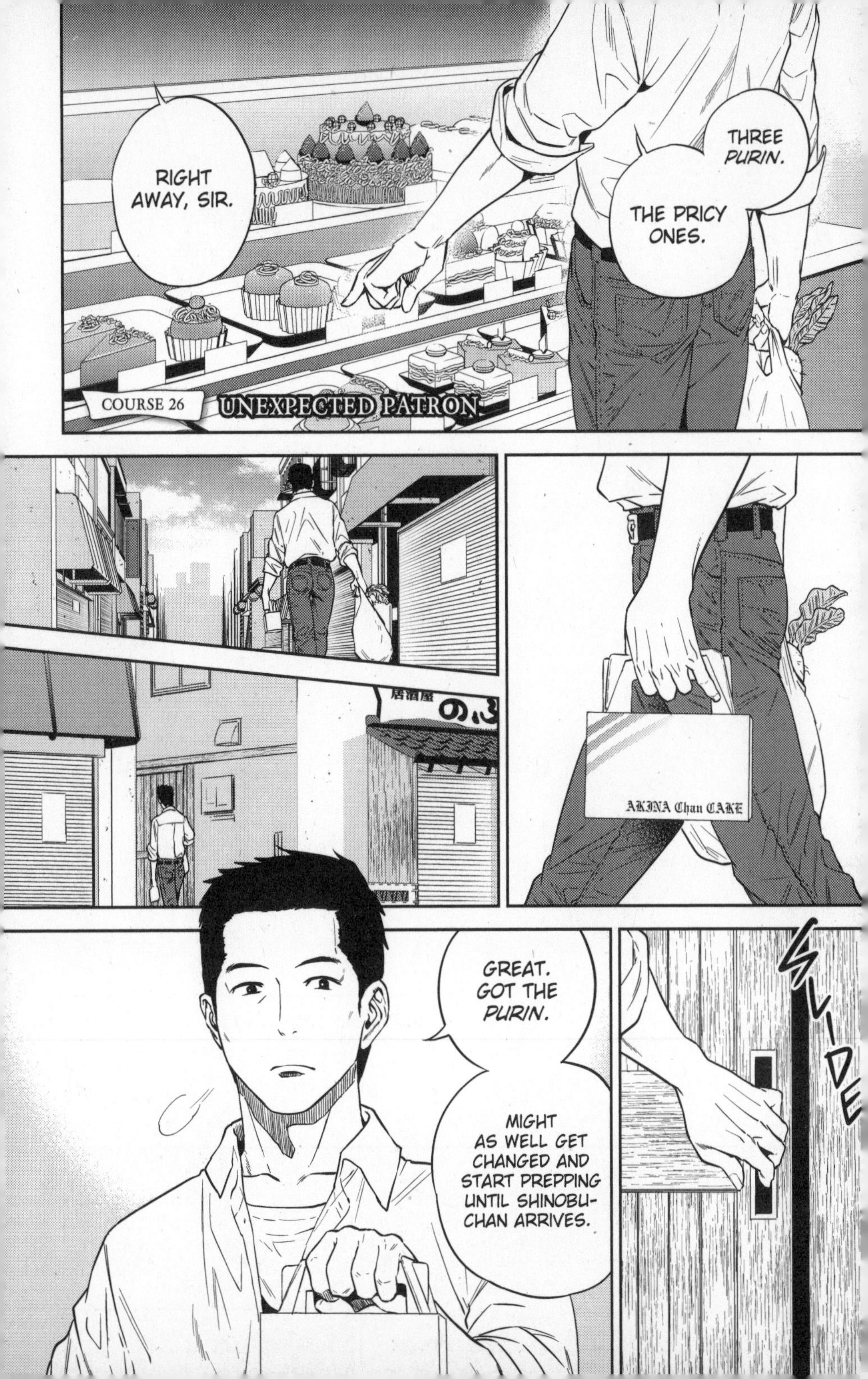
THREE PURIN.
THE PRICY ONES.
RIGHT AWAY, SIR.
COURSE 26
UNEXPECTED PATRON
AKINA Chan CAKE
SLIDE
GREAT. GOT THE PURIN.
MIGHT AS WELL GET CHANGED AND START PREPPING UNTIL SHINOBU-CHAN ARRIVES.

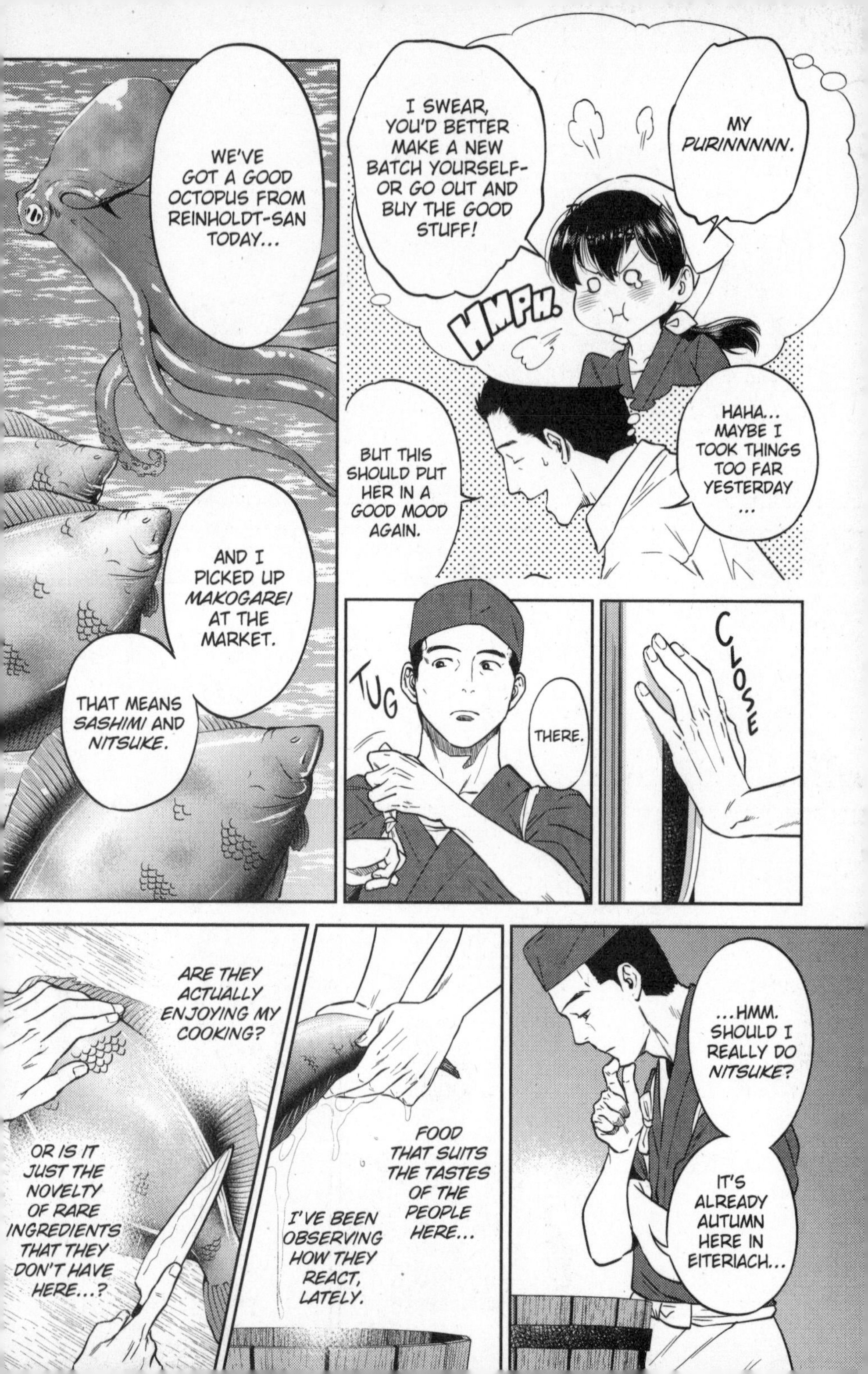
MY PURINNNNN.
I SWEAR, YOU'D BETTER MAKE A NEW BATCH YOURSELF- OR GO OUT AND BUY THE GOOD STUFF!
HMPH.
HAHA... MAYBE I TOOK THINGS TOO FAR YESTERDAY ...
BUT THIS SHOULD PUT HER IN A GOOD MOOD AGAIN.
CLOSE
TUG
THERE.
WE'VE GOT A GOOD OCTOPUS FROM REINHOLDT-SAN TODAY...
AND I PICKED UP MAKOGAREI AT THE MARKET.
THAT MEANS SASHIMI AND NITSUKE.
...HMM. SHOULD I REALLY DO NITSUKE?
IT'S ALREADY AUTUMN HERE IN EITERIACH...
FOOD THAT SUITS THE TASTES OF THE PEOPLE HERE...
I'VE BEEN OBSERVING HOW THEY REACT, LATELY.
ARE THEY ACTUALLY ENJOYING MY COOKING?
OR IS IT JUST THE NOVELTY OF RARE INGREDIENTS THAT THEY DON'T HAVE HERE...?

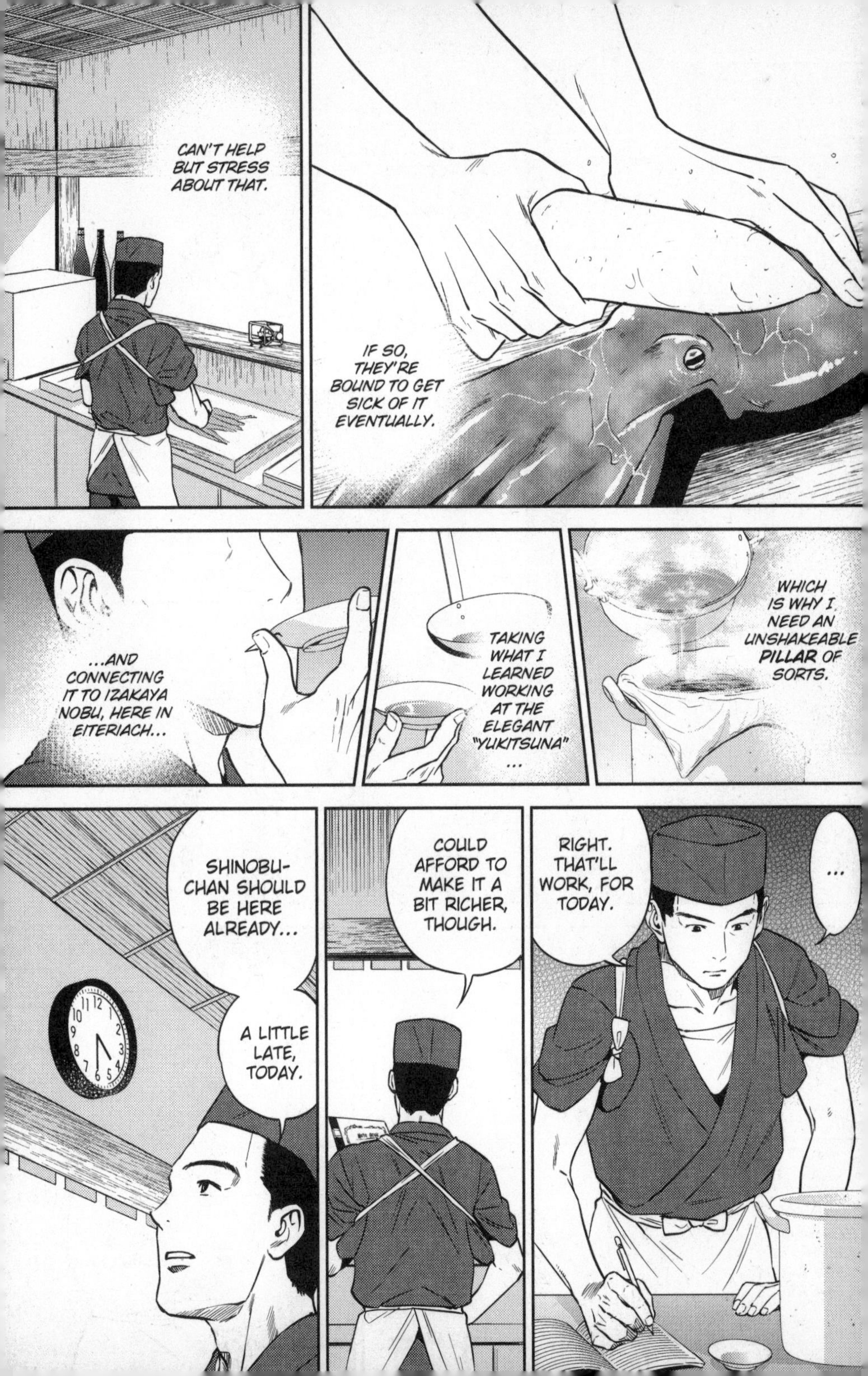
IF SO, THEY'RE BOUND TO GET SICK OF IT EVENTUALLY.
CAN'T HELP BUT STRESS ABOUT THAT.
WHICH IS WHY I NEED AN UNSHAKEABLE PILLAR OF SORTS.
TAKING WHAT I LEARNED WORKING AT THE ELEGANT "YUKITSUNA" ...
...AND CONNECTING IT TO IZAKAYA NOBU, HERE IN EITERIACH...
...
RIGHT. THAT'LL WORK, FOR TODAY.
COULD AFFORD TO MAKE IT A BIT RICHER, THOUGH.
SHINOBU-CHAN SHOULD BE HERE ALREADY...
A LITTLE LATE, TODAY.

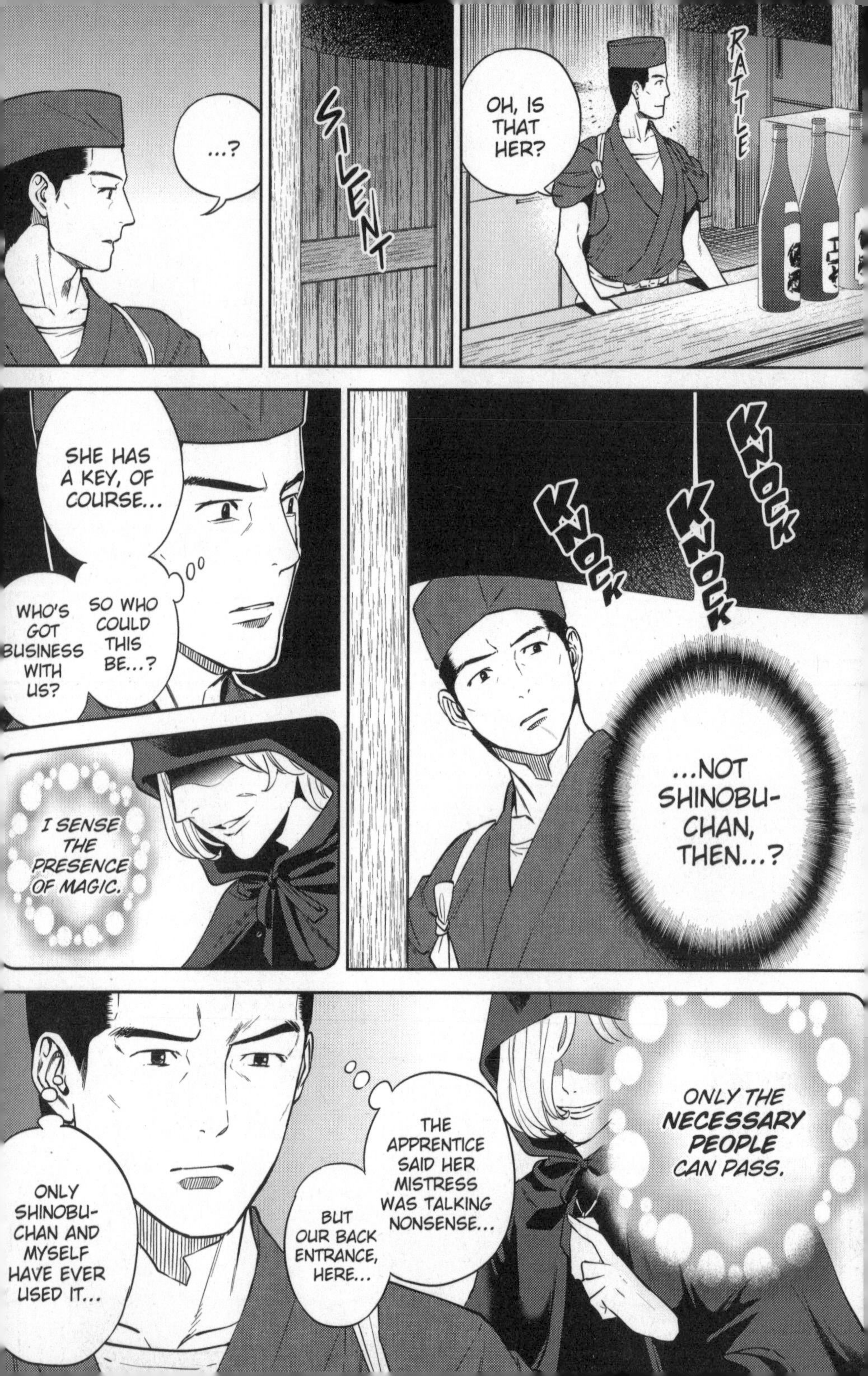
RATTLE
OH, IS THAT HER?
SILENT
...?
KNOCK
KNOCK
KNOCK
...NOT SHINOBU-CHAN, THEN...?
SHE HAS A KEY, OF COURSE...
SO WHO COULD THIS BE...?
WHO'S GOT BUSINESS WITH US?
I SENSE THE PRESENCE OF MAGIC.
ONLY THE **NECESSARY PEOPLE** CAN PASS.
THE APPRENTICE SAID HER MISTRESS WAS TALKING NONSENSE...
BUT OUR BACK ENTRANCE, HERE...
ONLY SHINOBU-CHAN AND MYSELF HAVE EVER USED IT...

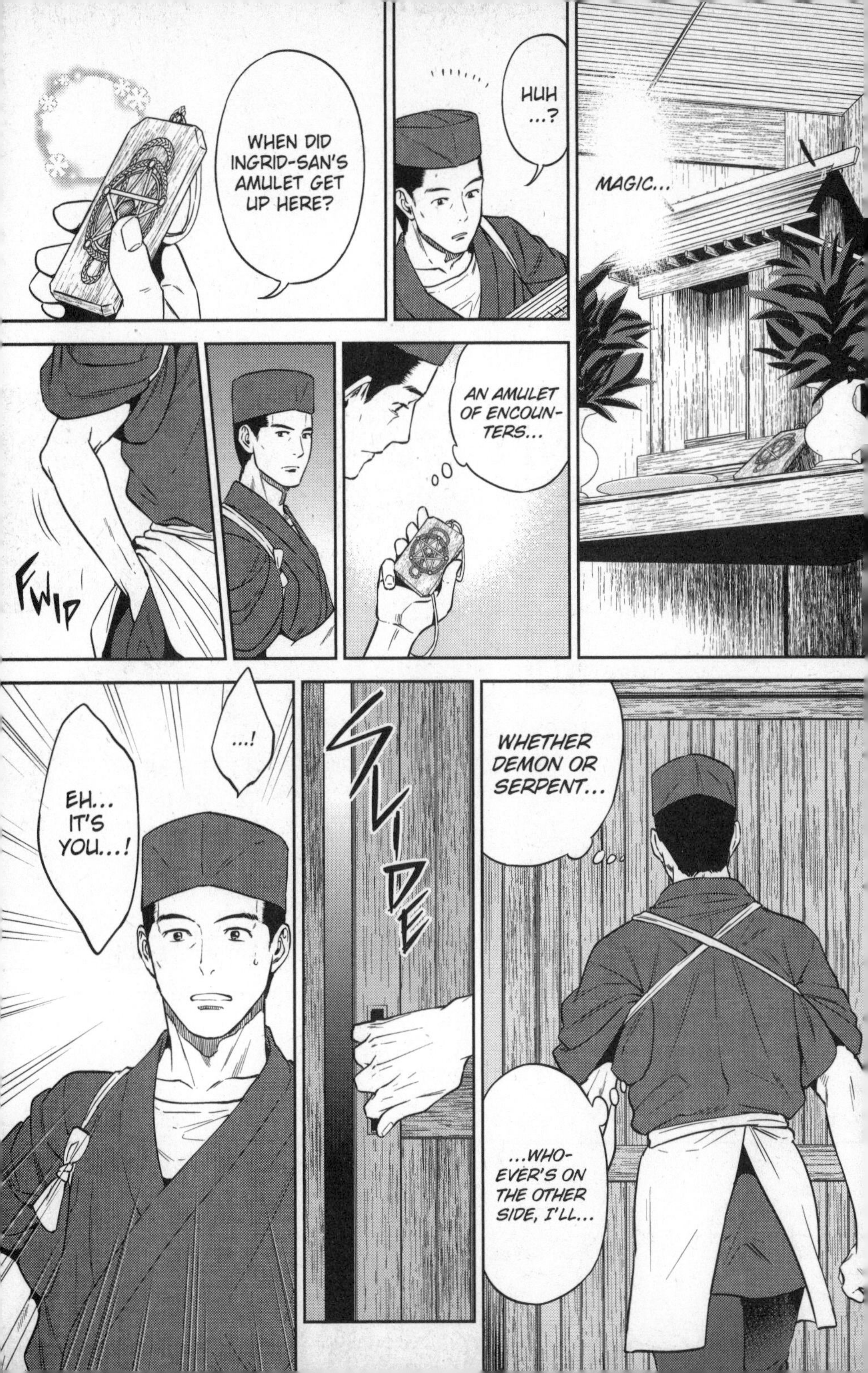
MAGIC...
HUH ...?
WHEN DID INGRID-SAN'S AMULET GET UP HERE?
AN AMULET OF ENCOUNTERS...
FWIP
WHETHER DEMON OR SERPENT...
...WHOEVER'S ON THE OTHER SIDE, I'LL...
SLIDE
...!
EH... IT'S YOU...!

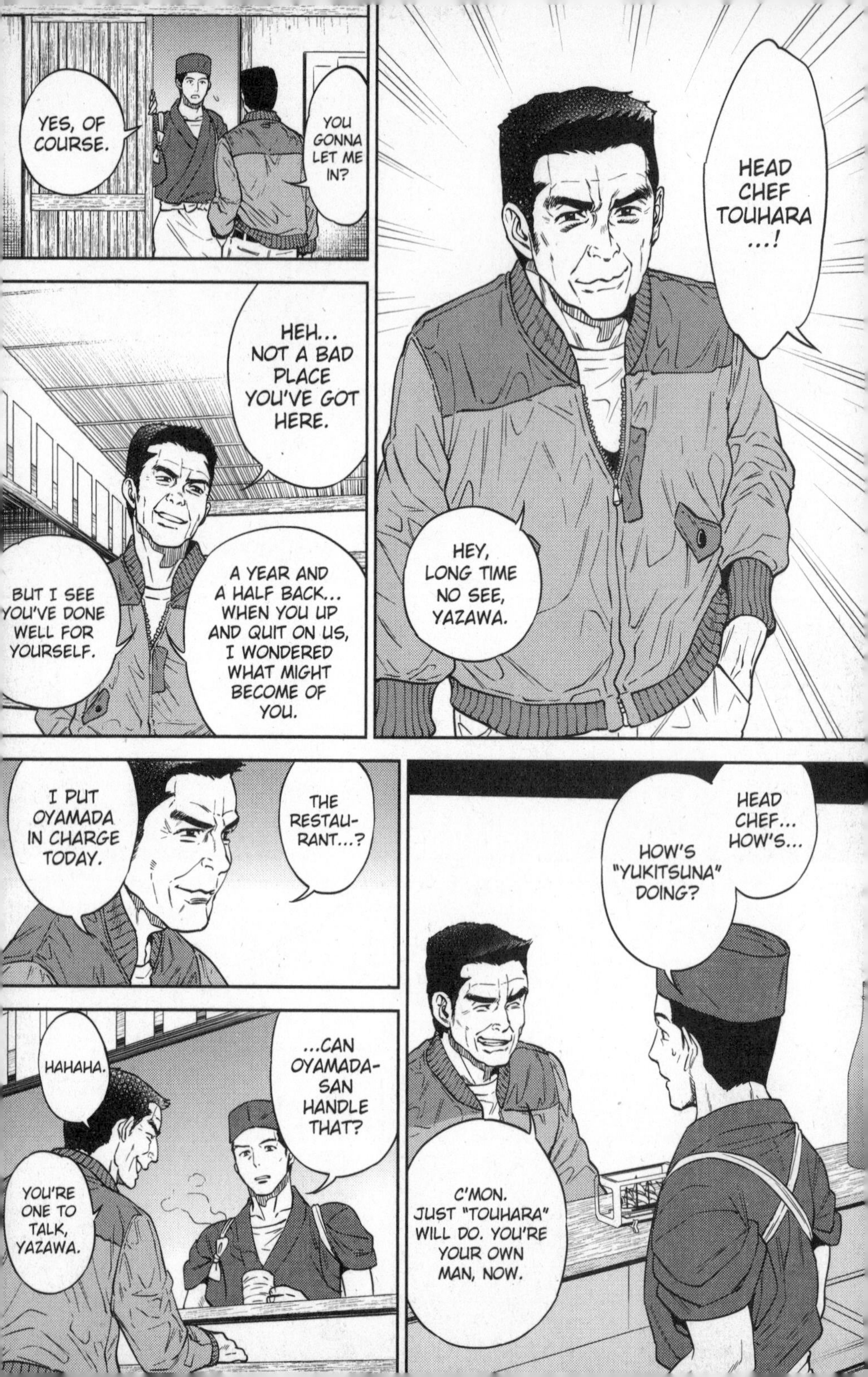
HEAD CHEF TOUHARA ...!
HEY, LONG TIME NO SEE, YAZAWA.
YOU GONNA LET ME IN?
YES, OF COURSE.
HEH... NOT A BAD PLACE YOU'VE GOT HERE.
A YEAR AND A HALF BACK... WHEN YOU UP AND QUIT ON US, I WONDERED WHAT MIGHT BECOME OF YOU.
BUT I SEE YOU'VE DONE WELL FOR YOURSELF.
HEAD CHEF... HOW'S...
HOW'S "YUKITSUNA" DOING?
C'MON. JUST "TOUHARA" WILL DO. YOU'RE YOUR OWN MAN, NOW.
THE RESTAU-RANT...?
I PUT OYAMADA IN CHARGE TODAY.
...CAN OYAMADA-SAN HANDLE THAT?
HAHAHA.
YOU'RE ONE TO TALK, YAZAWA.

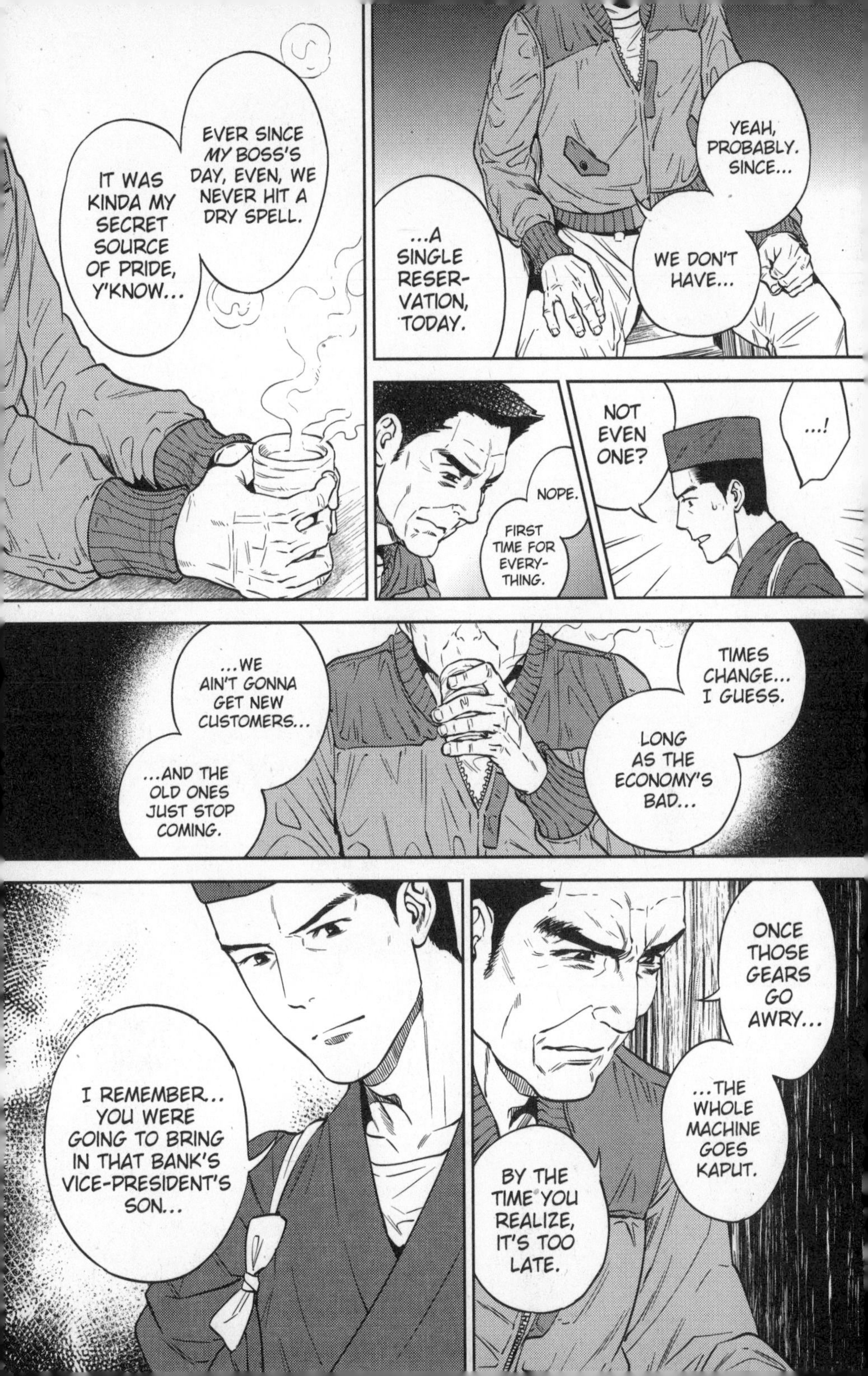
YEAH, PROBABLY. SINCE...
WE DON'T HAVE...
...A SINGLE RESER-VATION, TODAY.
...!
NOT EVEN ONE?
NOPE.
FIRST TIME FOR EVERY-THING.
EVER SINCE MY BOSS'S DAY, EVEN, WE NEVER HIT A DRY SPELL.
IT WAS KINDA MY SECRET SOURCE OF PRIDE, Y'KNOW...
TIMES CHANGE... I GUESS.
LONG AS THE ECONOMY'S BAD...
...WE AIN'T GONNA GET NEW CUSTOMERS...
...AND THE OLD ONES JUST STOP COMING.
ONCE THOSE GEARS GO AWRY...
...THE WHOLE MACHINE GOES KAPUT.
BY THE TIME YOU REALIZE, IT'S TOO LATE.
I REMEMBER... YOU WERE GOING TO BRING IN THAT BANK'S VICE-PRESIDENT'S SON...

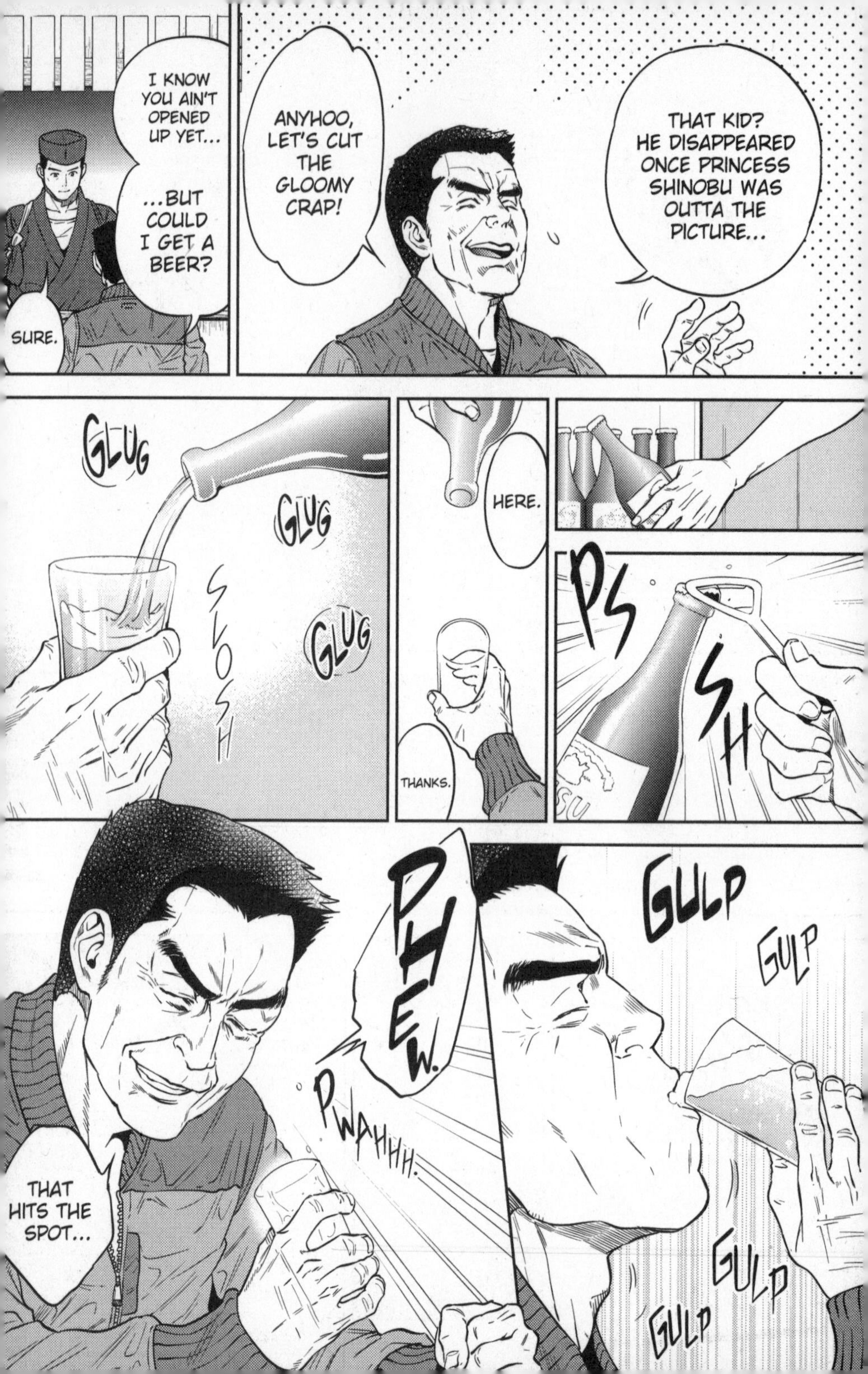
THAT KID? HE DISAPPEARED ONCE PRINCESS SHINOBU WAS OUTTA THE PICTURE...
ANYHOO, LET'S CUT THE GLOOMY CRAP!
I KNOW YOU AIN'T OPENED UP YET...
...BUT COULD I GET A BEER?
SURE.
PSSH
HERE.
THANKS.
GLUG
GLUG
SLOSH
GLUG
GULP
GULP
GULP
GULP
PHEW.
PWAHHH.
THAT HITS THE SPOT...

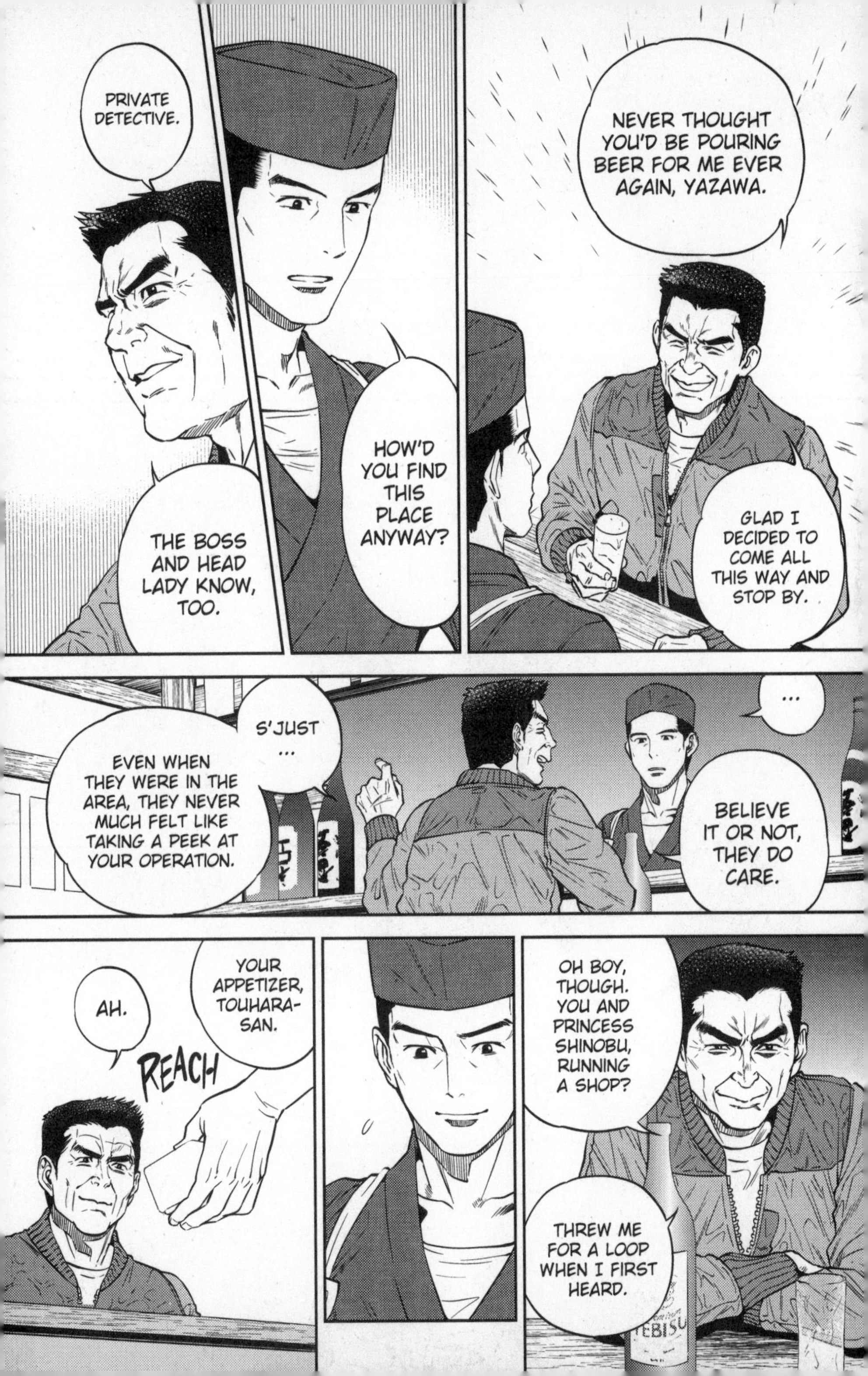
NEVER THOUGHT YOU'D BE POURING BEER FOR ME EVER AGAIN, YAZAWA.
GLAD I DECIDED TO COME ALL THIS WAY AND STOP BY.
HOW'D YOU FIND THIS PLACE ANYWAY?
PRIVATE DETECTIVE.
THE BOSS AND HEAD LADY KNOW, TOO.
...
BELIEVE IT OR NOT, THEY DO CARE.
S'JUST ...
EVEN WHEN THEY WERE IN THE AREA, THEY NEVER MUCH FELT LIKE TAKING A PEEK AT YOUR OPERATION.
OH BOY, THOUGH. YOU AND PRINCESS SHINOBU, RUNNING A SHOP?
THREW ME FOR A LOOP WHEN I FIRST HEARD.
YOUR APPETIZER, TOUHARA-SAN.
AH.
REACH

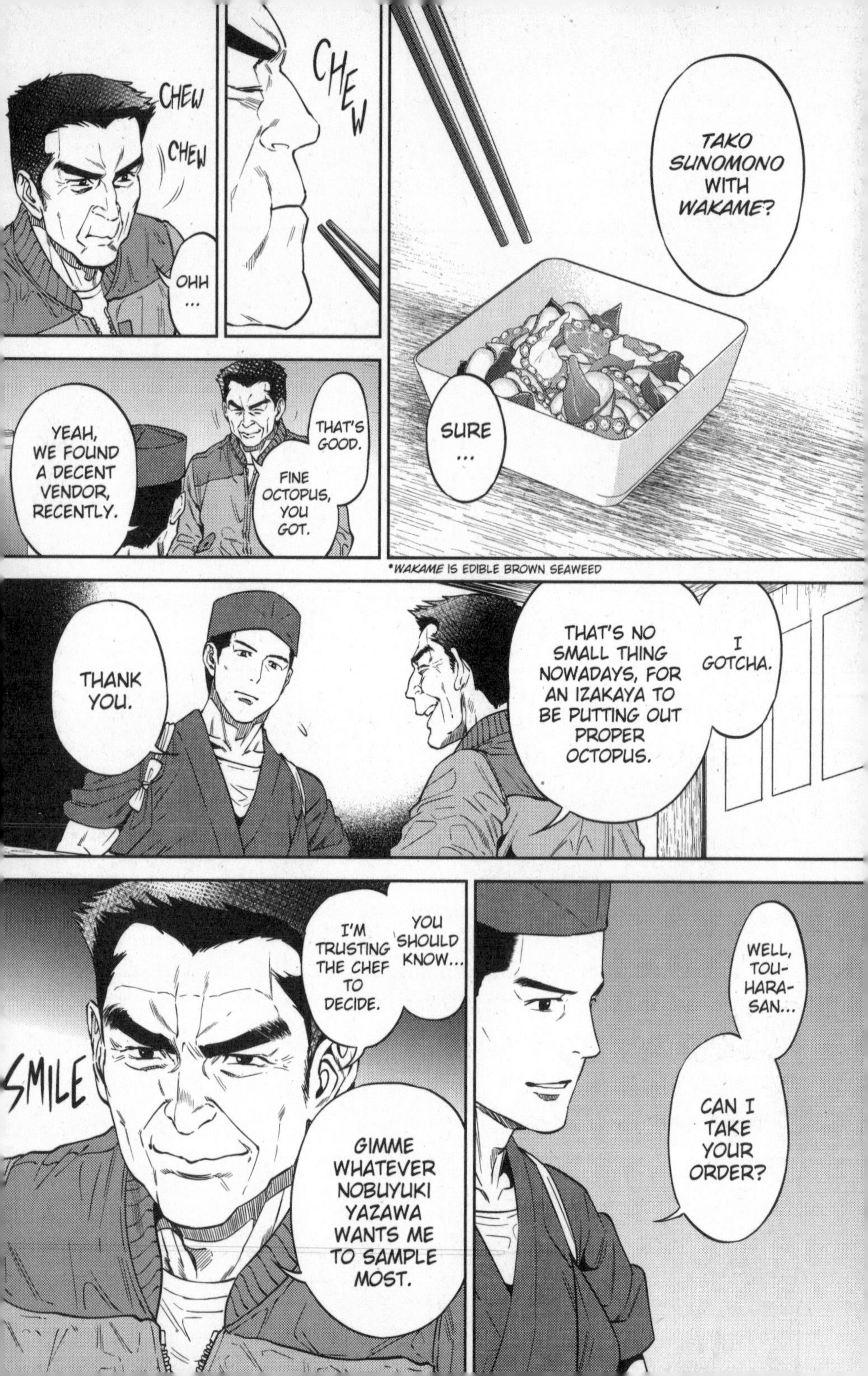
TAKO SUNOMONO WITH WAKAME?
SURE ...
CHEW
CHEW
CHEW
OHH ...
THAT'S GOOD.
FINE OCTOPUS, YOU GOT.
YEAH, WE FOUND A DECENT VENDOR, RECENTLY.
I GOTCHA.
THAT'S NO SMALL THING NOWADAYS, FOR AN IZAKAYA TO BE PUTTING OUT PROPER OCTOPUS.
THANK YOU.
WELL, TOU-HARA-SAN...
CAN I TAKE YOUR ORDER?
YOU SHOULD KNOW...
I'M TRUSTING THE CHEF TO DECIDE.
GIMME WHATEVER NOBUYUKI YAZAWA WANTS ME TO SAMPLE MOST.
SMILE

*WAKAME IS EDIBLE BROWN SEAWEED

...UNDER-
STOOD.

...!

YOU STARTED AT
YUKITSUNA RIGHT
OUTTA HIGH SCHOOL,
AFTER ALL.

SO I WANNA
SEE HOW YOU'VE
EXPANDED ON WHAT
YOUR OLD BOSS
TAUGHT YOU.

CHEW

CHEW

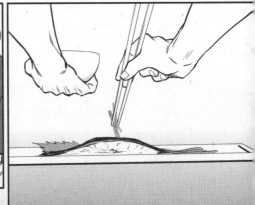

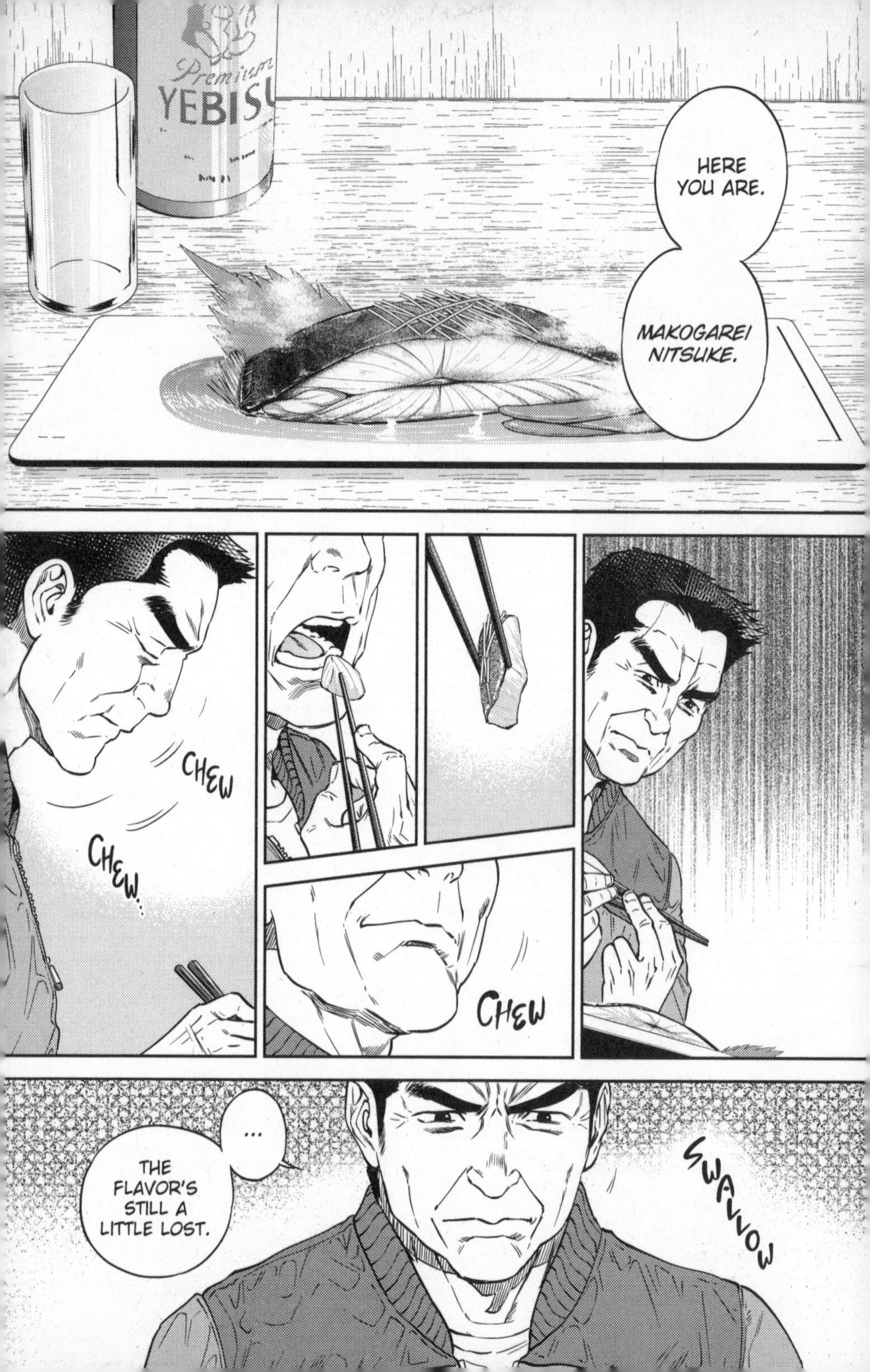
Premium
YEBISU
HERE YOU ARE.
MAKOGAREI NITSUKE.
CHEW
CHEW
CHEW...
SWALLOW
...
THE FLAVOR'S STILL A LITTLE LOST.

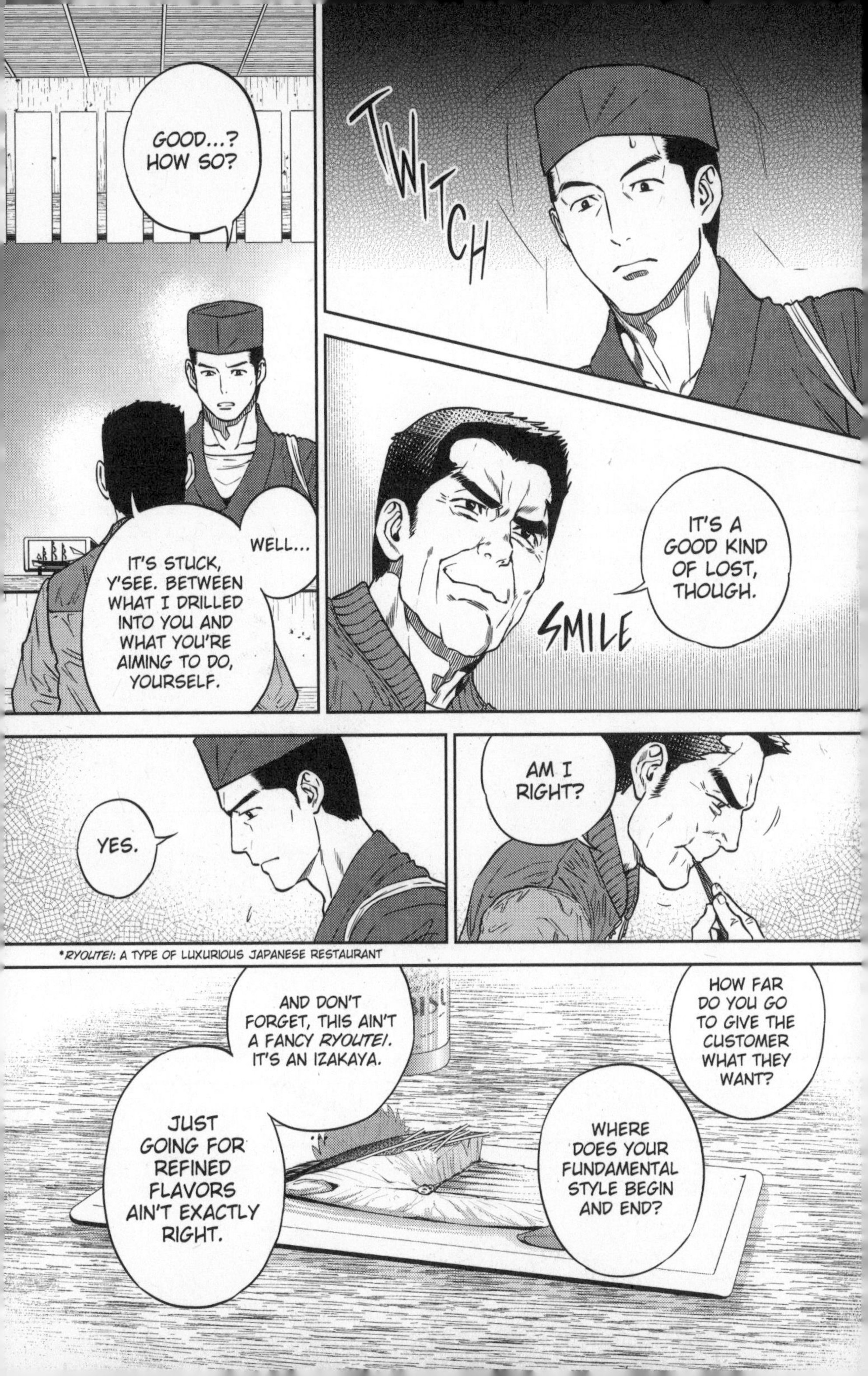
TWITCH
SMILE
IT'S A GOOD KIND OF LOST, THOUGH.
GOOD...? HOW SO?
WELL...
IT'S STUCK, Y'SEE. BETWEEN WHAT I DRILLED INTO YOU AND WHAT YOU'RE AIMING TO DO, YOURSELF.
AM I RIGHT?
YES.
*RYOUTEI: A TYPE OF LUXURIOUS JAPANESE RESTAURANT
HOW FAR DO YOU GO TO GIVE THE CUSTOMER WHAT THEY WANT?
WHERE DOES YOUR FUNDAMENTAL STYLE BEGIN AND END?
AND DON'T FORGET, THIS AIN'T A FANCY RYOUTEI. IT'S AN IZAKAYA.
JUST GOING FOR REFINED FLAVORS AIN'T EXACTLY RIGHT.

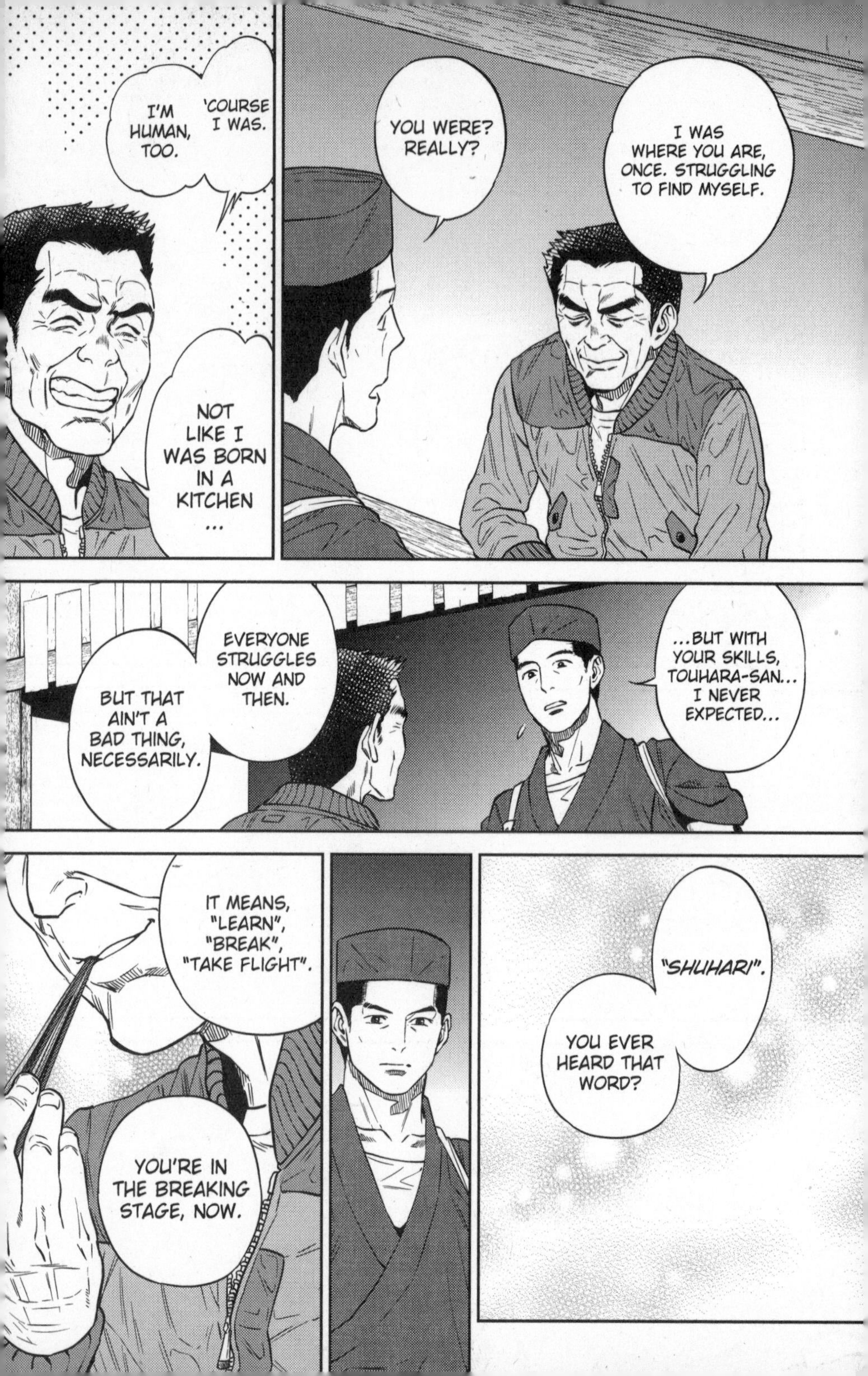
I WAS WHERE YOU ARE, ONCE. STRUGGLING TO FIND MYSELF.
YOU WERE? REALLY?
'COURSE I WAS.
I'M HUMAN, TOO.
NOT LIKE I WAS BORN IN A KITCHEN ...
...BUT WITH YOUR SKILLS, TOUHARA-SAN... I NEVER EXPECTED...
EVERYONE STRUGGLES NOW AND THEN.
BUT THAT AIN'T A BAD THING, NECESSARILY.
"SHUHARI".
YOU EVER HEARD THAT WORD?
IT MEANS, "LEARN", "BREAK", "TAKE FLIGHT".
YOU'RE IN THE BREAKING STAGE, NOW.

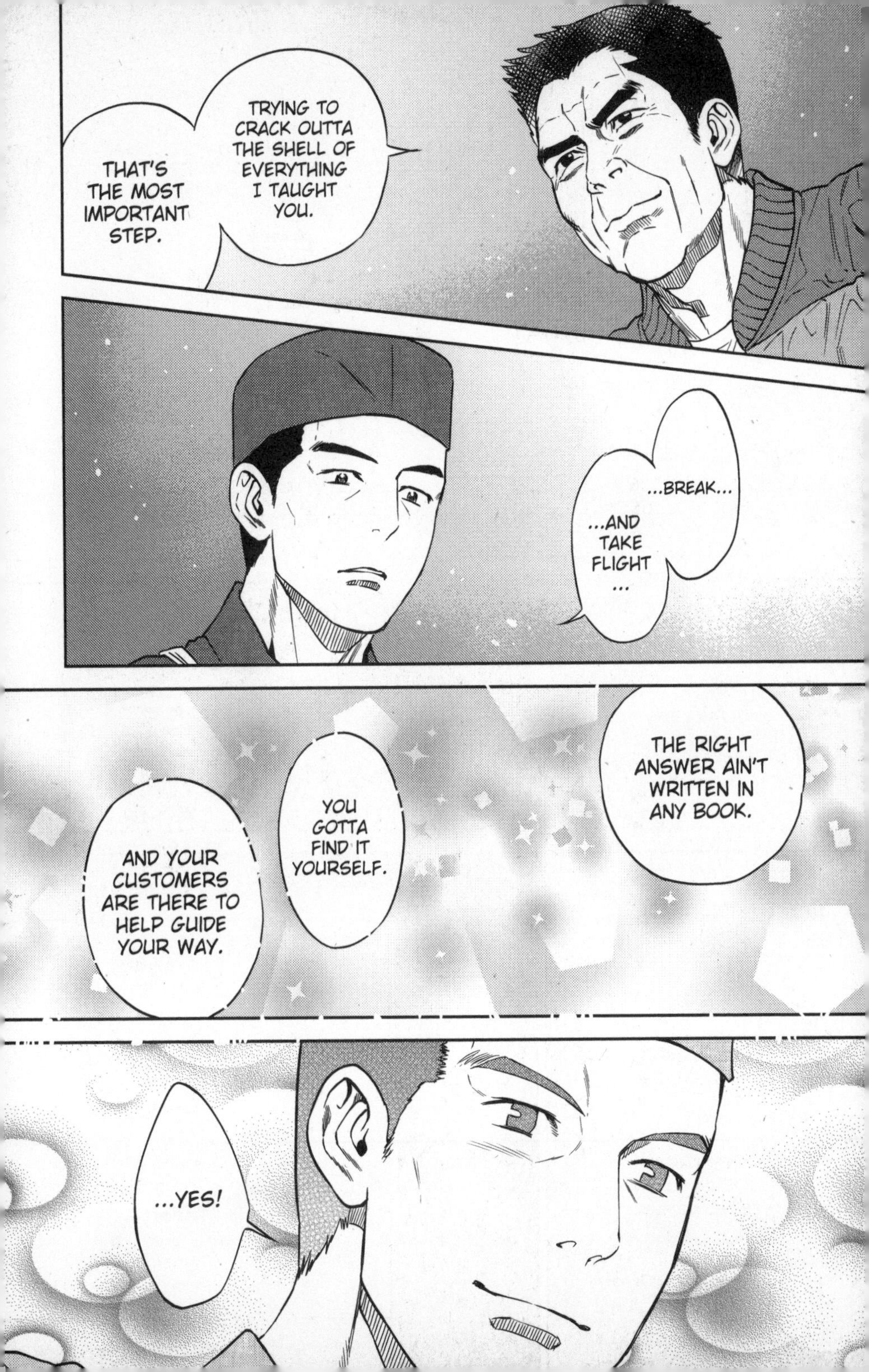
TRYING TO CRACK OUTTA THE SHELL OF EVERYTHING I TAUGHT YOU.
THAT'S THE MOST IMPORTANT STEP.
...BREAK...
...AND TAKE FLIGHT ...
THE RIGHT ANSWER AIN'T WRITTEN IN ANY BOOK.
YOU GOTTA FIND IT YOURSELF.
AND YOUR CUSTOMERS ARE THERE TO HELP GUIDE YOUR WAY.
...YES!

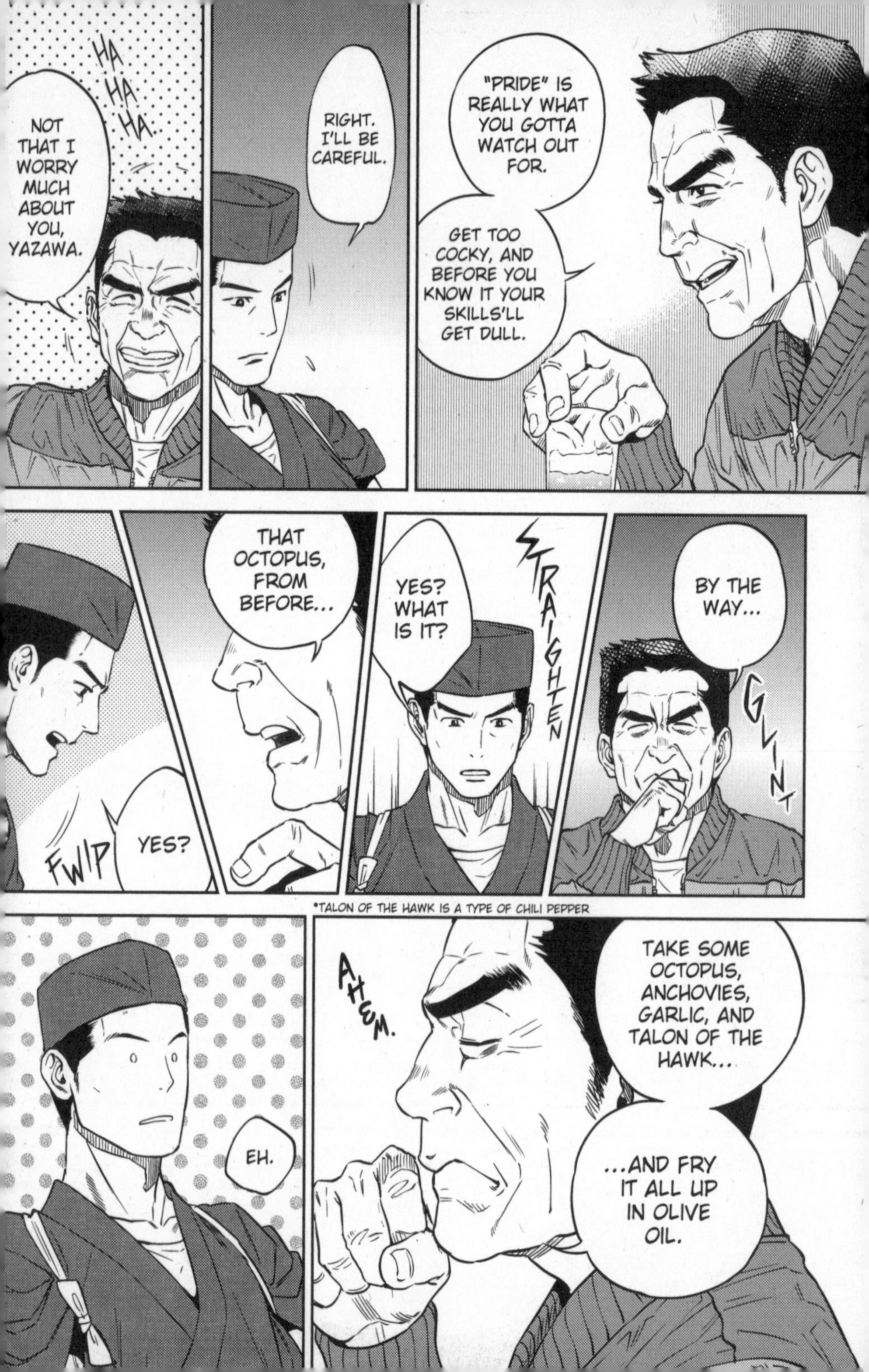
"PRIDE" IS REALLY WHAT YOU GOTTA WATCH OUT FOR.
GET TOO COCKY, AND BEFORE YOU KNOW IT YOUR SKILLS'LL GET DULL.
RIGHT. I'LL BE CAREFUL.
HA HA HA.
NOT THAT I WORRY MUCH ABOUT YOU, YAZAWA.
BY THE WAY...
GLINT
STRAIGHTEN
YES? WHAT IS IT?
THAT OCTOPUS, FROM BEFORE...
YES?
FWIP
AHEM.
TAKE SOME OCTOPUS, ANCHOVIES, GARLIC, AND TALON OF THE HAWK...
...AND FRY IT ALL UP IN OLIVE OIL.
EH.
*TALON OF THE HAWK IS A TYPE OF CHILI PEPPER

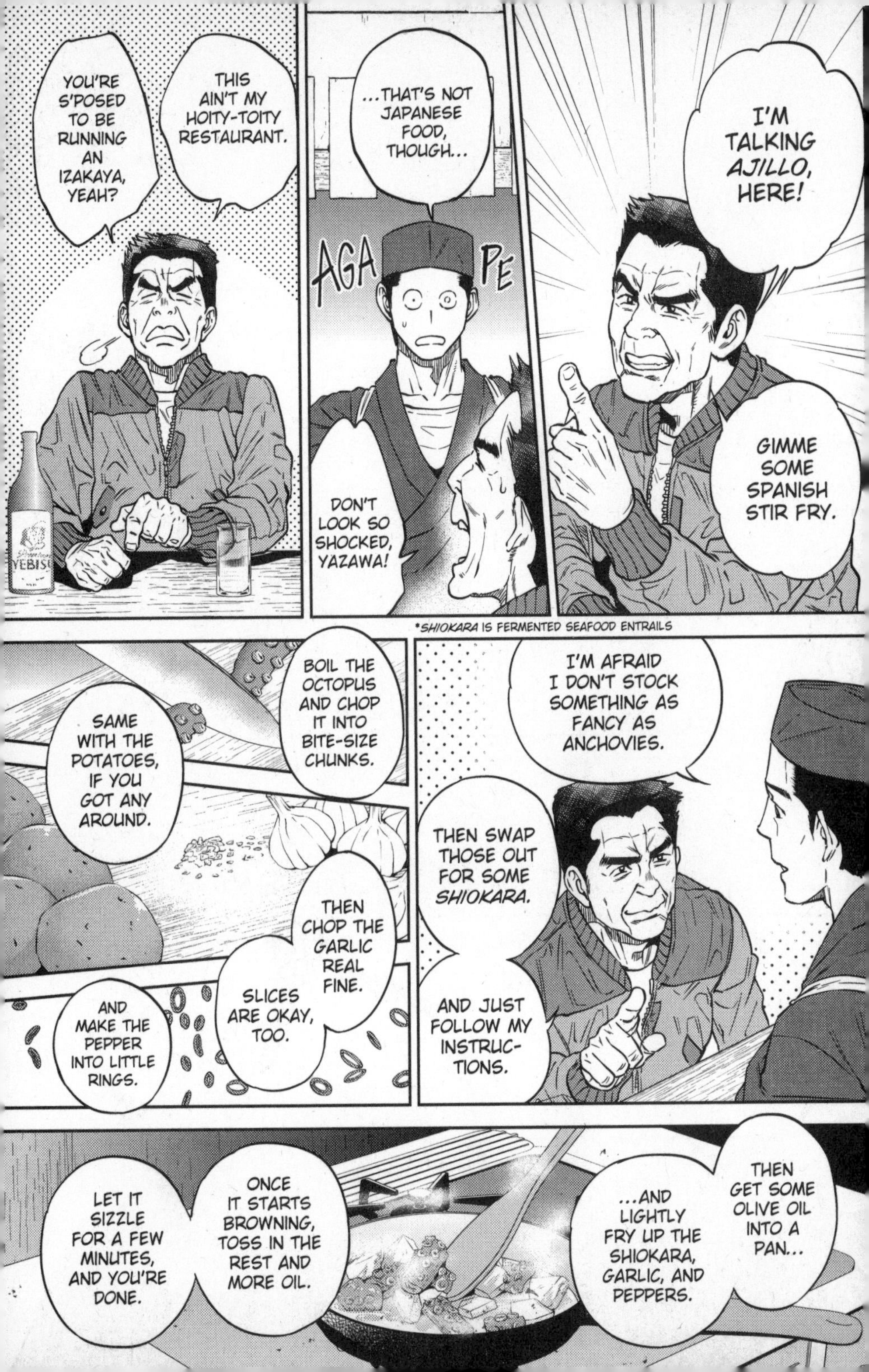
I'M TALKING *AJILLO*, HERE!
GIMME SOME SPANISH STIR FRY.
...THAT'S NOT JAPANESE FOOD, THOUGH...
AGA PE
DON'T LOOK SO SHOCKED, YAZAWA!
THIS AIN'T MY HOITY-TOITY RESTAURANT.
YOU'RE S'POSED TO BE RUNNING AN IZAKAYA, YEAH?
I'M AFRAID I DON'T STOCK SOMETHING AS FANCY AS ANCHOVIES.
THEN SWAP THOSE OUT FOR SOME *SHIOKARA*.
AND JUST FOLLOW MY INSTRUC-TIONS.
BOIL THE OCTOPUS AND CHOP IT INTO BITE-SIZE CHUNKS.
SAME WITH THE POTATOES, IF YOU GOT ANY AROUND.
THEN CHOP THE GARLIC REAL FINE.
SLICES ARE OKAY, TOO.
AND MAKE THE PEPPER INTO LITTLE RINGS.
THEN GET SOME OLIVE OIL INTO A PAN...
...AND LIGHTLY FRY UP THE SHIOKARA, GARLIC, AND PEPPERS.
ONCE IT STARTS BROWNING, TOSS IN THE REST AND MORE OIL.
LET IT SIZZLE FOR A FEW MINUTES, AND YOU'RE DONE.

**SHIOKARA* IS FERMENTED SEAFOOD ENTRAILS

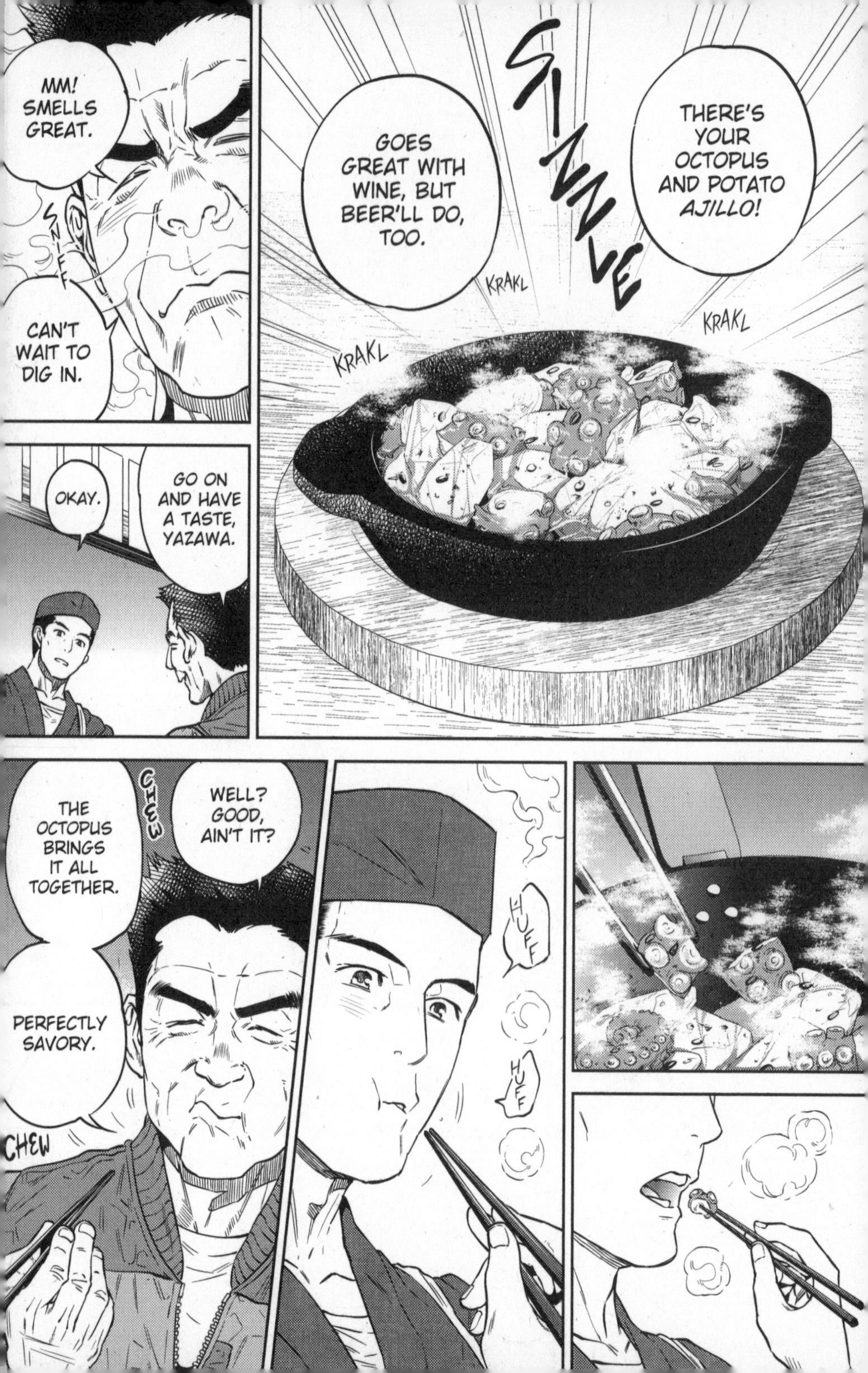
THERE'S YOUR OCTOPUS AND POTATO AJILLO!
GOES GREAT WITH WINE, BUT BEER'LL DO, TOO.
KRAKL
KRAKL
KRAKL
MM! SMELLS GREAT.
SNIFF
CAN'T WAIT TO DIG IN.
GO ON AND HAVE A TASTE, YAZAWA.
OKAY.
WELL? GOOD, AIN'T IT?
HUFF
HUFF
CHEW
THE OCTOPUS BRINGS IT ALL TOGETHER.
PERFECTLY SAVORY.
CHEW

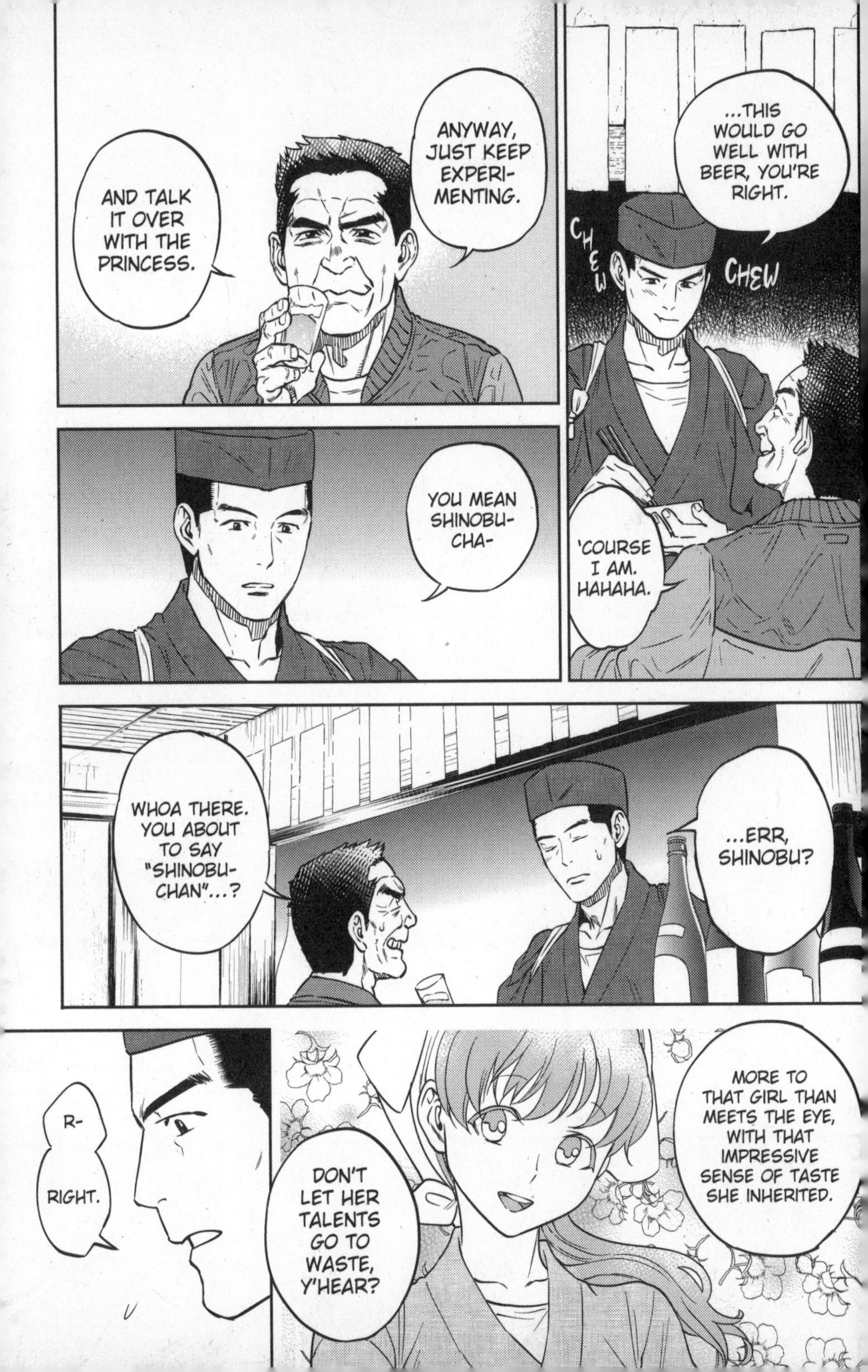
...THIS WOULD GO WELL WITH BEER, YOU'RE RIGHT.
CHEW
CHEW
'COURSE I AM. HAHAHA.
ANYWAY, JUST KEEP EXPERI-MENTING.
AND TALK IT OVER WITH THE PRINCESS.
YOU MEAN SHINOBU-CHA-
...ERR, SHINOBU?
WHOA THERE. YOU ABOUT TO SAY "SHINOBU-CHAN"...?
MORE TO THAT GIRL THAN MEETS THE EYE, WITH THAT IMPRESSIVE SENSE OF TASTE SHE INHERITED.
DON'T LET HER TALENTS GO TO WASTE, Y'HEAR?
R-
RIGHT.

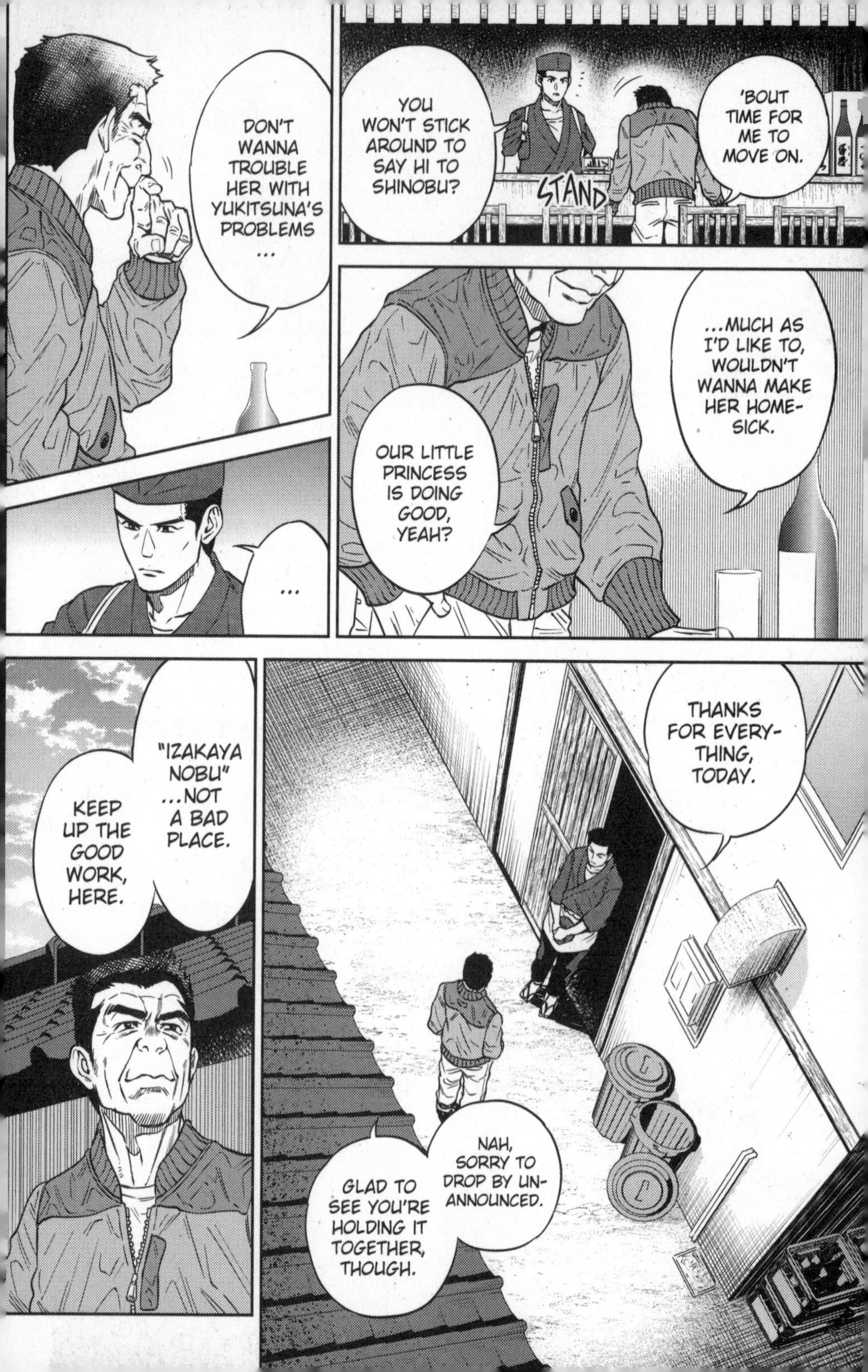
'BOUT TIME FOR ME TO MOVE ON.
YOU WON'T STICK AROUND TO SAY HI TO SHINOBU?
STAND
DON'T WANNA TROUBLE HER WITH YUKITSUNA'S PROBLEMS ...
...MUCH AS I'D LIKE TO, WOULDN'T WANNA MAKE HER HOME-SICK.
OUR LITTLE PRINCESS IS DOING GOOD, YEAH?
...
THANKS FOR EVERY-THING, TODAY.
NAH, SORRY TO DROP BY UN-ANNOUNCED.
GLAD TO SEE YOU'RE HOLDING IT TOGETHER, THOUGH.
"IZAKAYA NOBU" ...NOT A BAD PLACE.
KEEP UP THE GOOD WORK, HERE.

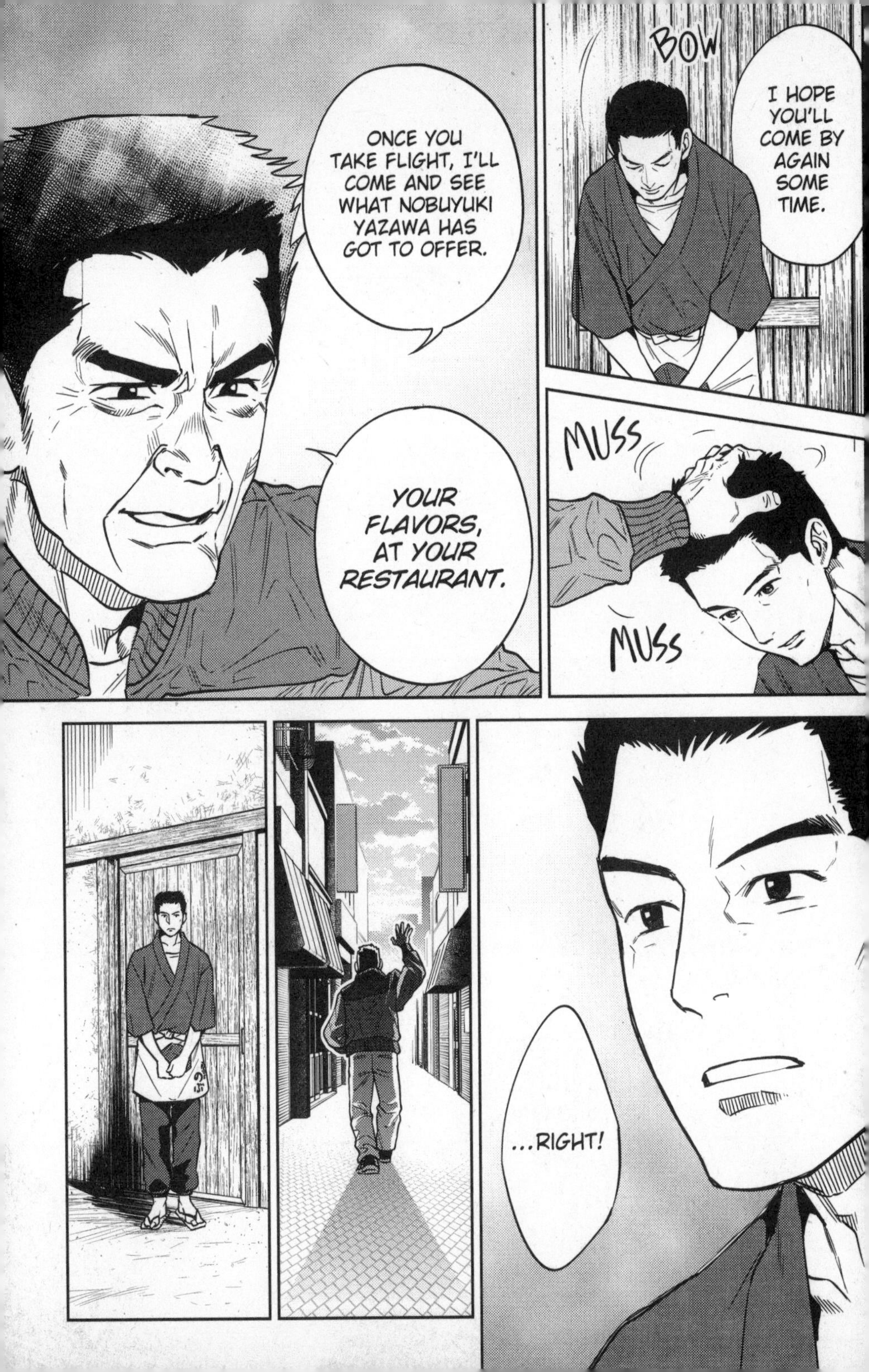
BOW
I HOPE YOU'LL COME BY AGAIN SOME TIME.
MUSS
MUSS
ONCE YOU TAKE FLIGHT, I'LL COME AND SEE WHAT NOBUYUKI YAZAWA HAS GOT TO OFFER.
YOUR FLAVORS, AT YOUR RESTAURANT.
...RIGHT!

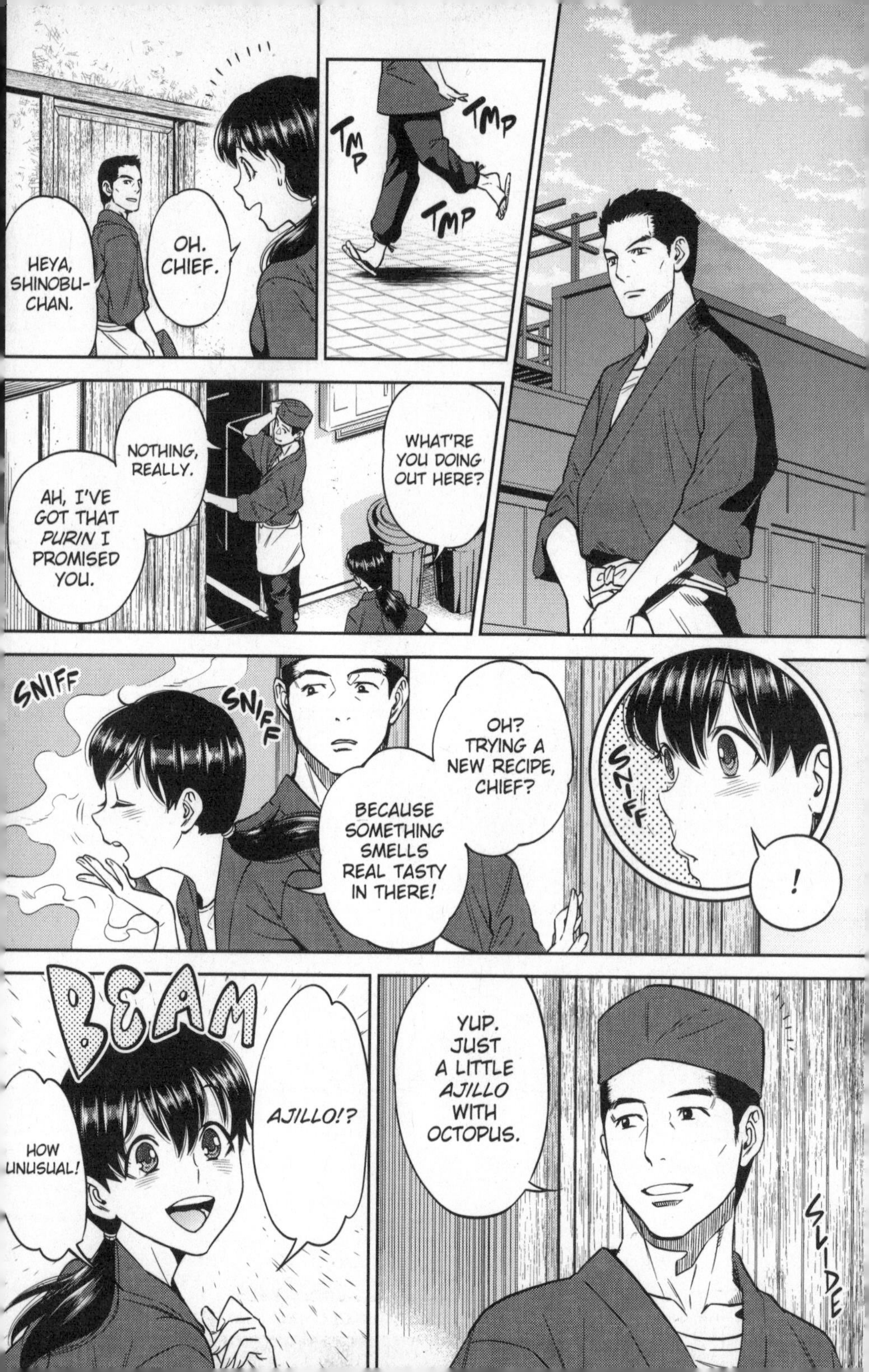
TMP
TMP
TMP
OH. CHIEF.
HEYA, SHINOBU-CHAN.
WHAT'RE YOU DOING OUT HERE?
NOTHING, REALLY.
AH, I'VE GOT THAT *PURIN* I PROMISED YOU.
SNIFF
!
OH? TRYING A NEW RECIPE, CHIEF?
BECAUSE SOMETHING SMELLS REAL TASTY IN THERE!
SNIFF
SNIFF
YUP. JUST A LITTLE *AJILLO* WITH OCTOPUS.
SLIDE
AJILLO!?
BEAM
HOW UNUSUAL!

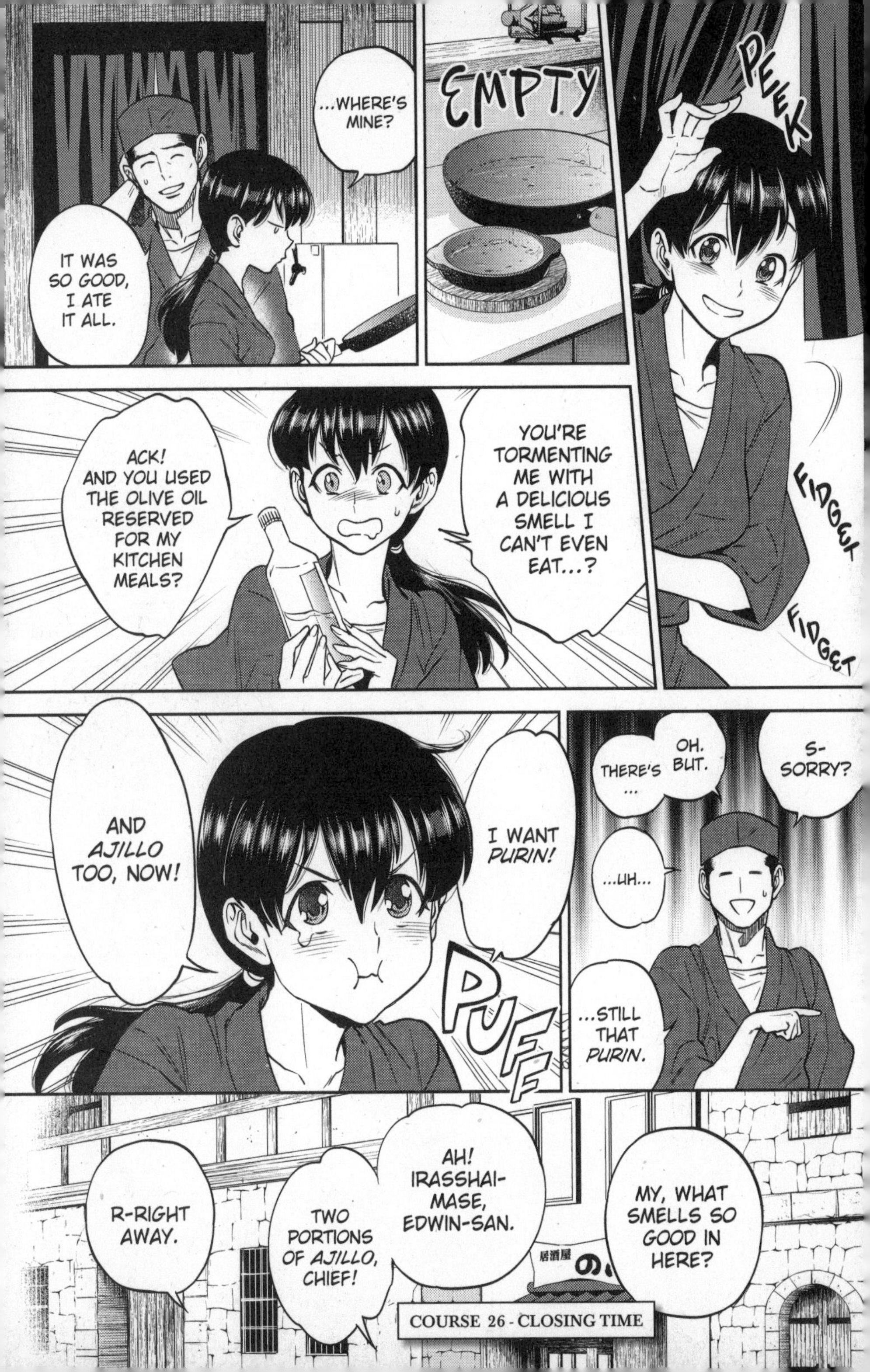
PEEK
FIDGET
FIDGET
EMPTY
...WHERE'S MINE?
IT WAS SO GOOD, I ATE IT ALL.
YOU'RE TORMENTING ME WITH A DELICIOUS SMELL I CAN'T EVEN EAT...?
ACK! AND YOU USED THE OLIVE OIL RESERVED FOR MY KITCHEN MEALS?
S-SORRY?
OH. BUT.
THERE'S ...
...UH...
...STILL THAT *PURIN*.
I WANT *PURIN*!
PUFF
AND *AJILLO* TOO, NOW!
MY, WHAT SMELLS SO GOOD IN HERE?
居酒屋
の
AH! IRASSHAI-MASE, EDWIN-SAN.
TWO PORTIONS OF *AJILLO*, CHIEF!
R-RIGHT AWAY.
COURSE 26 - CLOSING TIME

Octopus and Potato Ajillo

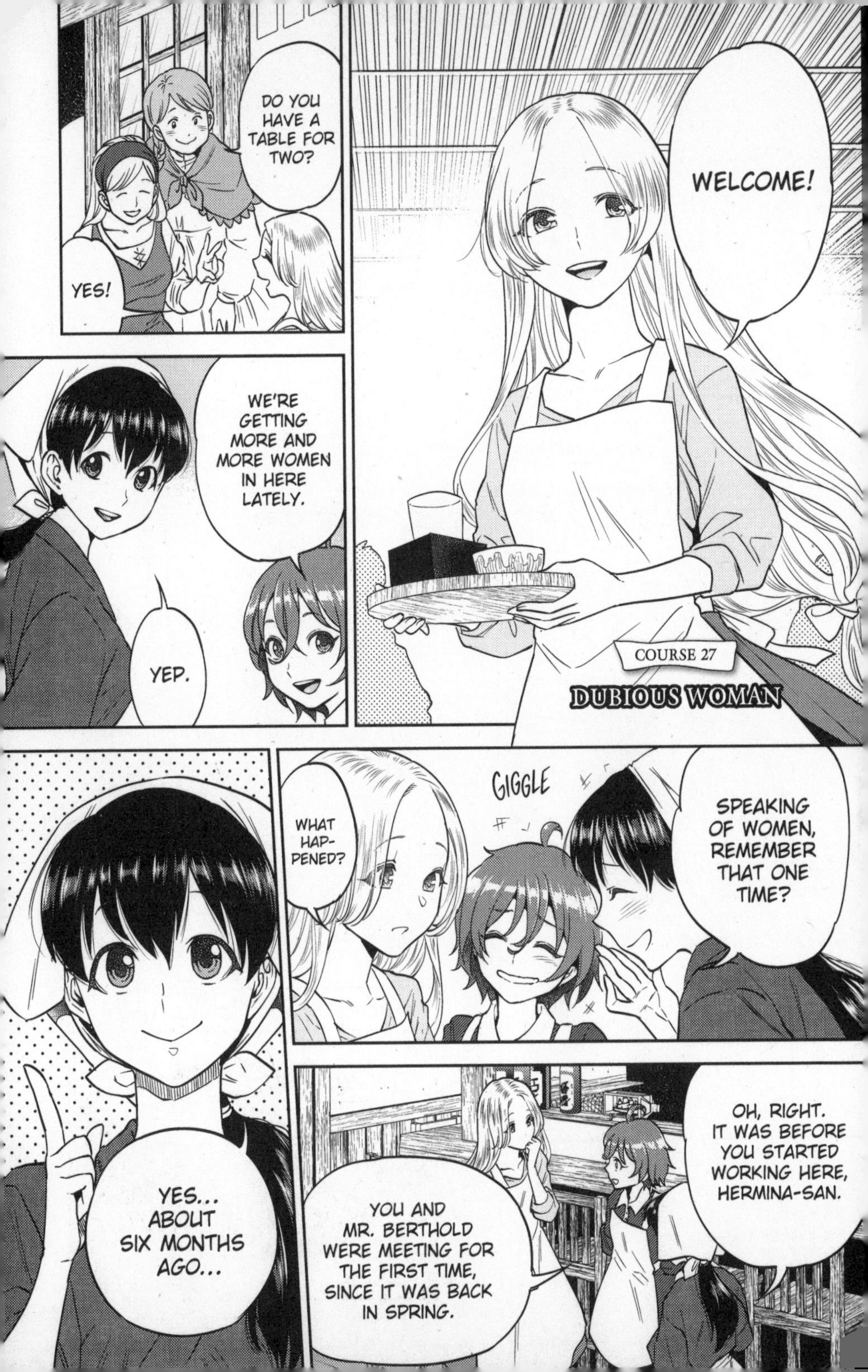
WELCOME!
COURSE 27
DUBIOUS WOMAN
DO YOU HAVE A TABLE FOR TWO?
YES!
WE'RE GETTING MORE AND MORE WOMEN IN HERE LATELY.
YEP.
SPEAKING OF WOMEN, REMEMBER THAT ONE TIME?
GIGGLE
WHAT HAP-PENED?
OH, RIGHT. IT WAS BEFORE YOU STARTED WORKING HERE, HERMINA-SAN.
YOU AND MR. BERTHOLD WERE MEETING FOR THE FIRST TIME, SINCE IT WAS BACK IN SPRING.
YES... ABOUT SIX MONTHS AGO...

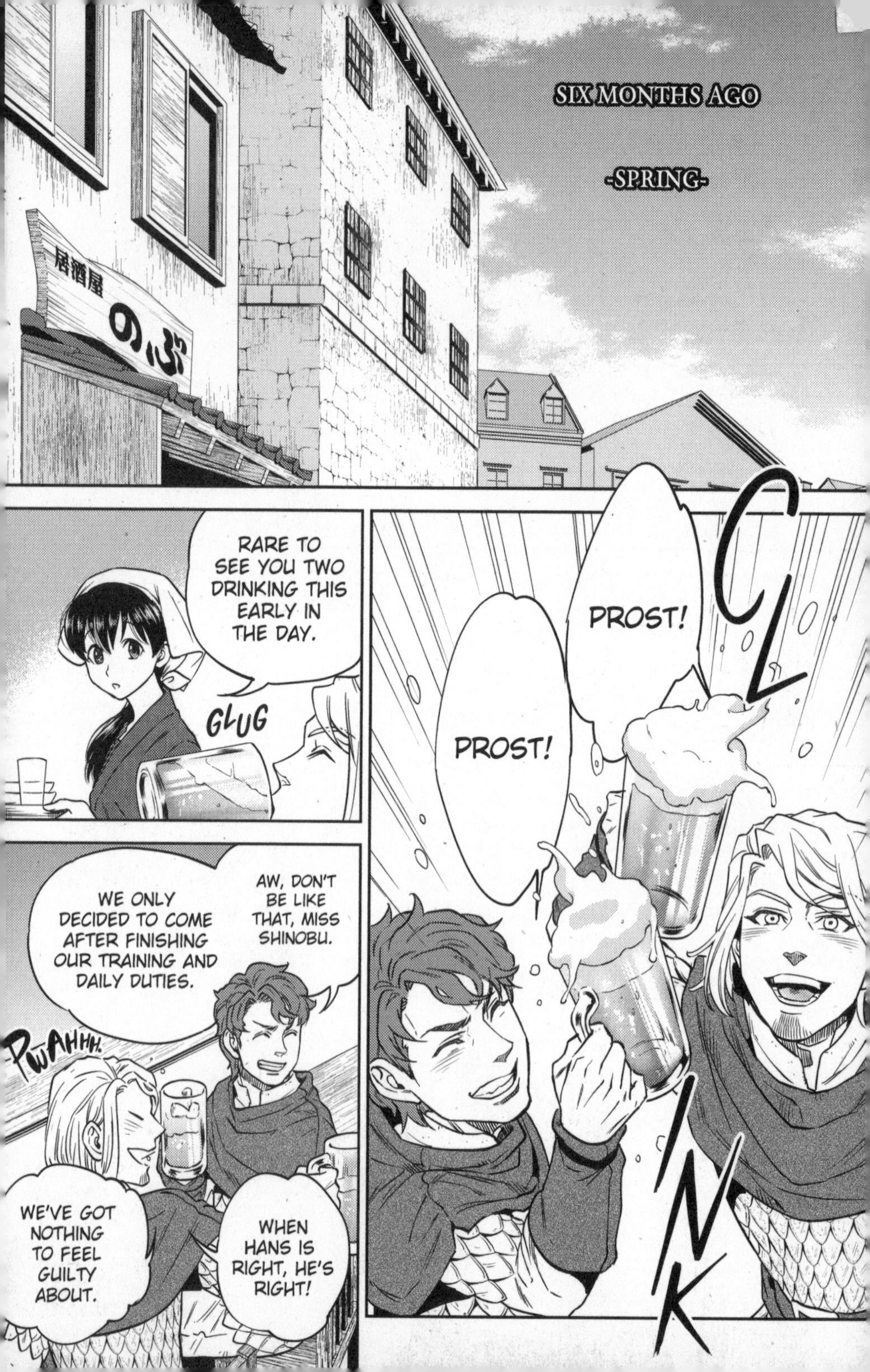
SIX MONTHS AGO
-SPRING-
居酒屋
のぶ
CLINK
PROST!
PROST!
RARE TO SEE YOU TWO DRINKING THIS EARLY IN THE DAY.
GLUG
AW, DON'T BE LIKE THAT, MISS SHINOBU.
WE ONLY DECIDED TO COME AFTER FINISHING OUR TRAINING AND DAILY DUTIES.
PWAHHH.
WHEN HANS IS RIGHT, HE'S RIGHT!
WE'VE GOT NOTHING TO FEEL GUILTY ABOUT.

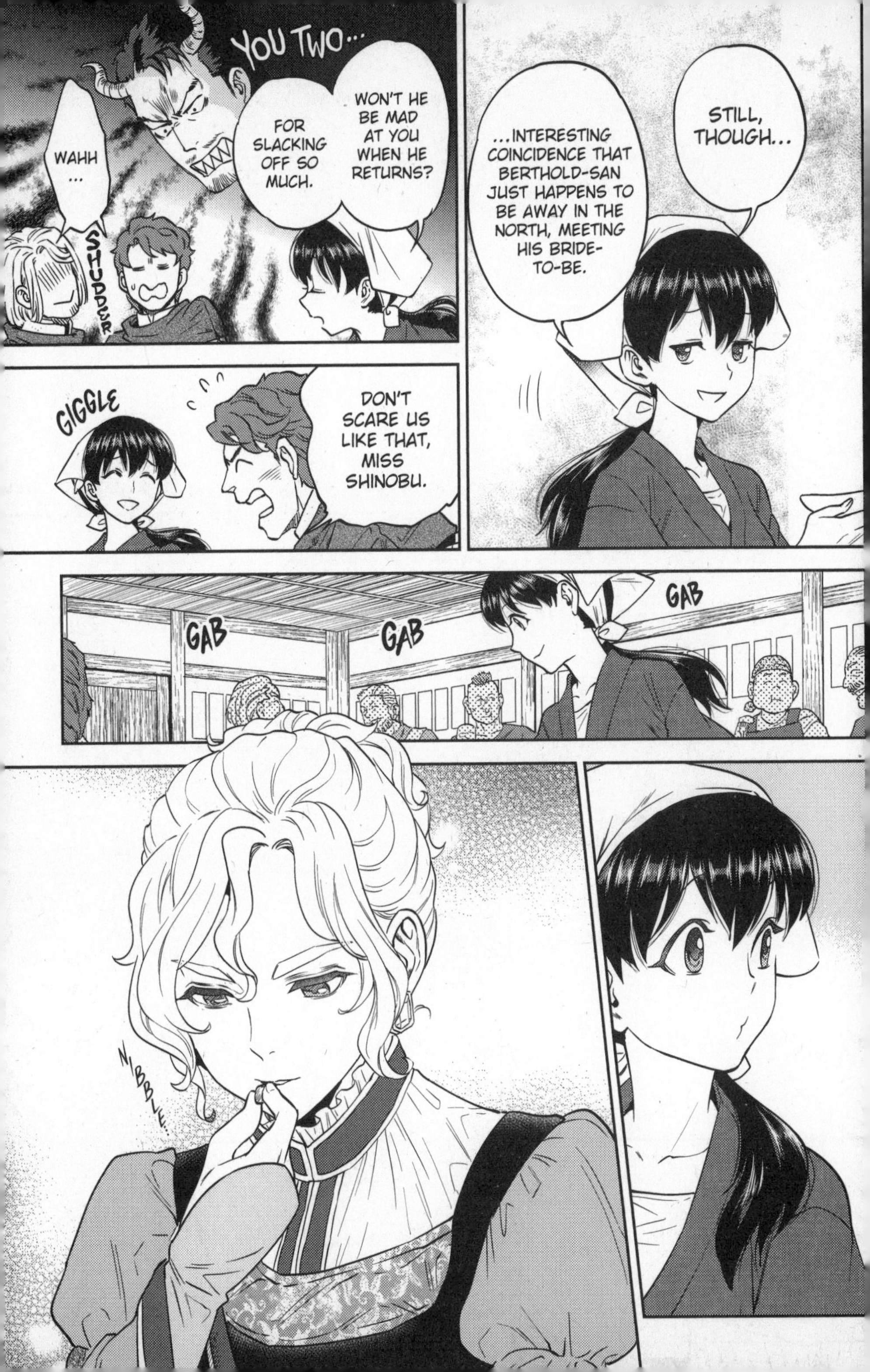
STILL, THOUGH...
...INTERESTING COINCIDENCE THAT BERTHOLD-SAN JUST HAPPENS TO BE AWAY IN THE NORTH, MEETING HIS BRIDE-TO-BE.
WON'T HE BE MAD AT YOU WHEN HE RETURNS?
YOU TWO...
FOR SLACKING OFF SO MUCH.
WAHH ...
SHUDDER
DON'T SCARE US LIKE THAT, MISS SHINOBU.
GIGGLE
GAB
GAB
GAB
NIBBBLE...

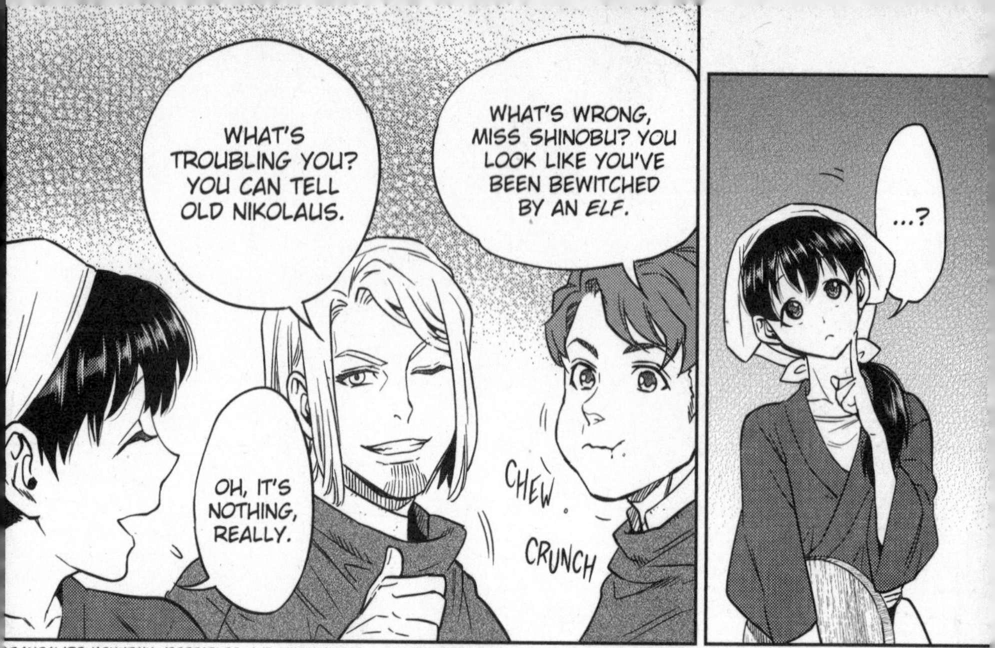
...?
WHAT'S WRONG, MISS SHINOBU? YOU LOOK LIKE YOU'VE BEEN BEWITCHED BY AN *ELF*.
WHAT'S TROUBLING YOU? YOU CAN TELL OLD NIKOLAUS.
CHEW
CRUNCH
OH, IT'S NOTHING, REALLY.

SANSAI ARE MOUNTAIN VEGETABLES, AND *KUSHIYAKI* IS A GENERIC TERM FOR FOOD GRILLED ON A SKEWER

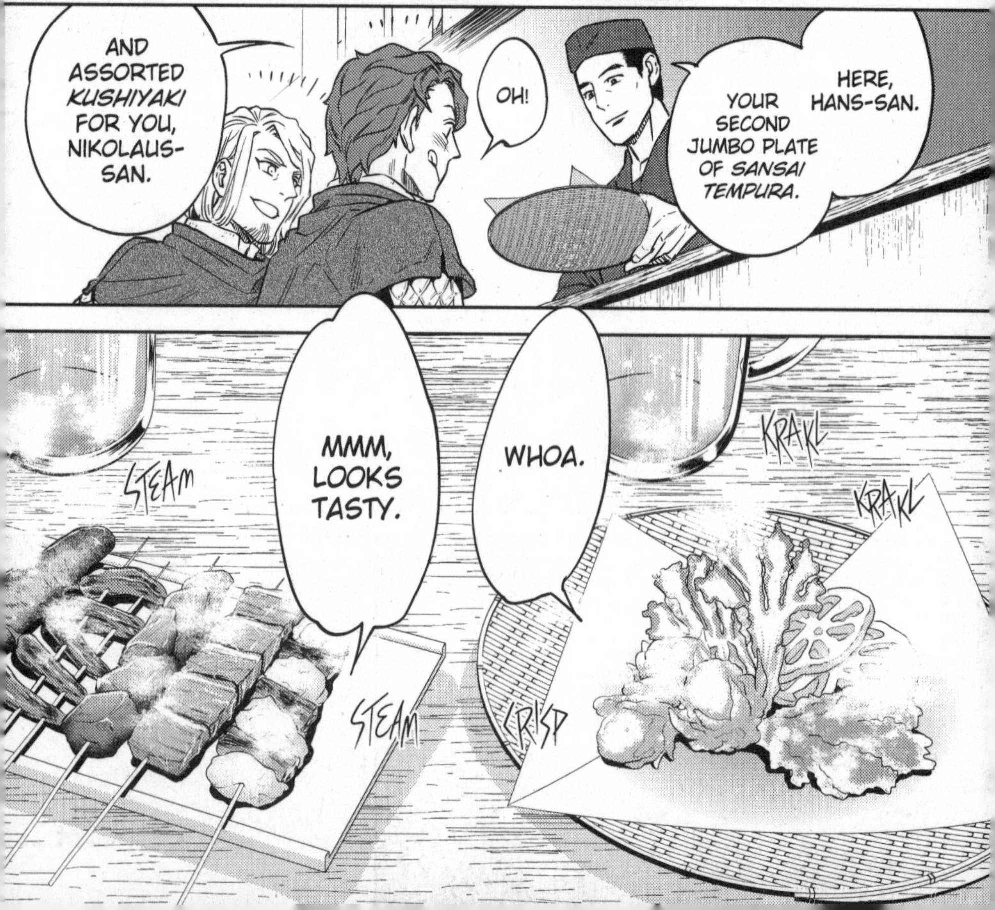
HERE, HANS-SAN. YOUR SECOND JUMBO PLATE OF *SANSAI TEMPURA*.
OH!
AND ASSORTED *KUSHIYAKI* FOR YOU, NIKOLAUS-SAN.
WHOA.
MMM, LOOKS TASTY.
KRAKL
KRAKL
STEAM
STEAM
CRISP

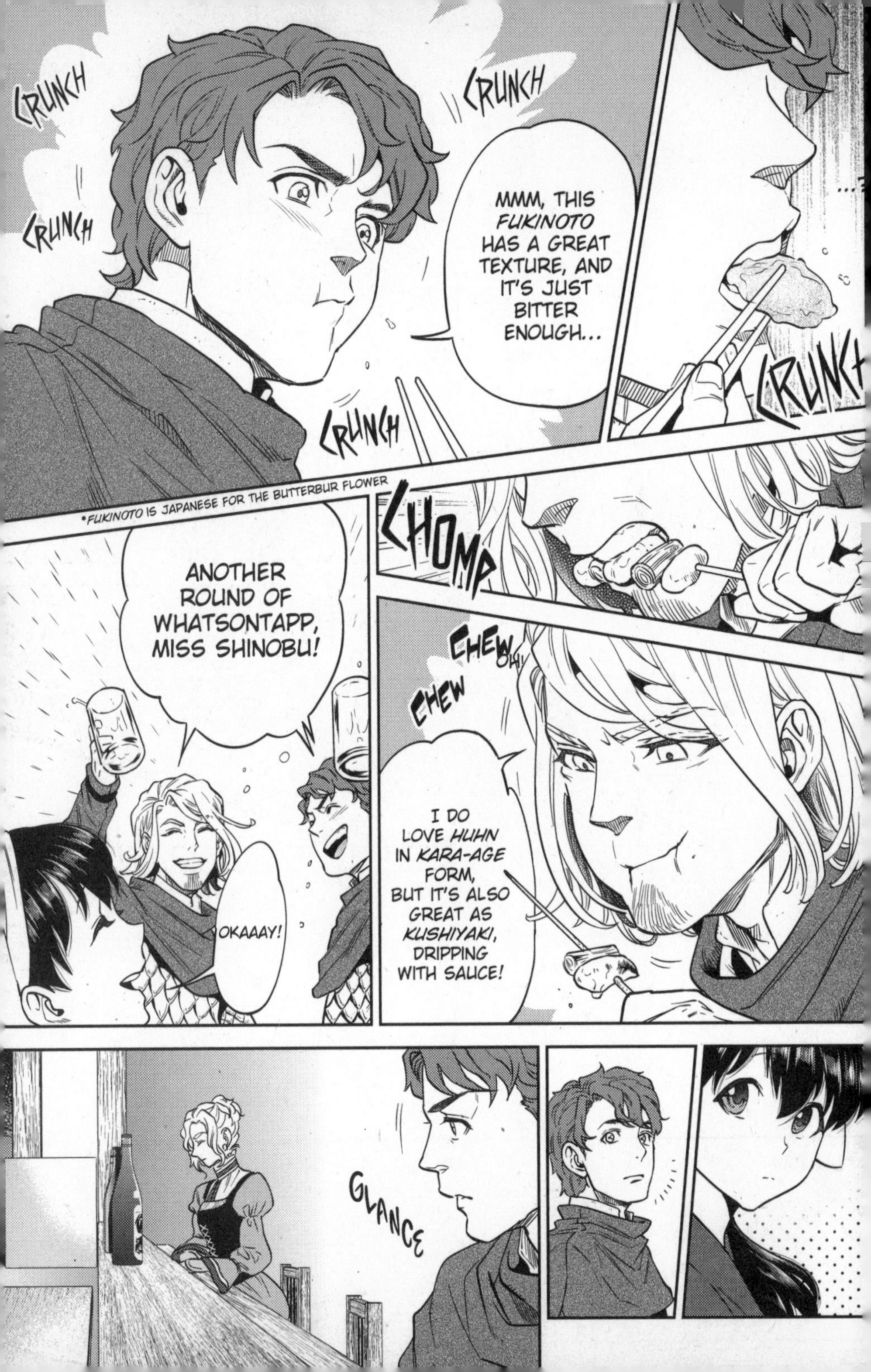
CRUNCH
CRUNCH
CRUNCH
CRUNCH
MMM, THIS FUKINOTO HAS A GREAT TEXTURE, AND IT'S JUST BITTER ENOUGH...
CRUNCH
*FUKINOTO IS JAPANESE FOR THE BUTTERBUR FLOWER
CHOMP
CHEW
OH!
CHEW
I DO LOVE HUHN IN KARA-AGE FORM, BUT IT'S ALSO GREAT AS KUSHIYAKI, DRIPPING WITH SAUCE!
ANOTHER ROUND OF WHATSONTAPP, MISS SHINOBU!
OKAAAY!
GLANCE

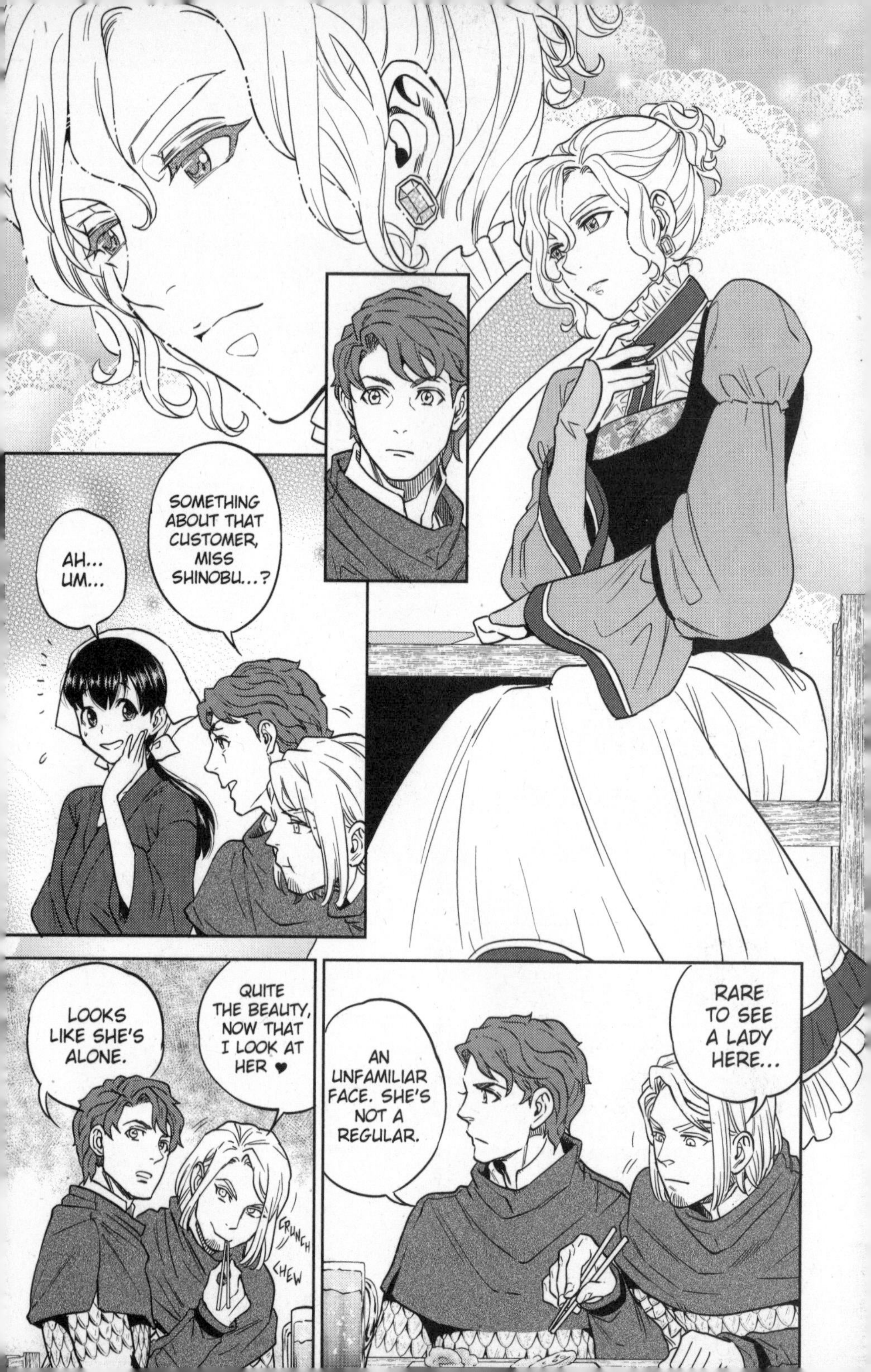
SOMETHING ABOUT THAT CUSTOMER, MISS SHINOBU...?
AH... UM...
RARE TO SEE A LADY HERE...
AN UNFAMILIAR FACE. SHE'S NOT A REGULAR.
QUITE THE BEAUTY, NOW THAT I LOOK AT HER ♥
LOOKS LIKE SHE'S ALONE.
CRUNCH
CHEW

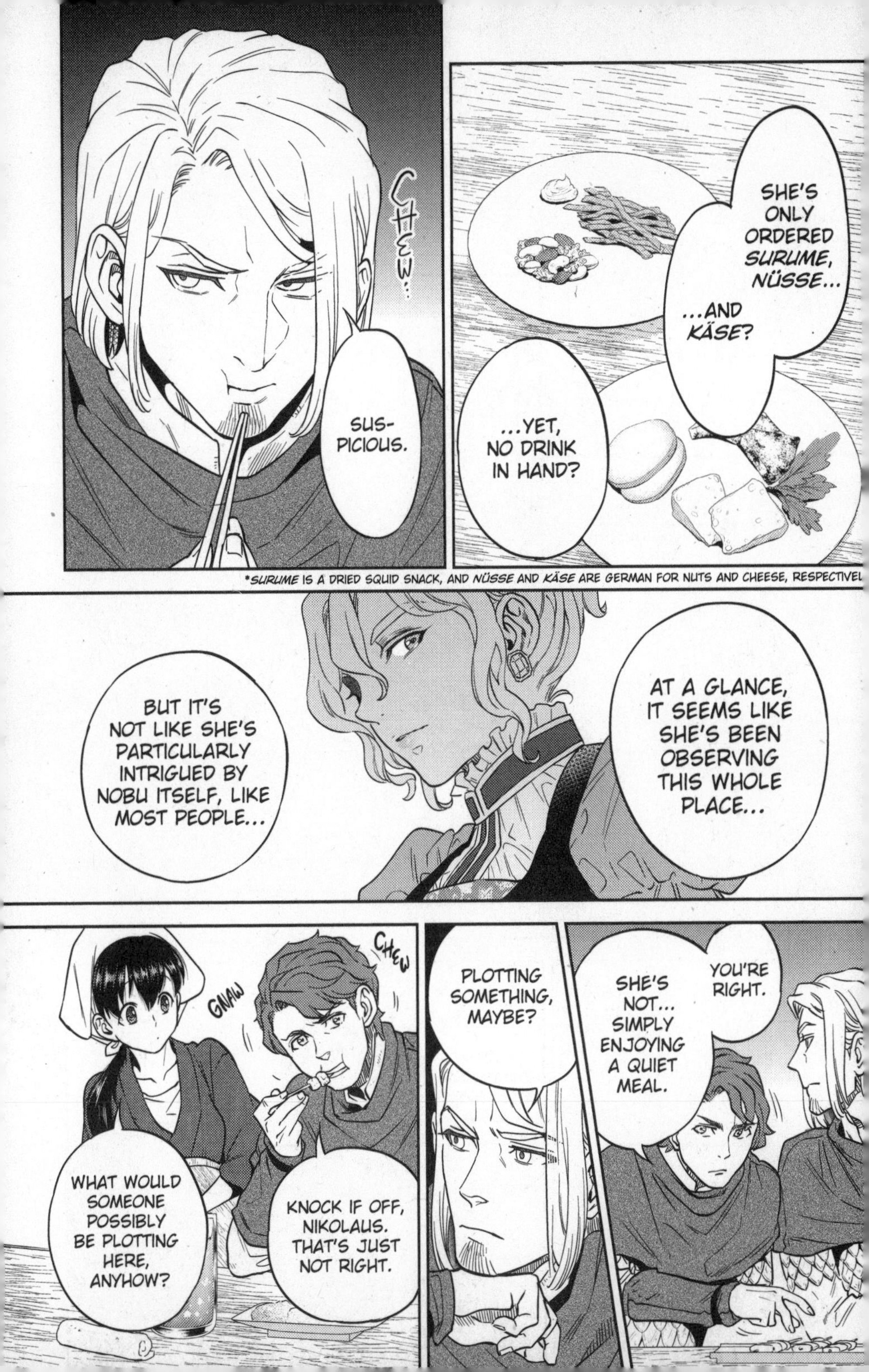
SHE'S ONLY ORDERED SURUME, NÜSSE...
...AND KÄSE?
...YET, NO DRINK IN HAND?
CHEW...
SUS-PICIOUS.
AT A GLANCE, IT SEEMS LIKE SHE'S BEEN OBSERVING THIS WHOLE PLACE...
BUT IT'S NOT LIKE SHE'S PARTICULARLY INTRIGUED BY NOBU ITSELF, LIKE MOST PEOPLE...
YOU'RE RIGHT.
SHE'S NOT... SIMPLY ENJOYING A QUIET MEAL.
PLOTTING SOMETHING, MAYBE?
CHEW
GNAW
KNOCK IF OFF, NIKOLAUS. THAT'S JUST NOT RIGHT.
WHAT WOULD SOMEONE POSSIBLY BE PLOTTING HERE, ANYHOW?

*SURUME IS A DRIED SQUID SNACK, AND NÜSSE AND KÄSE ARE GERMAN FOR NUTS AND CHEESE, RESPECTIVEL

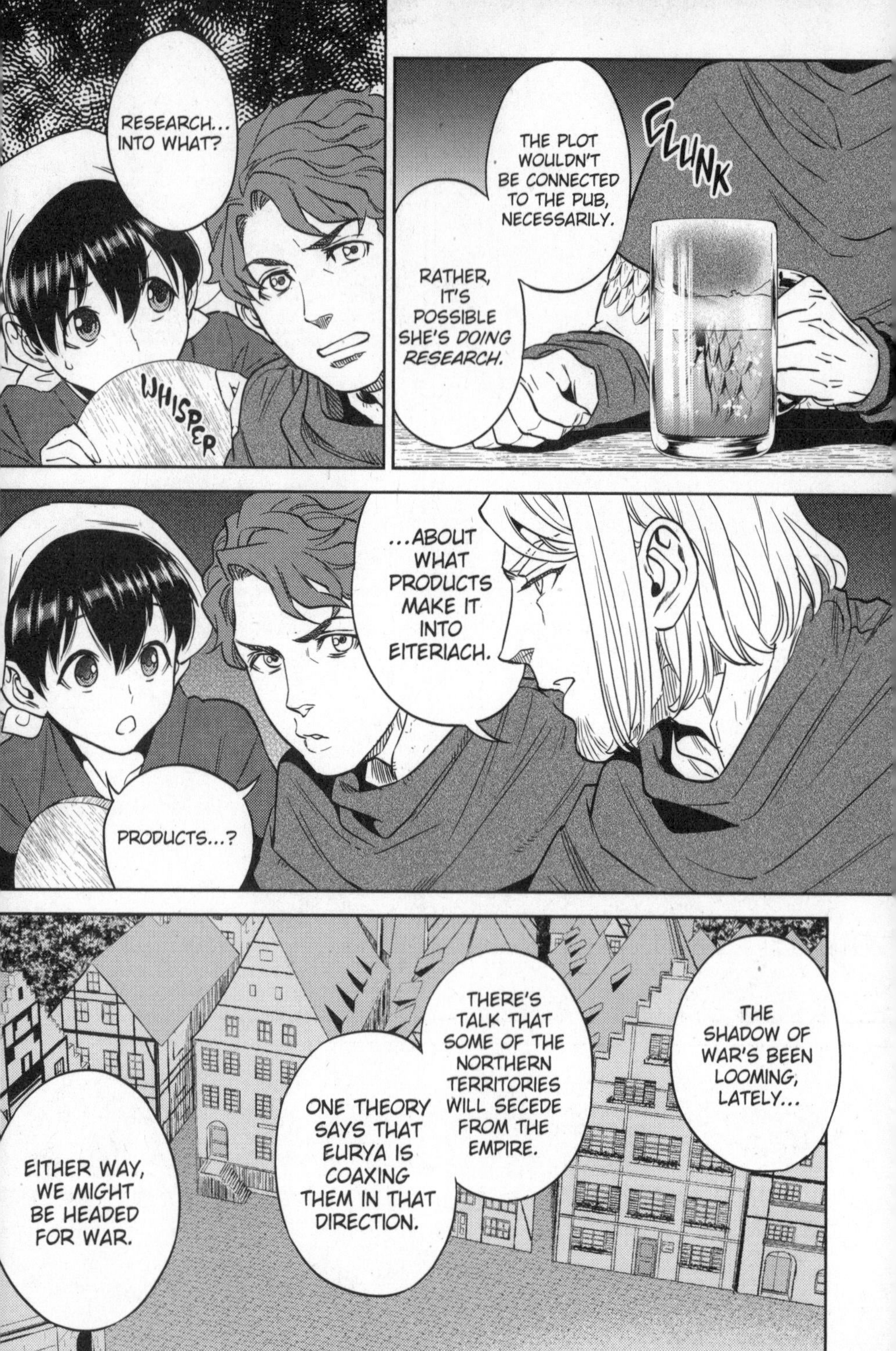
CLUNK
THE PLOT WOULDN'T BE CONNECTED TO THE PUB, NECESSARILY.
RATHER, IT'S POSSIBLE SHE'S *DOING RESEARCH.*
RESEARCH... INTO WHAT?
WHISPER
...ABOUT WHAT PRODUCTS MAKE IT INTO EITERIACH.
PRODUCTS...?
THE SHADOW OF WAR'S BEEN LOOMING, LATELY...
THERE'S TALK THAT SOME OF THE NORTHERN TERRITORIES WILL SECEDE FROM THE EMPIRE.
ONE THEORY SAYS THAT EURYA IS COAXING THEM IN THAT DIRECTION.
EITHER WAY, WE MIGHT BE HEADED FOR WAR.

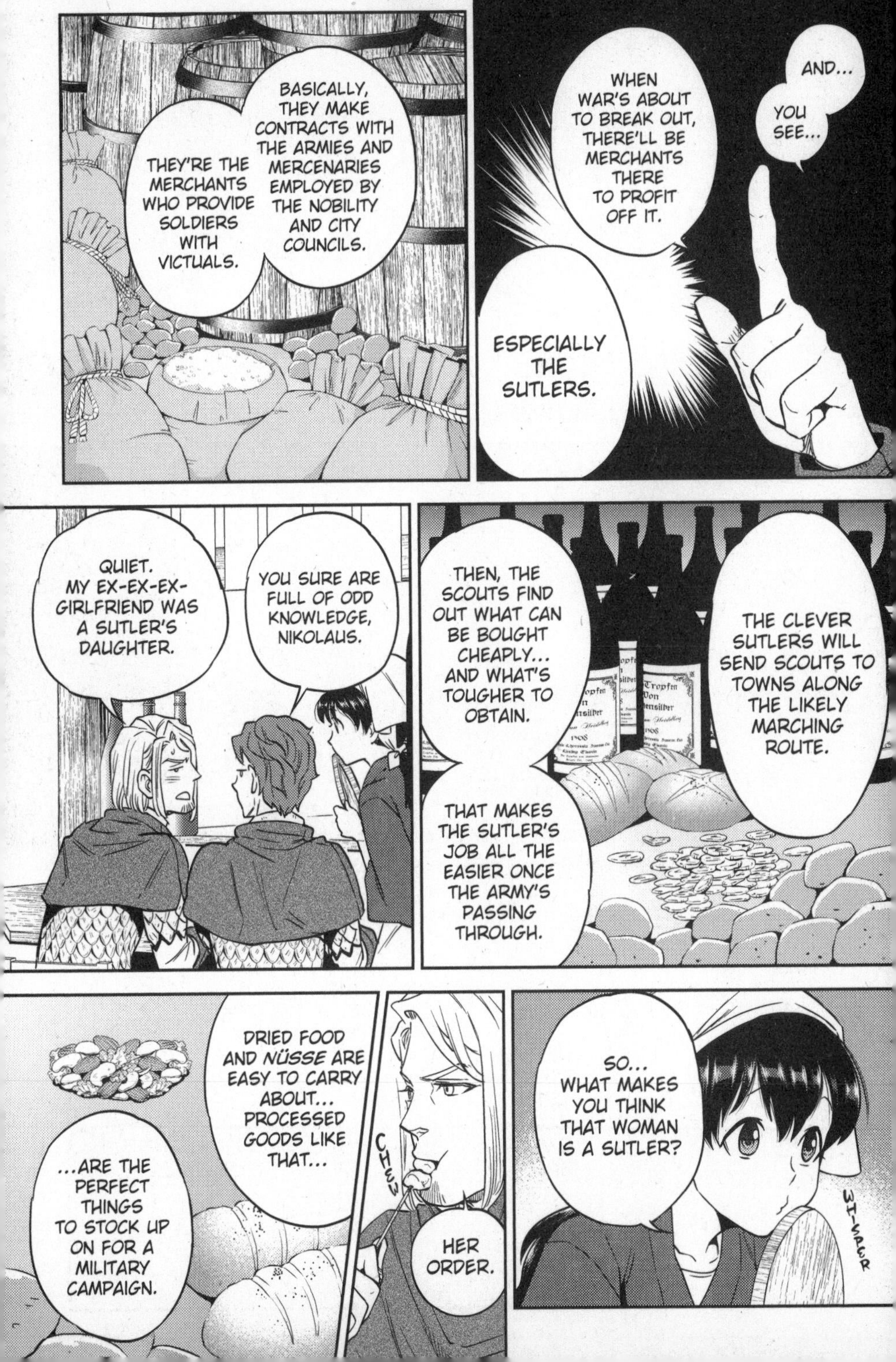
AND...
YOU SEE...
WHEN WAR'S ABOUT TO BREAK OUT, THERE'LL BE MERCHANTS THERE TO PROFIT OFF IT.
ESPECIALLY THE SUTLERS.
BASICALLY, THEY MAKE CONTRACTS WITH THE ARMIES AND MERCENARIES EMPLOYED BY THE NOBILITY AND CITY COUNCILS.
THEY'RE THE MERCHANTS WHO PROVIDE SOLDIERS WITH VICTUALS.
THE CLEVER SUTLERS WILL SEND SCOUTS TO TOWNS ALONG THE LIKELY MARCHING ROUTE.
THEN, THE SCOUTS FIND OUT WHAT CAN BE BOUGHT CHEAPLY... AND WHAT'S TOUGHER TO OBTAIN.
THAT MAKES THE SUTLER'S JOB ALL THE EASIER ONCE THE ARMY'S PASSING THROUGH.
YOU SURE ARE FULL OF ODD KNOWLEDGE, NIKOLAUS.
QUIET. MY EX-EX-EX-GIRLFRIEND WAS A SUTLER'S DAUGHTER.
SO... WHAT MAKES YOU THINK THAT WOMAN IS A SUTLER?
WHISPER
DRIED FOOD AND *NÜSSE* ARE EASY TO CARRY ABOUT... PROCESSED GOODS LIKE THAT...
CHEW
HER ORDER.
...ARE THE PERFECT THINGS TO STOCK UP ON FOR A MILITARY CAMPAIGN.

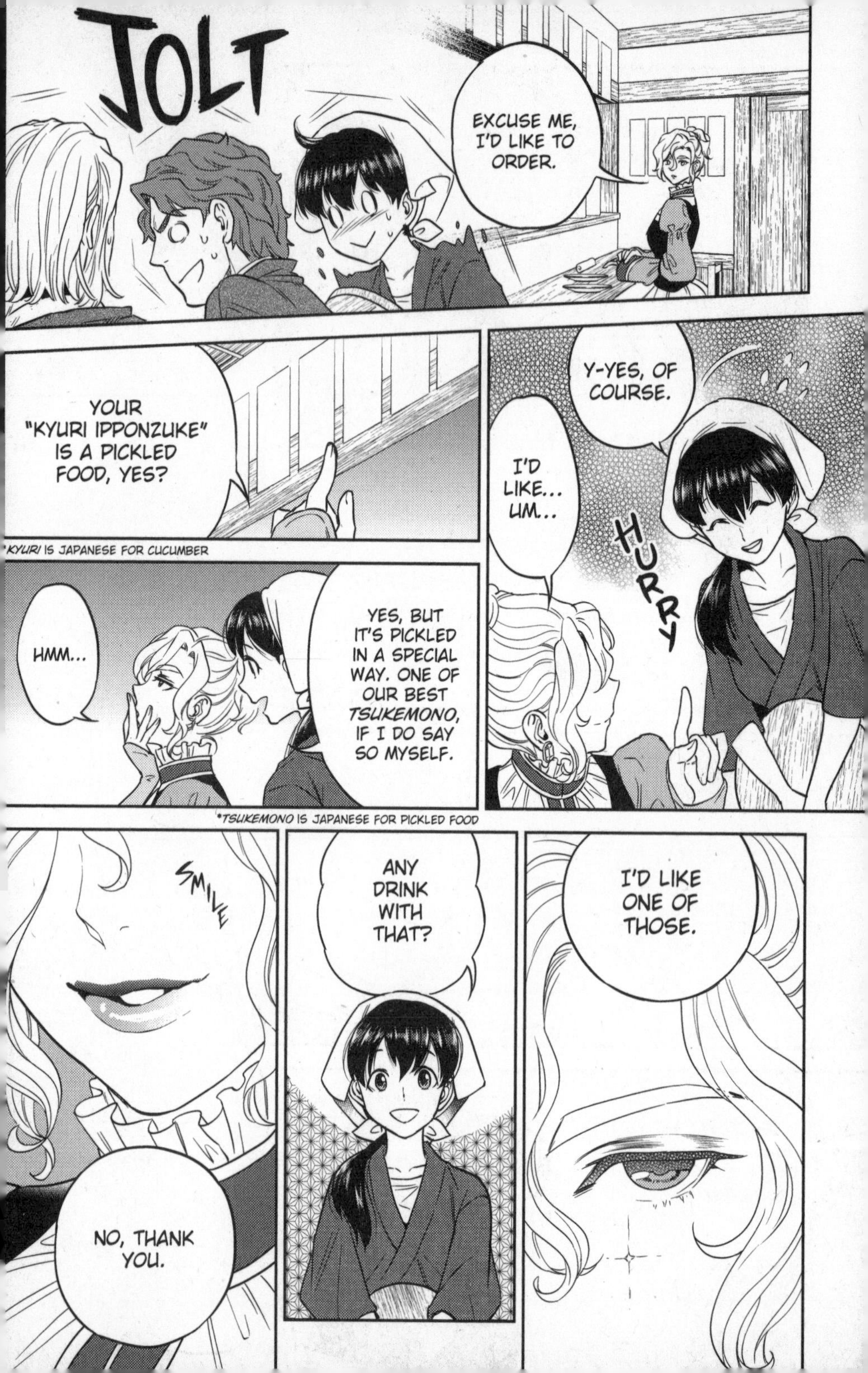
EXCUSE ME, I'D LIKE TO ORDER.
JOLT
Y-YES, OF COURSE.
I'D LIKE... UM...
HURRY
YOUR "KYURI IPPONZUKE" IS A PICKLED FOOD, YES?
*KYURI IS JAPANESE FOR CUCUMBER
YES, BUT IT'S PICKLED IN A SPECIAL WAY. ONE OF OUR BEST TSUKEMONO, IF I DO SAY SO MYSELF.
HMM...
*TSUKEMONO IS JAPANESE FOR PICKLED FOOD
I'D LIKE ONE OF THOSE.
ANY DRINK WITH THAT?
SMILE
NO, THANK YOU.

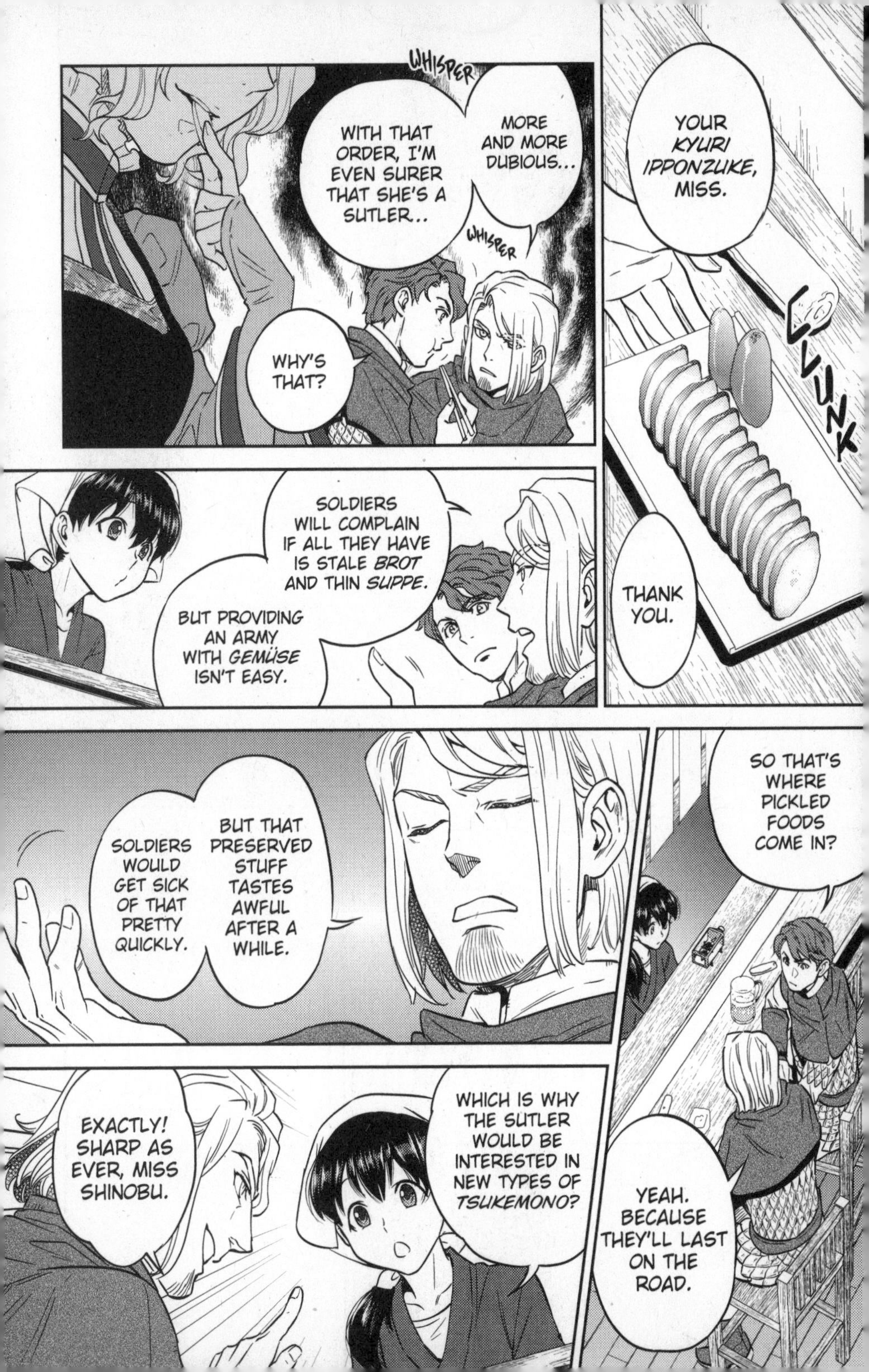
YOUR KYURI IPPONZUKE, MISS.
CLUNK
THANK YOU.
WHISPER
MORE AND MORE DUBIOUS...
WITH THAT ORDER, I'M EVEN SURER THAT SHE'S A SUTLER...
WHISPER
WHY'S THAT?
SOLDIERS WILL COMPLAIN IF ALL THEY HAVE IS STALE BROT AND THIN SUPPE.
BUT PROVIDING AN ARMY WITH GEMÜSE ISN'T EASY.
SO THAT'S WHERE PICKLED FOODS COME IN?
YEAH. BECAUSE THEY'LL LAST ON THE ROAD.
BUT THAT PRESERVED STUFF TASTES AWFUL AFTER A WHILE.
SOLDIERS WOULD GET SICK OF THAT PRETTY QUICKLY.
WHICH IS WHY THE SUTLER WOULD BE INTERESTED IN NEW TYPES OF TSUKEMONO?
EXACTLY! SHARP AS EVER, MISS SHINOBU.

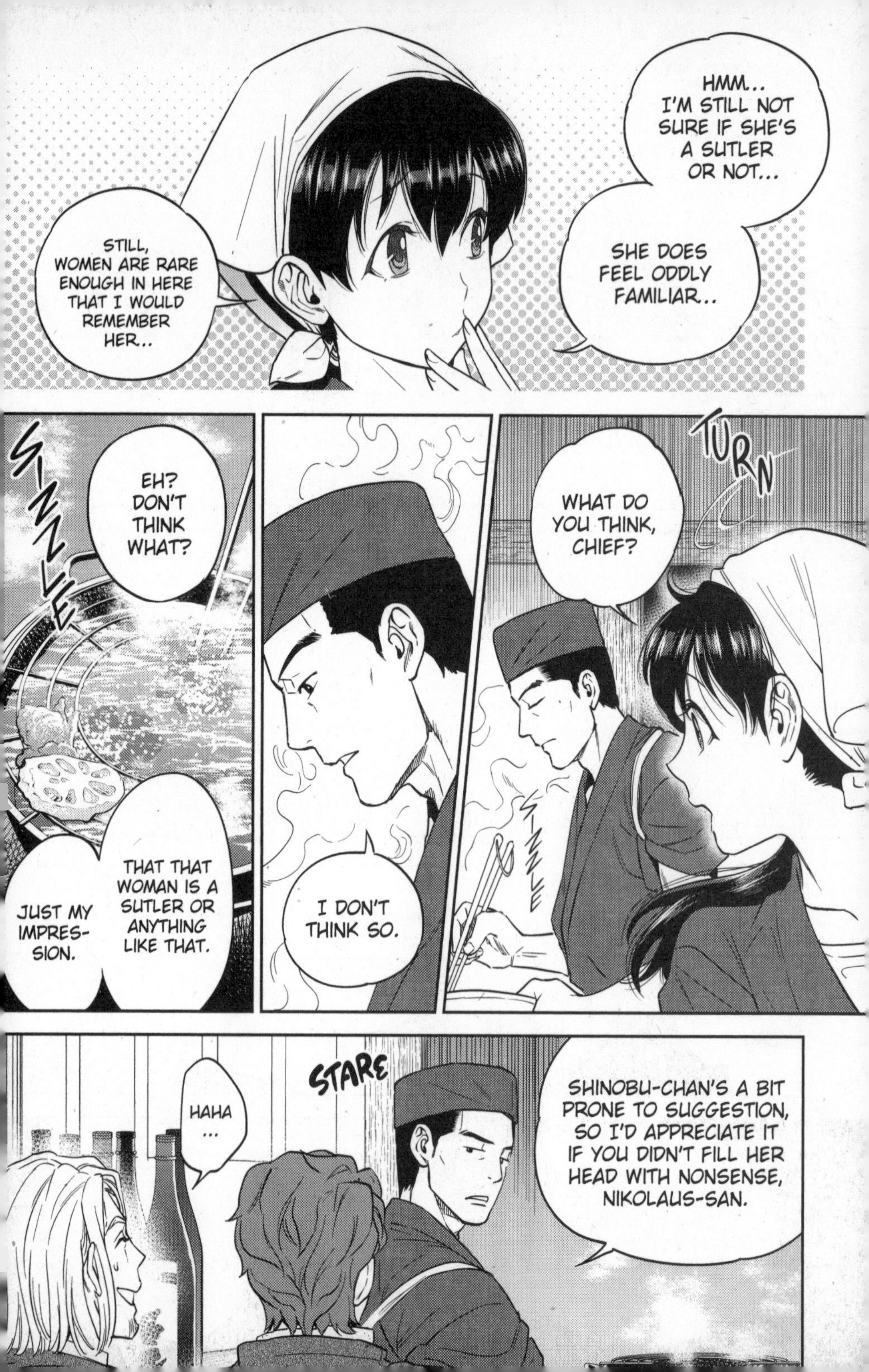
HMM... I'M STILL NOT SURE IF SHE'S A SUTLER OR NOT...
SHE DOES FEEL ODDLY FAMILIAR...
STILL, WOMEN ARE RARE ENOUGH IN HERE THAT I WOULD REMEMBER HER...
TURN
WHAT DO YOU THINK, CHIEF?
SIZZLE
I DON'T THINK SO.
EH? DON'T THINK WHAT?
SIZZLE
THAT THAT WOMAN IS A SUTLER OR ANYTHING LIKE THAT.
JUST MY IMPRES-SION.
SHINOBU-CHAN'S A BIT PRONE TO SUGGESTION, SO I'D APPRECIATE IT IF YOU DIDN'T FILL HER HEAD WITH NONSENSE, NIKOLAUS-SAN.
STARE
HAHA ...

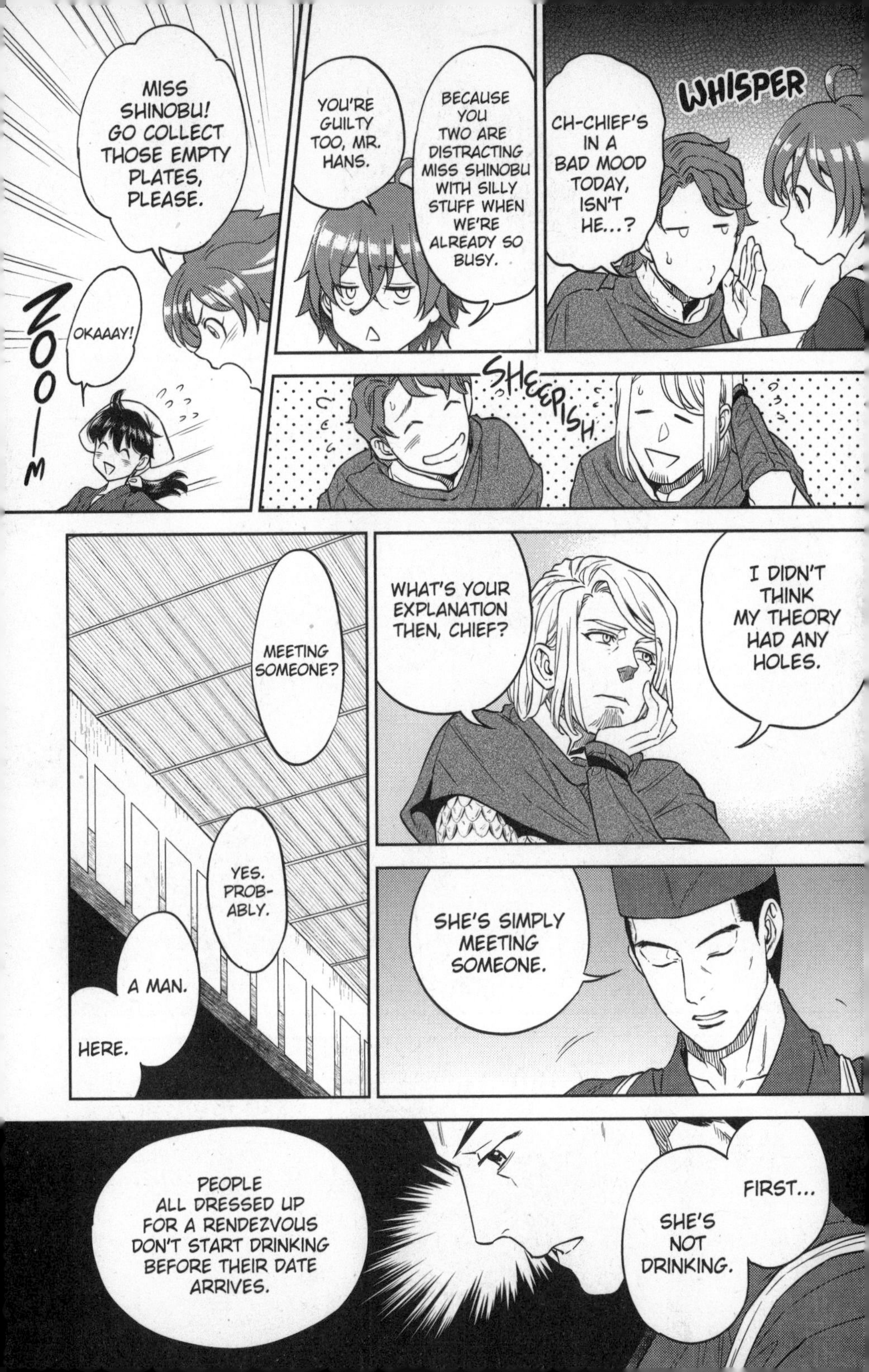
WHISPER
CH-CHIEF'S IN A BAD MOOD TODAY, ISN'T HE...?
BECAUSE YOU TWO ARE DISTRACTING MISS SHINOBU WITH SILLY STUFF WHEN WE'RE ALREADY SO BUSY.
YOU'RE GUILTY TOO, MR. HANS.
SHEEPISH
MISS SHINOBU! GO COLLECT THOSE EMPTY PLATES, PLEASE.
OKAAAY!
ZOOOM
I DIDN'T THINK MY THEORY HAD ANY HOLES.
WHAT'S YOUR EXPLANATION THEN, CHIEF?
SHE'S SIMPLY MEETING SOMEONE.
MEETING SOMEONE?
YES. PROBABLY.
A MAN.
HERE.
FIRST...
SHE'S NOT DRINKING.
PEOPLE ALL DRESSED UP FOR A RENDEZVOUS DON'T START DRINKING BEFORE THEIR DATE ARRIVES.

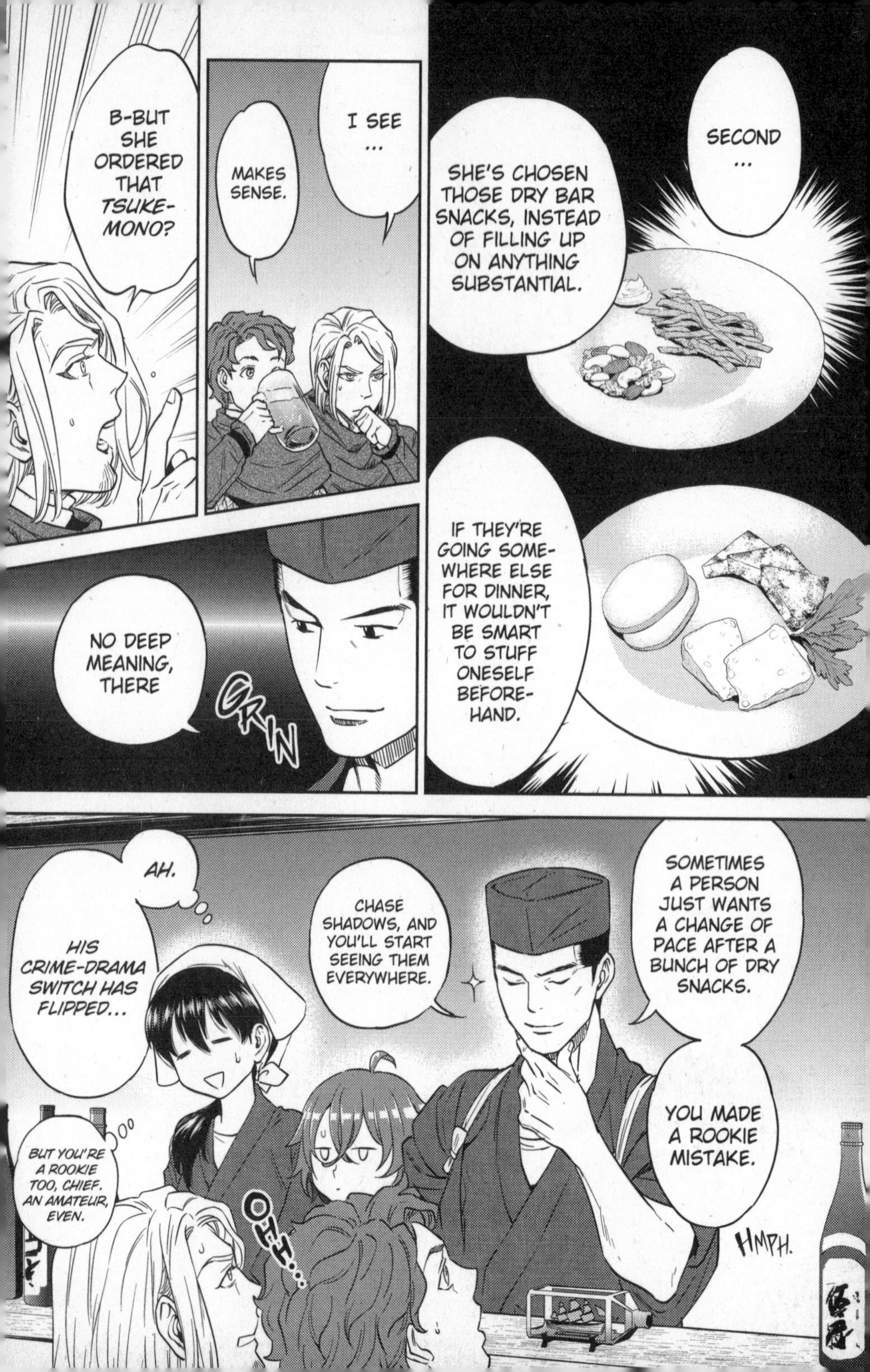
SECOND ...
SHE'S CHOSEN THOSE DRY BAR SNACKS, INSTEAD OF FILLING UP ON ANYTHING SUBSTANTIAL.
IF THEY'RE GOING SOME-WHERE ELSE FOR DINNER, IT WOULDN'T BE SMART TO STUFF ONESELF BEFORE-HAND.
I SEE ...
MAKES SENSE.
B-BUT SHE ORDERED THAT TSUKE-MONO?
NO DEEP MEANING, THERE
GRIN
SOMETIMES A PERSON JUST WANTS A CHANGE OF PACE AFTER A BUNCH OF DRY SNACKS.
YOU MADE A ROOKIE MISTAKE.
HMPH.
CHASE SHADOWS, AND YOU'LL START SEEING THEM EVERYWHERE.
AH.
HIS CRIME-DRAMA SWITCH HAS FLIPPED...
OHH...
BUT YOU'RE A ROOKIE TOO, CHIEF. AN AMATEUR, EVEN.

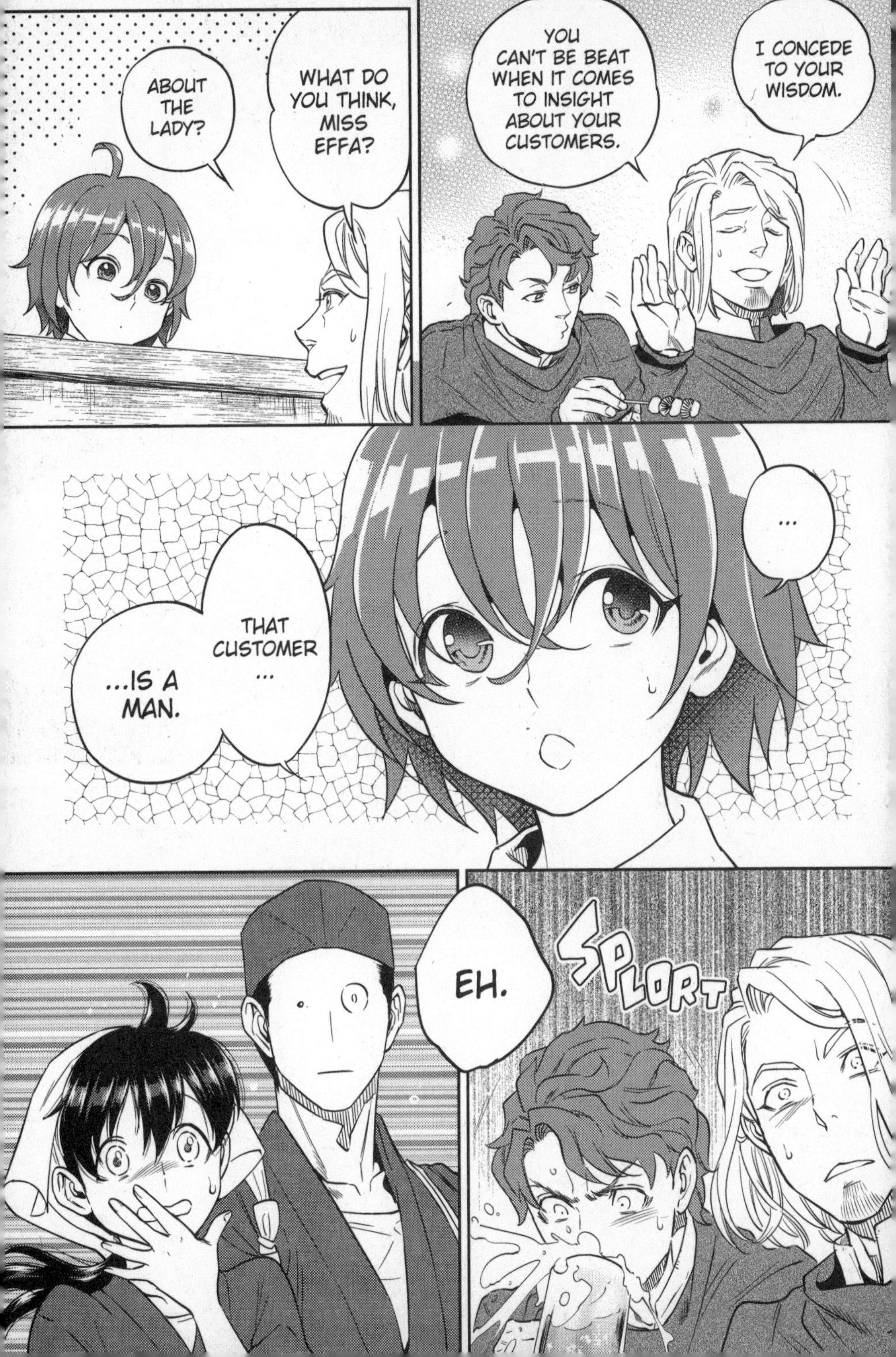
YOU CAN'T BE BEAT WHEN IT COMES TO INSIGHT ABOUT YOUR CUSTOMERS.
I CONCEDE TO YOUR WISDOM.
WHAT DO YOU THINK, MISS EFFA?
ABOUT THE LADY?
...
THAT CUSTOMER ...
...IS A MAN.
SPLORT
EH.

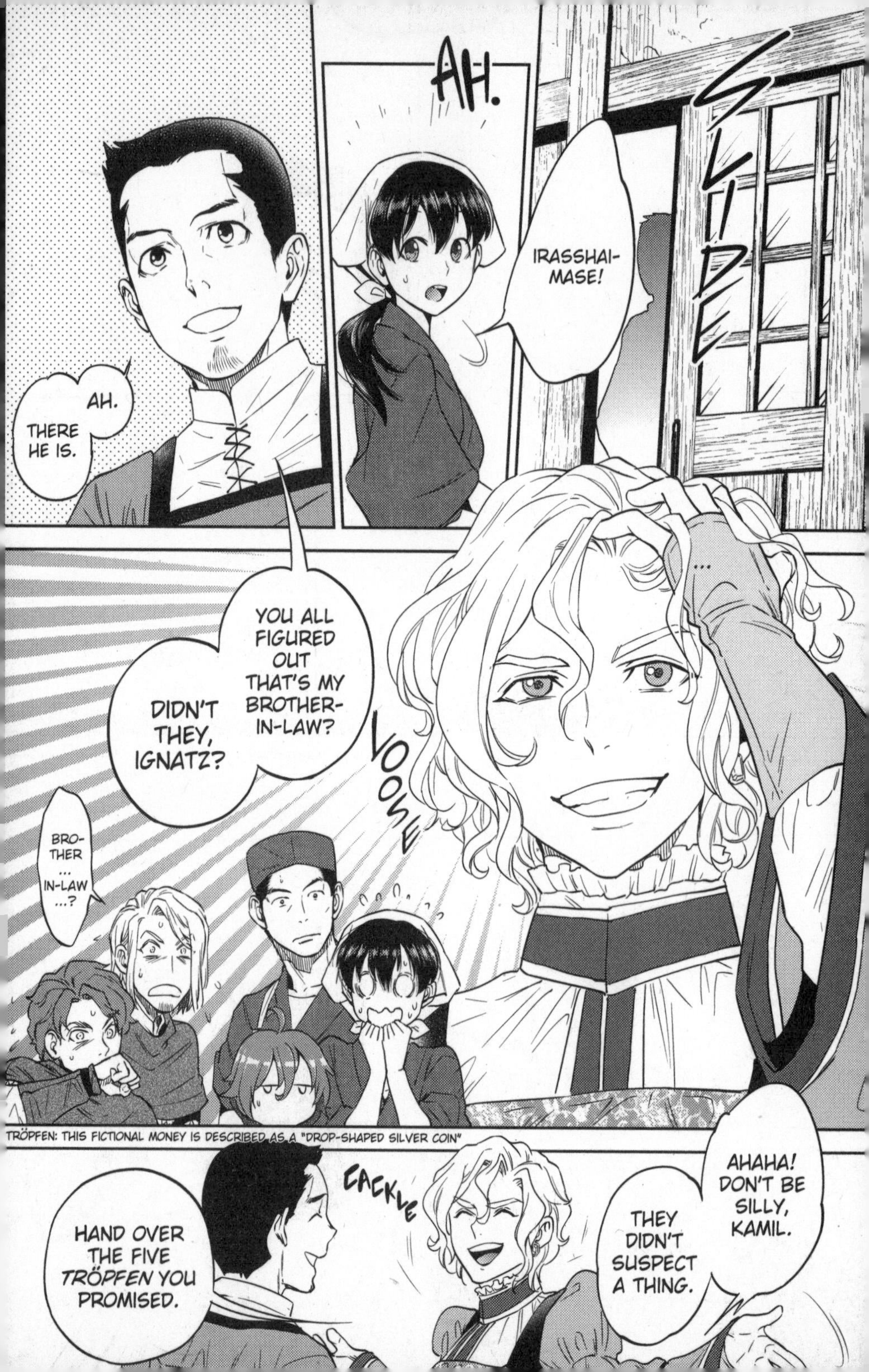
SLIDE
AH.
IRASSHAI-MASE!
AH. THERE HE IS.
...
YOU ALL FIGURED OUT THAT'S MY BROTHER-IN-LAW?
DIDN'T THEY, IGNATZ?
VOOOM
BROTHER ... IN-LAW ...?
AHAHA! DON'T BE SILLY, KAMIL.
THEY DIDN'T SUSPECT A THING.
CACKLE
HAND OVER THE FIVE *TRÖPFEN* YOU PROMISED.
TRÖPFEN: THIS FICTIONAL MONEY IS DESCRIBED AS A "DROP-SHAPED SILVER COIN"

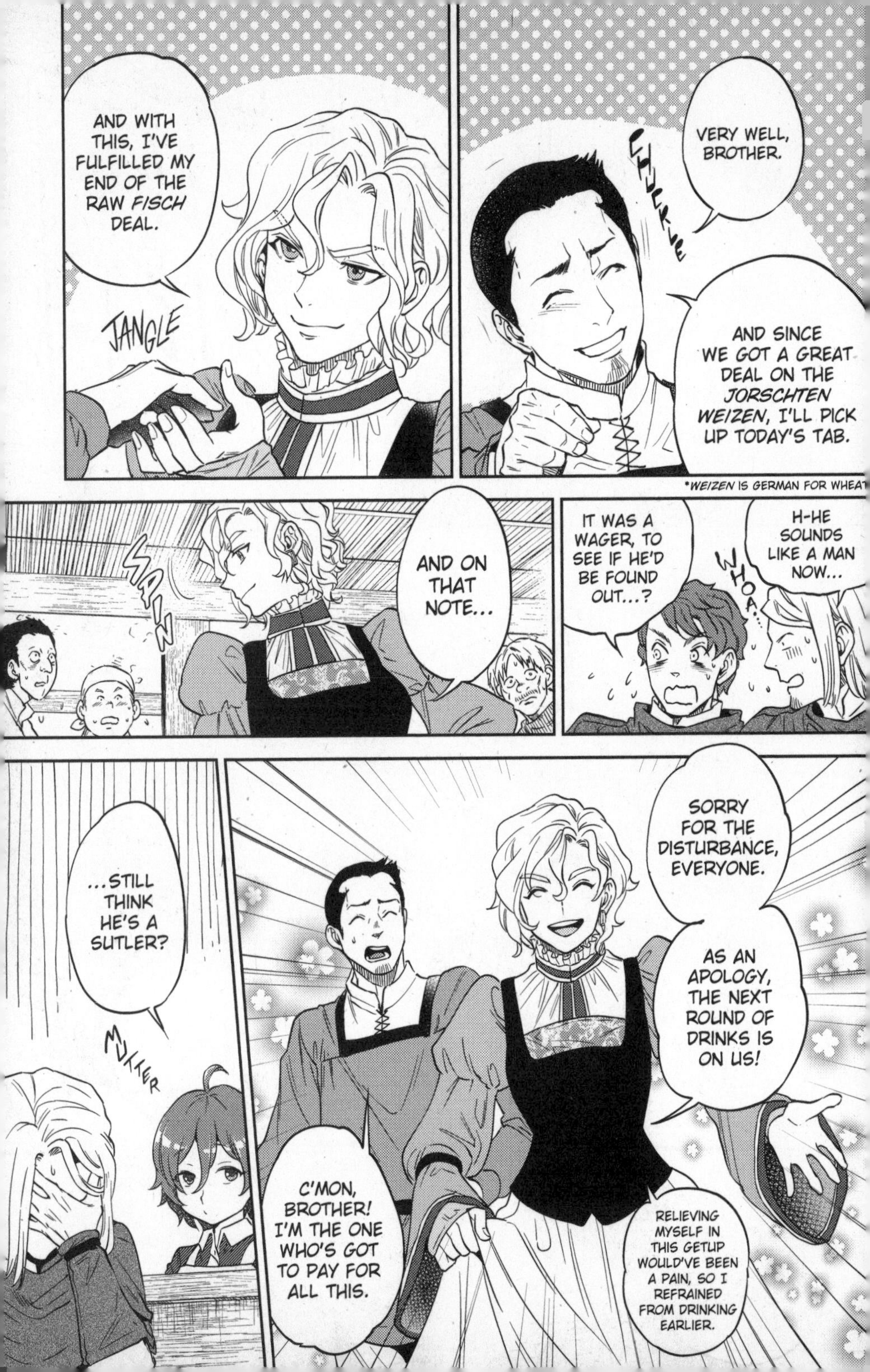
CHUCKLE
VERY WELL, BROTHER.
AND SINCE WE GOT A GREAT DEAL ON THE JORSCHTEN WEIZEN, I'LL PICK UP TODAY'S TAB.
AND WITH THIS, I'VE FULFILLED MY END OF THE RAW FISCH DEAL.
JANGLE
*WEIZEN IS GERMAN FOR WHEAT
H-HE SOUNDS LIKE A MAN NOW...
WHOA...
IT WAS A WAGER, TO SEE IF HE'D BE FOUND OUT...?
AND ON THAT NOTE...
SORRY FOR THE DISTURBANCE, EVERYONE.
AS AN APOLOGY, THE NEXT ROUND OF DRINKS IS ON US!
RELIEVING MYSELF IN THIS GETUP WOULD'VE BEEN A PAIN, SO I REFRAINED FROM DRINKING EARLIER.
C'MON, BROTHER! I'M THE ONE WHO'S GOT TO PAY FOR ALL THIS.
...STILL THINK HE'S A SUTLER?
MUTTER

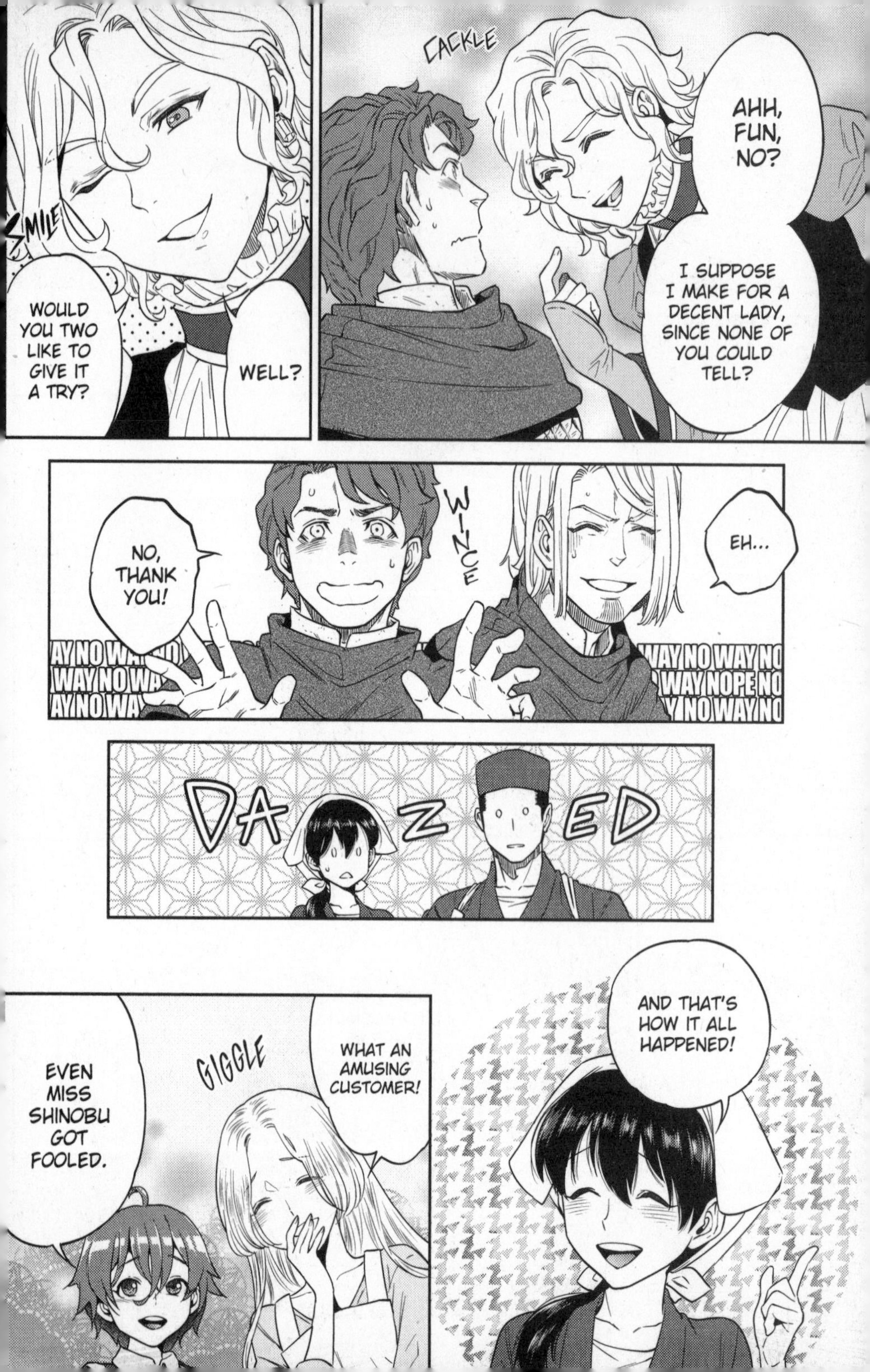
CACKLE
AHH, FUN, NO?
I SUPPOSE I MAKE FOR A DECENT LADY, SINCE NONE OF YOU COULD TELL?
SMILE
WOULD YOU TWO LIKE TO GIVE IT A TRY?
WELL?
EH...
WINCE
NO, THANK YOU!
WAY NO WAY NO
WAY NOPE NO
NO WAY NO
AY NO WAY NO
WAY NO WA
AY NO WA
DAZED
AND THAT'S HOW IT ALL HAPPENED!
WHAT AN AMUSING CUSTOMER!
GIGGLE
EVEN MISS SHINOBU GOT FOOLED.

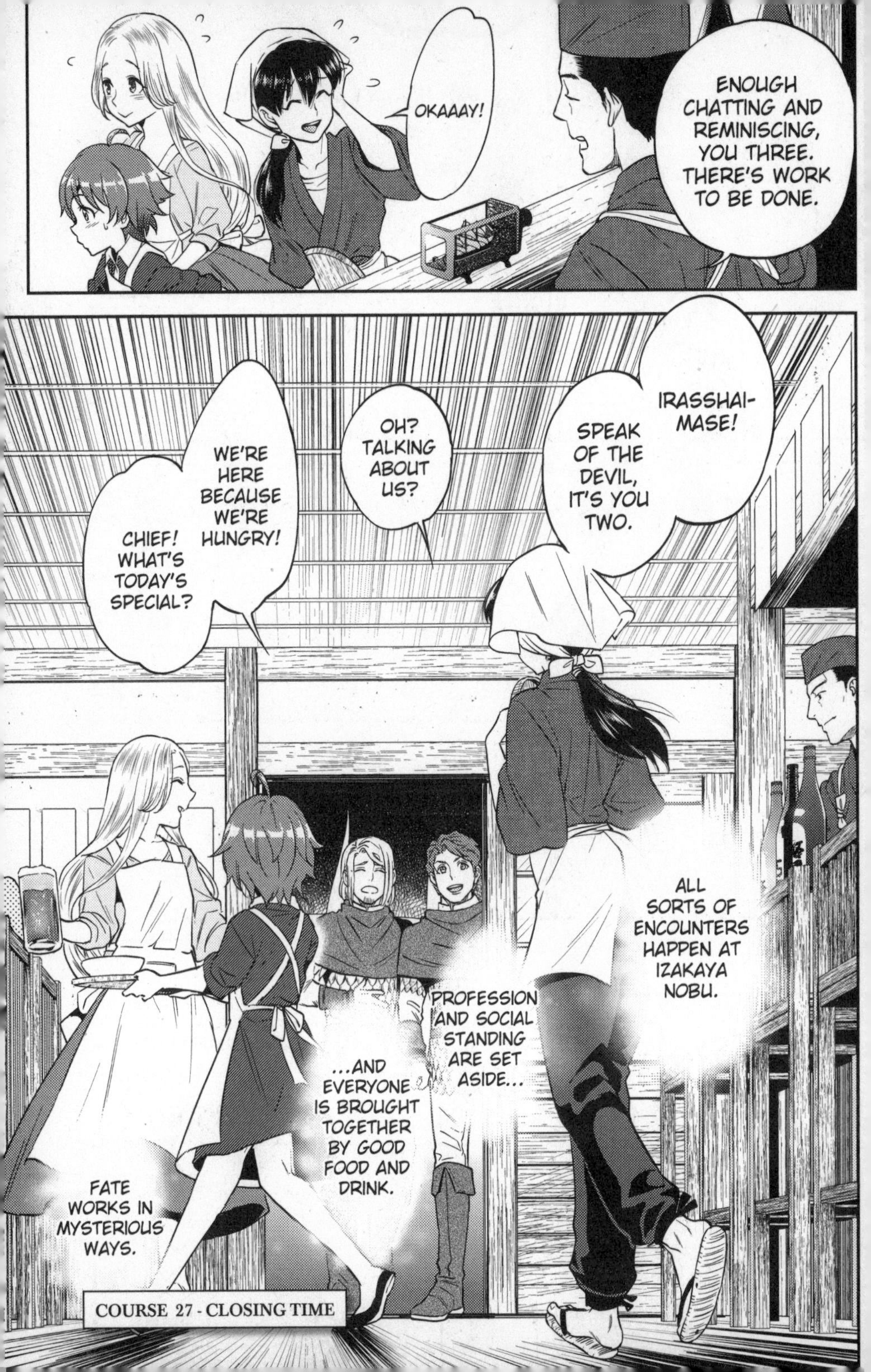
ENOUGH CHATTING AND REMINISCING, YOU THREE. THERE'S WORK TO BE DONE.
OKAAAY!
IRASSHAI-MASE!
SPEAK OF THE DEVIL, IT'S YOU TWO.
OH? TALKING ABOUT US?
WE'RE HERE BECAUSE WE'RE HUNGRY!
CHIEF! WHAT'S TODAY'S SPECIAL?
ALL SORTS OF ENCOUNTERS HAPPEN AT IZAKAYA NOBU.
PROFESSION AND SOCIAL STANDING ARE SET ASIDE...
...AND EVERYONE IS BROUGHT TOGETHER BY GOOD FOOD AND DRINK.
FATE WORKS IN MYSTERIOUS WAYS.
COURSE 27 - CLOSING TIME

OTHERWORLDLY IZAKAYA NOBU ROUGH CHARACTER DESIGNS 8

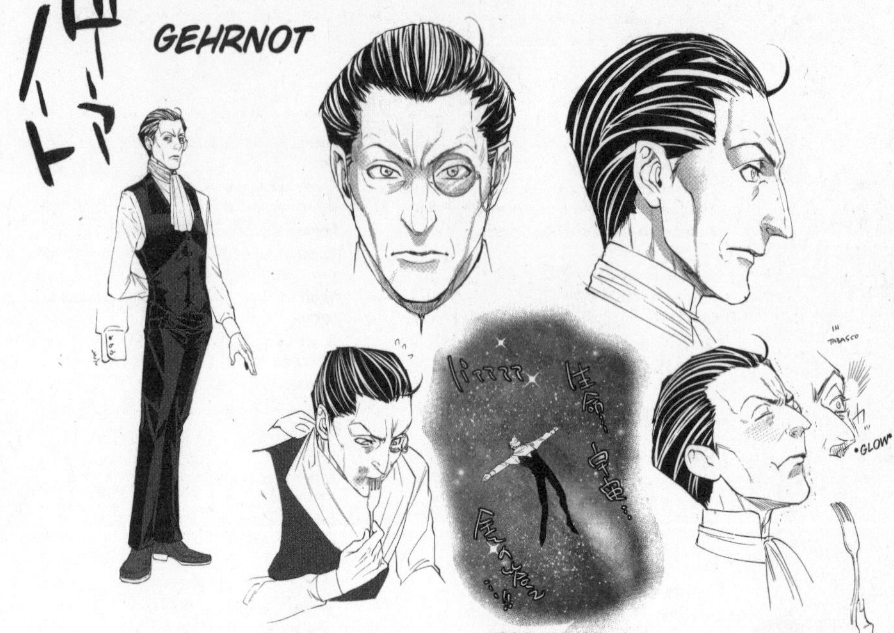
ゲーアノート
GEHRNOT
TABASCO
GLOW

THIS IS LIFE...
THE UNIVERSE...
EVERYTHING...

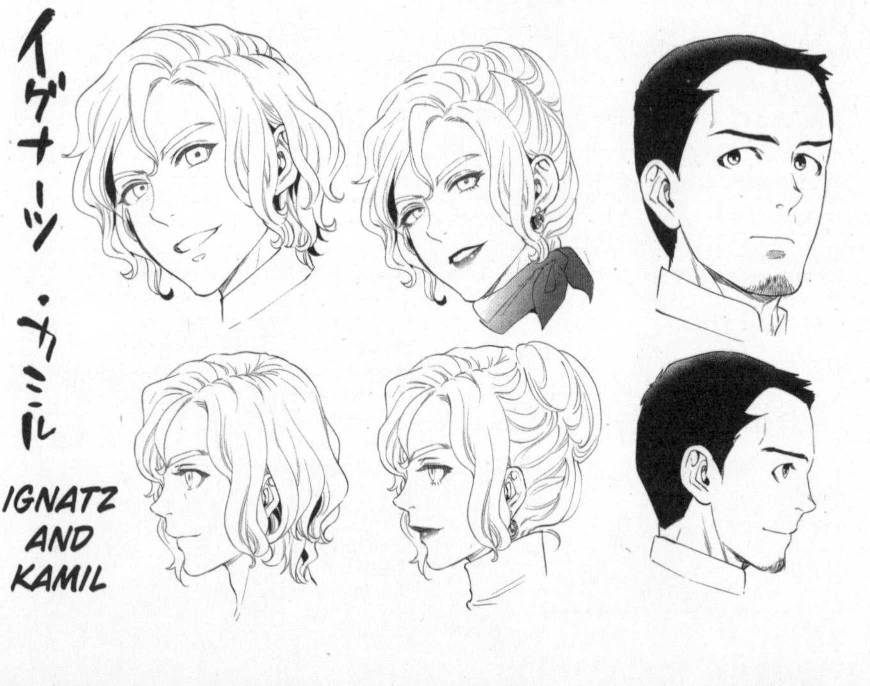
イグナーツ・カミル
IGNATZ AND KAMIL

MENU

FOOD VOCABULARY ENCOUNTERED IN THIS BOOK:

The fantasy world of "Nobu" brings together speakers of Japanese and German for a delicious cross-cultural exchange. Hans, Nikolaus, Chief, Shinobu, and the gang use a variety of foreign food vocabulary throughout, so here's a quick review of what came up in this volume, including a few terms from French and Spanish!

JAPANESE

Chawanmushi: savory steamed egg custard filled with mushrooms and chicken

Chicken Nanban: kara-age dipped in a sweet and sour sauce and topped with tartar sauce

Chikuzenni: an appetizer of braised chicken and vegetables

Daikon oroshi: grated daikon (large, Japanese radish)

Fukinoto: edible flower of the butterbur plant

Gohan: hot, cooked, white rice

Ipponzuke: generic term for any number of pickled vegetables, like cucumber or radish

Kara-age: one style of Japanese fried food (not limited to chicken)

Kimosui: eel-liver soup

Kinpira gobo: chopped burdock root cooked in sugar and soy sauce

Kushiyaki: generic term for food that's skewered and grilled

Kyuri: cucumber

Makogarei: marbled sole (fish)

Nitsuke: fish or vegetables boiled in soy sauce

Oden: a hot stew of fishcakes and root vegetables

Oshibori: the hot, rolled towels provided to restaurant customers before the meal

Purin: a chilled, flan-like custard with a layer of caramel sauce

Reishu: chilled sake

Sanma gohan: bits of mackerel pike, steamed in rice

Sanma shioyaki: mackerel pike, grilled and salted

Sansai: wild, mountain vegetables

Sashimi: slices of raw seafood served on their own, distinct from sushi

Satoimo: taro, a root vegetable similar to potato

Satoimo nikkorogashi: small taro cooked and rolled about in a thick, sweet sauce

Shiokara: fermented seafood entrails

Surume: salty, dried squid; a common bar snack

Tako: octopus

Takowasa: raw octopus heavily flavored with wasabi

Tako sunomono: octopus salad with pickled vegetables

Tempura: Japanese deep-frying technique that uses flour and egg batter

Tsukemono: pickled food

Umaki: eel wrapped in a rolled omelet

Unagi kabayaki: eel dipped in a soy-based sauce and broiled

Unagi shirayaki: broiled eel, seasoned only with salt

Ushiojiru: a thin fish soup boiled in seawater

Wakame: edible brown seaweed

FRENCH

Amuse-gueule: a complimentary appetizer chosen at the chef's discretion

Bouillabaisse: fish stew originally from Marseille, France

Fond: soup stock

Dry Bar Snacks

SPANISH

Ajillo: literally chopped garlic, but in this case, a type of tapas stir-fry with oil, garlic, and hot peppers

GERMAN

Aal: eel

Bonbon: candy

Brot: bread

Ei(er): eggs

Essig: vinegar

Fisch: fish

Fischsoße: fish sauce

Gans: goose

Garnele: shrimp

Gemüse: vegetables

Gurke(n): cucumber(s)

Huhn: chicken

Ingwer: ginger

Käse: cheese

Krake: octopus

Meeresfrüchte: seafood

Milch: milk

Nüsse: nuts

Obst: fruit

Safran: saffron (spice)

Skorpionfisch: scorpionfish

Suppe: soup

Tintenfisch: squid

Tomate(n): tomato(es)

Wein: wine

Weizen: wheat

Weizenbrei: wheat porridge

Zucker: sugar

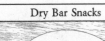

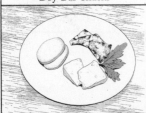

CEAC

ENGLISH EDITION
Translation: CALEB D. COOK
Typesetting: MIYOKO HOSOYAMA
Sound Effects: EK WEAVER
Associate Editor: M. CHANDLER

Original Story
NATSUYA SEMIKAWA

UDON STAFF
Chief of Operations: ERIK KO
Director of Publishing: MATT MOYLAN
VP of Business Development: CORY CASONI
Director of Marketing: MEGAN MAIDEN
Japanese Liaisons: STEVEN CUMMINGS
ANNA KAWASHIMA

Manga
VIRGINIA NITOUHEI

Character Design
KURURI

ISEKAI IZAKAYA "NOBU" Volume 4

©Virginia-Nitouhei 2017
©Natsuya Semikawa,Kururi/TAKARAJIMASHA

First published in Japan in 2017 by KADOKAWA CORPORATION, Tokyo.
English translation rights arranged with KADOKAWA CORPORATION, Tokyo
through TUTTLE–MORI AGENCY, INC., Tokyo.

English language version published by UDON Entertainment Inc.
118 Tower Hill Road, C1, PO Box 20008
Richmond Hill, Ontario, L4K 0K0 CANADA

www.UDONentertainment.com

First Printing: August 2019
ISBN-13: 978-1772941074
ISBN-10: 1772941077

Printed in Canada